Russia under the Last Tsar

Russia under the Last Tsar

Opposition and Subversion 1894–1917

Edited by Anna Geifman

BLACKWELL Publishers

First published 1999

2 4 6 8 10 9 7 5 3 1

Blackwell Publishers Ltd
108 Cowley Road
Oxford OX4 1JF
UK

Blackwell Publishers Inc.
350 Main Street
Malden, Massachusetts 02148
USA

British Library Cataloguing in Publication Data

A CIP catalogue record for this book is available from the
British Library.

Library of Congress Cataloging in Publication Data

Russia under the last tsar: opposition and subversion, 1894–1917/
edited by Anna Geifman.
p.   cm.
Includes bibliographical references and index.
ISBN 1-55786-994-4 (alk. paper). – ISBN 1-55786-995-2
(pbk. : alk. paper)
1. Russia – Politics and government – 1894–1917.   2. Government,
Resistance to – Russia.   I. Geifman, Anna, 1962–
DK262.R87   1999
947.08'3 – dc21   99-11162   CIP

Typeset in 10½ on 12 pt Photina
by Best-set Typesetter Ltd, Hong Kong
Printed in Great Britain by MPG Books Ltd, Bodmin, Cornwall

This book is printed on acid-free paper

Contents

List of Contributors

Aleksandr Bokhanov is Senior Researcher at the Institute of Russian History, Russian Academy of Sciences, Moscow

Jonathan Daly is Assistant Professor in the History Department, University of Illinois

Gregory L. Freeze is Professor of History at Brandeis University, Massachusetts

Anna Geifman is Associate Professor of History at Boston University

Alexandra S. Korros is Professor of History at Xavier University, Ohio

André Leibich is Professor of International History and Politics at the Graduate Institute of International Studies, Geneva

Aleksandr Lokshin is Senior Researcher at the Israel and Jewish Diaspora Department of the Institute of Oriental Studies, Russian Academy of Sciences, Moscow

Michael Melancon is Associate Professor of History at Auburn University, Alabama

John Morison is Senior Lecturer in the Department of Hisotry, University of Leeds

Dmitri B. Pavlov is Senior Researcher at the Russian Independent Institute of Social and National Problems, Moscow

Melissa Stockdale is Associate Professor of History at the University of Oklahoma

Theodore R. Weeks is Associate Professor of Russian and East European History at Southern Illinois University

Robert C. Williams is Professor of History at Davidson College, North Carolina

Acknowledgements

The authors and publishers gratefully acknowledge the following for permission to reproduce copyright material:

Peter Lang Publishing, Inc., for permission to reprint Robert C. Williams "Bolshevism in the West: From Leninist Totalitarians to Cultural Revolutionaries," first published in Robert C. Williams, *Russia Imagined: Art, Culture, and National Identity*, P. Lang, 1997.

Quotations and archival references from: Anna Geifman, *Thou Shalt Kill: Revolutionary Terrorism in Russia, 1893–1917*. Copyright © 1993 by Princeton University Press. Reprinted by permission of Princeton University Press.

The publishers apologize for any errors or omissions in the above list and would be grateful to be notified of any corrections that should be incorporated in the next edition or reprint of this book.

Introduction

If there was anything surprising about Nicholas II's ascension to the throne of the Russian Empire after the death of his father, Alexander III, in 1894, it was a widespread sentiment – a premonition perhaps, discernible from the earliest days of his rule – that the new tsar was not to have a peaceful reign. In fact, while it is not entirely clear when his nickname – "Nicholas the Last" – was first employed to indicate what seemed a groundless belief in his imminent downfall, the fact that the label stuck was as revealing as it was apposite in its retrospectively appreciated accuracy. Indeed, there must have been something in the outwardly unruffled political situation around the turn of the twentieth century that made this prediction seem a probability. This volume's primary objectives are thus to depict the Russian domestic scene during the reign of the country's last imperial ruler; to analyze the various factors that combined to evolve into an impending crisis that eventually swept away his regime; and to examine the various factions involved in the sociopolitical conflict – the tsar's numerous adversaries struggling against his loyal (and not so loyal) supporters.

The book is comprised of a series of original analytical articles by eminent American, West European, and Russian scholars, surveying the range of political forces during the final years of the tsarist regime. It may be of interest to both the educated general reader and academic audiences, as it brings together in a single volume the most recent scholarship on all the major political forces active during the reign of Nicholas II – from the most radical and violent opponents of the regime to its most conservative supporters, and incorporates new discoveries from the wealth of archival materials opened to historical investigation in the course of the few volatile years after the collapse of the Soviet Union. The book thus presents fresh perspectives on the key political issues, pivotal events, and prominent personalities just prior to and after the turn of the twentieth century – one of the most turbulent eras in Russian history. On numerous occasions throughout the volume, the authors' viewpoints challenge the existing scholarly assumptions and conventional interpretations.

This book may also serve as a new, useful textual source for university and college students, filling a gap that has been left by the prevalent academic tendency toward narrow topics and excessive detail: although there are a number of excellent single-theme works focusing on individual parties and important political personalities, many of the existing monographs are somewhat dated and largely descriptive. The collection's emphasis on analysis, enveloping the entire political spectrum and addressing a large variety of controversial issues, provides a wealth of material for classroom reading and discussion, without bogging the student down with the voluminous detail typical of large works with a narrow focus.

Leaving aside its analytical approach, this volume does not have a unifying philosophy, even less an "ideology"; nor are the chapters written in a single form. The introduction and each of the sections are personal-view essays, in which the authors frequently express opinions contradictory to those advocated by other contributors. Some parts of the book are based entirely on new and extensive archival research; many sources have never been used before. Other chapters are "analytical essays," which do not contain much scholarly apparatus, yet are of course based on the authors' prolonged research and reflection. The diversity of views and styles presented here introduces readers to contemporary scholarly polemics in the field of Russian studies and allows them to develop their own informed opinions on controversial topics.

One such topic is the continuing controversy over the relative importance of personalities versus large-scale social movements as the essential agents of political change. Owing, in the main, to the thematic requirements of this volume, most contributors tend to focus on broad-ranging political problems and strictly practical issues associated with the revolutionary process in Russia. Little attention is devoted to personalities and in particular to the intricate phenomenon of individuals developing oppositionist sentiments and becoming opponents of the establishment. In analyzing the revolutionary process, it would seem to be misleading to concur with those scholars who rely primarily on more than questionable *post factum* rationalizations offered by the oppositionists themselves in order to justify their involvement in antigovernment struggle. Nor does it seem legitimate simply to explain their participation in the revolutionary process by pointing to the numerous problems in the domestic situation in tsarist Russia and the various abuses on the part of its ruling classes and elites: historians (of Russia and elsewhere), although hardly oblivious to the strictly pragmatic factors contributing to political crises, have repeatedly demonstrated that these alone do not account for society's radicalization, as had been assumed by adherents of the notion that personal and collective consciousness is necessarily dependent on and determined by "the being." While emphasizing the grave agrarian and urban problems, the general process of modernization, and the transformation of the political consciousness, along with the unexpected and devastating effects of the Russo-Japanese war of 1904–5, all leading to the outbreak of revolution, it is equally essential to stress, as some scholars do, that "objective circumstances *per se* are not a sufficient, perhaps not even a necessary condition" for the escalation of political extremism and violence.[1]

In this general introduction to the book as a whole, it is therefore essential to outline the importance of some overlooked alternative, or rather, complementary factors, including those that are generated in the realm of psychology. Indeed, it would hardly be justifiable to omit from the context of the book a discussion of the deep yet unexpressed aspirations or ulterior motives of the various political participants solely because of the obvious difficulties in subjecting them to "objective analysis."[2]

From the plethora of primary sources – diaries, correspondence, and memoirs – one may infer that among the Russian intellectuals who alleged heartfelt compassion for the "oppressed toiling masses" and profound grief for their miserable existence, a very large (and thus indicative) number knew or at least instinctively sensed that the people were far from appreciating the concern of their self-appointed benefactors. Sources reveal that these champions of the people's cause could not escape the feeling of being entirely alien to the common folk, who were at best indifferent and more often suspicious and hostile to the intelligentsia's efforts and aspirations. An all too obvious illustration of this disparity is the famous "To the People" movement in the summer of 1874, when the revolutionaries' attempted wholesale mobilization of the countryside for the socialist cause turned into a fiasco, once again revealing the entirely apolitical nature of the Russian peasants: instead of following the radicals along the revolutionary path, the villagers mistrusted the educated strangers, attacked them, and turned them over to the police.

It might be argued that the "mad summer" of 1874 was a failure for the revolutionary cause because the radical intellectuals had not yet had a chance to establish a close connection with the masses. Yet nearly two decades later – the period of intense subversive agitation and propaganda, as well as antigovernment violence – the peasants were still no more willing to listen to fiery mutinous speeches or enlist as fighters for the cause of the revolution. During a severe famine following a crop failure in 1891, coupled with devastating cholera and typhus epidemics that ravaged European Russia in 1891–2, a significant number of radicals seized the opportunity and sought to set in motion a wave of revolutionary activity by turning the hungry masses against the tsarist regime. Revolutionary circles emerged everywhere in the provinces affected by the famine; their members energetically printed and distributed antigovernment literature and openly agitated for violence against state officials, the police, and the wealthy, blaming them for the misfortunes of the peasants and the poor townsfolk.

Both the authorities and the revolutionaries recognized the famine and epidemics of 1891–2 as the impetus for an increase in radical thinking and activity in the central Russian regions. There was, however, a major obstacle to the spread of radicalism, for even the most idealistic believers in the progressive nature of the Russian peasantry had to admit that the villagers saw no connection between their misfortunes and the central administration, and in fact were grateful for material assistance from the government, calling it the "tsar's ration." The peasants thus once again proved themselves to be the complete opposite of a "conscious revolutionary force," causing many opponents of the tsarist regime to question their ability to mobilize the still sleeping Russian masses. The most revealing paradox, however, was that, far from prompting them to recognize the people's inclinations and therefore to forego the unsupported revolutionary struggle, the radicals stubbornly and zealously continued on their chosen path – the liberation of mankind – regardless of whether or not it wished to be liberated. Indeed, after the failure to reach the people in 1891–2, government opponents began actively to seek alternative means of fighting the hated regime, at which point it returned to the late 1870s–early 1880s idea about the necessity to ignite the revolutionary flame on behalf of the people by means of individual acts of political violence, or terrorism.[3]

It seems appropriate here to leave aside any discussion of the various ways in which common criminals, society's riffraff, the miscellaneous misfits and pariahs, charlatans, and various other shady elements become part of what may be called "the seamy side" of any sociopolitical movement, regardless of its orientation and ideological coloring. Instead, a legitimate general question at this point seems to be as follows: what is it that drives honorable and sincere people, individuals who are conscientious and selfless, to take up activities aimed at undermining the establishment? Why do they strive so zealously toward an objective that no one is interested in or asking for? Why are they so intent on presenting a "gift to the people" which – and they could not be blind to this – is unwanted and may be returned to them at an opportune moment brusquely, and perhaps even aggressively?

Among those tormented with an insatiable thirst for sociopolitical activity, a certain personality type is found so frequently that it may well be perceived as a prototype. This is a rather "thin-skinned" person who is sensitive and emotionally vulnerable enough easily to discern the glaring depravity, ugliness, and vulgarity in the world around him.[4] (For even incurable optimists, who are far from being predisposed to melancholy and despondency, may be keenly aware of and be appalled by the deep and numerous ethical and aesthetic flaws in their environment.) Significantly, what may traumatize this kind of person the most is that, contrary to his genuine desire to avoid any encounter with the repugnant sides of life, his very unavoidable physical dependence on the environment constantly forces him to experience and confront what he perceives as vice. Moreover, at the core of his predicament is the frustrating realization that life in the corrupt world inevitably renders him helpless to protect his inner self; for, owing to his inability to resist the terrible impact of the outside world, his own inmost being is constantly exposed to evil and gradually absorbs it.

And so this individual, by no means a villain, and indeed often a person of sensitive and soaring soul, which in its fragile way reacts sharply and painfully to any encounter with iniquity, arrives at a desperate conclusion about the possibility of eradicating the world's imperfections by way of altering its political, economic, and/or social arrangements, or – to put it in more general terms – to change his life's repugnant "external circumstances." And this, after all, is what any revolutionary seeks to achieve. Having armed himself with a variety of theoretical or ideological schemes, which delineate the fundamental corruption in the world order, along with ways in which to correct it, such a person sets out to struggle against, and ultimately break, his environment's sociopolitical, economic, religious, or any other conventions. The purpose is to transform the world in accordance with his personal vision and preference (the most righteous ones, no doubt) and primarily *for his own sake*. As one scholar of the Russian antigovernment movement has it:

> The question of what motivated people to become revolutionaries . . . is intriguing. The general revolutionary movement itself and even the liberal reform movement demonstrate severe alienation on the part of large segments of Russian society. Despair about the oppressive political and social system motivated social critics. . . . Although speculative, it is nevertheless probable that there was an element of self-actualization in their mental gymnastics.[5]

For a very large number of revolutionaries political activity was conceivable only within a broader cultural and psychological context, particularly that of the Russian Silver Age – a period of intellectual turmoil,
aesthetic decadence, and spiritual vigor. This was the time when many
intense personalities and highly turbulent minds sought to fulfill themselves by what may be seen as ardent experimentation with various sub-
stitutes for the recently rejected official religion and the Orthodox church.
For an increasing number of educated Russians the passionate (and often
painful) search for a "different spirituality" and an iconoclastic ideology,
which would provide a new meaning to their existence, was a process by
which they discovered and embraced the idea of sociopolitical revolution
as a suitable guiding concept for shaping their outlook and actions. Thus,
for someone like Ivan Kaliaev, known among his comrades as "the Poet,"
who became a worldwide celebrity when he assassinated Nicholas II's
uncle, Grand Duke Sergei Aleksandrovich, in February 1905, political participation was primarily a solution to his inner turmoil, eliminating in his
mind a possible conflict between the revolutionary's license to murder and
his own fervid efforts to compose prayers in verse, exalting the glory of
Almighty God. Many of Kaliaev's comrades shared his spiritual approach
to the revolution: terrorist Mariia Benevskaia was an ardent Christian, who
never parted with the message of the Gospels; and Egor Sazonov explained
in a letter written to his parents from prison:

> My Socialist-Revolutionary beliefs merged with my religion. . . . I think that
> we, the socialists, continue the work of Christ, who . . . died for the people as
> a political criminal . . . We, the socialists . . . want the kingdom of Christ to
> come to earth. . . . When I heard my teacher saying: take up your cross and
> follow me . . . I could not abandon my cross.[6]

A newly made revolutionary, then – if it is still possible to talk of a prototype – is clearly disinclined to perceive himself or his environment in a
detached (and somewhat more balanced) way – something that might
perhaps cause him to doubt the assumed singularity, depth, and subtlety
of his own exceptionally refined sentiments and unique spiritual torments.
Preoccupied entirely with himself (as he is driven by his primary inner
motives), he is unable to recognize the person next to him; that is, he fails
truly to appreciate that another human being has an existence separate
from his own. This lack of empathy may be one reason why he tends to see
individuals primarily as an integral part of some abstract notion of "the
masses," and the complicated theories that he utilizes to validate this
attitude are but rationalizations of things far from cerebral.

Moreover, for all their lamentations about the suffering masses, many
among those who came to espouse the revolution around the turn of the
century began to demonstrate the type of mentality that was best sum-

marized by a popular motto: "the worse, the better" (*chem khuzhe, tem luchshe*). In essence, this meant that further deterioration of Russia's domestic situation was in the interests of all government opponents, as it contributed to the growing instability of the regime and thus benefited the revolutionary cause. This included the growing impoverishment of the tsar's subjects and additional hardships for them, as well as any official action damaging to the welfare of the people, whose relative proclivity for sociopolitical protest was assumed to have been directly proportionate to the degree of suffering. Accordingly, during the 1891–2 famine, many radicals rebuked the liberals for their aid to the starving peasants, arguing that it indirectly helped the government overcome the crisis and thus only strengthened the "sickly regime" in Russia.[7] Equally revealing is the reaction of radical émigrés to the news of Bloody Sunday, January 9 (22), 1905, when government troops killed and wounded hundreds of workers and their families marching to the Winter Palace to present a petition to Nicholas II. One of the revolutionaries later recounted: "Surprisingly, no one among the Russians was depressed. . . . On the contrary, [they] were in a lively, uplifted mood. It was clear that January 22 (9) would be the signal for a victorious struggle."[8] This attitude was not atypical among the government's opponents, one of whom was particularly explicit in a private letter: "If, God willing, we have a bad harvest this year, you'll see what a game will begin."[9]

Regarding the people exclusively as the means to achieve his objectives, the archetypal rebel develops a similarly extraneous attitude toward any single, nameless representative of these abstract masses. A classic literary example is Dostoyevsky's Ivan Karamazov, an iconoclast exasperated by the world's cruelty, who "returns God His ticket," yet minutes later impatiently kicks away the defenseless, piteous man, who had appealed for a bit of his kindness. The revolutionary, busy liberating humankind so as to accommodate his own vision of a better world, has no time to assimilate the notion that his next-door neighbor – that miserable individual whose single and separate life contributes extremely little, if at all, to "historical progress" – may be lonely, or sad, or afraid. Constrained by his own set of foregone assumptions, the revolutionary does not ask himself whether his position with regard to that particular person is humiliating, owing to its implicit denial of the individual's humanity or its purely theoretical (and therefore spurious and degrading) pity. Driven exclusively by his newly acquired ideological position – the product of his misplaced and rationalized deeper requirements – the radical is intent upon asserting his views at anyone else's expense. A glaring, if extreme, example of this attitude is that of Ekaterina Breshko-Breshkovskaia, venerated as an idol of the Russian revolution, who had abandoned her newborn son so as to be able to take part in activities aimed at bringing happiness to the people.

Even more paradoxical perhaps is that once the person burdened by yearnings to save the world joins a movement of like-minded individuals, he most frequently experiences an inner turnabout: he who had started out on the revolutionary path in response to his intense personal feelings of alienation and frustrated repression eventually forgets about other human beings for the sake of his own deeper need, rationalized and projected into a political goal; indeed, he gradually evolves into a person who, as part of this metamorphosis, merges with his new milieu and is no longer concerned even with himself.

Not only abstract and incorporeal "others," but even his own inner being no longer interests the individual who has discovered a way out of life's dilemma through the struggle against the external conditions of life itself. To a degree, the role played by sociopolitical activity here is analogous to that of the use of narcotics or perhaps cheap-thrill entertainment, both of which serve to distract attention from the inner self with extreme political activism, with all its exaggerated gestures, flamboyant colors and noises, and with its gripping, if garish, thrill. But the thrill generated by sociopolitical activity has one essential advantage over that of various traditional forms of entertainment, where running away from oneself cannot be sustained longer than the duration of an evening's entertainment. And so the problem persists: how to fill the intervals between periods of excitement? A political participant, on the other hand, *always* has, in the final goal, an objective, on which he habitually relies to justify his life, and toward which he strives incessantly.

An interesting question therefore poses itself: what would the revolutionaries do, if in fact, by a miracle, they managed to realize their programs in full? Such an outcome could turn into a genuine tragedy for people not concerned with the real-life individuals close to them and who have lost touch with their own tangible and unaffected selves. One wonders, therefore, whether there is some discernible connection between the various chimerical conceptions that these utopian thinkers and practitioners embrace and seek to realize and their reluctance to turn their eyes away from the external world and back to their inner selves: the more visionary the Utopia, the more its fervent adherents are afraid to be left on their own and without a purpose. This may be why they try their hardest to make sure that the promised paradise will remain forever out of reach. For even the most sincere defenders of the loftiest ideals, having succumbed to the urge for sociopolitical reform, rarely find the strength to recover themselves by escaping from the whirlwind, which twirls them around and carries them relentlessly from one "urgent" or "immediate" question of the day to another. But it is of no less import, of course, that a person thus justifying his flight from himself with high-minded rhetoric, does so at the expense of others – by way of using those whom he allegedly wishes to benefit as a result of his social experimentation. Indeed, one does not have to be Lenin to play with the lives of millions.

Regardless of what has been said about the revolutionaries' inner motives – something which may be applied to representatives of any organized ideological movement – many of those who had submerged themselves in the stormy waters of sociopolitical struggle were unquestionably upstanding and sincere people. Although unaware of their own obscured psychological needs, they may be respected for their refusal to accede to injustice and for their heroism in fighting it. In any case, in their ostensible altruism they were not at all like those skeptics who merely resigned themselves to a rather convenient idea about the futility of social participation.

It would hardly be an original approach to juxtapose the individualists and the social activists, of whom different writers had conflicting images. Dostoyevsky's *The Possessed* portrayed them as devils, beset by demons of destruction and self-annihilation. A century later Milan Kundera typified political zealots as "the Angels," who, unlike the individualist skeptics, believed that the world was not only invested with "rational meaning," but was also designed to be happy, "beautiful, good, and sensible"[10] – and would perhaps indeed be so with a little help from the altruists, who place collective interests before private ones. For his part, Ivan Turgenev, the renowned author of *Fathers and Children*, in his brilliant 1860 speech introduced two classical allegories, which seem to be particularly relevant for these psychological types, as they reveal vital antithetical extremes in the human character: the Hamlets and the Don Quixotes.[11]

"We would perhaps not be severely mistaken," Turgenev offers at the outset, "if we were to maintain that . . . in every one of us a primary place is occupied by either the personal 'I' or by something else, accepted as a higher ideal," and that for everyone "that ideal, that essence and purpose of one's existence is found either outside or within oneself." Aware that ideal types tend to fade away, usually not faring well amid the complexities of life, Turgenev is far from insisting on the rigidity of these categories; he seeks merely to outline the underlying priorities in human attitudes, essential for further discussion of his two paradigms. For whereas Don Quixote's *raison d'être* is an affirmation of the supreme principle or the eternal truth autonomous of the individual, Hamlet is torn by disbelief. Turgenev contrasts Cervantes' and Shakespeare's characters not only because the former is capable of conceptualizing the abstract ideal, whereas the latter doubts it, but because the main difference lies in the fact that Don Quixote is convinced that in our sinful world virtue and happiness can be fulfilled, if one devotes oneself to them entirely and unconditionally, while Hamlet – the great skeptic – discards this notion as a delusion.[12]

Each then acts in accordance with his convictions. Don Quixote is frantic in his efforts to establish the ultimate justice by striking with his sword at its would-be enemies. And his assumption that the nefarious world may be fundamentally transformed by direct (and, if need be, violent) intervention is a revolutionary concept, rendering Don Quixote a genuine radical. While intended to resurrect virtue and justice, his actions, however, often lead to an even greater evil and generate unmitigated wickedness. And if in rare cases (such as when he clumsily intervenes to save a peasant boy from his abusive master) he does fight – albeit in vain – against an unmistakable vice, the destruction he causes is more often than not merely for the sake of combating an entirely imaginary evil. An authentic revolutionary, Don Quixote is adamant about his illusions and chimerical schemes even though they cause a great deal of devastation and turn fictitious evil into a very real one.

Hamlet, on the other hand, while entirely skeptical about his abilities to fulfill the *a priori* questionable promise of happiness and justice – something which Don Quixote takes for granted – does not doubt the actuality of evil. It is crucial, however, that his attitude toward the various forms of wickedness is hardly a passive one; in fact, Hamlet takes a fatally active position against it – thereby implicitly contributing to the cause of goodness, which he so hesitates to uphold.[13] Equally critical is that he sees evil not only in external circumstances, but also as an integral part of his own soul; hence, his ceaseless efforts in the realm of the self-perception and his bitter "irony, in contrast to Don Quixote's enthusiasm." Hamlet fights and suffers: "he too has a sword in his hand" – the virulent weapon of self-analysis, with which he strikes at the vileness in himself, inflicting deep wounds.[14] Hamlet's struggle against evil is therefore deeper and more complex (if also ever more hopeless) than that of Don Quixote's belligerent antics – which are delirious, pathetic, and ludicrous.

In considering the archetypal revolutionary in turn-of-the-century Russia, one may reach an attitude similar to that toward the timeless Don Quixote, the character so admirable for his magnanimity and his determination in heroic deeds. He is both magisterial and pitiful; he deserves sympathy, if not succor; his image is touching, when he stands there with his eyes closed, as if blinded by the radiance of his own dream. But hardly anyone would be spellbound by the profundity of his personality or his cause.

Needless to say, this prototype has very little in common with representatives of the "seamy side" of any sociopolitical movement, who frequently become the controlling element during the process of its development. Certainly this was so in the Russian case. In general, this phenomenon may perhaps be attributed to the fact that the ideologists and organizers of a movement instinctively feel how flimsy their theoretical constructs really are and seek to convince themselves and others of these tenets' credibility by recruiting adherents to their cause, and – the more the better. The growing number of followers encourages the leaders to continue the brave march toward progress and happiness; the applause and the voices of support dim any doubts and maybe even pangs of conscience. In any event, rivals from opposing groups (for within every camp invariably there are adversaries, fighting for the common cause on "opposite sides of the barricade") will need to modify their arrogance: for when it comes to political movements, the truth is invariably measured by the number of raised hands . . . or weapons.

Supporters are thus very much in demand and actively sought, with leaders being entirely conscious of the fact that a fundamental condition for successful recruitment to any cause is that the movement's ideology must be made overt and simple, in fact straightforward to the point of being obtuse. Indeed, the more direct and brazen, the better, for this would ensure wider appeal and attract additional followers. With this idea in mind, the political leaders tend to render rudimentary their essential principles and methods. Such was clearly the case in Russia at the turn of the century, where numerous opponents of the government did not shy away from appealing to the most vulgar and primitive "mob instincts" and concepts of justice, including, for instance, the alleged popular yearning to "expropriate the expropriators." Moreover, to counterbalance the usual fiasco that resulted from attempts to mobilize the poor as conscientious fighters for the socialist cause, the Russian revolutionaries commonly resorted to the coarsest forms of propaganda and mass indoctrination by providing the barely literate populace with verses and chants ridiculing Nicholas II and his ministers in ways people were presumably quick to appreciate; for example, by alluding to the tsar's alleged imbecility or sexual inadequacies.[15]

Partly as a consequence of this proclivity to cater to the most crude or plebeian incentives and tastes, the Russian antigovernment camp gradually lost its initial elitism and transformed itself into a mass movement, as it opened itself up to people who had very little to do with its original ideals and tactics. They were driven largely by their personal goals, principles (if any), and judgments about suitable methods. In fact, for these radicals indiscriminate aggression, as it revealed itself in violence, became "so addictive that it was often carried out without even weighing the moral questions posed by earlier generations."[16] Many of their activities were entirely alien to the initial spirit of the movement, which they merely made use of to provide themselves with excuses for illicit or degenerate behavior. A murderer thus casually turned into a terrorist; a bank robber effortlessly became an expropriator; a psychopath suddenly transformed into a passionate orator.

Differentiating between revolutionaries and criminals in this period can thus be difficult, especially in cases involving individuals with lengthy police histories. Such a person might be arrested as a common criminal initially, then return to the court system several years later to be sentenced to a lengthy term of imprisonment for a political crime, and finally end up in court again on rape charges.[17] Nor was it unusual, for example, for a young revolutionary planning a bank robbery and calling it expropriation to count on using half of the loot to help the downtrodden proletarians, and the other half to buy himself an estate abroad, reasoning that, "as much as he sympathizes with the socialists . . . he considers their hope for a just social order totally unrealizable, [and] as much as he hates the bourgeoisie . . . he cannot help but envy it."[18] Equally revealing perhaps is that along with the criminal element attracted to the Russian revolutionary movement, a surprisingly large number of individuals who were evidently psychologically unbalanced also joined the movement. Many of them exhibited unquestionably psychopathic and sadistic behavior aimed at perverse personal gratification, which was concealed behind lofty rhetoric.[19]

Such were, as popular cliché had it at the time, the "lower depths" of the movement, its "seamy side," but its shady representatives gradually yet steadily pushed out and took the place of those who personified its more acceptable exterior. In the end, the initiators of the movement, isolated as they were from its core and its majority, faced a dilemma: either to adapt to the new modes of behavior, which by then dominated their political creation, or leave.

Patterns of political activity in early twentieth-century Russia seem to substantiate these (admittably arguable) generalizations. In analyzing the complex domestic situation in the empire, bloodstained with the revolutionaries' efforts to bring down Nicholas II's government despite its desperate retaliation, it is necessary to shift the emphasis from the radical rhetoric, which in the main only reveals what the oppositionists *wished* us to believe about themselves. Instead, it is of paramount importance to deal with the "lower depths" of the revolution, its fundamental aspect that for the most part remains obscured from historiography. A careful consideration of this element allows for the construction of a more balanced picture of the Russian revolutionary tradition in its new phase prior to the 1917 collapse of the old regime. Contrary to the tendency of many historians to concentrate their attention on the elevated and idealistic rhetoric of the antigovernment camp and accept at face value what its members chose to reveal about themselves, it now seems appropriate to demystify and deromanticize the Russian revolutionary movement, and consequently the revolution itself and its participants, all of whom have been glorified by far from impartial memoirists and sympathizers.

When one disassociates from the influence of lofty talk about the liberation of mankind, an attempt at a reconstruction of the more prosaic reality is possible. It was not unusual for a wide variety of shady individuals, adventurers, opportunists, as well as common criminals, hooligans, and the riffraff of Russian society, frequently collectively referred to as the "petty rabble" (*shpanka*), to join the ranks of the radicals and to use high-minded slogans to justify actions that in fact were outright banditry, noteworthy, if only because of their tremendous impact on the course of revolutionary developments in the country. Indeed, it is hardly possible to ignore what a prominent Russian liberal politician around the turn of the century, Petr Struve, appropriately termed a "new type of revolutionary that developed unnoticed by society . . . in the prerevolutionary years and finally emerged during 1905–1907." This new type of radical was "a blending of revolutionary and bandit, [marked by] the liberation of revolutionary psychology from all moral restraints." Initial signs of this tendency already present in the nineteenth century, were perceptively noted by Dostoyevsky and depicted in *The Possessed*. The process – which quickly became obvious even to Russian radicals themselves – reached its apogee in the post-1905 period when the militant practices of increasing numbers of activists qualified them as the "new type of revolutionaries."[20]

These radicals came to differ significantly from most of their revolutionary predecessors who had operated between the 1860s and the late 1880s (excepting, of course, a few pathological types such as the infamous Sergei Nechaev, father of the new type of extremism in Russia, upon whom Dostoyevsky based the sinister Petr Verkhovenskii).[21] The new political activists exhibited a considerably inferior level of intellectual and ideological awareness, as well as less inclination toward selfless idealism and dedication to the cause, prompting many radicals to lament the by then evident fact that the revolutionary organism was infected with Nechaevism, a "terrible disease . . . the degeneration of the revolutionary spirit."[22] Although the anarchists and activists from obscure radical groups represented the new type of extremism more frequently than any other revolutionaries, there was not a single party on the left wing of the Russian political scene whose numerous members did not qualify as this "new type of revolutionary," who bore primary responsibility for the pervading atmosphere of antigovernment violence and bloodshed in the empire in the first decade of the century – a period when close to 17,000 people became victims of terrorist activities alone.[23]

Needless to say, none of the above is in any way to suggest that the government of Nicholas II was exempt from a large share of responsibility for the acute domestic crisis in the empire and the eventual collapse of its political order in 1917. This attempt to delineate the archetypal psychological traits of so many of those who took part in the opposition movement merely aims to complement the strictly "political focus" of this volume, which converges on the administration's domestic policies and the oppositionists' alternative programs. As far as the former is concerned, several contributors to this volume vividly demonstrate that late imperial Russia did witness a great deal of administrative rigidity, official bigotry, and bureaucratic incompetence – to a large degree serving as a catalyst for confrontation. At the same time, it is impossible to deny that a revealingly sizable number among the participants in Russian political life during the reign of Nicholas II were unstable personalities going through considerable personal turmoil, as they struggled to realize their inner ambitions during this tumultuous period. By virtue of this seemingly typical (and agonizing) experience, these nonconformists and dissidents "were extremely estranged from society, and could not envision a satisfactory place for themselves in the future, if Russia were to remain as it was."[24]

Notes

1   Walter Laqueur, *Terrorism* (Boston-Toronto: Little, Brown, 1977), 145.
2   I am grateful to Princeton University Press for permission to use research materials originally published by the author in *Thou Shalt Kill: Revolutionary Terrorism in Russia, 1893–1917* (Princeton, NJ: Princeton University Press, 1993).
3   See Geifman, *Thou Shalt Kill*, 13–14. This process was very similar to the evolution of the populist propagandists of the 1870s into practitioners of terror. According to Sof'ia Perovskaia, one of the leaders of the notorious People's Will, she and her comrades resorted to terrorism as the only means to awaken the masses after vain attempts to do so by way of agitation (Viacheslav Venozhinskii, *Smertnaia kazn' i teror* (St Petersburg, 1908), 25; see also Franco Venturi, *Roots of Revolution: A History of the Populist and Socialist Movement in Nineteenth-Century Russia* (New York: Knopf 1960), 505, 577). In general, observers have noted that the "inability of those who identify with the plight of the poor or the victims of discrimination to mobilize the support of those segments of society most adversely affected by these circumstances . . . has led radicals in various parts of the world to constitute themselves as terrorists" (Leonard Weinberg and William Eubank, "Political Parties and the Formation of Terrorist Groups," *Terrorism and Political Violence* 2(2) (1990): 126).
4   Third person masculine is often used throughout the article for stylistic purposes only, and the central arguments proposed in this essay apply to both male and female opponents of the tsarist regime.
5   Sherron Nay, "The Maximalists," unpublished MS, 27.
6   For a discussion of the spiritual crisis in turn-of-the-century Russia see Geifman, *Thou Shalt Kill*, 19; Sazonov's letter cited in ibid., 49.

7   O. V. Aptekman, "Partiia 'Narodnogo Prava'," *Byloe* 7(19) 1907: 189; see also G. Ul'ianov, "Vospominaniia o M. A. Natansone," *Katorga i ssylka* 4(89) (1932): 71.

8   O. Piatnitskii, *Zapiski bol'shevika* (Moscow, 1956), 65.

9   "Iz otcheta o perliustratsii dep. politsii za 1908 g.," *Katorga i ssylka* 2(27) (1928): 156.

10 Milan Kundera, *The Book of Laughter and Forgetting* (New York: Penguin Books, 1981), 61–2.

11 I. S. Turgenev, "Gamlet i Don-Kikhot," in *Sobranie sochinenii*, vol. 6 (Moscow: Iz-vo "Pravda", 1968), 289–306.

12 Ibid., 290–1.

13 Ibid., 298–9.

14 Ibid., 292–3.

15 See, for instance, S. Iakov, *1905 g. v satire i karikature* (n.p., 1928). For similar examples of the reliance on the cruder forms of public taste see such 1906 publications as *Sekira, Gudok, Signal, Zabiiaka*, and *Nagaechka*; specific archival references may be found in Geifman, *Thou Shalt Kill*, 262n, 326n.

16 Norman M. Naimark, "Terrorism and the Fall of Imperial Russia," lecture presented at Boston University (April 14, 1986), 21.

17 See, for example, E. Koval'skaia, "Po povodu stat'i M. P. Orlova 'Ob Akatui vremen Mel'shina'," *Katorga i ssylka* 52 (1929): 164.

18 V. I. Sukhomlin, "Iz tuiremnykh skitanii," *Katorga i ssylka* 55 (1929): 104. P. Murashev cites similar examples in "Stolitsa Urala v 1905–1908 gg.," *Katorga i ssylka* 4(65) (1930): 49, 51.

19 For detailed discussion of criminal practices and psychological unbalanced behavior in the Russian liberation movement see Geifman, *Thou Shalt Kill*, 154–72.

20 Cited in Geifman, ibid., 6.

21 For an excellent analysis of Nechaev's personality and activities see Philip Pomper, *Sergei Nechaev* (New Brunswick, NJ: Rutgers University Press, 1979).

22 Cited in Geifman, *Thou Shalt Kill*, 7.

23 "New type of radical" in Russia is an underlying theme in Geifman, *Thou Shalt Kill*; for a discussion of the extent of political violence in the late imperial period see ibid., 20–2.

24 Nay, "The Maximalists," 29.

PART I

Radical Socialists

CHAPTER ONE

The Mensheviks

André Liebich

At its Second Congress in 1903 the Russian Social Democratic Labour Party (RSDRP, founded 1898) split into the Bolshevik, or majority faction, and the Menshevik, or minority one. Thereafter the two groupings continued to be so inextricably linked that they have been seen, on both sides of the divide, as *alter egos* or mirror images of each other. Here I propose to examine some of the historiographical issues regarding Menshevism, particularly in its relation to Bolshevism, before looking at Menshevik attitudes, policies, and doctrines between 1903 and 1917. The argument I should like to make is that the differences between Bolsheviks and Mensheviks in that period are not nearly as fundamental as we have assumed in the light of later historical events.

I

From the very outset the spokesmen of the two factions defined their differences in binomial terms. The earliest self-designation contrasted "hard" or "narrow" Bolsheviks with "soft" or "broad" Mensheviks.[1] Later labels opposed "dogmatists" to "pragmatists," or "orthodox" Marxists against "opportunists," although these terms were used interchangeably. Indeed, the accusations which the warring factions made against each other were often identical, as each charged the other with deepening the split between them. Epithets hurled at the opposing faction quickly became a foil with which one defended oneself.[2]

Each faction sought to underpin its accusations, and its own self-image, by elaborating theoretical arguments. Both the Bolsheviks and the Mensheviks claimed to speak on behalf of the working class and dismissed their opponents as intellectuals. To the extent to which each faction conceded that its rivals enjoyed a working-class following, it explained such allegiance in terms of the workers' immaturity. Significantly, however, "immaturity" in Menshevik parlance meant adventurism or excessive radicalism on the part of the workers, whereas in Bolshevik vocabulary it signified reformism or gradualism.[3]

Among the most frequent categories invoked in these debates were those of "spontaneity" and "consciousness." These terms too were highly ambivalent. Spontaneity generally corresponded to the Menshevik belief in workers' initiatives or "self-activity"; consciousness referred to Bolshevik emphasis on organization, centralization, and discipline. But the two terms could be used with diametrically opposite intent. Up to and including 1917, the Bolsheviks' spontaneity expressed itself in their willingness to ride with instinctive mass protest movements, even as the Mensheviks showed themselves partisans of "consciousness" in relying exclusively on the working class.[4]

Partisans and historians have developed further contrasts between the two factions. The Mensheviks have been routinely presented as the Westernized wing of Russian social democracy, whereas the Bolsheviks are considered more properly Russian, a label which may carry either positive or negative connotations.[5] It is true that the Bolshevik faction included more ethnic Russians, but this was of little consequence within a movement founded on class principles and Western socialists did not necessarily identify with the Mensheviks.[6] A variant on the theme of Westernization lies in the argument that the Mensheviks saw Russia as experiencing a Western-type development, both economically and politically.[7] This is true but misleading. Both Mensheviks and Bolsheviks were faithful to the classic Marxist tenets of their time and, until 1914, ardent admirers of German social democracy. Both factions looked to the West for guidance, inspiration, and approval.

Among the most common distinctions, suggested with ever-increasing frequency over the years, is that between Menshevik moderation and Bolshevik radicalism. Moderation in what, one might ask? The fact that many Bolsheviks condoned sensational measures condemned by most Mensheviks, such as "expropriations" or armed robberies, is not sufficient grounds to characterize them, especially since neither faction adopted an unequivocal stance on this issue.[8] Both factions prided themselves on being authentic revolutionaries, unconditionally committed to a radical overthrow of the existing order. Both were proud of their commitment to the principle of the dictatorship of the proletariat, and of the fact that the RSDRP was the only Marxist party of its time to incorporate this slogan into its program. Their differences lay in regard to tactics and strategies – the use of legal versus underground organizations, for example. Even strategies often coincided, either concurrently or with a time lag. In all cases, policies were defended on grounds of efficacy. No Menshevik before 1917 would have invoked "moderation" as grounds for his or her behavior.[9]

Attempts have been made to distinguish the two factions in terms of objective or social criteria. Differences in the estimated numerical strength or in the social composition of the factions are not striking. For example, in the course of 1906 Bolshevik strength varied between 13,000 and 33,000 members whereas Menshevik forces numbered 18,000 to 43,000. Gentry representation was roughly similar among Bolsheviks and Mensheviks (22 percent/19 percent), townspeople were more numerous among the Mensheviks (55 percent/39 percent), while there were more peasants among the Bolsheviks (38 percent/26 percent).[10] A Menshevik historian (who was originally a Bolshevik) writes, with reference to the year 1904, that "*in practice* the social composition of the organizations led by the Bolsheviks and by the Mensheviks was about the same."[11] Distinctions in ethnic composition may have been more significant; for example, at the Fifth or London Party Congress in 1907 the proportion of ethnic Russians was more than twice as high (78 percent/34 percent) and the proportion of Jews more than half as low (11 percent/23 percent) among the Bolsheviks as among the Mensheviks. A striking characteristic then, as later, was the prominence of Georgians among the Mensheviks (29 percent as compared to 3 percent among the Bolsheviks).[12] In occupational terms, the Mensheviks had more members from the intelligentsia and skilled workers but educational levels between the two factions overall were the same. One Menshevik leader has recalled that Menshevism appealed to the advanced metal workers of the south and to highly trained printers, whereas Bolshevism drew its strength from textile workers in the heart of the country and from the backward Ural metal workers.[13] A thorough comparison of the factions' profiles would need more information than is available and would require distinguishing between periods as well as between party cadres and the rank and file.[14]

A contrast between the factions comes out more clearly when one compares their respective leaders. First, it is significant that the Mensheviks could not be as closely indentified with a single leader as could the Bolsheviks. Although Lenin was regularly opposed within Bolshevik ranks and he might occasionally represent a minority position within his own faction, one can refer to Bolsheviks as "Leninists" from very early on. Among the Mensheviks, L. Martov (pseudonym of Iulii Osipovich Tsederbaum) did not emerge as a comparable leader until after 1917. In previous years he shared leadership with others, such as Pavel Axelrod and Aleksandr Potresov, or Georgii Plekhanov, the father of Russian Marxism, who did not fit comfortably into either faction. In terms of personality too, Martov and Lenin represent stark contrasts. Martov's biographer has referred to him as the "Hamlet of democratic socialism," whereas decisiveness may be considered Lenin's most characteristic trait. Nevertheless, the dreamy intellectual Martov waged war against his former friend and ally Lenin as relentlessly as the latter did against the Mensheviks. Moreover, once Martov had taken control of the defeated Mensheviks after the November Bolshevik takeover, he imposed strict discipline upon them.[15]

The most telling feature of the literature delimiting Mensheviks from Bolsheviks is the tendency to attribute abstract, ahistorical features to each faction. One is almost led to believe that Menshevism and Bolshevism existed from all time as philosophical categories, psychological types, or moral options. Of course, the distribution of heroes and villains is neatly reversed in Soviet and Western scholarship.[16] In both cases, however, the opposition between the factions assumes primordial and paradigmatic status as one contrasts the factions in terms of vice and virtue.[17] This historiographic tendency has developed exponentially over the years. Only rarely has it been subjected to self-criticism, as in the case of an early Bolshevik who wryly stated that the factional opposition was one between "respect for parents, legal marriage, educating children," as against "disrespect for parents, deflowering virgins, breaking youths' heads against stones."[18]

II

Attempts to reconstruct the specificities of menshevism (and bolshevism) usually begin with the Second Congress of the RSDRP. Historians have called the congress a milestone in world history, even as they have expressed bewilderment that apparently minor and random differences there could have produced a schism of such magnitude.[19]

The Second Congress marked the victory within the RSDRP of the *Iskra* current, to which both Lenin and the future Menshevik leaders belonged. In the preceding period the editors of the *Iskra* journal had led a relentless struggle against trends within the party favouring reformism, economic struggle, and workers' autonomy. The Iskrists' manifesto was Lenin's recent booklet, *What Is To Be Done?*, a spirited defense of the primacy of politics and of the role of intellectuals within the party. Discipline, centralization, leadership were the Iskrists' common watchwards.[20]

Disagreements within the Iskrist camp first appeared at the congress over the definition of a party member, with Lenin favouring a narrower definition over Martov's broader one. The issue was hotly debated but participants, including Lenin, conceded that the differences between the variants were not fundamental. In the event, Lenin lost and accepted his defeat. Indeed, until 1917 both Mensheviks and Bolsheviks shared a common party program and a common party statute, incorporating first the Menshevik and then, as of 1907, (with Menshevik assent) Lenin's definition of a party member.[21]

The actual division came over the issue of restructuring *Iskra*'s editorial board. Martov objected to Lenin's proposal of reducing the board and of easing out some of its less effectual editors, although Martov's own place was not threatened. Thanks to a fortuitous walk-out by some of the congress delegates Lenin was able to obtain a majority. It was thus on the basis of a chance vote regarding an issue of personnel and organization, not doctrine, that Lenin's adherents acquired the name Bolsheviks (majoritarians), relegating their opponents to the status of Mensheviks (minoritarians). Martov refused to accept the outcome of the vote or to take up his place on the newly constituted editorial board. His departure was temporary, however, because within four months Lenin's only ally on the board, Georgii Plekhanov, reversed position, removing *Iskra* from Lenin's hands and turning it over to Martov and the Mensheviks.

"The schism came like a thunderbolt from a clear blue sky," wrote Leon Trotsky, who initially opted for the Mensheviks before going off on his own and ending up as a Bolshevik in 1917.[22] Trotsky's incredulity was shared at all levels of the party as well as by many later commentators. Both Lenin and Martov had behaved in an overwrought and unreasonable manner and their quarrel did not appear to involve matters of principle.[23] Historical accounts have therefore had to grapple with the incommensurability between the causes of the disagreement and its effects. They have done so by reading differences back to the pre-congress period, by presenting its events as a "moment of truth," or by resorting to metaphors about the "seeds" of divison that were planted at the congress.[24] None of these explanations has been entirely successful.

The incipient factional positions were swept away in the excitement of the 1905 Revolution. Nothing underscored better the irrelevance of the Menshevik/Bolshevik division than their common incapacity to come to terms with events. Their shared belief had been that social democrats should not, at this historical stage, aim for power but for "hegemony" or dominance within a coalition of opposition forces.[25] In the course of 1905, however, neither faction could resist the temptation of toying with the idea of seizure of power.[26]

According to a schematic notion of the 1905 Revolution, Bolsheviks proved more radical and Mensheviks more cautious. Moreover, the Bolsheviks put their hopes on alliance with the peasantry whereas the Mensheviks counted on liberal-bourgeois forces. Lenin's transfer of hopes from the bourgeoisie to the peasantry, then as later, is considered to mark a watershed between Bolshevism and Menshevism.[27] Generally speaking, however, their differences proved less significant than their similarities, and differences did not always correspond to the Menshevik/Bolshevik divide. Divergences came out primarily in nuances. For example, both Bolsheviks and Mensheviks supported the soviets or workers' councils which had arisen independently of the social democratic movement. The Bolsheviks saw the soviets, however, as the embryo of a future government whereas the Mensheviks viewed them as organs of workers' self-government. Both factions fiercely resisted concessions to the government. The Mensheviks justified this stance in terms of preserving acquired positions; the Bolsheviks defended it by warning that concessions would sap revolutionary zeal.[28] In some respects the factions departed from stereotypes. Both made plans for an insurrection but it was the Bolsheviks who sought to husband their strength whereas the Mensheviks tried to unleash revolutionary forces.[29] Most importantly, however, the revolution of 1905 proved to be a defeat as much for one faction as for the other.

After the dramatic revolutionary events of 1905, the following years could only be anticlimactic. Traditional intelligentsia support for the revolutionary movement declined and the new rules of Russian politics threw all revolutionary parties off balance. The Mensheviks took up more readily new opportunities, such as that of participating in elections to the Duma. Lenin eventually came around to the same position, in spite of fierce opposition from the majority of his own faction; he even persisted in his decision when its justification was undermined by a reactionary turn in government policies in 1907.[30] The factions stood opposed with respect to the peasantry, with the Mensheviks successfully advocating that the party program endorse the principle of municipalization of land, as against Bolshevik arguments for nationalization. In the circumstances of the time this debate had no practical impact and it is even difficult to connect it directly to the Mensheviks' alleged "peasantophobia."[31] The key issue which emerged concerned the mobilization of trade unions and other open workers' organizations, such as cooperatives and welfare societies. In this area the Mensheviks seized the initiative early on only to lose it to the Bolsheviks in later years.[32]

The Bolsheviks (and Soviet historiography) have put the question of "liquidationism" as the heart of the party struggle between 1905 and

1914. Mensheviks are reproached for having purportedly worked to "liquidate" the underground party, thereby surrendering independent party structures and renouncing all prospects for revolution. In fact, liquidationism represents, at most, one of three or four currents within the Menshevik faction. Moreover, Western scholars have argued that the notion itself is simply a polemical slur. All Mensheviks agreed that struggle had to be waged on "two fronts," both legal and underground. Differences were ones of emphasis and they really revolved around the question of what sort of party structures were appropriate in given circumstances. They also contrasted trade union *praktiki* or activists with cadres, whose allegiance went first and foremost to the party itself, and who were more often theoretically inclined than the typically pragmatic workers' representatives. Most significantly, the debate was one between Mensheviks at home, keen to take advantage of existing legal possibilities, however few, and Mensheviks in emigration, by the nature of their situation cut off from such activity.[33]

Most telling with respect to the blurring of lines between Mensheviks and Bolsheviks is the fact that it is difficult to tell exactly when the two factions emerged as separate parties. In 1906 The Fourth Party Congress, known as the Stockholm "Reunification" Congress, put an end to the split on Menshevik terms, although the Menshevik majority only lasted until the next congress the following year. Of course, the split had never really ended, as each faction maintained its own secret organization and recriminations flew ever faster. The Mensheviks condemned party-inspired armed robberies, notably the dramatic Tiflis State Bank expropriation of 1907, but only some saw this as sufficient reason to break with Lenin.[34] A further unification agreement in 1910 capsized at the very last minute. The Menshevik liquidators who were to join the Central Committee in fulfillment of the agreement withdrew and the Bolsheviks declared the agreement invalid. According to Lenin's wife, Nadezhda Krupskaia, it was then that he decided upon a separate party, rather than simply a separate faction. According to a prominent Menshevik woman, the Menshevik leaders had already given up interest in unity.[35]

In the view of the official Communist Party history, as well as of some Western historians, it was at the Prague Party Conference of 1912 that the Bolsheviks created an independent party.[36] The legitimacy of this meeting was highly doubtful but the riposte to it, a Vienna Conference organized mainly by Trotsky, was weak. By 1913 the anti-Bolshevik August bloc created at Vienna, consisting of Mensheviks and others, had disintegrated. Moreover, it was in that year that the party's last unified central institution, the Social-Democratic caucus of Duma deputies consisting of seven Mensheviks and six Bolsheviks, also split through the efforts of a police agent in the guise of a Bolshevik deputy.[37] In 1914 the Socialist

International was preparing its own effort at reconciling the Russian factions. Had war not come the Bolsheviks would probably have been faced with a choice between unification or expulsion from the socialist movement.[38]

The First World War imposed new alignments on Russian social democracy. In Lenin's words, "chauvinism" versus "antichauvinism" represented the new dividing line and this did not necessarily correspond to a Bolshevik/Menshevik division.[39] The Duma Social-Democratic caucus rediscovered its unity (all the more easily as its *agent provocateur* deputy had fled) and took a common antiwar stance in contrast to the "chauvinist" positions of Social-Democratic parliamentarians elsewhere in Europe. Soon it turned out, however, that "internationalist" opposition to the war could take many different forms since the Mensheviks, and many Bolsheviks, would not go as far as Lenin in envisaging the defeat of Russia with equanimity. As these issues were being discussed by Social Democrats abroad, notably by Lenin and Martov, party members at home were faced with a dilemma reminiscent of earlier debates. The creation in Russia of "war industries' committees" with worker participation opened up the possibility of legal labour activity and set off a controversy reminiscent of that concerning "liquidationism" a few years earlier. Preoccupied by these issues, Social Democrats were caught off guard by the outbreak of the February Revolution of 1917.[40]

III

As late as 1917 many members of the RSDRP disregarded, for practical purposes, the Menshevik/Bolshevik division. At the grassroots level the movement towards unification became a surge in the course of that revolutionary year. Meanwhile, at the summit of the party Bolshevik leaders adopted "semi-Menshevik" positions whereas top Mensheviks maintained, even retroactively, that Bolsheviks were still sound Social Democrats in 1917.[41] Even the foremost Menshevik historian confessed that after having studied the era of the birth of Menshevism and Bolshevism for over ten years "you often wonder what people were fighting over. They all say almost the same things. Their fights are over shades yet from these shades arise different movements."[42]

Does this mean that both Western and Soviet historiography have been misguided in making the Bolshevik/Menshevik division the key to understanding Russian social democracy until 1917? Such a conclusion does not necessarily follow. One can indeed identify a number of political and ideological distinctions between the two factions. At the very least, one can speak of diverging outlooks. The weakness of the dominant approach lies in its reluctance to recognize the fundamental interdependence between Menshevism and Bolshevism. The two factions were not only opposed, they were also inseparable.

The political distinctions between Mensheviks and Bolsheviks began as differences in emphasis on matters of organization. They evolved by leaps and bounds until the issue came to be seen as one of attitudes towards democracy. The fundamental insight in this respect, however, came from Trotsky, a most doubtful Menshevik, under the name of "substitutionism." According to this analysis, the party would substitute itself for the proletariat, the central committee would substitute itself for the party, and the leader would substitute himself for the central committee.[43] Most other political divergences – regarding Duma or trade union participation, for example – raised the same question of democracy but democracy by itself was never a final goal or an unconditionally defended principle within the party. Mensheviks should not be confused with liberal democrats.

Ideological distinctions between the factions developed within a common Marxist framework. The belief in laws of historical development which dictated that Russia should pass through given stages of evolution is more readily attributed by historians to the Mensheviks but it was a shared postulate. Both factions believed, notably, that Russia needed to experience a bourgeois revolution before it undertook a proletarian or socialist revolution. The fact that the Mensheviks were more fearful of the peasantry (the petty bourgeoisie, in Marxist terms) and less suspicious of the liberal bourgeoisie than were the Bolsheviks made a difference in terms of strategy but not in terms of goals. Indeed, one of the last surviving Mensheviks has argued that Marxist doctrine as such did not dictate Menshevik policies in 1917. Rather, it provided the intellectual prism through which Russian Social Democrats, of all complexions, viewed struggling social forces.[44] At the crucial moment, the Bolsheviks proved ready to bend this prism but, at least in their own minds, they remained within it.

Marxists themselves have suggested that many of the differences between the two factions can be understood in terms of psychological outlook rather than politics. It is the psychological explanations that ring true in the various accounts by Social Democrats of the reasons which led them to join one faction or another.[45] It is also psychology, including the psychology of opportunism, which may explain why individuals moved from one faction to the other, some from Bolshevism to Menshevism in the aftermath of 1905, many more from Menshevism to Bolshevism after 1917. Precisely the fact that such movement was widespread, however, raises questions regarding the psychological approach. What can one surmise regarding Menshevik psychology as one considers the later careers of such ex-Mensheviks as the notorious Soviet prosecutor

Andrei Vyshinskii, the future foreign commissar Georgii Chicherin, or the fanatic Bolshevik planner Iurii Larin? Psychology may be a better instrument than party doctrine to explain the moral scruples of many Mensheviks, for example, but circumstances may provide an even better explanation.[46]

An alternative approach to a definition of the differences between menshevism and bolshevism would take its point of departure in the dual nature of the tasks confronting the RSDRP. This duality was incorporated in the party program which established a minimum and a maximum agenda. Among the former stood the establishment of a democratic republic, political and civil rights, the separation of church and state, free obligatory schooling; among the latter appeared the socialist revolution, the dictatorship of the proletariat, the socialization of means of production, a non-commodity planned economy. The party was thus staking out, in a perfectly self-conscious way, the two extreme poles between which it defined its activity. Factions would gravitate closer to one pole or another, but this did not mean they had abandoned the party banner or, at least at the outset, that they saw their activity as ultimately incompatible.

The dual nature of the tasks undertaken by the RSDRP is the theme of a subtle and reflective analysis, written late in life and in a self-critical spirit, by one of the exiled historic Menshevik leaders. In his *Origins of Bolshevism* Fedor Dan distinguishes between social democracy's general-democratic or political goals and its class-socialist or social mission. In Dan's reconstruction it was the Bolsheviks who incarnated the general-democratic current of social democracy down to 1917, with their willingness to place themselves at the head of non-proletarian forces and their readiness to use purely political weapons; at that time the Mensheviks, mindful of the autonomous interests of the proletariat, concentrated on the party's class-socialist mission. After the November revolution these roles were reversed, as the Bolsheviks sought to push through a socialist transformation, while the Mensheviks acted as guardians of social democracy's commitment to political emancipation.[47]

One need not accept Dan's verdict that both factions were "right, each in its own way, because with all its one-sidedness each one of them was expressing a certain essential need of Russian political life." But one would do well to ponder Dan's portrait of Mensheviks and Bolsheviks as "Siamese twins," fighting bitterly and yet dependent on each other, an image which echoes Karl Kautsky's references to the factions as "warring brothers."[48] Logically, a majority (*bol'shinstvo*) implies a minority (*men'shinstvo*), and it is therefore not surprising that in the course of their development each faction of the RSDRP defined itself in relation to the other and neither was able to shake off the intimacy born of opposition.

Notes

1 The early use of "hard/soft" is explained in a note to *Pis'ma P. B. Aksel'roda i Iu. O. Martova*, ed. F. Dan, B. Nikolaevskii, L. Tsederbaum-Dan (Berlin: Russkii revoliutsionnyi arkhiv, 1924), 88–91. See also the interesting graphic representation of the "hard/soft" division (as well as other party cleavages) in Robert V. Daniels, *The Conscience of the Revolution: Communist Opposition in Soviet Russia* (Cambridge, Mass.: Harvard University Press, 1960), 436.

2 The barrage of mutual accusations was carried on in the pages of the party journal *Iskra*. It was sustained on the Bolsheviks' part by Lenin's 1904 broadside, *One Step Forward, Two Steps Backward: The Crisis in Our Party*. For examples and accounts see: Israel Getzler, *Martov: A Political Biography of a Russian Social Democrat* (Cambridge: Cambridge University Press, 1967), 83–5; Abraham Ascher, *Pavel Axelrod and the Development of Menshevism* (Cambridge, Mass.: Harvard University Press, 1972), 198–205; Samuel H. Baron, *Plekhanov: The Father of Russian Marxism* (Stanford: Stanford University Press, 1963), 247–52. Pavel Axelrod's seminal statement of the factional differences by a leading Menshevik has been translated in part: "The Unification of Russian Social Democracy and Its Tasks," in Abraham Ascher, ed., *The Mensheviks in the Russian Revolution* (Ithaca, NY: Cornell University Press, 1976), 48–52.

3 In addition to the sources mentioned above see also: J. L. H. Keep, *The Rise of Social Democracy in Russia* (Oxford: Clarendon Press, 1963), 143–8. Theodore Dan, *The Origins of Bolshevism*, ed. and trans. Joel Carmichael (New York: Harper & Row, 1964; 1st Russian edn, 1946), 249–63.

4 Spontaneity and consciousness are pivotal concepts in Leopold H. Haimson, *The Russian Marxists and the Origins of Bolshevism* (Cambridge, Mass.: Harvard University Press, 1955), see especially 182–4. See further, T. Dan, *Origins of Bolshevism*, 249–407 *passim*. Haimson has recently reiterated the point that these concepts are heuristically more useful than those of Menshevik "determinism" versus Bolshevik "voluntarism," invoked by both Soviet and Western scholars. "Men'sheviki i bol'sheviki (1903–1917): Formirovanie mentalitetov i politicheskoi kul'tury," in Z. Galili, A. Nenarokov, L. Kheimson, eds, *Men'sheviki v 1917 godu*, vol. 1 (Moscow: progress-Akademiia, 1994), 27.

5 In his classic work Bertram D. Wolfe, *Three Who Made a Revolution: A Biographical History* (New York: Stein and Day, 1948), 160, refers to the Menshevik/Bolshevik clash as one of the "changing forms of the protean battle between Westernizer and Slavophile." E. H. Carr, the leading British historian of the Soviet Union and, unlike Wolfe, unsympathetic to the Mensheviks writes: "Almost the only indisputable generalization on this point [Mensheviks vs. Bolsheviks] is that while the Mensheviks stood nearer to Western conceptions and models of social democracy, the Bolsheviks had a keener instinct for what would work in Russian conditions." Review of S. Schwarz, *The Russian Revolution of 1905*, *History* 54 (1968): 118.

6   The high priest of orthodox German Marxism, Karl Kautsky, found himself
     in such a quandary as to which faction to support that he was inclined to cast
     a plague on both. See Moira Donald, *Marxism and Revolution: Karl Kautsky
     and the Russian Marxists 1900–1924* (New Haven: Yale University Press,
     1993).

7   The exiled Menshevik leader Raphael Abramovitch, *The Soviet Revolution*
     (New York: International Universities Press, 1962), 1, writes: "Russia on the
     eve of the war was well advanced on the path of evolution toward a modern
     democratic state. Had the war not intervened, she could have advanced much
     further, peacefully, through the pressures of the growing labor movement, the
     liberal middle classes, and the socially conscious intelligentsia." The author-
     itative presentation of this view by Alexander Gerschenkron, "Problems and
     Patterns of Russian Economic Development," in Cyril Black, ed., *The
     Transformation of Russian Society* (Cambridge, Mass.: Harvard University
     Press, 1960), 42–71, has been challenged by Leopold Haimson, originally in
     "The Problem of Social Stability in Urban Russia 1905–1917 (part 1)," *Slavic
     Review* 23 (1964): 619–42.

8   On the ambivalence of Menshevik attitudes to terror and to other unortho-
     dox practices, see Anna Geifman, *Thou Shalt Kill: Revolutionary Terrorism in
     Russia 1894–1917* (Princeton: Princeton University Press, 1993), 97–101.

9   On the later development of the image of Menshevik moderation, see André
     Liebich, *From the Other Shore: Russian Social Demcocracy After 1921*
     (Cambridge, Mass.: Harvard University Press, 1997), ch. 8.

10   David Lane, *The Roots of Russian Communism: A Social and Historical Study of
     Russian Social Democracy 1899–1907* (Assem: Van Gorcum, 1969), 12–21.
     This is still the most detailed study of the composition of the party.

11   Solomon M. Schwarz, *The Russian Revolution of 1905: The Workers' Movement
     and the Formation of Bolshevism and Menshevism* (Chicago: University of
     Chicago Press, 1967), 211.

12   *Politicheskaia istoriia rossii v partiiakh i litsakh*, ed. Rossiiskii nezavisimyi insti-
     tut sotsial'nykh i natsional'nykh problem (Moscow: "Terra," 1993), 13.

13   Dan, *Origins of Bolshevism*, 259.

14   A recent prosopographic study of Social-Democratic women does not gener-
     ally bother with the distinction between Mensheviks and Bolsheviks. Beate
     Fieseler, *Frauen auf dem Weg in die Russische Sozialdemokratie 1890–1917; eine
     Kollektive Biographie* (Stuttgart: Franz Steiner Verlag, 1995).

15   Martov's sympathetic biographer recognizes that, "for all his high purpose,
     he [Martov] did not avoid low politics," (Getzler *Martov*, 56). It is significant
     that members of each faction admired the leader of the other. (Cf. the
     Menshevik N. V. Valentinov, *Encounters with Lenin* (London: Oxford University
     Press, 1968; first Russian edn 1953), and the Bolshevik A. V. Lunacharskii,
     "Iulii Osipovich Martov (Tsederbaum)," in *Revoliutsionnye siluety* (Moscow:
     Deviatoe ianvaria, 1923): 63–70).

16   The first doctoral thesis in Russia to systematically criticize Soviet precedents
     in this respect also ends up merely reversing heroes and villains (V. Kh.
     Turmarinson, *Men'sheviki i Bol'sheviki: nesostoiavshiisia konsensus* (Moscow:
     "Luch," 1994).

17 Merle Fainsod, *How Russia is Ruled* 2nd edn (Cambridge, Mass.: Harvard University Press, 1963; 1st edn 1953), a textbook used by generations of students defines Bolshevism in terms of elitism, high centralization, tight discipline, absolutism, intolerance, manipulativeness, subordination of means to ends, the drive for total power. In Lenin's complete works, references to Menshevism have been classified under such headings as opportunism, splinterism, disorganizing activities, perversion of Marxist theory, appeasement, social chauvinism. *Polnoe sobranie sochinenii*, 5th edn, *spravochnyi tom*, pt 1 (Moscow: Izd. politicheskoi literatury, 1964) 373–83.

18 P. N. Lepeshinskii, "Partiinaia likhoradka 20-let tomu nazad," *Proletarskaia revoliutsiia* 25 (1924): 43–4.

19 Cf. the eminent political philosopher Isaiah Berlin, "in 1903 there occurred an event which marked the culmination of a process which has altered the history of the world," "Political Ideas in the Twentieth Century," *Foreign Affairs* 28 (1950): 364; and a Soviet writer: "the birth of the first proletarian party of a new type in the world . . . is the main historical result of the Second Congress," Iu. K. Malov, "Protiv fal'sifikatsii istorii II-ogo s'ezda RSDRP v sovremennoi anglo-amerikanskoi istoriografii," *Voprosy istorii KPSS* 7 (1973): 103.

20 A. Potresov, the *Iskra* editor who was later to be Lenin's most implacable opponent among the Mensheviks, wrote: "I've read your little book twice running and straight through and I can only congratulate its author. The general impression is superlative," cited in Dan, *Origins of Bolshevism*, 238.

21 The minutes of the Second Congress are available in English as (Russian Social-Democratic Labour Party) 1903: *Second Ordinary Congress of the RSDLP*, trans. and annotated by Brian Pearce (London: New Park Publications, 1978).

22 Cited in Keep, *Rise of Social Democracy*, 133.

23 Note the harsh judgment by a historian basically sympathetic to the Mensheviks: "All Iskrites, including the future Mensheviks, were fully compromised by their endoresement of Lenin's dictatorial principles of party organization. . . . Moreover, once dictatorship from the top downwards was accepted as the principle of organization, it was logical enough that Lenin should be that dictator," Leonard Schapiro, *The Communist Party of the Soviet Union* 2nd rev. edn (New York: Random House, 1971; 1st edn, 1960), 54.

24 Getzler, *Martov*, 64–7, searches for earlier differences between Lenin and Martov. Keep, *Rise of Social Democracy*, 126–7, says of Martov at the congress: "Now it was as though the scales were suddenly lifted from his eyes." Cf. a Soviet commentator's image of a "kernel" of division with Wolfe's reference to a "germ." W. Bystranski, *Die Menschewiki und die Sozial-Revolutionäre in der Russischen Revolution* (Hamburg: Verlag der Kommunistischen Internationale, 1922), 11, and Wolfe, *Three Who Made a Revolution*, 248.

25 The notion of hegemony had been developed by Plekhanov, Axelrod, and Lenin before the 1903 split. See Ascher, *Axelrod*, 134–7.

26 In particular they proved susceptible to Trotsky's theory of "Permanent Revolution" which linked the Russian Revolution to a simultaneous socialist revolution in the advanced Western countries (See Dan, *Origins of Bolshevism*,

345, Schwarz, *Russian Revolution of 1905*, 101–3, and Getzler, *Martov*, 101–3).

27   Schwarz, *Russian Revolution of 1905*, 30, writes that "radical versus cautious" is how the factions were *seen* by the rank and file. Schwarz also analyzes (21–8) the limitations of Lenin's evolution.

28   Dan, *Origins of Bolshevism*, 356–61.

29   Ibid., 350. Dan connects this difference to a more "political" conception of the insurrection among the Mensheviks and a more "military-technical" one among the Bolsheviks.

30   Daniels, *Conscience of the Revolution*, 13–28, and Schapiro, 93, 102.

31   See Esther Kingston-Mann, *Lenin and the Problem of Marxist Peasant Revolution* (New York: Oxford University Press, 1983).

32   Haimson, "Problem of Social Stability in Urban Russia," 629–36.

33   Geoffrey Swain, *Russian Social Democracy and the Legal Labour Movement 1906–1914* (London: Macmillan, 1983), 92, writes that the terms Bolshevik and Menshevik were by the end of 1909 increasingly anachronistic. Schapiro, *Communist Party of the Soviet Union*, 114, maintains that "liquidationism" was nothing but a Bolshevik term of abuse.

34   Getzler, *Martov*, 120, cites Martov as referring to the Tiflis State Bank expropriation as "a very convenient basis for an honest split which would be fully understood by the public."

35   On the aborted agreement, Dan, *Origins of Bolshevism*, 395. Krupskaia cited in R. C. Elwood, *Russian Social Democracy in the Underground: A Study of the RSDRP in the Ukraine* (Assem: Van Gorcum, 1974), 33. Interview with Lydia Dan, who was the sister of Martov and the wife of another Menshevik leader, Fedor Dan. In Leopold H. Haimson, ed., *The Making of Three Russian Revolutionaries: Voices from the Menshevik Past* (Cambridge: Cambridge University Press, 1987), 212–14.

36   *History of the Communist Party of the Soviet Union / Bolsheviks /: Short Course*, ed. A Commission of the C. C. of the C.P.S.U. (B.) (Moscow; Foreign Languages Publishing House, 1939), 138–43. Adam B. Ulam, *Lenin and the Bolsheviks: The Intellectual and Political History of the Triumph of Communism in Russia* (London: Secker & Warburg, 1965), 283–4.

37   On this agent, Roman Malinovsky, see Wolfe, *Three Who Made a Revolution*, ch. 31.

38   Schapiro, *Communist Party of the Soviet Union*, 138–42.

39   Lenin, *Polnoe sobranie sochinenii*, vol. 49, 64.

40   See Lewis H. Siegelbaum, *The Politics of Industrial Mobilization in Russia, 1914–1917: A Study of the War-Industries Committees* (London: Macmillan, 1983), esp. ch. 7.

41   "Semi-menshevik," is the term used, for example, by the Soviet dissident Roy Medvedev with reference to Stalin and Kamenev in 1917. *Let History Judge: The Origins and Consequences of Stalinism* (New York: Random House, 1971) 8. On sound Social Democrats, Th. Dan, "Das Ende der Opposition," *Der Kampf* 21 (February 1928): 1–2.

42   B. I. Nikolaevskii, discussion of R. Abramovich, "Perspektivy bol'shevizma i nashi zadachi," lecture at Berlin Menshevik Club, February 17, 1931, tran-

script in *Protokoly Berlinskoi Organizatsii* (available at International Institute of Social History, Amsterdam, and Nicolaevsky Collection, Hoover Institution).

43 See Baruch Knei-Paz, *The Social and Political Thought of Leon Trotsky* (Oxford: Clarendon Press, 1978), ch. 5.

44 Boris Sapir, "Notes and Reflections on the History of Menshevism," in Leopold H. Haimson, ed., *The Mensheviks; From the Revolution of 1917 to the Second World War* (Chicago: University of Chicago Press, 1974), 365.

45 There is a huge memoir literature on this subject. Amongst it note the publications already cited here: Haimson, ed., *The Making of Three Russian Revolutionaries* and Valentinov, *Encounters with Lenin.*

46 Daniels, *Conscience of the Revolution*, demonstrates that moral scruples were not a Menshevik monopoly.

47 Dan, *Origins of Bolshevism*, 259.

48 Ibid. and, citing Kautsky, Getzler, *Martov*, 134.

CHAPTER TWO

The Bolsheviks

Robert C. Williams

Two master narratives dominate the story of Lenin, the Bolsheviks, and their unanticipated rise to power in 1917. The first is the Soviet master narrative which deified Lenin as the omniscient leader of a small group of efficient Marxist revolutionaries who overthrew a bourgeois government, won a civil war against allied counterrevolutionaries, and launched the Soviet Union on the path of socialism or communism. The second is the Western master narrative which demonized Lenin as the Jacobin dictator whose ruthless band of obedient followers seized power, subdued all other political parties, and created a totalitarian police state that ruled workers and peasants with an iron hand. Bolshevik triumph and the defeat of all opposition to their rule bred both master narratives which emphasized the individual (Lenin) and the defining moment of revolution (1917) when history displayed either inevitability or accident. Bolshevism was equated with Leninism, the 1917 Revolution divided two sharply discontinuous pre- and postrevolutionary eras, and Stalinism was the logical outcome.

More recently, however, multiple historical narratives have sprung up to succeed the less sustainable Soviet and Western myths of a bygone era. These revisions tend to shift from the individual to the collective, from Lenin to classes and masses, and from discontinuity to continuity. In part, the new narratives derive from the collapse of the former Soviet Union and the end of the Cold War. But they also reflect the varying shapes of the discipline of history and the turn from event-making individuals and politics to broader and longer historical trends in society and culture.

Yet the central questions still remain: who was and was not a Bolshevik? How much control did Lenin exert over his own party? Was Bolshevism identical with Leninism? What influence did Bolshevism have inside and outside Russia, in the capital cities and in the provinces? Why did the Bolsheviks succeed in 1917? Was their success inevitable? Was the Bolshevik revolution a seizure of power, a socioeconomic transformation, or a cultural revolution? How much mass support did the Bolsheviks receive from workers and peasants? Were they a Jacobin elite or a mass party? Did Bolshevism lead to Stalinism or was there a Bolshevik alternative?

In addressing these questions, the master narratives emphasized Lenin's dominance and his link with Stalin, for good or for evil. The revolution was either an inevitable good thing or an accidental and conspiratorial bad thing. The new narratives stress the polyphony of the other Bolsheviks with their cacophonous discourse, Russian social democracy in the context of European socialism, the Bolsheviks as a vanguard of the working class, Bolshevism as a mass mobilization movement, and the Bolshevik revolution as a cultural revolution akin to millenarianism that links the deep structure of Russian religion with intelligentsia culture and popular myth. The center can no longer hold. In the story of Bolshevism, the preeminence of Lenin as a causal explanation has given way to the meaning of cultural transformation as public carnival and popular discourse. Historians naturally continue to hold a variety of views on these matters. But the unmistakable trend in Western historiography on Bolshevism appears to be away from individuals and toward a social and cultural history whose *longue durée* renders less significant the old defining personalities and moments of Bolshevism.

I

In the beginning there was Lenin – the underground alias of V. I. Ulianov (1870–1924) – a 33-year-old former attorney from Samara and Simbirsk on the lower Volga whose searing personality and theory of party organization in 1903 split the Russian Social Democratic Workers' Party into Bolshevik and Menshevik factions. Lenin was the old man, the leader, the event-making individual, the revolutionary Jacobin from the University of Kazan whose bald head seemed to burst with invective and conspiracy. Bolshevism was biography, and Lenin was its subject. Or so it seemed to the Mensheviks. Just as Lenin labeled Menshevism a minority faction in order to define his own faction of the party as a majority, so the Mensheviks imagined Bolshevism as the illegitimate offspring of one man, Lenin, a perversion of Marxism and socialism whose ancestry lay deep in the Russian psyche. Lenin created Bolshevism in his own image and with Bolshevism the seeds of totalitarianism. The Mensheviks created the master narrative that dominated Western scholarship on Bolshevism for decades after Lenin's death.

After the Bolsheviks came to power in November 1917, their political opponents elaborated on the Menshevik scheme. The Bolsheviks were said to be Jacobin dictators, not democratic socialists, whose "commissarocracy" continued tsarist autocratic traditions. Bolshevism was identical to Leninism. Lenin the dictator resembled Caesar, Napoleon, Pugachev, Arakcheev, Bakunin, and Robespierre. The Party of Social Revolutionaries (PSR), whose support came from the peasantry, saw Bolshevism as a dictatorship of the city over the countryside, of the industrial worker over the peasant, and of the state over the people. The Constitutional Democrats (Kadets) viewed the Bolsheviks as illegitimate heirs of the 1917 liberal–socialist Provisional Government, a menace to European order and to freedom, law, and constitutional government. The monarchists considered Bolshevism an offspring of the forces of darkness, Antichrist and the Jews. All imagined Bolshevism to be the child of Lenin, a malicious political manipulator with the "cynicism and genius of the executioner."[1]

Lenin continued to dominate Western views of Bolshevism in the interwar and Cold War periods. Bolshevism and fascism seemed linked in their militant opposition to democracy and the liberal democratic state. Leon Trotsky, writing in exile, noted that "Bolshevism created the type of the authentic revolutionist who subordinates to historic goals irreconcilable with contemporary society these conditions of his personal existence, his ideas, and his moral judgements." For Trotsky, Lenin's role was critical during the armed insurrection of November 1917. Lenin assured that all Bolsheviks maintained a "vigilant irreconcilability" with bourgeois ideals. The British historian E. H. Carr, writing in 1950, considered Lenin the "spokesman and creator of Bolshevism," who ensured that Bolshevik "men of action" triumphed over the Menshevik theorists. Likewise, the American historian Donald Treadgold equated Bolsheviks and Leninists, observing that they were "peasant minded" in 1905. Lenin's violently coercive tactics made the Bolshevik party a "conspiratorial military brotherhood rather than a group competing in the marketplace with discussion and argument," in the minds of political scientists Carl Friedrich and Zbigniew Brzezinski. "If 'to make the revolution' means to conceive and build the machine that seized power in 1917," wrote Bertram D. Wolfe in 1964, the year of N. S. Khrushchev's political demise as leader of the Soviet Union, "then Lenin is without peer" in creating a "centralized hierarchical organization of 'professional revolutionaries.'"[2]

During the Cold War most Western observers agreed with political scientist Adam Ulam's observation in *The Bolsheviks* (1965) that "the history of the Bolsheviks and of the Russian Revolution has to be focussed around the life of one man: Vladimir Ulyanov – Lenin." The image of Lenin the Jacobin dictator who single-handedly created Bolshevism in the manner of a Robespierre or a P. N. Tkachev (a nineteenth-century Russian revolutionary) provided the same biographical emphasis as the Lenin cult inside the Soviet Union. Lenin was the "founder and leader of Bolshevism," a hypnotic and ascetic revolutionary in the tradition of Russian religious-schismatic Old Believers whose cult celebrated an "immortal exemplary leader, while his living successors in the Kremlin bear the burden of power."[3]

Yet in the 1980s, Western historians began to modify their views of Lenin as the single dominating figure of Bolshevism. Robert Service in his two-volume biography of Lenin noted that he lacked "omnipotence" while wielding a "pre-eminent influence" within Bolshevism; Lenin "had never, not even in late 1903, held a monopoly of power in the Bolshevik faction." Lenin was a "political genius" whose impact on Bolshevism had been exaggerated in most accounts. His political opponents' image of him as the dominating figure of Bolshevism and the October Revolution was "an exaggerated image." Nonetheless, Service concluded that Lenin exhibited a "real superiority of impact over his colleagues and his party: no one matched him in importance."[4]

Other historians still asserted that Lenin's foresight and organization were critical to Bolshevism and that Bolshevism and Leninism were virtually identical. The Lenin cult survived the revisionism of perestroika inside the Soviet Union, where Lenin himself took on a kinder, gentler aspect as a reformer whose New Economic Policy (1921–8) was an antecedent of Mikhail Gorbachev's efforts. Novelists like Vasily Grossman continued to view Lenin as a consequence of 1,000 years of Russian servitude.[5] But the Lenin cult lasted as long as the Soviet Union and disappeared only with the latter's demise.

More recently the retired Soviet army general Dmitri Volkogonov has revived the traditional Cold War view of Bolshevism and Stalinism as the offspring of Lenin. For Volkogonov, who had access to newly opened Russian archives, Lenin remained a "Russian Jacobin" who was "the source of the totalitarian ideology of intolerance," a utopian who sought power through violence and terror, and was the high priest of Bolshevism. Bolshevism and Leninism remained identical movements which led ultimately to Stalinism. Trotsky too was no longer a prophetic alternative to Lenin and Stalin, but an arrogant, brutal, and contemptuous orator who helped create the Stalinist system which murdered him and who thought he was the last real "bolshevik-Leninist" even in exile and death. An American historian in the 1990s could still write that Lenin "ultimately emerged as the sole acknowledged leader" of Bolshevism, that Leninism led to Stalinism, and that Lenin "brought the Bolsheviks to victory in the struggle for power in 1917."[6] Yet other voices who did not accept the Menshevik and totalitarian master narrative of Lenin the Jacobin leader of a subordinate political party were now clamoring to be heard.

II

The other Bolsheviks (everyone but Lenin) by no means accepted Lenin's views as orthodoxy before 1917. In fact, they articulated their own Marxist positions on many issues. Historians intrigued by Bolshevik alternatives to Leninism have focused on two crucial periods: 1905–17, when the party was divided and defeated in the wake of the 1905 Revolution, for which the Bolsheviks were quite unprepared, and 1921–8, when the New Economic Policy sparked considerable discussion and debate about the future of socialism in the USSR. For these historians, Lenin was not the only Bolshevik leader nor even the dominant one. The political historian Stephen Cohen, in his 1973 biography of Nikolai Bukharin, was among the first to question the Menshevik-totalitarian master narrative, or paradigm, which had informed most studies of Bolshevism. Cohen argued in great detail that Bukharin was a reformer whose views on economic development, if carried out, would have provided a Bolshevik alternative to both Leninism and Stalinism. The idea that Bolshevism was a "united, homogeneous, singleminded group of men and women" was a myth. Bolshevism before 1917 had featured "endless disputes over fundamental issues, particularly between Lenin and his fellow leaders." Bolshevism was not Leninism, but a "diverse movement led by dissimilar men and women."[7]

Turning to the 1917 Revolution, Alexander Rabinowitch also discovered that the Bolsheviks were not simply Leninist conspirators, but had strong popular support among the masses. The Bolshevik central committee was "simply unable to control the behavior of major regional organizations," and the party was a "relatively free and flexible structure" that was "internally relatively democratic, tolerant and decentralized."[8] Other Bolshevik leaders were therefore worth studying: Roman Malinovskii, the Polish double agent for the Okhrana and the Bolsheviks who led the Bolshevik Duma delegation in 1913–14 and was shot on Lenin's orders in 1918; A. V. Lunacharsky, a prolific writer and poet whose Nietzschean views informed his later career as Commissar for Public Enlightenment; Savva Morozov, the Old Believer millionaire friend of Maxim Gorky who funded Bolshevik operations after 1905; Inessa Armand, the wealthy Bolshevik feminist who befriended Lenin in Paris in 1909; Maxim Litvinov, the revolutionary smuggler who refused to represent the Bolsheviks at the congress of the Second International in 1914; and Leonid Krasin, the engineer who organized Bolshevik underground operations (printing, gun running, and bank robberies – known as expropriations, or "exes"). Krasin, like many other Bolsheviks, was no obedient Leninist. His ultimate loyalty was to "his own perception of socialist revolution" more than to party cohesion.[9]

Historians also discovered a current of "left Bolshevism" grounded in European syndicalism that was quite distinct from Leninist authoritarianism. The French syndicalist Georges Sorel, a great admirer of Lenin, attracted the attention of many other Bolsheviks before 1914, much to Lenin's disgust. The other Bolsheviks read and translated syndicalist texts and emphasized the role of worker experience through strikes, rather than party authority through hierarchy and conspiracy. Syndicalists opposed participating in parliamentary elections as a bourgeois sham. Around 1980, Jack J. Roth and K. D. Bracher, European historians, noted the similarity of Bolshevism and syndicalism as political ideologies. Other historians traced the syndicalist influences on the other Bolsheviks during 1905–14 and identified a current of anti-Leninist Bolshevism around the Geneva exile journal *Vpered* (Forward) that was as legitimate an offspring of the Bolshevism of 1903 as Leninism.[10]

The other Bolsheviks were particularly drawn to Aleksander Bogdanov, Lenin's rival for control of Bolshevism, a physician who developed his own Marxist philosophy based on the teachings of the Austrian philosopher Ernst Mach. Bogdanov urged the RSDRP to "boycott" the elections to the First and Third Dumas (parliaments) and to "recall" deputies already elected. In contrast to Leninist absolutism, Bogdanov was a relativist thinker who believed that socialism was a useful myth that organized mass experience. Ideas were as important as economic classes and forces of production. Bolshevism was not Marxist orthodoxy, but socialist mythmaking for the working classes. Lenin assaulted and distorted Bogdanov's views in his famous *Materialism and Empiriocriticism* (1909). Bogdanov responded by resigning from the Bolshevik Center and the *Proletarii* (Proletarian) editorial board, and organizing his own party schools for underground workers in the Italian safety of Capri (where Gorky had a home) and Bologna. In the 1980s, Bogdanov spawned a virtual industry within the history profession. A translated edition of his utopian science fiction novel *Red Star* (1908) characterized Bogdanov as "a major prophet of the Bolshevik movement and one of its most versatile writers and thinkers." Another historian characterized Bolshevism as "a fractious and divided movement of emigre intellectuals and white-collar professionals who continually disagreed over matters of ideology, organization, and money"; Bogdanov represented a collectivist strand of Bolshevik thinking that was quite at odds with Lenin's Jacobinism and emphasized intellectual

organization of mass experience more than party hierarchy and discipline.[11] The other Bolsheviks thus emerged as thinkers independent of
Lenin, whether or not they disagreed with him on particular tactical issues
such as the wisdom of bank robberies, participation in Duma elections, or
the strike movement.[12]

Focus on the other Bolsheviks stimulated a parallel discussion of the
distinction between Leninism and Bolshevism. Moshe Lewin in 1984
observed that "'Bolshevism' applies to the party as a whole, which
espoused Leninism by and large as its ideology of struggle, but bolshevism
included factions which often proposed divergent interpretations of the
Marxist canons as well as of the theoretical and strategic positions that
derive specifically from Leninism." Lewin noted that there were in fact
many Leninisms, since Lenin changed his position constantly before and
after 1917. Stephen Cohen argued at about the same time that neither
Bolshevism nor Leninism implied Stalinism as a future development,
and reiterated his argument that Bukharin represented "a more liberal,
humane variant of Russian Communism, with its native authoritarian
traditions." In contrast to Robert Tucker's view of Stalin as a hero-
worshipper of Lenin, Robert Himmer argued that before 1914 Stalin was
more of a left Bolshevik who was "increasingly disenchanted with Lenin,"
dissatisfied with his "temporizing" leadership of the Bolshevik faction of
the Russian Social Democratic Workers' Party (RSDRP), and at odds with
Lenin's positions on the land question, the Duma, and Bolshevism generally. Robert McNeal's thorough biography of Stalin likewise argued that
Stalin was not simply a Lenin follower, but an "ultra-militant" from
Georgia who played the moderate in early 1917 and had virtually no role
in October, even though he remained "near the top of the ruling party."
Dmitri Volkogonov also considered Stalin an unknown party functionary
who "in the Bolshevism of October" was "a centrist who knew how to sit
and wait and adapt himself."[13]

In 1990, Philip Pomper, in an updated triple biography of Lenin, Stalin,
and Trotsky reminiscent of Bertram Wolfe's classic *Three Who Made a
Revolution* (1948), characterized Lenin as a Jacobin who "looked like both
a heretic and a candidate for dictatorship" before 1905. Lenin's "drive for
authority" underlay his psychobiography and helped explain Bolshevism's
hatred for both the intelligentsia and the peasantry. By the time of the
Fourth (Unification) Congress of the RSDRP in 1906 at Stockholm, Lenin
was "a kind of outcast among the leaders of the Russian Social Democratic
movement." Bolshevism and Leninism were two distinct phenomena.
Bolshevism existed briefly before 1905 and then was reborn in 1908–11
but quite in conflict with the views of its original founder, Lenin.[14] Other
historians shared Pomper's view,[15] and the new historiography thus
identified the other Bolsheviks as an independent group of revolutionaries

whose emphasis on strikes, changeable myth, relativistic philosophy, and mass appeal was quite distinct from Lenin's Jacobinism. Bolshevism was neither as unified nor as obedient as the Leninist model of Bolshevism suggested.

III

The Bolsheviks were a particular breed of social democrat in imperial Russia, a squabbling and ambitious faction of a left-wing socialist political party. Historians thus view Lenin and the Bolsheviks within the larger context of the RSDRP, their Menshevik rivals, the European socialists of the Second International, and the political party structure of the Duma years (1906–17) of constitutional monarchy and limited parliamentary elections. The Bolsheviks were defined not only by their relationship with Lenin, but by their participation in a larger political party.

Already in 1963, the historian Richard Pipes argued that Bolshevism grew out of the Social-Democratic labor movement in St Petersburg and Poland in the 1880s and 1890s and was grounded in Russian populism as much as in Marxism. Pipes claimed that Lenin's importance had been "grossly exaggerated and distorted," that he was not a leader of the Union of Struggle for the Emancipation of Labor or any other social democratic organization, and that he was a writer, not a labor leader. Thus Lenin's famous 1902 pamphlet *What is to be Done?*, defining the organizational principles of a conspiratorial revolutionary party, marked a sharp break with his "economist" past. In the beginning, Lenin's Bolsheviks resembled Martov's Mensheviks.[16] In studying the RSDRP inside Russia before 1917, David Lane cited many examples of Bolshevik–Menshevik collaboration in the provincial towns.[17] Abraham Ascher's biography of Pavel Akselrod also emphasized the similarities between Bolshevism and Menshevism, noting that there were "too many switches from one faction to another for us now to accept the assertion that the two movements were at all times clearly divided over ideological matters."[18]

But if the Bolsheviks and Mensheviks were so similar, then what caused their frequent internecine quarrels? Dietrich Geyer's meticulous 1981 compilation of materials from Karl Kautsky's archives in Amsterdam set the stage for a wide-ranging discussion of these quarrels and showed that they derived in large measure from disputes over funds acquired from fictitious marriages with wealthy women and from bank robberies or "exes" conducted by the Bolsheviks inside Russia after 1905. The three German trustees of these funds forced Lenin to make concessions to the Mensheviks and to close down the Bolshevik Center and the journal *Proletarii*, while accepting Bolshevik–Menshevik parity in the Central

Organ, the Foreign Bureau, and the Russian Board of the RSDRP. Geoffrey Swain's study of Russian social democracy and the labor movement concluded that "Lenin's party" was virtually destroyed in 1909 and that the RSDRP by 1914 was more Trotsky's creation than Lenin's. Leninism was a subset of Bolshevism. Swain wrote: "The Bolshevik faction had virtually dissolved itself. From now on, the terms Bolshevik and Menshevik were increasingly meaningless. The hierarchy of control, that Lenin had been struggling to prevent falling into Bogdanov's hands, was simply dismantled."[19]

In the 1880s, Russian populists and Marxists had often engaged in mutual cooperation despite their varying emphases on peasants and urban workers. Subsequently, as Social Democracy spread to the provincial towns, Jacobinism mattered less than political realism, foreign émigrés had little influence on events inside Russia, and all radicals operated in a common spirit of ideological flexibility, mutual aid, and tolerance against their common enemy, the imperial regime. By the time of the London Congress (1907), the RSDRP claimed 150,000 members belonging to 145 local organizations. With the outbreak of World War I, Bolsheviks joined Mensheviks and Trudoviks in remaining faithful to the antiwar spirit of the socialist Second International of European working-class parties. Like other parties and factions, the Bolsheviks were divided about whether or not to resist the war; many of them were even so-called *defensisty* who supported the government's war effort. On the whole, the Bolsheviks were certainly no more antiwar than other socialists, who encouraged collaboration among Mensheviks, Bolsheviks, and Social Revolutionaries. In short, recent scholarship has demonstrated common activity by Russian socialists and far more cooperation than was thought among Bolsheviks and Mensheviks.[20]

The Bolsheviks and Mensheviks thus retained their sense of membership in a common RSDRP until 1917. They represented branches of a single Russian social democratic movement, in contrast to the regional and national socialist organizations, such as the Jewish Bund or the Lithuanian Social Democratic Party. Their joint efforts in exile before 1905 nurtured a common enterprise. Revolutionary terrorism was another thread linking Bolsheviks, Mensheviks, Social Revolutionaries, and anarchists. Even the Kadets at times condoned terrorism. Revolutionary action thus crossed political party boundaries. The Bolsheviks matured in the underground conspiratorial atmosphere of bank robbery, counterfeiting, and murder which found its fruition in both Leninism and Stalinism. Only after 1917 did the Mensheviks become victims of Bolshevik persecution and the Bolsheviks a "party without a clearly defined social base" that failed to unite or control a divided peasant Russia and turned into a "product of Lenin's doctrinairism."[21]

IV

As a faction of the RSDRP, the Bolsheviks claimed to be a workers' party drawing its class support from the labor movement in urban areas. Lenin, living in Austrian Galicia, was especially aware of the upswing in labor unrest in Russia after 1911. Around 1970, Western social historians began to realize that worker support for Bolshevism was not a fiction created by Leninism and Soviet official history. Bolshevism had more worker support than Cold War historiography on both sides might have suggested. The general turn toward social history in the 1970s within the historical profession involved a new focus on large statistical sampling, the lives of ordinary working people, women, the family, peasants and the group norms, processes, and structure of society that underlay political history. Historians of Bolshevism now began to emphasize strikes, labor unions, soviets, and the workers' control movement in 1905 and 1917 in order to demonstrate the working-class basis of a political movement.

Workers replaced Bolsheviks as the heroes or villains of 1917. Tsuyoshi Hasegawa in his history of the February Revolution noted that the Bolsheviks were not monolithic, lacked coordination between central and local organizations, and failed to react effectively to the strike movement. The French historian Marc Ferro considered the Bolshevik revolution from the point of view of social history, rather than as an inevitable and legitimate political triumph or an accidental seizure of power. Ferro argued that "the role of political parties, including the Bolsheviks, was not necessarily decisive" in 1917. Rather, the October Revolution was a "test of strength between a government without a state and a state without a government." Bolshevism was a kind of "embryo state" through which the masses came to power. In his study of the revolution in Baku, Ronald Suny showed that Bolshevism was a "moderate" part of the labor movement that showed a "sensitivity toward workers' economic desires." Bolsheviks and Mensheviks cooperated within the Baku RSDRP. Neither faction was tightly organized or conspiratorial. Both had considerable worker and Moslem support. Diane Koenker in her 1981 study of Moscow workers in 1917 argued that workers became Bolshevik supporters because of rational and logical choices based on the political and economic pressures of their society. Like the Bolsheviks, workers were diverse and often mutually antagonistic. But workers were attracted to Bolshevism for perfectly rational, rather than irrational or conspiratorial, reasons.[22]

By the early 1980s, social historians had reached a consensus that the Bolshevik revolution was no accident precipitated by an individual conspirator, Lenin, but a social upheaval in which workers were major players. Laura Engelstein wrote that Bolshevik leadership and intelligentsia activism were only two of many forces shaping workers' experience and perception in 1905; the Bolsheviks were long on the rhetoric of armed insurrection and short on action, but capable of recruiting Moscow workers into the trade unions and the strike movement. Victoria Bonnell likewise showed that worker support for the Bolsheviks increased on the eve of World War I, but that "the Bolsheviks cannot be credited with having radicalized workers; the disposition to embrace radical solutions arose out of the workers' own experience with employers and the state." Sheila Fitzpatrick concluded that the Bolsheviks were neither totalitarians nor modernizers, but a workers' party defined by Lenin's ideas and personality, and led by the intelligentsia, a party which after the revolution created a "broad channel for working-class upward mobility."[23]

Workers played a critical role in 1917 with or without Bolshevik leadership. The Bolsheviks did exert some influence on workers through their legal daily newspaper *Pravda* (Truth) and the Fourth Duma. In Petrograd the organized working class, not the Bolsheviks, held real power in the factories and the streets. David Mandel portrayed the Russian Revolution as a struggle for state power led by workers who acted and made choices based on their own experience; the July Days, not Bolshevik orders, pushed workers away from revolutionary democracy in the direction of proletarian dictatorship. Nor was this immature, irrational, chiliastic or anarchist behavior. Workers gave a "fundamentally reasoned response to a changing situation." Likewise workers' militias, Rex Wade demonstrated, acted quite independently of the Bolsheviks in organizing Red Guard units, providing a "critical mass of socially cohesive, politically determined armed workers who could and would support a radical revolution in the name of 'soviet power.'" Such studies showed in detail how the Bolsheviks had greater social and worker support than had previously been assumed. In 1917, only the Bolsheviks reflected and articulated mass aspirations. They were not willful conspirators but alert politicians. The new social history revealed a growing social polarization between upper and middle classes and the mass of workers, soldiers, and peasants. "The Bolsheviks came to power," concluded Ronald Suny, "not because they were superior manipulators or cynical opportunists, but because their policies as formulated by Lenin in April and shaped by the events of the following months placed them at the head of a genuinely popular movement."[24]

Radical workers thus replaced the Bolsheviks as the major force behind the 1905 and 1917 Revolutions. Under the new paradigm of social history, the Bolsheviks were revolutionaries acutely sensitive to rational popular demands, not omniscient leaders of irrational mobs. The Bolsheviks were an open, mass party, at times undisciplined and disorganized, but appealing to the broad spectrum of urban workers. In 1905, in both St Petersburg and Moscow, they were reluctant prisoners of events who worked with the strike movement only after it had taken independent shape. Socialists followed where workers led. Party lines mattered little. By 1910, the Bolsheviks were largely an émigré faction, Lenin an isolated figure; the party had little influence on the workers' movement in the cities. "Party labels," concluded Diane Koenker in her study of the strike movement in 1917, "were significantly absent from strike activity."[25]

In the 1990s, historians continued to show that Russian workers lacked political party leadership in both 1905 and 1917, that political parties were disorganized and poorly funded, and that the Bolsheviks did not direct the workers' movement. Odessa workers in 1905 "acted politically without necessarily following the lead of socialist activities." Red Guards were as apt to be Mensheviks as Bolsheviks, and both factions frequently cooperated in the factories. Factory committees and trade unions were primarily workers' organizations that drifted toward the Bolsheviks only late in 1917. Some workers in 1918 thought that the RSDRP was divided into two factions, Bolsheviks and Communists. Lenin's ideas had very little influence on how the workers' movement was led, although workers turned increasingly toward the Bolsheviks in the summer of 1917. A few historians still argued that socialist parties did provide mass leadership in 1917. But most agreed that the "working class" of later Soviet mythology was in fact a regionally distinct, internally divided, and professionally diverse social group, acting quite independently of the socialist parties, and that the Bolshevik influence on workers until the late summer was much less than had been thought.[26]

V

The workers were the most obvious social class supportive of the Bolsheviks in 1917. Yet historians in recent years have also turned their attention to the role of the masses generally, especially the peasants of rural Russia. The masses represented the deep structure of Russian society, the long run of history, and the popular mythology of social justice. John Keep's seminal 1976 study of the Russian Revolution focused on Bolshevik mass mobilization, ordinary men and women, the chaos and anarchy of the 1917–21 period. Keep argued that the Bolsheviks had "captured the energies" of mass organizations, that the October Revolution was less of a watershed than assumed, and that the Bolsheviks did not become a mass party until 1918. "The Bolsheviks alone," he concluded, "were schooled in the techniques of organized manipulation and knew more or less what they wanted to achieve."[27] The masses were of crucial importance, but the Bolsheviks remained in control.

The 1980s witnessed a number of studies emphasizing the role of the masses under Bolshevik guidance. Robert Edelman's work on peasants in the right bank of Ukraine in 1905 showed that the Bolsheviks showed more interest in peasantry than did the Mensheviks, but that peasant unrest was spontaneous, disorganized, and broad. Alan K. Wildman's massive work on the end of the imperial army and the role of soldiers in the revolution again emphasized that Bolshevism was not a monolithic and voluntarist power-oriented conspiracy, but a complex and divided movement of mass mobilization aimed at workers, peasants, and soldiers, whose longing for peace was epitomized by one man's query: "What good is land and freedom to me if I'm dead?" William Rosenberg in a collection of readings on Bolshevik visions of the future observed that "the Bolsheviks came to power not only because they identified with militant workers and peasants in rejecting the premises of liberal rule, but also because they associated themselves directly with mass social and cultural aspirations." Peter Kenez showed that the Bolshevik "propaganda state" was a result of extended mass mobilization by men who were masters of persuasion and treated the masses with condescension. Likewise, Donald J. Raleigh in his local history of the revolution in one provincial town, Saratov, demonstrated that the masses could rarely distinguish between Bolsheviks and Mensheviks, since Bolshevism in Saratov remained only "skin deep" even in 1917. The masses opted for soviet power, not Bolshevik dictatorship.[28]

By 1990, the new paradigm of social history stressed the masses, the long view, mentalities of the peasantry, social context, continuities, and comparison. Many historians accepted the view that Bolshevism had never been a monolithic command center, but a diverse group of revolutionaries responsive to differing views within the party and to a shifting social context. Lenin no longer appeared to be an ideologue whose model was a dictatorship of the proletariat, but a member of a party that emphasized libertarian themes of popular empowerment. Russian peasants, workers, and soldiers were no longer pawns of political parties, but autonomous agents making rational choices. Mass aspirations from below were more important than propaganda from above. The Bolsheviks themselves were vibrant, chaotic, divided, and democratic in their daily activities. Moshe Lewin characterized them as men and women unsure about whether or not a revolution would occur and what it would bring, bickering intellectuals who held elections, conferences, congresses, and debates. The peasants were ultimately the crucial factor in saving the Bolshevik revolution by underwriting the regime Bolshevism engendered, the necessary and sufficient condition for Bolshevik power. While Richard Pipes and other historians hardly agreed, social historians generally saw Bolshevism as a diverse political movement with broad appeal, not a small band of conspirators with no base of support in society. "The social historians," wrote Dominic Lieven, "provide many new and useful insights. The danger only comes if they threaten to monopolize the field."[29] Certainly in the 1990s, the social history of Bolshevism was a significant trend, if not a monopoly.

VI

The idea of Bolshevism as a cultural revolution originated before the Bolshevik Revolution with the Bolshevik claim to build a new proletarian or soviet culture. The classic work *The Mind and Face of Bolshevism* (1926) by René Fueloep-Miller argued that Bolshevism claimed to realize the redemption and happiness of all through revolution, producing a "radical change of the whole of human life in all its fundamental aims and interests." While stressing the importance of Lenin in shaping Bolshevism, Fueloep-Miller emphasized the millenarian and quasi-religious impulses behind the movement and treated it as a cultural, as well as political, phenomenon. The Chinese cultural revolution of the 1960s inspired a later generation to refocus on Bolshevism as a cultural movement, rehabilitating some of Lenin's writings from the 1920s, the Proletkult (proletarian culture) movement launched by Bogdanov after 1917 and the Bukharin alternative to Stalinism. Sheila Fitzpatrick studied the First Five Year Plan (1928–32) as a cultural revolution from below, emphasizing the rise of a new class to positions of power in an industrializing society.[30]

Most historians focused on the cultural consequences of the Bolshevik Revolution. Both Lenin and Bukharin had called for a cultural revolution in the 1920s, but neither favored Bogdanov's version of proletarian culture that grew out of the civil war experience. Robert Tucker treated Bolshevism as a culture in the making even before 1917, a millenarian movement with Lenin as its prophet, Bolshevism as a mental structure, and Lenin's idea of the state as a "culture-building culture." Richard Stites's richly textured 1989 study of Bolshevism in terms of its revolutionary dreams, utopian vision, and experimental life emphasized the Bolsheviks as underground revolutionaries in a land of peasants, utopians seeking power, intellectuals who spun their own fantasies and voiced their own dreams, dreams which in power became nightmares. Lynn Mally's work on the Proletkult movement studied this version of utopia spawned by the revolution with its grass roots activities in workplace, school, theater, and home. Bernice Rosenthal saw Bolshevism as part of a much broader revolution of the spirit, grounded in Nietzsche's will to power and belief in man's ability to create his own culture. Others interpreted Bolshevism as a new messianism that manipulated apocalyptic thinking and sought to control all aspects of time, including the calendar and the days of the week, in order to provide a secular alternative to Christianity. More recently, David Pretty has shown that Russian workers were often drawn to Bolshevism because of their Orthodox Christian background and their predilection for an ascetic lifestyle.[31]

The notion of Bolshevism as a quasi-religious movement with millenarian mass appeal in a culture long accustomed to eschatological thinking about apocalyptic events forms a particular variant of the cultural revolution approach. Mikhail Agursky has linked the Bolsheviks with the antistate Old Believers as a sectarian and millenarian response to the periodic crises of Russian history. Jay Bergman has shown that Lunacharsky and other Bolsheviks used Jesus as a revolutionary martyr capable of physical resurrection in their party literature and in designing the Lenin cult. Zenovia Sochor traced the god-building tendency of Bolshevism to the Bogdanov–Lenin controversy of 1907–14 and identified cultural transformation with Bogdanov and Bukharin more than Lenin and Stalin. John Marot also explored the influence of Bogdanov's proletarian culture ideas on Bolshevism as an example of the complicated relationship between the intelligentsia and the workers. Bogdanov's collectivism, noted Andrzej Walicki, was thoroughly grounded in Marxist thought as a program of universal human liberation. Bogdanov was a complex and original thinker whose notion of cultural revolution was a kind of "antiauthoritarian totalitarianism." Bogdanov in power might well have turned out much like Lenin.[32]

As historians paid greater attention to the story of popular culture, they saw that Bolshevik power and cultural forms were symbiotically related. The Bolsheviks, concluded Richard Stites, saw popular culture as a functional and purposeful structure grounded in economics, class, and power, while the left Bolsheviks dreamed of a utopian proletarian culture. Bolshevik culture both drew upon popular forms and sought to transform society, but in the end barely narrowed the gap between the elite and the masses in revolutionary Russia. The Bolsheviks inherited the Christian dream of salvation and victory over death, manipulated the notion of Lenin as a new Lazarus, and extended the god-building dreams of the "immortality seeking intelligentsia" to an official culture of longevity, necrophilia, ancestor worship, and salvation through history. Bolshevik festivals found that older symbols had popular resonance. The myth of October was grounded in the Russian fairground and circus, as much as French Revolution festivals and mystery plays. Katerina Clark argued that St Petersburg intellectuals launched a cultural revolution based on millenarianism and romantic anticapitalism that dreamed of transcending time and space but ended up creating the transformist basis of Stalinism.

Stalin's cultural revolution was grounded in the visions of the Russian avant-garde, the intelligentsia's great experiment, which respatialized and inverted the world and moved culture from the capital to the provinces, but also served as a major factor in the imminent undoing of the movement's numerous supporters.[33]

Were the Bolsheviks then cultural revolutionaries? John Marot noted that postmodern approaches to the Bolshevik Revolution have emphasized mass support for the Bolsheviks and moved from political to social history. They ignore the activist role of the party in making a revolution. Marot emphasized that the masses made rational choices among competing political parties, among which the Bolsheviks played a decisive role by steering the revolutionary process to a successful conclusion.[34] The cultural revolution combined Bolshevik manipulation and mass articulation. What modern scholarship suggests is that the Bolsheviks were caught up in a massive cultural revolution that they tried to engineer but never quite controlled.

VII

Over the course of the twentieth century, Bolshevism has ceased to mean the Marxist ideology of one individual, Lenin, and has come to mean the cultural transformation of an entire society which has now disintegrated. Historians now see with the advantages of hindsight that a movement to seize power in one country led by one man was also a cultural transformation of Eurasia. Leninism, Bolshevism, socialism, workers' soviets, and mass cultural revolution provide concentric circles of master narratives to describe the complex story of Russia's revolutionary transformation through war, civil war, industrialization, collectivization, and purges. Whereas the Cold War created two competing master narratives of heroic Leninism and accidental totalitarianism, Bolshevism before 1917 appears in retrospect more internally divided and disputatious, more popular and less conspiratorial, linked more with society and less with ideology, than imagined. Of all the political parties of imperial Russia, Bolshevism may have seemed the most unlikely to seize power in 1917. Yet a deeper and more extensive knowledge of Russian society and culture has made it possible for historians to discover roots of social support and cultural resonance in a movement previously associated with raw political power. We now know that Bolshevism was more diverse and disputatious than orthodox Leninism, less distinct from Menshevism within the socialist party, more supported from below by workers and peasants, and more embedded in the deep structure of Russian culture than we had thought. The frigid dialogue of Soviet and Cold War historiography has given way to a competing polyphony (sometimes cacophony) of voices in search of a new audience. Such voices have not yet created an acceptable paradigm for Bolshevism, but they are and will be heard.

Notes

1   Jane Burbank, *Intelligentsia and Revolution: Russian Views of Bolshevism, 1917–1922* (Oxford: Oxford University Press, 1992), 19–22, 48–9, 119, 149–150. P. N. Miliukov, *Bolshevism* (New York: Scribner, 1920).

2   Francesco Nitti, *Bolshevism, Fascism and Democracy* (New York: Macmillan, 1927), 163. Maurice Parmelee, *Bolshevism, Fascism and the Liberal-Democratic State* (New York: John Wiley, 1934). Waldemar Gurian, *Bolshevism* (New York: Macmillan, 1932). Leon Trotsky, *The Russian Revolution* (Garden City: Doubleday, 1959), 303. E. H. Carr, *The Bolshevik Revolution, 1917–1923: A History of Soviet Russia*, vol. 1 (New York: Macmillan, 1950), 50. Donald W. Treadgold, *Lenin and his Rivals: The Struggle for Russia's Future, 1896–1906* (New York: Praeger, 1955), 82, 105, 200. Carl J. Friedrich and Zbigniew J. Brzezinski, *Totalitarian Dictatorship and Autocracy* (Cambridge: Harvard University Press, 1956), 25. Bertram Wolfe, *Three Who Made a Revolution: A Biographical History* (New York: Dell, 1948; 1964), 4, 165.

3   Adam Ulam, *The Bolsheviks: The Intellectual and Political History of the Triumph of Communism in Russia* (New York: Macmillan, 1965), vii. Astrid von Borcke, *Die Ursprunge des Bolschewismus: Die jakobinischer Tradition in Russland und die Theorie der Revolutionare Diktatur* (Munich, 1977). Nina Tumarkin, *Lenin Lives! The Lenin Cult in Soviet Russia* (Cambridge, Mass.: Harvard University Press, 1983), 40, 268.

4   Robert Service, *Lenin: A Political Life.* vol. I *The Strengths of Contradictions* (Bloomington: Indiana University Press, 1985), 9, 193. vol. II *Worlds in Collision.* xii, 334. See also Service's edition of Lenin's *What is to be Done?* (London/New York: Penguin, 1988) and his *Society and Politics in the Russian Revolution* (London: Macmillan, 1992).

5   Paul Le Blanc, *Lenin and the Revolutionary Party* (London: Humanities Press, 1990), 2. Donald Raleigh, ed., *Soviet Historians and Perestroika: The First Phase* (Armonk: M. E. Sharpe, 1989). John Gooding, "Lenin in Soviet Politics, 1985–1991," *Soviet Studies* 44(3) (1992): 403–22.

6   Dmitri Volkogonov, *Lenin: A New Biography* (New York: Free Press, 1994), xxx, xxxviii, 27, 55, 60, 182. Dmitri Volkogonov, *Trotsky: The Eternal Revolutionary* (New York: Free Press, 1996). George Jackson, "The Influence of the French Revolution on Lenin's Conception of the Russian Revolution," in Gail M. Schwab and John R. Jeanneney, eds, *The French Revolution of 1789 and its Impact* (Westport-London: Greenwood Press, 1995), 273. See also Neill Harding, *Lenin's Political Thought* (London: Macmillan, 1977), *Leninism* (Durham: Duke University Press, 1996), and Ronald W. Clark, *Lenin: The Man behind the Mask* (London: Faber and Faber, 1988).

7   Abbott Gleason, *Totalitarianism: The Inner History of the Cold War* (Oxford: Oxford University Press, 1995), 138–40. Stephen F. Cohen, *Bukharin and the Bolshevik Revolution: A Political Biography, 1888–1938* (New York: Knopf, 1973), xvi, 3, 5. Donny Gluckstein, *The Tragedy of Bukharin* (London: Pluto Press, 1994).

8   On the Bolsheviks and German money, see Semion Lyandres, *The Bolsheviks' "German Gold" Revisited: An Inquiry into the 1917 Accusations* (Pittsburgh: Center for Russian and East European Studies, Carl Beck Papers no. 1106, 1995), which concludes that accusations that the Bolsheviks received German funding were "never substantiated" and the Provisional Government's case against them "lacked validity" (102, 104). Alexander Rabinowitch, *Prelude to Revolution: The Petrograd Bolsheviks and the July 1917 Uprising* (Bloomington: Indiana University Press, 1968), and *The Bolsheviks Come to Power: The Revolution of 1917 in Petrograd* (New York: Norton, 1976), xvii, xx, 311, 313.

9   Ralph Carter Elwood, *Roman Malinovsky: A Life without a Cause* (Newtonville, MA: Oriental Research Partners, 1977). A. L. Tait, *Lunacharsky: Poet of the Revolution (1875–1907)* (Birmingham: Birmingham Slavonic Monographs no. 15, 1984). Jo Ann Ruckman, *The Moscow Business Elite: A Social and Cultural Portrait of Two Generations, 1840–1905* (DeKalb: Northern Illinois University Press, 1984), 68, 138, 169. Ralph Carter Elwood, *Inessa Armand: Revolutionary and Feminist* (New York: Cambridge University Press, 1992). Hugh D. Phillips, *Between the Revolution and the West: A Political Biography of Maxim M. Litvinov* (Boulder: Westview Press, 1992). Timothy O'Connor, *The Engineer of Revolution: L. B. Krasin and the Bolsheviks, 1870–1926* (Boulder: Westview Press, 1992), 51, 55. On Krasin, see also G. S. Usyskin, *Vyborgskii uznik: dokumental' naia povest' o L. B. Krasine* (Leningrad: Lenizdat, 1984).

10   Jack J. Roth, *The Cult of Violence: Sorel and the Sorelians* (Berkeley: University of California Press, 1980), 141–78. Karl Dietrich Bracher, *The Age of Ideologies: A History of Political Thought in the Twentieth Century* trans. E. Osers (New York: St. Martin's, 1980), 59–60. Robert C. Williams, "Collective Immortality: The Syndicalist Origins of Proletarian Culture, 1905–1910," *Slavic Review*, 39 (September 1980): 389–402. Avraham Yassour, "Lenin and Bogdanov: Protagonists in the 'Bolshevik Center'," *Studies in Soviet Thought*, 22 (February 1981): 1–32. John Biggart, " 'Anti-Leninist Bolshevism': The *Forward* Group of the RSDRP," *Canadian Slavonic Papers/Revue Canadienne des Slavistes*, 23(2) (June 1981): 134–53.

11   Gereon Wolters in Ernst Mach, ed., *Die Analyse der Empfindungen und das Verhaltnis des Physischen zum Psychischen* (Darmstadt: Wissenschaftliche Buchgesellschact 1985 (Leipzig, 1886)), and authored "Ernst Mach and the Theory of Relativity," *Philosophia Naturalis*, 21 (1984): 630–41, and "Atome und Relativitat – Was meinte Mach?," in R. Haller, F. Stadler, eds, *Ernst Mach: Werk und Wirkung* (Wien: Holder–Pinchler–Temsky 1988), 484–507. Aileen Kelly, "Empiriocriticism: A Bolshevik Philosophy?," *Cahiers du monde russe et sovietique*, 21 (January–March 1981): 89–118. Michael M. Boll, "From Empiriocriticism to Empiriomonism: The Marxist Phenomenology of Aleksandr Bogdanov," *Slavonic and East European Review*, 59 (January 1981):

41–58. Alexander Bogdanov, *Red Star: The First Bolshevik Utopia*, ed. Loren Graham and Richard Stites, trans. Charles Rougle (Bloomington: Indiana University Press, 1984), citation 1. Robert C. Williams, *The Other Bolsheviks: Lenin and his Critics, 1904–1914* (Bloomington: Indiana University Press, 1986), 1. Also, Williams, "Lenin," in Joel Krieger, ed., *The Oxford Companion to Politics of the World* (New York: Oxford University Press, 1993), 534–6. On Bogdanov, see also Kenneth M. Stokes, *Paradigm Lost: A Cultural and Systems Theoretical Critique of Political Economy* (Armonk: M. E. Sharpe, 1995).

12   For a lively debate regarding Bogdanov's role within Bolshevism see: James D. White, "The First *Pravda* and the Russian Marxist Tradition," *Soviet Studies*, 26 (April 1974): 181–204; David G. Rowley, *Millenarian Bolshevism: Empiriomonism, God-Building, Proletarian Culture* (New York: Garland, 1987), 355, 359; Robert V. Daniels, "Lost Branches of History," *Russian Review*, 49(4) (October 1990): 469–73, citation 470; Raimond Sesterhenn, *Das bogostroitel'stvo bei Gor'kij und Lunacarskij bis 1909* (Munich: Otto Sagner, 1982); Aileen Kelly, "Red Queen or White Knight? The Ambivalences of Bogdanov," *Russian Review*, 49(3) (July 1990): 311.

13   Moshe Lewin, "Le Leninisme et le bolschevisme à l'épreuve de l'histoire et du pouvier," in René Gallissot, ed., *Les Aventures du marxisme* (Paris: Syros, 1984), repr. as "Leninism and Bolshevism: The Test of History and Power" in Lewin, ed., *The Making of the Soviet System: Essays in the Social History of Interwar Russia* (New York: Pantheon, 1985), 191. Stephen F. Cohen, *Rethinking the Soviet Experience: Politics and History since 1917* (New York, 1985), 91. Robert Himmer, "On the Origin and Significance of the Name 'Stalin'," *Russian Review*, 45 (1986): 271, 283. Robert H. McNeal, *Stalin: Man and Ruler* (New York: New York University Press, 1988), 18, 20, 40. Dmitri Volkogonov, *Stalin: Triumph and Tragedy*, ed. and trans. Harold Shukman (New York: Grove Weidenfeld, 1988), 22–3, 33.

14   Philip Pomper, *Lenin, Trotsky, and Stalin. The Intelligentsia and Power* (New York: Columbia University Press, 1990), 74, 80.

15   See, for example, Ronald I. Kowalski, *The Bolshevik Party in Conflict: The Left Communist Opposition of 1918* (London: Macmillan, 1991), 10, 188; and Richard Sawka, "Bolshevism of the Left and Right," *Russian Review*, 51(3) (July 1992): 420.

16   Richard Pipes, *Social Democracy and the St. Petersburg Labor Movement, 1885–1897* (Cambridge, Mass.: Harvard University Press, 1963), 122.

17   David Lane, *The Roots of Russian Communism: A Social and Historical Study of Russian Social-Democracy, 1898–1917* (University Park: Pennsylvania State University Press, 1968), 210.

18   Abraham Ascher, *Pavel Axelrod and the Development of Menshevism* (Cambridge, Mass.: Harvard University Press, 1972), 213–14, 382. See also Ralph Carter Elwood, *Russian Social Democracy in the Underground: A Study of the RSDRP in the Ukraine, 1907–1914* (Assen: Van Gorcum, 1974).

19   Dietrich Geyer, *Kautsky's Russisches Dossier: Deutsche Sozialdemokraten als Treuhander des russischer Parteivermogens, 1910–1915* (Frankfurt, 1981). Geoffrey Swain, *Russian Social Democracy and the Legal Labour Movement, 1906–1914* (London: Macmillan, 1983), 78, 188.

20 Norman Naimark, *Terrorists and Social Democrats: The Russian Revolutionary Movement under Alexander III* (Cambridge, Mass.: Harvard University Press, 1983), 239–40. Abraham Ascher, *The Revolution of 1905: Russia in Disarray* (Stanford: Stanford University Press, 1988), 183. D. A. Longley, "The Russian Social Democrats' Statement to the Duma on 26 July (8 August) 1914: A New Look at the Evidence," *English Historical Review*, 102 (July 1987): 615–16. Michael Melancon, *The Socialist Revolutionaries and the Russian Anti-War Movement, 1914–1917* (Columbus: The Ohio State University Press, 1990), 180. Ziva Galili y Garcia, *The Menshevik Leaders in the Russian Revolution: Social Realities and Political Strategies* (Princeton: Princeton University Press, 1989), 397.

21 Leonas Sabaliunas, *Lithuanian Social Democracy in Perspective, 1893–1914* (Durham: Duke University Press, 1990). Frank Ortmann, *Revolutionare im Exil: Der 'Auslands-bund russischer sozialdemokraten' zwischen Autoritarem, Fuhrungsanspruch und Politischer Ohnmacht (1888–1903)* (Stuttgart: Franz Steiner Verlag, 1994). Anna Geifman, *Thou Shalt Kill: Revolutionary Terrorism in Russia, 1894–1917)* (Princeton: Princeton University Press, 1993), 96, 256. Vladimir N. Brovkin, ed. and trans., *Dear Comrades: Menshevik Reports on the Bolshevik Revolution and Civil War* (Stanford: Hoover Institution Press, 1991). Brovkin, *The Mensheviks after October: Socialist Opposition and the Rise of the Bolshevik Dictatorship* (Ithaca: Cornell University Press, 1987), 299. Brovkin, *Behind the Front Lines of the Civil War: Political Parties and Social Movements in Russia, 1918–1922* (Princeton: Princeton University Press, 1994), 414, 421. On the civil war, see also Geoffrey Swain, *The Origins of the Russian Civil War* (London: Longman, 1996).

22 Tsuyoshi Hasegawa, *The February Revolution: Petrograd, 1917* (London/Seattle: University of Washington Press, 1981), 109, 579. Ronald G. Suny, *The Baku Commune, 1917–818: Class and Nationality in the Russian Revolution* (Princeton: Princeton University Press, 1972), xii, 344. Marc Ferro, *The Bolshevik Revolution: A Social History of the Russian Revolution* trans. Norman Stone (London: Routledge and Kegan Paul, 1980), 273. Diane Koenker, *Moscow Workers and the 1917 Revolution* (Princeton: Princeton University Press, 1981), 358–9, 362. Maurice Brinton, *The Bolsheviks and Workers' Control, 1917–1921: The State and Counter-Revolution* (London: Solidarity, 1970), xii, 85.

23 Laura Engelstein, *Moscow, 1905: Working Class Organization and Political Conflict* (Stanford: Stanford University Press, 1982), 3, 222. Victoria E. Bonnell, *Roots of Rebellion: Workers' Politics and Organizations in St. Petersburg and Moscow, 1900–1914* (Berkeley: University of California Press, 1983), 428, 437–8. Sheila Fitzpatrick, *The Russian Revolution, 1917–1932* (Oxford: Oxford University Press, 1982), 6, 25, and 1994 edn, 11, 30.

24 S. A. Smith, *Red Petrograd: Revolution in the Factories, 1917–1918* (Cambridge: Cambridge University Press, 1983), 259. David M. Mandel, *The Petrograd Workers and the Fall of the Old Regime* (London: Macmillan, 1983), 1, 178. Mandel, *The Petrograd Workers and the Soviet Seizure of Power: From the July Days 1917 to July 1918* (London: Macmillan, 1984), 414. Rex A. Wade, *Red Guards and Workers Militias in the Russian Revolution* (Stanford: Stanford

University Press, 1983), 207. Ronald G. Suny, "Toward a Social History of the October Revolution," *American Historical Review*, 88(1) (February–December 1983): 52.

25 Daniel H. Kaiser, ed., *The Workers' Revolution in Russia, 1917: The View from Below* (Cambridge, Mass.: Cambridge University Press, 1987), 18, 77. Diane Koenker and William G. Rosenberg, *Strikes and Revolution in Russia, 1917* (Princeton: Princeton University Press, 1989), 328. Henry Reichman, *Railwaymen and Revolution: Russia, 1905* (Berkeley-Los Angeles: University of California Press, 1987), 203–4. Robert B. McKean, *St. Petersburg between the Revolutions: Workers and Revolutionaries, June 1907–February 1917* (New Haven: Yale University Press, 1990), 49, 484–5. Gerald Surh, *1905 in St. Petersburg: Labor, Society, and Revolution* (Stanford: Stanford University Press, 1989), 411.

26 Robert Weinberg, *The Revolution of 1905 in Odessa: Blood on the Steps* (Bloomington: Indiana University Press, 1993), 122–3, 195, 230. Heather Hogan, *Forging Revolution: Metalworkers, Managers, and the State in St. Petersburg, 1890–1914* (Bloomington: Indiana University Press, 1993). S. A. Smith and Diane Koenker, eds, *Notes of a Red Guard* (Urbana: University of Illinois Press, 1993), 186. Gennady Shkliarevsky, *Labor in the Revolution. Factory Committees and Trade Unions, 1917–1918* (New York: St. Martin's, 1993). Lewis H. Siegelbaum and Ronald G. Suny, eds, *Making Workers Soviet: Power, Class, and Identity* (Ithaca: Cornell University Press, 1994). James D. White, *The Russian Revolution, 1917–1921: A Short History* (London: Edward Arnold, 1994), 21, 125, 167, 252. Michael Melancon, "Who wrote What and When? Proclamations of the February Revolution in Petrograd, 23 February–1 March 1917," *Soviet Studies*, 40(3) (July 1988): 479–500. D. A. Longley, "The Mezhraionka, the Bolsheviks and International Women's Day: In response to Michael Melancon," *Soviet Studies*, 41(4) (October 1989): 633. James D. White, "The February Revolution and the Bolshevik Vyborg District Committee (In Response to Michael Melancon)," *Soviet Studies*, 41(4) (October 1989): 602–24. Michael Melancon, "International Women's Day, the Finland Station Proclamation, and the February Revolution: A Reply to Longley and White," *Soviet Studies* 42(3) (July 1990): 583–9.

27 John L. M. Keep, *The Russian Revolution: A Study in Mass Mobilization* (New York, 1976), 470–1.

28 Robert Edelman, *Proletarian Peasants: The Revolution of 1905 in Russia's Southwest* (Ithaca: Cornell University Press, 1987), 162. Alan K. Wildman, *The End of the Russian Imperial Army* vol. I *The Old Army and the Soldiers' Revolt (March–April 1917)* and vol. II *The Road to Soviet Power and Peace* (Princeton: Princeton University Press, 1980 and 1987), esp. vol. I, 380 and vol. II, 402–4. William G. Rosenberg, *Bolshevik Visions* (Ann Arbor: Ardis, 1984), 18. Peter Kenez, *The Birth of the Propaganda State. Soviet Methods of Mass Mobilization, 1917–1929* (Cambridge, Mass.: Cambridge University Press, 1985), 5, 7. Donald J. Raleigh, *Revolution on the Volga: 1917 in Saratov* (Ithaca: Cornell University Press, 1986), 132–9, 323, 329.

29 John Keep, "Social Aspects of the Russian Revolutionary Era (1917–1923) in Recent English-Language Historiography," *East European Quarterly*, 24 (June 1990): 159–84. Edward Acton, ed., *Rethinking the Russian Revolution*

(London/New York: Edward Arnold, 1990). E. R. Frankel, J. Frankel, and B. Knei-Paz, eds, *Revolution in Russia: Reassessments of 1917* (Cambridge, Mass.: Cambridge University Press, 1992), 301, 353, 388–405. Moshe Lewin, *Russia/USSR/Russia: The Drive and Drift of a Superstate* (New York: New Press, 1995), 59–60, 62. Dominic Lieven, "Western Scholarship on the Rise and Fall of the Soviet Regime: The View from 1993," *Journal of Comparative History*, 29(2) (April 1994): 195–227, 200.

30 René Fueloep-Miller, *The Mind and Face of Bolshevism: An Examination of Cultural Life in Soviet Russia* (New York: Harper and Row, 1965 (1926)), ix, 27. Carmen Claudin-Urondo, *Lenin and the Cultural Revolution*, trans. Brian Pearce (Atlantic Highlands: Humanities Press, 1977), 63. Sheila Fitzpatrick, *Cultural Revolution in Russia, 1928–1931* (Bloomington: Indiana University Press, 1978).

31 John Biggart, "Bukharin and the Origins of the 'proletarian culture' Debate," *Soviet Studies*, 39(2) (April 1987): 240. A. Gleason, P. Kenez, and R. Stites, eds, *Bolshevik Culture* (Bloomington: Indiana University Press, 1985), 25–6, 37 (Robert Tucker). Richard Stites, *Revolutionary Dreams: Utopian Vision and Experimental Life in the Russian Revolution* (New York: Oxford University Press, 1989), 85, 254. Lynn Mally, *Culture of the Future: The Proletkult Movement in Revolutionary Russia* (Berkeley: University of California Press, 1990). Bernice Rosenthal, ed., *Nietzsche in Russia* (Princeton: Princeton University Press, 1986), 4. Rosenthal and M. Bohachevsky-Chomiak, eds, *A Revolution of the Spirit: Crisis of Value in Russia, 1890–1924* (New York: Fordham University Press, 1990), viii. Robert C. Williams, "The Russian Revolution and the End of Time," *Jahrbucher fur Geschichte Osteuropas*, 43(3) (1995): 364–401. David Pretty, "The Saints of the Revolution: Political Activists in 1890s Ivanovo-Voznesensk and the Path of Most Resistance," *Slavic Review*, 54(2) (Spring 1995): 304.

32 Mikhail Agursky, "L'Aspect Millenariste de la Revolution Bolchevique," *Cahiers du Monde russe et sovietique*, 29(3–4) (July-December 1988): 487–514. Jay Bergman, "The Image of Jesus in the Russian Revolutionary Movement. The Case of Russian Marxism," *International Review of Social History*, 35 (1990): 239, 241. Zenovia Sochor, *Revolution and Culture: The Bogdanov-Lenin Controversy* (Ithaca: Cornell University Press, 1988), 229. Sochor, "On Intellectuals and the New Class," *Russian Review*, 49(3) (July 1990): 287. John Marot, "Alexander Bogdanov, *Vpered*, and the Role of the Intellectual in the Workers' Movement," *Russian Review*, 49(3) (July 1990): 241–64; "The Bogdanov Issue: Reply to My Critics," *Russian Review*, 49(4) (October 1990): 457–65; "Politics and Philosophy in Russian Social Democracy. Alexander Bogdanov and the Sociotheoretical Foundations of *Vpered*," *Canadian Slavonic Papers*, 33 (September–December 1991). John Biggart, "Alexander Bogdanov and the Theory of a 'New Class'," *Russian Review*, 49(3) (July 1990): 265–82. Andrzej S. Walicki, "Alexander Bogdanov and the Problem of the Socialist Intelligentsia," *Russian Review*, 49(3) (July 1990): 299, 302.

33 Richard Stites, *Russian Popular Culture: Entertainment and Society since 1900* (Cambridge, Mass.: Cambridge University Press, 1992), 206. Irene Masing-Delic, *Abolishing Death: A Salvation Myth of Russian Twentieth-Century*

Literature (Stanford: Stanford University Press, 1992), 7. James Van Geldern, *Bolshevik Festivals, 1917–1920* (Berkeley: University of California Press, 1993). Katerina Clark, *Petersburg, Crucible of Cultural Revolution* (Cambridge: Harvard University Press, 1995), 30, 242.

34 John Marot, "A 'Postmodern' Approach to the Russian Revolution? Comment on Suny," *Russian Review*, 54(2) (April 1995): 264.

CHAPTER THREE

The Bund in the Russian-Jewish Historical Landscape

Aleksandr Lokshin

The All-Jewish Workers' Union in Lithuania, Poland, and Russia, better known as the Bund (Yiddish for "union"), was founded in September 1897 in Vilna by Jewish Social Democrats representing Jewish socialist groups in several towns within the Pale of Settlement. The history of the Bund, however, goes back to the 1880s and the rise of the movement of Jewish artisans and workers.

At the end of the nineteenth century, about a third of the working Jewish population in the Pale were employed in industry and crafts, another third were merchants, shopkeepers, petty traders, and the like. Slightly more than 10 percent were workers at various enterprises, people working at home, and employers. About 10 percent were *luftmentshen* ("people of the air"), who lived by their shrewdness alone, availing themselves of any opportunity to earn some bread, and lacking any permanent source of livelihood.

At the end of the century, of the approximately 300,000 Jewish workers about 50,000 worked in medium- and large-size enterprises; the rest were employed in small workshops. Much like Russian proletarians, Jewish workers toiled under the most adverse conditions. The working day lasted for about 16 hours and longer. Wages were extremely low, sanitary conditions and safety were remarkably primitive.

The labor movement among Jewish artisans and workers in Vilna and Minsk started around 1886–8. Strikes took place here by carpenters, upholsterers, mechanics, printers, and stocking-makers, demanding that the working day be reduced to ten hours. It was not accidental that the first propaganda circles to educate workers in a Social-Democratic vein emerged in Vilna in those years. In order to assure a mass following for the workers' movement, the first propagandists in Vilna referred to the factory legislation adopted in the reign of Catherine the Great which prohibited more than ten hours of work a day in workshops. In the early 1890s the mayor of Vilna was forced to acknowledge the fact in a special declaration. The strike movement then became widespread in the Northwestern region. The movement was purely economic and had no political undertones.

Simultaneously, there emerged a large group of radically minded assimilated Jewish intellectuals in the Pale. This Jewish intelligentsia was entirely Russified, the intellectuals spoke and thought only in Russian, and although Yiddish was their native language, they were brought up on Russian literature.[1] Initially associated with the Russian populists, the Jewish socialists were distancing themselves from them at the time and evolving towards Marxist Social Democracy. It was these people who began to organize discussion circles for the most intellectually inclined Jewish workers, drawn chiefly from among printers and typesetters. The circles operated on several levels, beginning with mini-courses on Russian literacy and natural history; only at the final stage did discussions turn into socialist propaganda. When possible, sessions were held in Russian largely because the circles' intention was to produce cadres for the Russian revolutionary camp. Tsemakh (Timofei) Kopelzon, one of the Jewish leaders, remembered half a century later: "We were for assimilation; we did not even dream of a special Jewish mass movement."[2]

On the strength of the populist doctrine, most Jewish radicals of the previous decade regarded their fellow Jews as members of a parasitical class without any revolutionary potential. Yet, there was also another opinion. Aaron Liberman, a graduate of the rabbinical school in Vilna, whom the Bundists would later regard as their predecessor, reached the conclusion that it was necessary to carry on socialist propaganda among the Jews themselves. Accordingly, in 1877 he published the socialist journal *HaEmet* (The Truth) in Hebrew. Still, the issue of language was one of the first problems encountered by the Jewish propagandists who began to work in a Jewish milieu. In order to appeal to the toiling masses, it was necessary to address them in their native tongue – Yiddish – and make propagandist literature available in this language.

The need to move from narrow theoretical propaganda to practical work among the masses was announced in Vilna on May Day in 1892 and became an object of intense debate. The idea provoked opposition (chiefly from among members of the workers' circles) in favor of the established methods, i.e. training politically conscious workers who would naturally attract a following from the rest of the masses. By 1894, however, the notion of large-scale agitation won general recognition. Jewish Social Democrats concurred entirely with Georgii Plekhanov's 1892 pamphlet entitled "On the Tasks of Socialists," which emphasized the need to conduct revolutionary agitational activities among the masses: "A sect can be satisfied with propaganda in the narrow sense of the word; a political party never . . . A propagandist gives many ideas to one or a few people but an agitator gives only one or only a few ideas to a mass of people . . . History is made by the masses."[3]

Attaching priority to agitational activities settled the crucial problem of language. The decision to appeal to the working masses in their native Yiddish and publish propaganda literature in this language had far-reaching implications for the ideological and political evolution of the party-to-be.

The new trend was set forth in two hand-written pamphlets: "A briv tsu agitatorn" (A letter to agitators) by Samuel Gozhanskii (Lonu), and "Ob agitatsii" (On agitation) by Aaron (Arkadii) Kremer. Both argued that Yiddish, the language of mass agitational activities, opened up new strata of Jewish society as potential supporters for the movement – people from what could vaguely be defined as "semi-intelligentsia circles," including former students of rabbinical schools, the so-called *eshibotniki* who knew Hebrew and Yiddish and were quite close to the working masses.

While dealing with the issue of the national evolution of Jewish Social Democracy, historians attach much importance to a well-known May 1895 speech by Iulii Martov (Tsederbaum), then a leader of the revolutionary movement in Vilna. Made before worker-agitators, the speech was printed in 1900 under the title "A Turning Point in the History of the Jewish Labor Movement" and in Yiddish as "New Epoch in the History of the Jewish Labor Movement." Martov pointed out that, as it becomes more democratic and mass-scale, a movement inevitably assumes a national character. The logical outcome of this development would be the rise of "a separate Jewish labor organization which would lead and teach the Jewish proletariat in the struggle for economic, civil and political liberation."[4]

The Jewish Social-Democratic Group, also known as the Vilna Group, was the immediate predecessor of the Bund. It consisted of intellectuals and workers who would organize the Bund, introduce conspiratorial methods and discipline into the party, and determine its tactics for many years to come. Among others, this group included Kremer, "the father of the Bund," Kopelzon, Samuel Gozhanskii, Matle Srednitskii (Pati), and his future wife. In the next few years the group expanded to include a few college students, such as the young ideologist Vladimir Kosovskii (real name Nahum Levinson), Abram Mutnikovich (Gleb Mutnik), Jekuthiel (Noikh) Portnoi, Pavel Berman, Pinai Rosenthal (Pavel), and Anna Heller,

Rosenthal's future wife. Historian Henry Tobias wrote of the Vilna radicals: "The group included the major organizers, editors, and polemicists of the first generation of Bundists, and six of its members served on the Central Committee of the Bund at one time or another before 1905.[5]

The intellectuals who joined the Vilna group as translators, public speakers, agitators, and propagandists played an important part in lending the movement a mass character. Among these mention should be made of A. Litvak (real name Khaim Yankel Helfand) and Sendor Zeldov (Nemanskii). Among other intellectuals, they gave the movement an increasingly nationalist coloring, considering Yiddish to be more than just a means for agitation; for instance, Litvak organized small libraries of books in Yiddish and sought to acquaint workers with the rich Yiddish literature of the time, naturally focusing on works with social undertones.

By the mid-1890s Jewish Social-Democratic organizations had arisen in many parts of the Pale. Links and contacts between intellectuals and workers increasingly acquired organizational forms. It was the decision of the Bund's future organizers to join the economic struggle, which was already being actively waged by workers and craftsmen, a move which played a significant part in the growth and development of the future Jewish Social Democracy. The most important organizations emerged in Warsaw, Belostok, and Vitebsk. In 1892 Jewish workers celebrated May Day for the first time at a mass gathering in Vilna. At the same time, the movement's conventions, ethical standards and principles were also developing along lines which were very different from the legacy of traditional Jewish life. Jewish revolutionary songs began to appear. In 1902, Sh. Ansky (Rappaport), writer and revolutionary, composed *The Oath*, a poem which became the Bund's hymn.

Earth with its heaven hears.
Witness; the bright stars,
And our oath of blood and tears.
We swear. We swear.

To the Bund, our hope and faith, we swear
Devotedly to set men free.
Its flag, bright scarlet, waves up there,
Sustaining us in loyalty.

According to a contemporary, "The Party was a Temple, and those who served socialism had to have clean hands, clean thoughts, pure qualities, and to be pure in their relations with one another."[6]

The establishment of an illegal Bund press was a major success even before the party was formally constituted. The newspaper *Arbeter Bletl*

(Workers' Newsletter) was printed on a hectograph in Minsk. The first issue of *Der Yidisher Arbeter* (Jewish Worker) appeared in December 1896. It was compiled in Vilna, with 1,000 copies printed abroad. Two years later this journal became the organ of the Bund's Foreign Committee and continued to exist until 1904. The most important achievement in those years was the publication of *Der Arbeter Shtimme* (The Workers' Voice) in August 1897. Until 1905 this newspaper served as the official organ of the Bund Central Committee.

In the early period of their activity the Jewish Social Democrats did not pay any serious attention to the national question, believing that the overthrow of autocracy and the establishment of a socialist order would solve the Jewish problem automatically. However, during 1893–4, the issue led to an increasingly passionate debate among Jewish intellectuals. In setting up a political organization of Jewish workers they were determined to preserve it as a specific part of the revolutionary movement of the Russian empire. As Israeli historian Jonathan Frankel notes, "Vilna Social Democrats developed their ideology in the process of building a movement" as distinct from Palestinophilism, an ideology of early Zionism, which soon became one of the chief political rivals of the Social Democrats in the Jewish political camp which "created the movement after the ideology."[7]

The joint conference of Jewish Social-Democratic groups in Vilna and Minsk held in June 1895 reflected the tendency towards the movement's consolidation. At the same time, its participants harbored quite a few doubts as to the need to set up a separate organization. Indeed, there was virtually no borderline between Russian and Jewish Social-Democratic movements. Despite the existence of the so-called Jargon Committee (as Yiddish was usually referred to at the time) and the publication of Yiddish propaganda literature, Russian remained the main language of communication between Jewish Social Democrats; Yiddish became the working language of party conferences only shortly before World War I.

In the mid-1890s the future "founding fathers" of the Bund, Kremer above all, were racked by doubts concerning the need to set up an independent organization of Jewish workers. In particular, Kremer feared that the Jewish movement might become isolated by not being able to match the speed with which the Russian liberation movement was developing. He believed that only as an autonomous part of the All-Russian party could the Jewish movement effectively solve any general or specific problems of the revolutionary process. The imminent formation of a single Social-Democratic party in Russia provided an impetus for the convening of the first congress of the Bund.

The congress was held in the suburbs of Vilna at the end of September 1897. Of the 13 participants, one or two exceptions aside, all the delegates were residents of Vilna or participants in the Vilna group. The congress delegates justified the founding of a separate "union" of the Jewish proletariat (the revolutionaries preferred this title to that of a "party") by referring to the specific interests of Jewish workers. They voiced the opinion that a Russian Social-Democratic organization, unfamiliar with the needs of Jewish workers, would be unable to deal properly with them.

The name of the newly formed union was among the controversial questions discussed at the congress. In accordance with Kremer's proposal, the congregation adopted the name All-Jewish Workers' Union (Bund) in Russia and Poland (Lithuania was added to the title in 1901). The words "and Poland" were added in response to a motion by the delegates from Warsaw. The viewpoint of the Warsaw delegates reflected the sharp rivalry between Jewish Social Democrats and the Polish Socialist Party (PPS) which, among other things, accused the Jewish propagandists teaching Jewish craftsmen Russian language of deliberate "Russification." The adopted party name, Frankel wrote, "Left no doubt that its goal was to organize the Yiddish-speaking proletariat throughout the western regions of the empire, specifically including the strongholds of the PPS."[8] The congress stated that it was ready to join the union of Russian Social Democrats abroad in which the leading part was played by Plekhanov's group.

In March 1898 Minsk was the venue of the first congress of the Russian Social-Democratic Workers' Party attended by three delegates from the Bund (Kremer, Mutnikovich, and Samuel Katz). The Bund envoys suggested that the new party be called not *Russkaia*, as the other delegates had originally proposed, but *Rossiiskaia*, emphasizing that the party should represent the interests of workers of different nations living in the empire. At the congress the Bund was acknowledged as being part and parcel of the party, but autonomous on questions specifically concerning the Jewish proletariat. The Bund supported the party manifesto which declared the right of each nation to self-determination.

By the end of 1900 there were Bund organizations in the Vilna, Minsk, Kovno, Grodno, Vitebsk, Mogilev, and Suvalki provinces, as well as in Warsaw and Lodz. Party work in the towns was directed by local committees which set about publishing their own periodicals at this time. By mid-1900, the total circulation of the underground Bund press, including local and central organs, reached 45,000.

A specific feature of the Jewish workers' movement in the Pale was the active part played by women, this representing a sharp contrast to the situation in the Russian workers' movement. The active role of females may be explained partly by the specific kinds of production prevalent in the Pale. Stocking-making, tailoring, garment-making, and millinery were developed in the towns and Jewish settlements, where cigarette and envelope factories also represented important features of the local economy.

All these enterprises employed thousands of Jewish girls and young women who were subject to cruel exploitation. They were at the lowest social level in traditional Jewish society. At the same time, Jewish female workers were particularly eager to acquire an education and also took an active part in the activities of the Bund organizations. One of the leaders of the Bund, Ester Frumkina, recalled how she taught young female workers who would come to the illegal study groups after a long and difficult working day:

> With what rapt attention they listened to the talks on cultural history, on surplus value, commodity, wages, life in other lands. How many questions they would ask! What joy would light their eyes after the circle leaders produced a new number of *Yidisher Arbeter* . . . or even a brochure! How proud a girl was when she would be given a black book to take home.[9]

Similarly, American historian Zvi Gitelman noted that the Bund fulfilled a psychological need by giving the Jewish workers – whose low status and increasing radicalism isolated them from the "respectable" Jewish community – a sense of dignity and a reassuring feeling of belonging to a cohesive, supporting group. More and more the Bund became a "counter-culture" of sorts, offering enlightenment and social opportunities and evolving an alternative Jewish identity and social life.[10]

The Bund's position with regard to the nationality issue in effect became the central question at the union's Fourth Congress, held in Belostok in April 1901. The idea of national autonomy as opposed to territorial autonomy discussed at the Brünn party congress of the Austrian Social Democrats in 1899 had a strong impact on debates at the Bund gathering, since the Austrian Social Democrats had achieved a revolutionary change akin to that in the minds of the socialists of many countries, including the ideologists of the Bund. Indeed, up until that time, the Social Democrats had believed that any national demands were nothing short of a "harmful maneuver" by the bourgeoisie seeking only to confuse the proletariat. Yet, a percentage of the Bund delegates in Belostok proposed to include the demand for national autonomy in the program immediately. However, the final version of the party resolution stated that in the future Russia must "be transformed into a federation of nationalities with full national autonomy for each, regardless of the territory it lives on." The congress acknowledged that the concept of "nationality can be applied to the Jewish people." However, the viewpoint of the congress concerning the question of national autonomy was eventually reflected in the statement that "the demand for national autonomy was premature for the Jews under existing circumstances." The congress deemed it sufficient at the time "to struggle to abolish all laws aimed against Jews . . . avoiding fanning national sentiment which would only obscure the proletariat's class consciousness and lead to chauvinism."[11]

Joseph (John) Mill and Ben-Tsion Hofman (Zivion) were among the most avid supporters of the national approach in the party. Hofman wrote many years later that "the Bundist intelligentsia . . . was particularly interested in the national question which was debated more than any other in their clashes with the Zionists."[12] The Bundist intellectuals were often the principal critics of Hertzl's Zionism in Russian émigré "colonies," although they were themselves under the influence of these ideas.

The Fourth Congress stated the official party attitude toward Zionism as a movement inflaming national feelings and preventing the development of class self-awareness. Nevertheless, the decisions of the congress showed that the Bund rejected the assimilation tendency prevalent in socialism and offered its own vision of the solution of the national question in the Russian Empire.

The congress's attitudes toward other questions were also highly revealing. The delegates firmly spoke out in favor of political struggle independent of economic struggle, and also against economic terror (attacks against factory owners, administrators, and the like) which "obscures workers' Social-Democratic awareness, lowers their moral standards and discredits the workers' movement." The Bund's attitude to political terrorism was also unequivocal at the time. It firmly renounced terrorism as an appropriate tactic.

Nonetheless, the assassination attempt by a Bund member against Vilna Governor-General Viktor von Val' in May 1902 changed the party's position for a while. After von Val' ordered 28 arrested people (22 Jews and six Poles) flogged for having taken part in a May Day demonstration, cobbler Girsh Lekert shot and wounded him. The official floggings had provoked a feeling of despair and frustration among Jews – and among workers in particular – and for this reason Lekert's assassination attempt had been regarded by them as an act defending Jewish honor and dignity. Despite all protests, however, Lekert was sentenced by a military tribunal to be hanged.

The act of vengeance and Lekert's subsequent execution stirred universal distress in the Jewish community. In the Bund organizations Lekert became a popular hero, a symbol of the heroism of Jewish workers. For decades the Jewish proletarian movement commemorated the anniversary of his death. An appeal by the Bund Central Committee and its central organ *Der Arbeter Stimme* ("How to Respond to Flogging") partly justified extreme forms of the antigovernment struggle. A conference in Berdichev in August 1902 adopted a similar resolution, supporting "organized vengeance," but the committee abroad unequivocally rejected this position, thus underlining the differences regarding the question of terrorism between the Central and the Foreign Committees. Generally, however, the Bund did not follow the road of terrorism, and the Fifth Party Congress held a year later annulled the decisions of the Berdichev conference.

Around 1901 the Bund gradually began to lose its "revolutionary monopoly in the Jewish community," as Moishe Rafes (Soviet historian and himself formerly a prominent Jewish revolutionary) correctly noted in his history of the Bund.[13] Various Zionist groups of socialist orientation began to revise their Zionist platform under the influence of the Bund. A group of Russian Zionist workers first spoke out at their convention in 1902. Adherents of the Zionist movement insisted on the necessity to integrate the Zionist ideal with a concern for the situation of Jews in areas where they lived.

For its part, the Russian government, and particularly interior minister Viacheslav von Plehve, sought to use the Zionist movement in the empire as a means of channeling discontent and discouraging Jews from taking part in the political struggle against autocracy. A part of this effort was the initiative of the Moscow Okhrana chief, Sergei Zubatov, to organize in July 1901 a group of former Bund members in Minsk into the so-called Jewish Independent Workers' Party (JIWP). The manifesto of the JIWP announced that the party did not pursue political aims, but sought to raise the economic and cultural level of the Jewish proletariat by promoting legal labor unions, raising workers' funds, and conducting other activities under the revealing slogan "Bread and Knowledge." The success of the first economic strike in Minsk, secured by the pressure applied by the chief of the local gendarmes on employers, attracted many Jewish workers in the city to the JIWP for a while and weakened the Bund's influence. The Bund declared a boycott against the JIWP, regarding its members as *agents provocateurs*.

The new Bund's position vis-à-vis the nationality question led to sharp debates on the pages of *Iskra*, which later became the RSDWP's central mouthpiece. In early 1902 the Bund published a pamphlet by a leading ideologist V. Kosovskii entitled "To the Question of National Autonomy and Transformation of the RSDWP along Federal Lines." The author sharply criticized *Iskra*'s standpoint and developed the Bund's views on the nationality question: "National autonomy is self-government in issues of language and culture" which should be supervised only by a "national body", i.e. the sum total of people freely acknowledging their national identity, while the rest of the questions – not national or cultural – would be directed by general government or local bodies. In June–July 1903 the Fifth Bund Congress considered, among other issues, the question of the attitude toward the RSDWP and drew up the charter of the party as a national organization. This charter was to serve as a guide for the delegates to the all-party congress.

The Second Congress of the RSDWP was held in July 1903. Of the 45 delegates, six (Vladimir Medem, Kosovskii, Isaiah Aizenshtat, Mark Liber (Mikhel Goldman), Portnoy, and Kremer were from the Bund. The Bund delegates insisted that theirs was a Social-Democratic organization of the Jewish proletariat, not limited in its activities to a certain locality; it joined the RSDWP as its only representative of Jewish workers. Still, the majority of the congress delegates supported Martov, who came out against the federative principle in party-building. The resolution Martov submitted to the Second Congress, "On the Place of the Bund in the Party," and approved by a majority (only the Bund delegates voted against it, in fact) read:

> The Second Congress of the Russian Social-Democratic Workers' Party expresses its profound conviction that restructuring organizational relations between the Jewish and the Russian proletariat along federative lines would constitute a significant obstacle on the way to the fullest organizational merging of politically conscious proletarians of different races and would inevitably do great harm to the interests of the . . . Jewish proletariat of Russia. For that reason [the congress] firmly rejected as unpermissible in principle any possibility of federative relations between the RSDWP and the Bund as its integral part.[14]

The Bund delegation left the congress. Seeking to explain the break with the RSDWP to the rank-and-file Bundists, the Central Committee published 20,000 copies of its appeal "The Bund Leaves the Party," in which the leaders insisted that the "Bund delegates did everything they could not to leave the party; . . . they made concessions in their demands, reducing them to a minimum. . . . [But] the Russian Social Democracy recognizes the right of each nation to self-determination . . . [yet] deprives the Jewish proletariat of the most common and elementary right to have an independent organization."

Among the main causes of the break, the Bund leaders referred to the "rigorously straightforward centralism which suits a group seeking to make a revolution without the people . . . Such is the ideal . . . worshipped by a majority of the Russian delegates."[15] Thus, in retrospect, the episode with the Bund at the Second Congress of the RSDWP, whose faction would govern the former Russian empire 14 years later, proved to be symptomatic. In this case at least, the Bolsheviks and the Mensheviks agreed: the Bundists had become nothing more than "Zionists afraid of seasickness."

Under the crossfire of Zionist criticism, on the one hand, and the Social Democrats, particularly the Bolsheviks, on the other, Bund theoreticians focused attention on developing their own nationality program. A major contributing factor was the infamous Kishinev pogrom in April 1903, which had broad repercussions both in Russia and abroad.

Understandably, the Kishinev tragedy had a strong impact on the Bund: from 1904 onwards, the political slogan of "national autonomy" was widely used in its propaganda, and the party's influence spread from mainly the empire's northwestern regions to its southern areas.

The wave of pogroms which began in the spring of 1905 and assumed a larger scope following the Manifesto of October 17, enabled the Bund to strengthen its influence among the Jewish popular masses. For one thing, the Bund set up self-defense units in the Pale, as did Poalei-Zion. The party leadership regarded the struggle of the combat units not only as an effort to defend the Jews from the pogroms, but also as preparation for the prospective armed uprising against the tsarist government. As a Bund newspaper noted proudly: "Jews are no longer weak cowards who flee from the Gentiles. Jews can form self-defence organizations. Jews are building barricades."[16]

One of the surveys of the revolutionary movement compiled by the Police Department stated: "In the period between 1905 and 1906 . . . the Jewish masses were a body split into parties, factions, and groups. The life of the Jewish people in Russia was marked by extraordinary sensitivity and intensity of political activity."[17] The idea of national autonomy was used in a variety of ways in the programs of Jewish parties emerging in the course of the 1905 Revolution. In November 1905 the political Zionists, who had a more neutral attitude with regard to events occurring in Russia, decided to join the Russian liberation movement at the Helsingfors Congress and put forward the demand of national autonomy for minorities, including Jews. The Zionist movement had an impact chiefly on the middle class, petty bourgeoisie, and also in part, the intelligentsia, which tended to combine Zionist ideas with socialist-political and economic demands.

The Zionist-Socialist Workers' Party held its first congress in 1906. This new party, whose chief ideologist was Nachman Syrkin, aimed at setting up a Jewish state because only in such a state, its members believed, would the Jewish masses be able to take part in normal economic processes and participate in the building of socialist society. With time, members of this party began to gravitate towards what was known as "territorialism," denying the inevitable relation between Zionism and Palestine. They criticized the Bund for regarding the Jews in Russia as a separate nation, rather than as part of world Jewry, and for ignoring such a phenomenon as Jewish emigration. In Russia, however, the party only called for equality for the Jews.

In April 1906 the Socialist Jewish Workers' Party was founded. It regarded the Jews' desire to gain their own territory in the near future as a utopian dream and saw the solution of the Jewish problem in turning Russia into a federative state of different nationalities and setting up a *Sejm* for each of them. The *Sejm* must then become the supreme authority not only in questions of culture, but also in all other problems concerning the nation's domestic life. The Socialist Jewish Workers' Party considered the Bund insufficiently radical and demanded national-political autonomy for Russian Jewry.

Another party in the Jewish political camp was the Social-Democratic Jewish Workers' Party, Poalei-Zion, consolidated in 1906. It founded its program on the ideas of Ber Borokhov, whose thinking combined Marxism and Zionism. The basic assumption of this party's leaders was that Jewish social and economic life would be normalized, and consistent class struggle would be waged only if there were a unified territory for the nation – Palestine. As an immediate objective, however, Poalei-Zion favored broad economic, political, and cultural autonomy for Russian Jewry. This party became the Bund's chief rival in the years of the 1905–7 Revolution in the struggle for influence over the working masses.

The picture of Jewish political life in that era of political turmoil would not be complete if at least two liberal organizations were not mentioned. The first was the so called Folksgrupe (People's Group), which advocated civil rights for Jews and conditions for the unfettered development of national Jewish institutions. Its anti-Zionist position made it possible for the group to collaborate with the Bund, which at its Sixth Congress in October 1905 reaffirmed the need to struggle against Zionism in all its forms.

For his part, Shimon Dubnov, historian and well-known public figure, who supported the Zionists in accusing the People's Group of favoring assimilation, organized the so-called Folkspartai with a clear national orientation. The Folkspartai advocated "institutionalization of autonomy through self-governing local and federated community councils, that is, through *kehillas* (communities), which would be national rather than exclusively religious."

Despite a substantial similarity between the idea of autonomy as conceived by Dubnov and that proposed by the Bund, the party members firmly rejected the assertion that the Bund should merely adapt Dubnov's program to their own purposes.[18] Most likely, the Bundists refused to acknowledge Dubnov's influence because they regarded him as a liberal bourgeois. For his part, on many occasions Dubnov reproached the Bund for accentuating the class interests of Jewish workers instead of the national interests of the Jewish nation.

As if the confirm their primary allegiance to the socialist cause, the Bund's leadership reunited their forces with those of other Social-Democratic organizations at what came to be known as the "unifying" congress of the RSDWP in April 1906. Having joined the RSDRP again, the

Bund retained its special stand on the national question, as well as its autonomy in the organization's internal affairs.

In the period prior to the overthrow of the tsar's government, the Bund's maximum strength may be estimated at 34,000 people in 274 organizations in 1906. As a point of comparison, the Poalei-Zion had about 25,000 members at the time. Following the October 17 Manifesto, the Bund press began to develop rapidly, becoming almost exclusively legal. There appeared a party daily newspaper, *Der Wecker* (The Alarm), as well as weeklies in Yiddish and in Russian. Various groups promoting or sympathizing with the Bund operated abroad, particularly in Switzerland, France, Britain, Argentina, South Africa, and especially America, from where numerous clubs, societies, and fraternities rendered assistance (mostly financial) to the Bund in Russia.

The 1905–7 Revolution's defeat and the ensuing political crisis in the liberation movement had an immediate effect on the life of the Bund and that of other Jewish parties. The Zionist-Socialist and Socialist Jewish Workers' Parties were disbanded and Zionist activity discontinued. Most Bund organizations ceased to exist. The party organization in 1908 included no more than 800 members. A number of Bund-led labor unions, such as those of construction workers, stocking-makers, and tailors in Vilna, also in effect disappeared. The party crisis was deepened by government persecution and the arrest of hundreds and thousands of activists. The Bund also suffered a staggering blow at the hands of the secret police: at the end of 1908, famous spy-hunter Vladimir Burtsev discovered that Israel Kaplinskii, a founder of the underground Bund press and a man close to the Central Committee for many years had been an Okhrana agent.[19] This led to the further disintegration of the Bund: most professional revolutionaries and even high-ranking party members were forced to discontinue participation in the antigovernment movement, emigrate, or turn to non-political cultural activities. For example, one of the Bund leaders, Mark Liber, became a teacher of Latin and ancient Greek; ideologist A. Litvak resigned himself to teaching Jewish history and religion in a Vilna gymnasium.

In the period between the end of the 1905 Revolution and World War I the Bund took an active part in the national democratic movement together with members of liberal Jewish society, and in particular, in work to create a secular Jewish community. Such a community, the Bundists believed, could become the foundation for national-cultural autonomy, the attainment of which was one of the party's chief aims. Former revolutionaries became involved with such organizations as the "Society for the Spreading of Education Among Jews in Russia," the "Jewish Literary Society," and the "Music Society." The Bund regarded itself as representing the interests not only of the Jewish proletariat, but also of the broad masses as a whole. Consequently, the Bundists focused their major attention on efforts to secularize the Jewish community, especially by setting up different kinds of schools, courses, and lecture-clubs, as well as by advancing the cultural level of mass readership and by developing Yiddish as the Jewish literary language.

In the prewar period, when the Jewish question was further exacerbated in the empire, the Bund organized its supporters to fight official and public anti-Semitism. A total of 20,000 Jewish workers in different cities took part in the protest strike organized by the Bund against the Beilis trial in 1913.[20] Around the same time, in the new social atmosphere of awakening from political apathy the network of Bund organizations grew so strong that its leaders proposed to convene the next, Eighth Party Congress. The outbreak of World War I, however, prevented the congress from taking place.

As areas of the Pale became the theater of military operations, and Russian military authorities perpetrated cruel measures against the Jewish population, the wave of Jewish refugees led to the formation of an entire network of Jewish charity organizations aimed at helping the people who had been abandoned by the state. The Bund organizations took an active part in setting up various education and charity structures for Jewish refugees and thereby increased their influence in the community's leadership.

Despite a certain ambiguity in their position regarding the war, those leaders of the Bund remaining in Russia adhered predominantly to "revolutionary defensism." A declaration made by a meeting at the Bund Central Committee in May 1916 stated that the working class taking part in the country's defense was thereby waging a struggle for political power and liberation from tsarism. By taking part in the activities of the military-industrial committees, the Bundists actively involved themselves in Russia's economic and political life on the eve of the February Revolution.

Following the overthrow of the tsarist government, and as soon as opportunities for free political activity appeared, Bund organizations quickly revived their network covering the territory of the former Pale, which had been eliminated by the Provisional Government. The Bund even extended its activities to Central Russia, the Caucasus, and Siberia.

With its leadership displaying exceptional organizational abilities, the Bund was first among Russia's revolutionary parties to convene an all-Russian conference, which was held on April 10, 1917 in Petrograd. On most issues the Bund adhered to a Menshevik platform, firmly advocating the idea of revolutionary defensism. As far as the national question was concerned, the conference put forward the demand to introduce national-cultural autonomy for the Jewish people immediately as a burning political issue of the day and proposed, even before the convening of the Constituent Assembly, to begin setting up locally "organs of national-cultural autonomy for the Jewish nation on the basis of universal suffrage for citizens of both sexes attaining 20 years of age and identifying themselves with the Jewish nationality."[21] On the eve of the Bolshevik takeover the Bund numbered 40,000 members and was one of the most influential parties in the country's Jewish community.

Subsequent events proved to be tragic for the Bund, as they were for other Jewish political parties, organizations, and groups in Soviet Russia. Relying on their ideological and political legacy, all of them became involved in a bitter internecine struggle. It is significant that despite serious ideological contradictions the Bund managed to preserve party unity from its founding in 1897 up to 1919–20. Right-wing Bundists emigrated; left-wing Bundists dissolved the Bund, and a few of them joined the Bolshevik Party. They did so, according to Ester Frumkina, "in order to save the idea of the Bund as *apparat* until the inevitable moment . . . when the Russian Communist Party will recognize . . . [the Bund's] organizational principle, in order to preserve the great treasure smeared with the blood and tears of the Jewish proletariat, soaked with the hopes and sufferings of the generation of fighters, with memories of ˙superhuman achievements."[22] However, the hopes of the ardent Ester and her colleagues were not destined to come true. In the 1930s most former Bundists were cruelly persecuted and perished: Frumkin was sent to the Soviet Gulag and died in Siberia in 1943.

The history of Russian Jewry developed quite differently from how the Bund had predicted it would. However, this failure in terms of practical politics should not depreciate the Bund's achievements as an organization and, above all, as an ideology. Having lent political weight to the theory of autonomy or extraterritorial self-government, the Bund's ideas were adopted virtually by all Jewish parties in Russia in 1905–6, and in 1918 by leaders of American Jewry in the shape of the "national rights" concept. Nor should it be forgotten that although autonomy was decisively rejected by Bolshevik theoreticians, the Bund's claim that the Jewish nation would realize itself through the development of a secular proletarian Jewish culture in the Yiddish language was embraced by official Soviet ideology in the 1920s.

Notes

1   Sh. Gozhanskii (Lonu), "Evreiskoe rabochee dvizhenie nachala 90-kh godov," in *Revoluitsionnoe dvizhenie sredi evreev* (Moscow: Vsesoiuznoe obshchestvo politkatorzhan i ssyl'no-poselentsev, 1930), vol. 1, 67.

2 T. M. Kopel'zon, *Evreiskoe rabochee dvizhenie kontsa 80-kh i nachala 90-kh godov"*, ibid., 71.

3 G. V. Plekhanov, *O zadachakh sotsialistov v borbe s golodom v Rosii* (Geneva: Izdanie Gruppy "Osvobozhdenie Truda," 1892), 58.

4 I. Martov, *Povorotnyi punkt v istorii evreiskogo rabochego dvizheniia* (Geneva: Izdanie Souza rus. sotsial' demokratov, 1900), 12.

5 Henry J. Tobias, *The Jewish Bund in Russia: From Its Origins to 1905* (Stanford: Stanford University Press, 1972), 11.

6 Quoted from Ezra Mendelsohn, *Class Struggle in the Pale: The Formative Years of the Jewish Workers' Movement in Tsarist Russia* (Cambridge: Cambridge University Press, 1970), 154.

7 Jonathan Frankel, *Prophecy and Politics: Socialism, Nationalism and the Russian Jews, 1862–1917* (Cambridge: Cambridge University Press, 1981), 182.

8 Ibid., 208.

9 Quoted from Zvi Y. Gitelman, *Jewish Nationality and Soviet Politics: The Jewish Sections of the CPSU, 1917–1930* (Princeton: Princeton University Press, 1972), 30.

10 Zvi Gitelman, *A Century of Ambivalence: The Jews of Russia and the Soviet Union, 1881 to the Present* (New York: Schocken Books, Inc., 1988), 23.

11 See *Sputnik izberatelia v Uchreditel'noe sobranie* (Petrograd: "Vserossiiskii soiuz gorodov," 1917), 106.

12 Cited in Frankel, *Prophecy and Politics*, 182.

13 M. Rafes, *Ocherki po istorii "Bunda"* (Moscow: "Moskovskii rabochii," 1923), 69.

14 Cited in ibid., 100.

15 Ibid., 353.

16 Cited in Gitelman, *Jewish Nationality and Soviet Politics*, 51.

17 State Archive of the Russian Federation (GARF), f. 102, op. 253, d. 8, 452, 458.

18 See S. M. Dubnov, *Pis'ma o starom i novom evreistve (1897–1907)* (St Petersburg: "Obshchestvenaiia pol'za," 1907).

19 For documents on the Bund's Azef see Aleksandr Seerebrennikov, ed., *Soblazn sotsializma: revolyutsiya v Rossii i evrei* (Paris-Moscow: YMCA-PRESS, 1995), 392–5.

20 Mendel Beilis was a Jewish brickmaker in Kiev accused by local anti-Semites of murdering a Christian boy allegedly to use his blood for the Passover rituals. The defamation was encouraged by the Ministry of Justice, which took part in fabricating evidence in support of the absurd and criminal accusation. The affair lasted from the discovery of the boy's body in March 1911 until – largely as a result of a worldwide scandal – Beilis was acquitted in 1913.

21 *Sputnik izbiratelia v Uchreditel'noe sobranie*, 111.

22 Cited in Gitelman, *Century of Ambivalence*, 110.

CHAPTER FOUR

Neo-Populism in Early Twentieth-Century Russia: The Socialist-Revolutionary Party from 1900 to 1917

Michael Melancon

From a welter of populist groups, descendants of the famous Land and Freedom and People's Will of the 1870s and 1880s, arose the neo-populist Party of Socialist-Revolutionaries (PSR or SRs). Party formation was gradual, characterized by the more or less random late 1890s unification of various groups and circles into ever larger entities; these proto-parties usually described themselves as "socialist-revolutionary" in reference to their core doctrine – a hallmark of Russian populism – that Russia's approaching revolution would be social (socialist) rather than merely political (bourgeois liberal). By 1900 the unification process virtually completed itself when the so-called Southern and Northern Unions of SRs joined together. Although the PSR did not hold its first congress until late 1905 and thus as yet had no official program, for all intents and purposes it had become and functioned as a political party, albeit, like the Social Democrats (SDs), an illegal and therefore underground one.[1]

Along with their analysis of the coming revolution as socialist, the SRs shared with their populist forbears a belief that, under Russian conditions, the peasantry were a potentially revolutionary class. At the turn of the century, the chief purveyor of the latter concept was Victor Chernov (the grandson of a peasant, a former Moscow University law student, and, somewhat later, prime SR theorist and organizer), who in the waning years of the last century carried out organizational work among the Volga peasantry. However, neither the writings of Chernov nor SR doctrine, largely the fruit of his lively intelligence, focused as single-mindedly on the peasantry as later commentary has averred. After all, even Land and Freedom, although it understood the peasantry to be the main revolutionary class, willingly turned to workers, artisans, and students in its recruitment; the People's Will viewed the peasantry, for the time being, as unsusceptible to revolutionary propaganda and consequently aimed its efforts almost entirely at workers and intellectuals, leaving the peasantry for the future. This last complex of attitudes precisely characterized not only the proto-SR groups of the late 1890s but the early SR party as well. Because of general SR indifference (not to say hostility) toward efforts among the peasantry, Chernov founded the Agrarian-Socialist League, a small group of SR-oriented leaders who insisted on plowing the fertile field of Russia's countryside. Only during 1902, after the red flame of peasant revolt raced across southern Russia, did the SRs reorient themselves to some degree toward the village, leading to the entry of the League into the PSR and completing the party's formation.[2]

Even so, Chernov, whose thinking and writings underlay SR theory and programs, carefully crafted a triadic social basis for Russia's revolution: the radical intelligentsia, the urban proletariat as the mass vanguard, and the peasantry as the main army. This, in fact, delineated neo-populism from early populism. The advance of industrialization had led to the growth of a significant urban proletariat that was ripe for political exploitation. This, together with the proletariat's concentration in and around major industrial cities, and its higher levels of literacy, rendered it a significant element in SR revolutionary algebra. Meanwhile, the bourgeoisie, although waxing, remained numerically small and politically timid, so that the original populist calculation that Russia's revolution would bypass a lengthy capitalist stage was reinforced rather than damaged by the entry of the workers onto the Russian scene as a major social force. But, as Chernov and other SR theorists reasoned, the working class remained too small to achieve the revolution unaided: a combination of radical intelligentsia, proletariat, and peasantry could provide the potent admixture that would both overthrow tsarism and propel the country toward socialism.[3]

Following the example of The People's Will, the SRs also determined to wield the sword of terrorism. The party's Central Committee created its famous Fighting Organization, which undertook to assassinate high-level officials of the late tsarist regime, eventually counting as its victims, among others, two successive ministers of the interior and a senior member of the Romanov family; local organizations followed suit with attacks on less famous persons deemed objectionable (military officers, prison wardens, police officials), finally running the count of deaths by terrorism into the thousands. The PSR, however, never visualized terrorism as a mode of overthrowing the tsarist regime, considering it an error of judgment on the part of The People's Will, whose lesson had been learned. Indeed, the SRs calculated that terrorism in conjunction with mass organization and propaganda would only serve to destabilize, demoralize, and thus hasten the downfall of the government. Although some SRs associated with the Fighting Organization – Boris Savinkov comes first to mind – created a kind of terrorist mystique, the PSR as a whole never fixated upon terror nor viewed it as the most lethal weapon in its arsenal, although SDs often made this accusation.[4] Mass revolution was the goal toward which the PSR strove and to which it devoted its heaviest material and human resources. By the early 1900s, it had no reason to doubt that the workers and peasants, with the leadership of socialist organizations such as itself, would deliver the blow that would fell the enemy.

During the several years prior to the revolutionary turmoil of 1905–7, the SR combination of worker–peasant organization, along with terrorism against persons symbolizing the old regime, led to considerable success as the party grew by leaps and bounds. From Saratov, its chief center on the Volga and one of the cradles of the entire party, by 1901 the SRs began forging methods of bringing their message of empowerment and land to the peasants; enormous quantities of literature for peasants poured out of the party's underground presses. This village activism quickly spread throughout the Volga-Urals region, over into Ukraine, Belorussia, the central and northern regions, and into Siberia. Already during 1902, local SR organizations throughout much of Russia began creating so-called SR Peasant Unions (not to be confused with the non-partisan Peasant Union of 1905). During the peasant disturbances of 1902–4, SR activists also led numerous armed peasant brotherhoods.

The SR approach to the peasantry was facilitated by the party's land program. This program was based upon the concept of land socialization, which called not for nationalization of the land, which signified state ownership, but for control of the land by peasant communes or commune confederations. The land itself would "belong to no one" and thus would be available for those actually using it. These and other aspects of the SR land program (unremunerated confiscation of all noble and other forms of land property and its transfer to the peasantry for use) closely fit traditional peasant thinking. The SRs aimed at eventual large-scale agricultural methods but insisted that these could be introduced only gradually and without coercion.[5] Of course, the SRs never entirely overcame the peasants' famous imperviousness to political organization, but they alone labored in the peasant vineyard, took into account peasant aspirations in the construction of their land program, and, more or less exclusively, garnered the fruit of peasant support. Notable were the sweeping scope of the PSR's successes among the peasantry, not remotely matched by any other political group, as well as the limitations of their accomplishments.

During this very same period, for a variety of reasons, the PSR witnessed considerable growth in its membership in the urban environment. The PSR's program for workers contained planks on minimum wages, the eight-hour day, the right to unions, and was also worded in terms that suggested workers' control of factories (a suggestion quite absent in SD programs). This program, along with the party's defiant use of violence against the tsarist regime, held the SRs in good stead in worker recruitment. The PSR reaped additional benefits from its open espousal of a political revolution that would quickly evolve toward socialism, at a time when the so-called "economist heresy" – that is, a focus on economic rather than political goals – played a certain role within Social Democracy. Yet another contributory factor, which even caused a significant SD to SR worker crossover during 1903–4, was the Menshevik–Bolshevik conflict; workers cared little for labels and polemics, preferring to see efforts expended directly on their cause rather than on seemingly esoteric squabbles among intellectuals. For many, the SR alternative filled the bill.

The SR following among workers certainly did not surpass that of the SDs on the eve of the 1905 disturbances (or thereafter). After all, SD efforts in the factories had continued on a widespread, unabated, and concentrated basis ever since the mid-1890s, whereas the SRs failed to present a united front until 1900. Upon its creation, the PSR inherited from its progenitor groups a certain worker following that had begun to gather already during the late 1870s; but the rapid 1890s growth of Russian Marxism in the form of the SD party had left the rival political movement far behind. Even so, although overall worker adherence to the SDs exceeded that of the SRs, in many areas the SRs now carved out a respectable worker following that in some important industrial centers fully rivaled that of the SDs.[6]

Much commentary – both contemporary and historiographical – has attributed worker support for SRs to a kind of anomaly connected to the constant recent arrival of workers from the village during Russia's heady industrial expansion; in this version, worker-peasants, dreaming of returning to the village, formed their socialist allegiance on the basis of their peasant identity rather than their still weak worker identity and thus joined the party that seemed best positioned to fulfill peasant aspirations. Somewhat later, the SRs themselves characterized their principal proletarian support during the 1900–7 era as connected with "gray" workers recently arrived from the villages. The kernel of truth in this analytical tendency serves to obscure a much more complicated reality.

Research about peasant migration into Russia's cities has demonstrated that newly arrived workers actively maintained ties with the village, often retained membership in the communes, and joined so-called *zemliachestva* (land brotherhoods of individuals from certain villages or districts formed to preserve elements of the home culture in the city environment). Even peasants who remained permanently in the factories and, often, their descendants into the second and third generations acted similarly. Naturally, the SR melding together of peasant and worker programs attracted many such individuals. Indubitably, during the early period of mass SR worker recruitment (1902–7), these workers were clearly both younger and less seasoned in respect to socialist consciousness than SD worker adherents; but this was an ephemeral phenomenon. Lengthy exposure to the city environment transformed SR worker cadres into seasoned proletarians no less conscious (and not much less numerous) than their SD counterparts.[7]

As noted, the SRs proclaimed the radicalized intelligentsia as one of the social bases of the coming revolution. However, during the heady days of the late 1890s and early 1900s, when both SD and SR movements took shape as national parties, Marxism enjoyed a distinct advantage as the students' preferred outlook. Thereafter, the Marxist tide ebbed, as oppositionist-minded students confronted an array of alternatives, ranging from the staunch liberalism of the Constitutional Democrats, through the varying shades of Marxist Social Democracy, to the reviving populist movement in the form of the PSR. For the balance of the late tsarist regime's existence, these movements seem to have vied on more or less equal terms, with the SRs yielding to none in the effort expended and numbers recruited.

Examples of SR efforts among the intelligentsia were the organization during 1902 of local SR Teachers' Unions (again, not to be confused with the non-partisan All-Russian Teachers' Union of several years later). This effort to reach the rural intelligentsia, which, according to Scott Seregny, far exceeded that of any other party, was aided by a significant SR presence in the zemstvos and, later, rural cooperatives, all of which also contributed to strengthening the ties with the peasantry. In the urban environment, SRs actively created student organizations in gymnasiums, institutes, and universities and entered various professional and clerical unions; in all these endeavors, the SRs competed with Social Democrats and liberals.[8]

Thus by the eve of 1905, the PSR was poised to play a role in the revolutionary events of that year and thereafter. During the course of the year itself, the PSR, like the other oppositionist parties, gradually adopted a more or less open status. Party committees in the capital, as well as in other major cities such as Moscow and Saratov, consolidated their positions and began publishing and distributing large quantities of revolutionary literature, followed later in 1905 and 1906 by newspapers. All the parties engaged in active recruitment, which had commenced during 1904, but which intensified throughout the entire 1905–7 "era of freedom." By fall of 1905, major party leaders such as Chernov, M. Natanson, and numerous others, had returned home to Russia in order to preside over the burgeoning organization (a similar process occurred among the Social Democrats).[9] Furthermore, with the issuing of the October Manifesto, socialist parties for the first time attained legal status within the Russian Empire.

As regards the 1905–7 Revolution, one can identify several main areas of mass socialist activism, namely, among the workers, the peasantry, the intelligentsia, and the armed forces. The worker milieu was characterized during this period by the widespread formation of SR- and SD-oriented party circles, groups and committees; in addition, labor unions of every imaginable profession took shape with heavy socialist involvement. The very first national labor union in Russia's history was that of the railroad workers, who already held their first all-Russian congress during the spring of 1905. This was a heavily SR-oriented union, although some SDs, anarchists, liberals, and non-party activists entered the national executive committee as well; the railroad workers adopted planks sufficiently similar to SR programs that Lenin complained that the SRs "had stamped their *iarlyk*" on the new union's program.[10]

However, most of the vast array of labor and artisanal unions that took shape during 1905 had greater SD than SR input, with Mensheviks leading the way. For one thing, as noted earlier, at this time SDs still maintained a distinct advantage over SRs in terms of the quality of their worker cadres, enabling the SD worker-activists to provide a greater degree of leadership in many union endeavors. Furthermore, despite the fact that SRs always espoused worker unionization and SR entry into unions, many SR activists denigrated this realm of endeavor as merely economic and reformist. SR involvement across the country nonetheless exceeded that of the Bolsheviks, who throughout the entire formative period of the labor union movement held themselves aloof from these non-party institutions.

A similar dynamic prevailed later in the year when the famous worker soviets arose in cities across the empire. Primarily Menshevik SDs had the leading roles, followed by the SRs, whereas the Bolsheviks initially held themselves aloof. Even so, significant numbers of large factories sent SRs into the Petersburg, Saratov, Moscow, and other soviets and some worker soviets (in Belorussia, and Ukraine) operated under outright SR influence. Additionally, the SRs usually shouldered the chief burden of organizing and leading the worker militias (precursors of the famous 1917 Red Guards) that arose in many cities, often as a kind of armed auxiliary of the soviets; consequently, SR activists led the armed workers when it came to fighting during 1905, as in Moscow, Saratov, and Ekaterinoslav.[11]

The SR position in the national railroad union gave the party the opportunity to play a key role in the transformation of the almost year-long strikes and demonstrations into revolution. During October, the railroad union executive committee, with its SR leaning, voted to issue the call for a national railroad strike; when the railroad workers struck in various cities, other workers, followed by white-collar personnel and students, did likewise, creating the national general strike that signaled the onset of the 1905–7 Revolution. The SRs were also largely responsible for calling and leading the December uprising in Moscow, which has erroneously been connected with the Bolsheviks, who had a much smaller role.[12]

During the spring and summer of 1917, vast peasant uprisings occurred that far outstripped the involvement of any one party or, for that matter, all of them put together. Nonetheless, the SR Peasant Unions and armed brotherhoods, not a few of which had leadership from rural teachers of SR-orientation, played a role that much surpassed that of any other party. One of the chief new characteristics of the 1905 peasant movement, aside from its exceptionally widespread nature, was the formation of the All-Russian Peasant Union. Arising at the summons of Moscow liberals, local Peasant Unions began to take shape during May; the PSR urged its members to enter the unions in order to influence them in a manner suitable to the party. The All-Russian Peasant Union held its first congress during late July of 1905; liberals, SDs, and SRs all jockeyed for position, whereas the mostly non-partisan peasant delegates tended to maintain their own outlooks on political and land questions, with the result that the resolutions were somewhat more moderate than those proffered by the SRs (and the SDs). The Peasant Union's second congress met during October, during renewed peasant disturbances. Here the chief political influences were exercised by liberals and SRs, with signs that the latter were gaining ground. The quite SR-oriented Saratov Peasant Union explained the militancy of the peasant movement there, provoking some delegates to criticize the violence of the Saratov movement. Regardless, the congress resolved to boycott the upcoming State Duma elections and in other ways indicated waxing SR influence.

In a related development, the PSR also urged its members to enter and influence the All-Russian Teachers' Union which, like the Peasant Union, took shape during the spring of 1905 and which held its first national congress during July. At this congress, some SRs argued that the Teachers' Union should adopt the PSR's program, whereas most delegates, including the majority of SRs, argued for the appropriateness of a non-sectarian approach. Meanwhile, the considerable SD fraction abandoned the congress and the All-Russian Teachers' Union because of its failure to adopt the SD program, leaving the field to the liberals and SRs; both at this congress and the second during December 1905, the SRs, although certainly not in direct control, exercised increasing weight.[13]

As the stormy year came to a close, the SRs opened their First Party Congress in Finland. The PSR had played a role in the 1905 events second to none; yet the goal of overthrowing the tsarist regime had eluded them. Still all was not lost, as both SDs and SRs looked forward to new opportunities; the revolutionary fires in Russia had not yet been quelled and the new laws opened up unaccustomed possibilities for organization and propaganda. The congress itself adopted the program that Chernov had worked out over the last several years, many aspects of which had already been published in various party newspapers and journals. The SRs also made several decisions about current events. The PSR maintained its course toward revolution, which, as before, it expected to be socialist. The SRs decided also to boycott the coming Duma elections, since the voting formulas discriminated against the laboring classes.[14]

During the congress, alternative positions on both the right and left wings of the party came to the fore. On the right, a number of intellectuals (primarily journalists, advocates, and academics) wished to renounce the revolutionary and illegal side of party activities in order to utilize the legal methods afforded by the October Manifesto. The majority's firm rejection of this reformism led this group to break off from the PSR in order to found the Popular Socialist Party; this small group, distinguished for its high intellectual calibre, found a following primarily among a part of the urban intelligentsia.

A far more serious threat to the party's organizational integrity was the leftist Maximalist heresy. Far from wishing to renounce revolutionary methods, the Maximalists espoused an even sterner position than the main body of the PSR. The Maximalists advocated factory and agrarian terrorism against capitalist-noble property, along with the other weapons in the SR arsenal. The Maximalist tendency had considerable support from within the Moscow and several other organizations; additionally, many workers and not a few peasants and soldiers favored the militancy of the Maximalists. Fortunately for the PSR, when the Maximalists followed the example of the Popular Socialists in leaving the party, most of the group's adherents remained with Chernov and the PSR. The Maximalists became an ongoing force in several locales such as Kronshtadt, Samara, and Izhevsk but never achieved the status of a mass party.[15]

Although during 1906 and 1907 both the SRs and SDs entertained the hope of reviving the workers' movement to the revolutionary proportions of fall 1905, the repression that brought about the demise of the soviets and other militant worker organizations such as the militias proved decisive in undercutting the workers' desire for further sacrifices. Strikes, demonstrations, and the wide entry of workers into the socialist parties, labor unions, and worker cooperatives continued throughout this so-called "era of freedom," whereas proletarian revolt was not on the agenda. Nevertheless, the continued peasant uprisings and the veritable tide of soldier and sailor mutinies led the SRs to believe that revolution was still possible. During 1906, the SRs espoused the creation of worker, soldier, and peasant soviets. Within the numerous garrisons and naval installations, the SRs and the SDs built underground groups that provided much of the organized leadership of the revolts. Likewise, although wave after wave of arrests destroyed the All-Russian Peasant Union and hindered its ability to give structure to the piecemeal peasant revolts, the SR Peasant Unions and armed brotherhoods continued their activism. After the dismissal of the First Duma, the SRs participated in the elections to the Second Duma, which held its sessions briefly during 1907, in order to utilize it as a propaganda forum (in these elections, the SRs did almost as well as the SDs in proletarian curia).[16]

In the end, all of the combined efforts of the various socialist parties came to naught. By late 1907, after the dismissal of the Second Duma, the Stolypin regime unleashed the full force of revived tsarism's repressive apparatus, not only against the socialist parties but against all the national structures so painstakingly built over the last several years. By the end of 1908, the socialist parties had been forced back into the underground and the railroad, teacher, peasant, and postal-telegraph unions had all been eliminated. Surviving local labor unions came under constant surveillance, with the threat of summary arrest and confiscation of resources hanging over their heads. Cossacks and loyal units had been used to suppress the mutinies in the armed forces; thousands had been arrested and hundreds executed, including many SR-oriented military activists. Punitive expeditions of Cossacks and army units roamed the countryside, finally quelling the peasant revolts that in some areas had burned for five and six years. Thus, by the end of 1908 the SRs had abandoned all hope for revolution in the short term. In evaluating the failure of revolutionary plans, during 1908 Chernov admitted that the SRs (and other socialist parties), long forced by tsarist repression into the underground, had failed in the task of coordinating the vast social forces they had helped unleash.[17]

During 1907 and 1908, the PSR held several national gatherings in order to reorient the party's priorities and direction in the new conditions. Under the leadership of a predominant group of leaders – Chernov, Natanson, and N. Rakitnikov – the party again came down firmly on the side of commitment to revolution through mass organization and the maintenance of the underground organizational structures. At the same time, the PSR called a *de facto* halt to the terror program. Although the party always asserted its right to renew the attack on tsarist officials, in fact for the balance of the old regime's existence the SRs rarely organized attacks on persons. This reflected ethical and practical considerations: the brutality of terrorism became repugnant to many party leaders and the cost to the party in terms of government reprisals was too high.

Additionally, the PSR launched a new program that emphasized the involvement of SR activists in the network of legal institutions such as labor union, cooperatives, and educational-cultural societies that alone survived the government's repression unscathed. Indeed, this did not so much alter SR policy (the party had always espoused activism, for revolutionary goals, in legal social institutions) as its practice. Many SR activists, prompted by the party's continued revolutionary militancy and its eschewing of participation in the Dumas (after the dismissal of the Second Duma, the PSR reverted to its boycott of the Russian half-parliament), forbore from participating in labor union and cooperative activities, preferring direct revolutionary organization. Under the prevailing conditions (the Stolypin repression), this was a costly attitude since underground party committees and groups came under heavy attack, the leadership had withdrawn again to Western Europe, and thousands of rank-and-file cadres languished in tsarist prisons, Siberian hard labor, or administrative exile.

The SR position on legal social institutions emphasized utilizing them for dual purposes: the given institution should work for the betterment of the social group involved and should serve as an organizing center for the PSR and for the future revolution. This stance exploited problems among the Social Democrats: many Menshevik activists began to view the legal institutions as ends in themselves (the so-called Liquidator tendency which aimed at de-emphasizing illegal, revolutionary activities), whereas the Bolsheviks largely ignored them. Thus it came to pass that precisely during 1908–11 the SRs won their maximum degree of influence within labor institutions; in many areas, including St Petersburg, they largely supplanted the Mensheviks as the predominant influence in many unions, clubs, and cooperatives.[18]

Nevertheless, this was overall the bleakest time in recent memory for the PSR, as for all the revolutionary parties. As noted, the organizations, replete with committees at all levels, newspapers, and printing presses, fell victim to repression. Although student organizations and the labor-oriented institutions provided a certain forum for continued work in the urban environment, peasant-oriented organizations suffered almost complete decimation. The government even purged the zemstvos of radical elements, removing an early neo-populist path to the peasantry. Rural cooperatives remained SR-oriented, but direct peasant organizational activities became quite hazardous and therefore limited. Likewise, the military organizations constructed by both the SRs and SDs suffered heavily. The Social Democratic military organizations, which had always had an uneasy status within the SD movement, suffered extinction, whereas the SR equivalents survived only in the deepest underground and with heavily curtailed activities. Symbolic of the PSR's efforts to maintain its contacts with soldiers and sailors was the publication of an underground newspaper, *Za Narod* (For the People), which was smuggled to the armed forces throughout the prewar years.[19]

However, for all practical purposes the supposedly peasant-oriented terrorist SR party had become an organization that operated largely in the urban environment, using tactics of mass organization of both a legal and an underground tendency. By virtue of necessity, the PSR now operated in a manner highly reminiscent of the SDs. A basis had been laid for future successes among the peasants and those in military uniform but for the time being those arenas remained closed.

The tactical maneuvers of the PSR after 1908 were not without controversy. For example, the effective cancellation of terrorism provoked a small group of party activists, calling themselves "Left SRs" (not to be confused with the Left SR movement and later party of 1914–18), to argue vociferously for the continuation of SR terror against tsarist officials. A more serious threat arose during 1909 when a sizable segment of the senior party leadership – A. Argunov, N. Sletov, M. Vishniak, E. Breshko-Breshkovskaia, and others – now repeated many of the arguments of the 1906 Popular Socialists (and of some moderate Mensheviks) in calling for an end to illegal activities in favor of a focus on legal action within the Duma and existing social institutions. This movement received much of its impetus from the revelation of the treachery of Azev; this formerly trusted party leader, who at one time led the terrorist Combat Organization, had finally been unmasked in 1909 as an informer who had heavily damaged the party's efforts through his continual betrayals to the police of its plans and leaders.

Eventually calling itself Pochin (New Beginnings), this reformist group, top-heavy with leaders, failed to attract much support among SR activist cadres, much less among the party's worker, soldier, and peasant following. The Azev affair, by the way, embarrassing as it was, by no means caused the catastrophe to the SR party that histories sometimes portray, although the intellectuals associated with the Pochin certainly attempted to describe the matter in those terms in order to justify the abandonment of all underground activities. However, the Chernov–Natanson–Rakitnikov leadership core kept the (somewhat creaky) SR ship afloat and steered it, through the storms of police repression and internal reformist heresy, toward revolution.[20]

The SRs fully participated in the rising urban movement noted by contemporary and historiographical commentary between 1910 and mid-1914. After the failure of an attempt during 1910 to establish the Central Committee inside Russia, the SRs relied instead upon local committees and groups, which now operated more successfully than before 1910. By 1911–12 the SRs in Petersburg and other cities began to issue worker-oriented newspapers, which played a cat-and-mouse game with the tsarist censorship (Social Democrats did the same). The police still reserved its worst for the SRs, arresting the editors and staffs of the SR Petersburg newspaper and imposing on them fines and jail sentences at more than twice the rate and severity levied upon the Bolshevik and Menshevik equivalents.

During 1912 the Bolsheviks altered their orientation toward legal labor institutions, much in the way the SRs had done several years earlier and with similar success. In Petersburg, the formerly predominant Mensheviks and SRs now found themselves ousted from the leadership of many organizations. These Bolshevik successes were temporary, however, and by no means extended to all of Russia. Nationwide, the SRs continued their activism, took part in the numerous strikes and demonstrations of the 1913–14 era, and issued quantities of illegal literature. By the early summer, citywide strike committees that consisted of SRs, Mensheviks, and Bolsheviks in Petersburg, Ekaterinoslav, and Baku heralded what some have called a revolutionary situation in Russia on the eve of the outbreak of World War I.[21]

Whatever the prospects for revolution as of mid-summer of 1914, the coming of the war itself led to a strong, if brief, outbreak of patriotism, granting the tsarist regime one final reprieve.[22] On this basis, the regime carried out the most thorough repression of all oppositionist groups and parties since the early 1880s. All SR committees and groups, their newspapers and printing presses, and hundreds of local leaders and activists were arrested; a similar process among the Social Democrats, anarchists and other parties signaled one of the darkest periods of the socialist movement. This time arrests even forced the closure of most labor unions and cultural societies. For a year or so, remnants of loosely connected underground organizations struggled to survive and issue occasional anti-tsarist and antiwar literature, with underground SR groups in no way lagging behind in this matter.

By early summer of 1915, after a year of unrelenting military reverses at the front and hardship at home, the atmosphere began to change. All the revolutionary parties noted a new openness to antiwar and antigovernmental agitation in the factories. For the next year and a half, socialist organizations gradually reshaped their organizations and, when possible, their local committees. None other than Aleksandr Kerensky, who enjoyed parliamentary immunity, aided considerably in the reestablishment of the SR organizations in the capital and throughout Russia. Of course, all party work was strictly conspiratorial; there could be no question of issuing newspapers as had occurred before the war's outbreak. Nevertheless, underground SR organizations in Petrograd, Moscow, Kharkov, Kiev, Tomsk, and many other places took shape, held secret conferences, and issued agitational leaflets.

Meanwhile, the sizable number of SR cadres and leaders in Western Europe met to work out a position on the war. These meetings witnessed severe debates, leading to a *de facto* split within the PSR. Leaders of the Pochin group, who had already abandoned the cause of revolution before the war, now insisted on the necessity of supporting the existing government for the duration of the war. This position, which had an even wider adherence among Mensheviks than among SRs (and not a few among Bolsheviks as well), came to be known as defensism. The Chernov–Natanson–Rakitnikov leadership group, which had shown its predominance in all party debates since 1906, argued for staunchly maintaining the party's revolutionary goals, even during the war and, in fact, because of the war, which would intensify social and economic pressures within the country. This position, called internationalism, became the predominant one among SRs both in the émigré Community and inside Russia and was shared by many Mensheviks and Bolsheviks. Furthermore, a group of radical SRs, under the guidance of Natanson and B. Kamkov (with a certain degree of cautious support from Chernov) called for the defeat of the Russian government in the war as a precursor to the government's overthrow; this so-called defeatist position, usually attributed solely to Lenin and some Bolsheviks, was quite independently worked out by the radical wing of the PSR. Inside Russia, a similar debate with similar outcomes occurred: many party intellectuals called for Russia's defense, whereas most party activists and much of the party's worker, soldier, and student following turned against any pursuit of victory in the war, preferring to concentrate on the overthrow of the tsarist regime. Literally, each passing month of the war added to the list of SR groups and organizations throughout the empire that adopted the internationalist stance and began issuing antiwar proclamations.

Within the factories, SR groups cooperated closely with SD groups (of both Menshevik and Bolshevik tendency) to organize the strikes that plagued Russia's war effort during the last 18 months before February 1917. The SRs and Bolsheviks further cooperated to agitate against the election of workers' groups to the War Industries Committees (an organization that aimed at promoting war production). The number of underground SR organizations in urban centers regularly issuing revolutionary proclamations aimed against the war, the tsar, and capitalism easily equaled the number of SD equivalents. Several Soviet-era historians have even noted somewhat begrudgingly that SR influence in large plants in Petrograd and elsewhere increased during 1915 and 1916. Although somewhat less is known about the student movement, the police noted that SR student organizations were staunchly opposed to the war. Occasionally, SR organizations issued leaflets aimed at the peasants, but efforts in the village remained limited.

In the realm of agitation in the armed forces, the SRs achieved perhaps their greatest success. On the basis of their still-existing underground military organizations and their superior standing in the eyes of innumerable peasant-soldiers, the SRs formed organizations behind all the fronts aimed at soldier agitation. One example was the Northern SR Military Organization that maintained outposts in Pskov, Novgorod, Petrograd, and Arkhangelsk. Although antiwar Bolsheviks and Mensheviks also engaged in this kind of activity, the SRs had a distinct edge. This turned out to be a matter of considerable importance since the involvement of soldiers was vital to the success of revolution. During the war, SRs sometimes criticized the SDs for having outmoded views of the coming revolution, which the latter conceived as consisting of worker revolts with barricades in the streets à la 1905. The SRs pointed out that the ubiquitous wartime garrisons rendered such an approach hopeless. Instead, the revolt could be carried out only with solider cooperation; thus the SR emphasis on soldier agitation. Needless to say, this was precisely the character of the revolt in Petrograd and elsewhere when it came.

A last aspect of the wartime SR movement concerns the question of intersocialist cooperation touched upon above. Perhaps because of the PSR's relatively catholic approach to social groupings (as opposed to the SDs' rather narrower focus on the proletariat) and its ideological eclecticism (incorporating into its outlook populist, general socialist, and Marxist aspects), the SRs always emphasized close cooperation with other socialist parties and even foresaw eventual socialist unification. Although no formulas were ever found for the latter, cooperation characterized the Russian socialist movement; formal and informal agreements were the watchword at all levels of activities, from factory cells to central committees. Characteristic was the repeated joint publication of leaflets by the SR and Bolshevik Petersburg committees during the first half of 1914. During the war, antiwar Mensheviks, Bolsheviks and SRs not only regularly coordinated activities in the large cities but at the fronts and in a network of cities and towns across the country, from Minsk to Vladivostok, from Kronshtadt to Astrakhan, formed intersocialist committees to issue leaflets and lead strikes and demonstrations. When, during early 1917, Minister of the Interior Protopopov referred to a pending revolt based upon joint socialist action, he correctly characterized the nature of the February Revolution.

As regards the SRs, by late summer of 1916 SR proclamations assumed the nearness of revolution and urged it; by late 1916 and early 1917, SR leaders in Petrograd, Moscow, and Kharkov issued direct calls for the revolutionary provisional government and laid down plans for a national newspaper and a national SR congress. During early February, the police reported that the Trudoviks (led by Kerensky) in the Duma had given up all legislative activities in favor of agitation for revolution, in respect of which they were consolidating ties to their populist allies, the SRs, who, noted the police, foresaw imminent revolution.[23] Indeed, shortly thereafter the SRs and SDs organized the strikes and demonstrations that overthrew the tsarist regime and then instituted the soviets that arose with the regime's end; thus the catastrophe of war had finally created the situation that had allowed Russia's revolutionary socialist movement to achieve its goal. The SR role had been a prominent (although not exclusive) one, as confirmed by that party's vast support after the February Revolution.

The SRs were a movement that fit early twentieth-century Russian reality. The country was not yet a capitalist state with a fully developed urban civil society; rather, the peasantry still dwarfed the growing middle and proletarian classes. For this very reason, after 1905 Lenin, to the horror of the Mensheviks, adopted aspects of neo-populist theory as regards the potential revolutionary role of the peasantry and the "over-growth" of the bourgeois revolution into a socialist one. In a certain sense, an orthodox Marxist movement in a country such as Russia with its over-whelmingly peasant population was an oddity. Mensheviks compensated for the theoretical dissonance by insisting – despite the Russian bour-geoisie's inability to make its own revolution – on the bourgeois nature of the imminent revolution, leaving socialism for a distant future. This relied upon the infinite patience of Russia's mass social elements, whereas, in the event, they displayed only finite forbearance; as the neo-populists had always expected, the combined worker, soldier, and peasant elements first overthrew the tsar and then (with Bolshevik, Left SR and Left Menshevik encouragement) ran roughshod over moderate socialist dilatoriness in moving the revolution toward a socialist denouement.

Precisely because of the broad social net they cast and their militant activism, the SRs did more than any other political group to bring about the collapse of tsarism, which, as noted, helps explain the prime position the party had among workers, soldiers, peasants, and radical intelligentsia after February. In this regard, the traditional historiographical tendency to describe the PSR as a peasant-oriented, terrorist, and intellectual-based organization has not only profoundly distorted the SR record but that of the entire revolutionary movement.

A full investigation of how the SRs managed during 1917 to alienate a sizable portion (but by no means all) of their hard won and well-earned support is beyond the purview of this study. A few comments will suffice. One of the party's chief merits – its relative social inclusiveness – became its Achilles' heel during the turbulent events of 1917. Attending to the aspirations and needs of the various politically awakened social strata (workers, peasants, soldiers, and intelligentsia) proved daunting, any attempt at which dissipated forces and resources. Another indirectly related problem lay in the PSR's ruinous post-February unification of the entire spectrum of right, center, and left SRs (a Menshevik–Bolshevik SD party would have been the unwieldy rival equivalent). Nevertheless, it is difficult to imagine a democratic government in Russia of that era, given its specific social make-up, to be without significant SR participation. The party's failures and defeats quickly translated into the nation's misfortunes.

Notes

1   Manfred Hildermeier, *Die Sozialrevolutionaere Partei Russlands: Agrarsozialismus und Modernisierung im Zarenreich (1900–1914)* (Cologne: Boehlau Verlag, 1978), 35–57; Maureen Perrie, *The Agrarian Policy of the Russian Socialist-Revolutionary Party from its Origins through the Revolution of 1905–1907* (Cambridge: Cambridge University Press, 1976), 5–13; Oliver Radkey, *The Agrarian Foes of Bolshevism: Promise and Default of the Russian Socialist Revolutionaries, February to October 1917* (New York: Columbia University Press, 1958), 47–56; Michael Melancon, "Athens or Babylon? The Birth of the Socialist Revolutionary and Social Democratic Parties in Saratov, 1890–1905," in Rex Wade and Scott Seregny, eds, *Politics and Society in Provincial Russia: Saratov, 1590–1917* (Columbus: Ohio State University Press, 1989), 75–84.

2   Perrie, *Agrarian Policy*, 14–50; Radkey, *Agrarian Foes*, 56–60; Michael Melancon, "The Socialist Revolutionaries from 1902–1907: Peasant *and* Workers' Party," *Russian History*, 12(1) (Spring 1985): 2–9; S. Sossinskii, "Pages from the Life of Victor Chernov," (PhD diss., Boston University, 1995).

3   Donald Treadgold, *Lenin and His Rivals* (New York: F. A. Prager, 1955), 60–86; Christopher Rice, *Russian Workers and the Socialist-Revolutionary Party through the Revolution of 1905–1907* (New York: St Martins Press, 1988), 23–7; Radkey, *Agrarian Foes*, 24–46; Hildermeier, *Sozialrevolutionaere Partei*, 68–108; Melancon, "Socialist Revolutionaries from 1902 to 1907," 11–14.

4   Anna Geifman, *Thou Shalt Kill: Revolutionary Terrorism in Russia, 1894–1917* (Princeton: Princeton University Press, 1993), 45–83; Hildermeier, *Sozialrevolutionaere Partei*, 58–67; Rice, *Russian Workers*, 21–3; Richard Spence, *Boris Savinkov: Renegade on the Left* (Boulder: East European Monographs, 1991), 28–73; K. V. Gusev, *Partiia eserov ot melko-burzhuaznogo revoliutsionarizma k kontr-revoliutsii* (Moscow: Mysl', 1975), 56–77.

5   Hildermeier, *Sozialrevolutionaere Partei*, 83–98; Melancon, "Athens or Babylon," 90–3; Perrie, *Agrarian Policy*, 34–69, 143–52; Gusev, *Partiia eserov* 40–9; Radkey, *Agrarian Foes*, 24–32; Maureen Perrie, ed., *Protokoly Pervogo S'ezda Partii Sostsialistov-Revoliutsionerov*, (London: Kraus International Publications, 1983), 363–4.

6   Rice, *Russian Workers*, 32–56, 71–4; Melancon, "Socialist Revolutionaries from 1902 to 1907," 14–19.

7 Melancon, "Socialist Revolutionaries from 1902 to 1907," 43–6; Rice, *Russian Workers*, 42–62; L. Haimson, "The Problem of Social Stability in Urban Russia, 1905–1917," (part 1), *Slavic Review*, 23(4) (December 1964): 635; Robert Johnson, *Peasant and Proletarian: The Working Class of Moscow in the Late Nineteenth Century* (New Brunswick: Rutgers University Press, 1979), 67–9.

8 Melancon, "Athens or Babylon," 81–3; Scott J. Seregny, *Russian Teachers and Peasant Revolution: The Politics of Education in 1905* (Bloomington: Indiana University Press, 1989), 91–2; Hildermeier, *Sozialrevolutionaere Partei*, 292–304.

9 Rice, *Russian Workers*, 57–63; Perrie, *Agrarian Policy*, 101–17; Melancon, "Socialist Revolutionaries from 1902 to 1907," 20–9; Hildermeier, *Sozialrevolutionaere Partei*, 193–205.

10 I. M. Pushkareva, *Zheleznodorozhniki Rossii v burzhuazno-demokraticheskikh revoliutsiiakh* (Moscow: Nauka, 1975), 111–24; Hildermeier, *Sozial-revolutionaere Partei*, 186; Rice, *Russian Workers*, 187–91.

11 Rice, *Russian Workers*, 191–2; Hildermeier, *Sozialrevolutionaere Partei*, 114, 187–92, 226; Melancon, "Socialist Revolutionaries from 1902–1907," 26–8, 32–4; Melancon, "Athens or Babylon," 104–6; Joseph L. Sanders, "The Moscow Uprising of December 1905: A Background Study," PhD diss., University of Washington, 1981.

12 Pushkareva, *Zheleznodorozhniki*, 150, 182, 194, 202–4; Melancon, "Socialist Revolutionaries from 1902–1907," 27–8; Hildermeier, *Sozialrevolutionaere Partei*, 254–7.

13 Perrie, *Agrarian Policy*, 101–42; Melancon, "Athens or Babylon," 107–11; Seregny, *Russian Teachers*, 158–70, 174–96; Hildermeier, *Sozialrevolutionaere Partei*, 119–21; Robert Edelman, *Proletarian Peasants: The Revolution of 1905 in Russia's Southwest* (Ithaca: Cornell University Press, 1986), 161–4.

14 Perrie, *Agrarian Policy*, 143–52; Hildermeier, *Sozialrevolutionaere Partei*, 83–104; *Protokoly Pervogo S'ezda*, 355–65.

15 Hildermeier, *Sozialrevolutionaere Partei*, 126–40, 145–9; Perrie, *Agrarian Policy*, 153–67; Rice, *Russian Workers*, 64–6.

16 Melancon, "Socialist Revolutionaries from 1902–1907," 34–42; Perrie, *Agrarian Policy*, 168–76; Rice, *Russian Workers*, 85–96.

17 Rice, *Russian Workers*, 63–4; Hildermeier, *Sozialrevolutionaere Partei*, 309–13; Radkey, *Agrarian Foes*, 79–80; *Protokoly pervoi obschepartiinoi konferentsii sotsialistov-revoliutsionerov, avgust 1908* (Paris: Izd. Tsen. kom. P.S.-R., 1908), 96–7.

18 M. Melancon, " 'Stormy Petrels': The Socialist Revolutionaries in Russia's Labor Organizations, 1905–1914," *The Carl Beck Papers*, no. 703 June 1988, 1–42; Radkey, *Agrarian Foes*, 80–1.

19 Radkey, *Agrarian Foes*, 80; M. Melancon, *The Socialist Revolutionaries and the Russian Anti-War Movement, 1914–1917* (Columbus: Ohio State University Press, 1990), 13–14.

20 Radkey, *Agrarian Foes*, 81–2; Hildermeier, *Sozialrevolutionaere Partei*, 324–40.

21 Melancon, " 'Stormy Petrels'," 21–42; Gusev, *Partiia eserov*, 75–7.

22   The following discussion of the wartime PSR is based upon Melancon, *The Socialist Revolutionaries and the Russian Anti-War Movement*. Other relevant secondary sources are L. M. Shalaginova, "Esery-internatsionalisty v gody pervoi mirovoi voiny," in A. L. Sidorov, ed., *Pervaia Mirovaia Voina* (Moscow: Nauka, 1968), 323–34; Gusev, *Partiia eserov*, 78–96; Radkey, *Agrarian Foes*, 88–126; M. Melancon, " 'Marching Together!': Left Bloc Activities in the Russian Revolutionary Movement, 1900 to February 1917," *Russian Review*, 49(2) (Summer 1990): 239–52; and Melancon, "Who Wrote What and When?: Proclamations of the February Revolution in Petrograd, 23 February–1 March 1917," *Soviet Studies*, XL(3) (July 1988): 499–500.

23   *Gosudarstvennyi arkhiv Rossiiskoi Federatsii*, POO, F 111, op. 5, d. 658, l. 230; d. 669, l. 230; d. 669a, l. 38.

PART II

The Other Adversaries

CHAPTER FIVE

The Anarchists and the "Obscure Extremists"[1]

Anna Geifman

"To demolish the contemporary order" absolutely, to do away with all laws and courts, all religion and churches, all property and property owners, all traditions and customs and their adherents, were the immediate objectives of all anarchists in the Russian Empire. Those who derived their name from the Greek *anarxia* (meaning "lawlessness," "absence of government") sought as their ultimate goal the complete liberation of man from all "artificial restraints," in order to render him totally independent from any form of political, economic, or spiritual authority. Emancipation of mankind from both God and the devil would be achieved by allowing citizens to unite in voluntary associations, which would impose no restraints on individuals' free development.[2] The anarchist means to these ends would be social revolution, defined by them as any direct action, particularly terrorism, expropriation of private and public property, and the destruction of state institutions, that would shake the foundations of the contemporary order. These direct actions would be taken "without entering into any compromises with the bourgeoisie and . . . without putting forth any concrete demands," and would lead to the final destruction of both capitalism and the state, followed by their replacement with an egalitarian communal society, free from oppression and even the minimal control necessarily exerted by any form of government.[3] According to the anarchist creed, man is naturally good and humane and therefore does not need to comply with norms established by compulsory institutions such as law, government, or church.[4]

According to Paul Avrich, the leading authority on Russian anarchism, "the very nature of the anarchist creed, with its bitter hostility toward hierarchical organization of any sort, impeded the growth of a formal movement." Indeed, Russian anarchism can barely be regarded as a movement at all, for no united anarchist organization existed, and there were no strictly defined or centrally coordinated policies on any programmatic or tactical issue. In accordance with their general belief that "the spirit of destruction is a creative spirit," the anarchists – that "varied assortment of independent groups, without a party program or a measure of effective coordination" – set forth little in the way of a positive program.[5]

Still, despite the fact that there were only roughly 5,500 active anarchists in the Russian Empire at the peak of the movement, in 1905–7[6] – rendering them numerically inferior in comparison with the SRs and the SDs – their impact on Russian life was enormous, if only in one respect: their role in promoting political violence was greater than that of any organized political formation in the country. The anarchists were responsible for many more acts of political violence than any of the larger subversive organizations or parties.[7]

It is impossible to estimate with any degree of precision exactly what percentage of the total number of terrorist acts were carried out by anarchists, for the local authorities seldom specified an individual terrorist's political sympathies in their reports. The anarchist groups themselves, isolated as they were from one another and with no central organizational structure, did not maintain accurate statistical records. There is little doubt, however, that the majority of the estimated 17,000 casualties of terrorist acts between 1901 and 1916,[8] were victims of anarchist attacks. Some of the individuals represented by these statistics had been carefully selected as assassination targets, but many were accidental casualties killed and wounded as bystanders at the scene of bomb explosions, revolutionary robberies, or shootouts between anarchists and the police. The influence of anarchism on Russian life in the opening decade of the twentieth century thus appears to have been "quite out of proportion to the number of its adherents."[9]

There were few anarchists in Russia prior to the twentieth century, with the first groups beginning to operate under the black banner of anarchism toward the end of 1903 in Belostok, Odessa, Nezhin, and other areas. They did not arise spontaneously, but rather as a result of defections from other political organizations, primarily the Party of Socialists-Revolutionaries and the various factions of the Social Democratic Workers' Party. With the outbreak of revolutionary disturbances in 1905, and throughout the next two violent years, anarchist groups, in the words of Belostok anarchist committee leader Iuda Grossman, "sprang up like mushrooms after rain," in cities, small towns, and villages.[10] According to Avrich, the pattern was the same throughout the empire. In Ukraine, in the Caucasus, and especially in the western provinces, where anarchism became widespread in Riga, Vilna, and Warsaw, as well as in smaller towns such as Gomel, Grodno, and Kovno, a handful of disaffected SRs or SDs united into small anarchist cells that then formed loose federations and plunged into radical activity of every sort, most notably terrorism.[11]

SRs and SDs chose to leave their organizations for a variety of reasons. Many from the lower strata of society, especially workers, had become alienated from party leaders who in their eyes were theorizing intellectuals, and who preferred ideological debate to any radical action, a fact which did nothing but divide the revolutionaries. Even party members who were slightly more theoretically inclined became disillusioned by the SRs' preoccupation with the agrarian question, and objected to the Marxist insistence upon the necessity of establishing parliamentary democracy that, according to socialist dogma, would mark the stage preceding the withering away of the state. Indeed, as the anarchists argued in one of their proclamations, since democracy protected capitalist oppression it was as much an enemy as autocracy. Therefore with both political systems "only one language was possible – violence." The working class should not make any distinction between the various forms of government, for a revolutionary worker should "enter the democratic parliament, the Winter Palace, or any police-state establishment only . . . with a bomb!"[12]

Tactically, the dissenters from the SR camp, while in complete agreement with their party's practice of political terror, wished to extend those methods to the economic sphere, and use them against capitalists and other exploiters.[13] Dissident SDs left the RSDRP in protest at its official antiterrorist stand and the consequent shortage of practical militant work.[14] Nevertheless, Avrich justifiably asserts that the "socialist parties of Russia, in contrast to those of Western Europe, with their strong reformist slant, were sufficiently militant to accommodate all but the most passionate and idealistic young students and craftsmen and the rootless drifters of the city underworld."[15] It was these restless, and primarily youthful, individuals, unable to control their rebellious spirit and conform to the rules and discipline of any structured political organization, who tended to leave the formal political parties to become anarchists, thus brushing aside all questions of ideology and tactics.[16]

The practitioners of anarchism in Russia had little concern for adhering to a strictly defined and thought out set of theoretical principles for the armed struggle against the establishment. Instead, they confined themselves to a few appeals in the style of the semi-Futurist manifesto issued in 1909, which complained of the "poisonous breath of civilization," and urged, "Take up the picks and hammers! Undermine the foundations of ancient towns! Everything is ours, beyond is only death . . . Everyone to the street! Forward! Destroy! Kill!"[17] Still, although miscellaneous groups and circles within the anarchist milieu generally adhered to this unsophisticated credo, different extremist organizations offered a diverse list of justifications for their tactics and practical activities.

Among the most notable anarchist groups, one of the least radical was a circle of followers of Petr Kropotkin, the leading theoretician of Russian anarchism, residing in London at the time. The group was headquartered in Geneva, and led by Georgian anarchist G. Gogeliia (K. Orgeiani) and his wife Lidiia. It published the monthly journal *Khleb i volia* (Bread and Liberty), and its members therefore came to be called Khlebovol'tsy. They considered themselves Anarchists-Communists, that is, adherents of Kropotkin's doctrine promoting a free communal society in which each person was to "live according to his abilities and be provided according to his needs." Like the SDs and the SRs, they attributed the primary role in the revolutionary movement to the masses, and although Kropotkin declared that he was "not afraid to proclaim: do whatever you like, act entirely in accordance with your own discretion," he warned his followers against acts of violence isolated from the mass liberation movement. In his opinion, individual acts directed against the state, as well as those aimed against the bourgeoisie, could produce no significant change in the existing sociopolitical order and certainly fell short of achieving the total elimination of private property – the ultimate goal of anarchism.[18] At the same time, the Khlebovol'tsy believed that efforts on the part of members of other revolutionary organizations to distinguish between acts perpetrated for the sake of political struggle and those whose purpose was economic liberation was inappropriate and artificial: it was the duty of the anarchists to struggle simultaneously against the state and capitalist exploitation – the two mutually enhancing and equally oppressive features of mass enslavement.

Nevertheless, the Khlebovol'tsy leaders openly sanctioned only "defensive violence," which encompassed retaliation against particularly odious representatives of the state, extraordinarily brutal exploiters, and their supporters among the radical monarchists; as a counter to this, they renounced indiscriminate attacks against petty servants of the establishment.[19] Like the SRs, the Khlebovol'tsy hoped and expected that their attacks would contribute to the revolutionary "propaganda by deed," awakening the masses and inciting them to further struggle.

The public renunciation of indiscriminate violence by Kropotkin and his followers was echoed by certain other anarchists, the most ardent of whom were the Anarchists-Syndicalists (Anarkhisty-Sindikalisty), whose leader in Russia was D. Novomirskii (Iakov Kirillovskii). According to him, under the circumstances prevailing at the time, the struggle for the liberation of the poor was to be economic, and therefore the immediate goal of the anarchists was to disseminate propaganda in the factories and organize labor unions as agents of the class struggle against the bourgeoisie. He renounced extremist conspiratorial tactics, for, in his opinion, random assassinations and confiscation of private property did nothing to educate the proletariat, and merely nourished "coarse and bloodthirsty instincts." On the other hand, the effective use of violence, according to Novomirskii and his followers, included not only labor strikes and boycotts, but also assaults on factory managers, sabotage, and expropriation of government funds and property.[20]

In their theoretical outlook, a number of anarchist groups thus appeared relatively restrained, unexpectedly more moderate than the SRs and, at least in the case of Novomirskii, approximated the general principles of the SDs. Such groups represented a minority in the anarchist forces, however; the great majority of the anarchists applauded indiscriminate, reckless, and boundless violence. The largest and most ardent of them was a federation of groups after 1903 dispersed primarily through the frontier provinces of the west and south, and known as Chernoe Znamia (Black Banner).

Like the Khlebovol'tsy, the Black Banner members, or Chernoznamentsy, considered themselves Anarchists-Communists. In their tactics, however, they were prepared to go beyond Kropotkin's idea of individual action merely as a supplement for the mass struggle against political and economic oppression, and adhere more closely to the principles of conspiracy and uninterrupted violence advocated by the late father of Russian anarchism, Prince Mikhail Bakunin (1814–76). Suspicious of large-scale organizations, they did not support the Anarchists-Syndicalists' claims regarding the leading role of the trade unions in the liberation of the proletariat, clearly preferring immediate sanguinary action to patient propaganda against the capitalists.

For the Chernoznamentsy, every act of violence against political oppression, however random and senseless it might appear to the general public, was justified in the atmosphere of universal conflict and mutual hatred in Russia between the rebellious slaves and their former masters. The liberators of the people, as the anarchists saw themselves, did not need special provocation to direct their vengeance against any agent of the autocracy. Political assassination was thus no longer to be used simply as a clearly motivated punishment for specific harsh or repressive measures on the part of a certain proponent of reaction; indeed, recognizing the arbitrary nature of violence that they promoted, the anarchists even assigned it a special label: "motiveless terror" (*bezmotivnyi terror*).

In accordance with this entirely new concept, which originated and became widespread around 1905, when the situation in Russia was approaching civil war, violence no longer required immediate and direct justification: anyone wearing a uniform was considered a representative of the establishment and was therefore subject to execution at any moment as an enemy of the people. The principle hailed by the bezmotivniki thus provided justification for any extremist who decided to toss a bomb into the middle of a military unit, a Cossack patrol, or a police squad. As one revolutionary recalled, some anarchists could not tolerate even the sight of a police officer passing by in the street. Indeed, perhaps the most common targets for random anarchist attacks after 1905 were street policemen, who were visible enough to attract the attention of anyone seeking an opportunity to express anger – actions amounting to mass political violence, complemented as it was by the anarchist struggle against economic oppression.

In the fight against private property, the anarchist creed justified the death of each and every industrialist, estate and factory owner, and even their managers, bankers, merchants, store-keepers, owners of tiny craft shops, and any other representatives of the capitalist world who were exploiters by the very nature of their occupation and social status. In accordance with the slogan of several Anarchist-Communist groups in Moscow and Odessa, "The death of the bourgeoisie is life for the workers," anyone who was not an unpropertied proletarian deserved to be killed. With this in mind, leaders of the Black Banner organization and similar groups, such as a militant sect called Beznachalie (Without Authority) and the Anarchists-Individualists (Anarkhisty-Individualisty), urged their followers to cast aside their scruples when throwing bombs into theaters or cafés, since it would be unusual for anyone who did not belong to the class of exploiters to frequent such places of entertainment for the bourgeoisie. In the words of one Beznachalie group member, it was sufficient "to see a man in white gloves . . . to recognize in him an enemy, who deserves death." The Anarchists-Individualists went still further and proclaimed themselves free to attack and kill anyone, even if the only aim behind the murder was personal gratification, for, in their perception, any violent act, without distinction, in its own way contributed to their final objective – destruction of the bourgeois world. Nor did they neglect the loathsome "spiritual foundation" on which that world rested, thus sanctioning unprovoked or motiveless violence against reactionary intellectuals, the clergy, and designating even the physical symbols of state and religious enslavement – triumphal arches and statues of civil and military leaders, church and synagogue buildings – all as appropriate targets for explosives.[21]

Although the anarchists frequently demonstrated great personal courage and willingness to sacrifice their lives in daring exploits undertaken for the revolutionary cause, their underlying motives were often less elevated than their lofty talk about the emancipation of the oppressed. As

Avrich notes, reckless and frustrated youths, among whom were certain "self-styled Nietzschean supermen," often "satisfied their desire for excitement and self-affirmation by hurling bombs into public buildings, factory offices, theaters, and restaurants."[22] Moreover, common banditry quickly became widespread in the anarchist ranks, much more so than among any other proponents of the revolution. Former vagabonds, professional thieves, and other denizens of the criminal world joined the anarchists in large numbers in accordance with Bakunin's recommendation that all the base rabble, all the shadowy and outcast elements and renegades of society, should be welcomed into the revolutionary milieu as brothers and comrades and potential fighters for the people's cause. The anarchists agitated for social justice among tramps and thieves, and when they themselves served time in prison and in hard labor, successfully recruited criminal convicts into the radical ranks.[23] And so, having undergone revolutionary transformation, those who had previously killed and robbed for selfish motives began to engage in similar activities for more progressive reasons. At the same time, however, the revolutionaries inevitably fell under the influence of the criminal underworld, to the extent that many anarchist groups deteriorated into semi-criminal gangs and began to occupy themselves with robbery and looting for personal profit. According to the St Petersburg police chief Aleksandr Gerasimov, these organizations, operating under the anarchist flag after 1906 were not at all revolutionary; they merely used anarchist rhetoric to justify pure banditry, as was the case with a group led by a certain Savel'ev, a convinced proponent of motiveless violence. To a large extent Savel'ev's group was composed of hard-core thieves and murderers, who had fled from the police and joined the anarchists: one of them was a deserter from the navy, who claimed responsibility for 11 murders; his girlfriend was a registered prostitute; another fugitive sailor had been sentenced to hard labor for taking part in killing a priest and robbing a church; and that convict's lover was a thief with a police record.[24] Considering that many similar anarchist groups, such as the Black Ravens (Chernye vorony), Hawks (Iastreby), Black Terror (Chernyi terror), Bloody Hand (Krovavaia ruka), or those which operated throughout the Russian provinces without a name, degenerated into bandit gangs engaged in rampant and exclusively profit-oriented violence, Georgii Plekhanov's words, written some 15 years prior to the outbreak of mass violence in 1905, proved apposite: "It is impossible to guess where a comrade anarchist ends and where a bandit begins."[25]

This characterization can be applied to the numerous groups operating outside the mainstream antigovernment movement throughout the Russian Empire after the turn of the century, and especially following the outbreak of revolutionary events in 1905. Having for diverse reasons isolated themselves or broken away from the major revolutionary parties and even the anarchist groups, various alienated individuals, too rebellious to remain within the framework of any political formation, banded together in small, loosely organized gangs of revolutionary extremists, prepared for the time being to cooperate in practical matters such as expropriations. Most of these radicals either deviated from the ideological principles advocated by the established revolutionary parties, or, more commonly, could not confine themselves to specific tactical programs, usually wishing to go beyond the limits of what these organizations considered legitimate and justifying revolutionary means. The primary point of disagreement as far as tactics were concerned was the issue of terror and expropriations, and the dissenters' attitude vis-à-vis these methods clearly betrayed them as extremists of a new type. These independent radicals had failed to develop any firm ideological principles differing from those advocated by the established political parties, and practiced uninterrupted violence without making any serious attempt to justify it with dogma, readily engaging in a range of criminal enterprises that had little to do with revolutionary goals and that were perpetrated instead for personal material profit.

The various groups classified as "obscure" included former representatives of the revolutionary organizations, but the overwhelming majority of independent extremists were dissidents from the Socialist-Revolutionary cells operating in the provinces after 1905. As was true of most defectors to the anarchist camp, many former SRs objected first of all to the control of terrorist activity by a party leadership empowered to regulate these actions in accordance with the overall political goals of the organization, initiating and halting them at will. Secondly, these nonconformists denounced the restrictions officially imposed by the PSR on economic terror, and specifically the prohibitions against the expropriation of private property. Even though these acts never ceased in practice, isolated individuals within the PSR still resented the obligation to adhere to its discipline, pay lip service to its tactical policies, and refrain from attractive ventures proscribed because they might stain the party's reputation.

Numerous SRs thus left the SR party to escape its centralized control of political violence. In the city of Gomel, for example, a number of defectors from the PSR united in 1905 into a group whose members called themselves Independent Socialists-Revolutionaries, and formed terrorist detachments that were autonomous from all the local SR combat forces. Along with terrorist attacks against police and civil authorities – acts that were quite in line with the SR methods – these extremists indulged in uncontrolled economic violence, often directing their wrath against estate managers, with their actions acquiring anarchist overtones. These independent revolutionaries were apparently disinterested in all aspects of socialist ideology, and this tendency, in combination with their use of coercion to secure funds from private individuals for terrorist operations, caused the local Socialists-Revolutionaries to dissociate themselves entirely from these obscure figures, and to deny any previous links with them.[26]

Many former SRs among the independent radicals drifted gradually toward anarchism. A group known as the Uncompromising Ones (Neprimirimye), formed in Odessa in November 1903, having formally broken from the local SR Committee over tactical matters, renounced or ignored all aspects of SR thinking, but retained their fascination with political murders. In addition, they embraced such anarchist goals as the systematic destruction of factories and plants as a necessary part of the antibourgeois struggle.[27] Oriented almost exclusively toward violence, some of these tiny autonomous bands were led by genuinely criminal types, such as the notorious criminal from the small town of Klintsy, a certain Comrade Savitskii, a born gang-leader, nicknamed for his exploits "the new Nat Pinkerton and Rinaldo-Rinaldini" by the local press.[28]

Similarly, following the outbreak of violence in 1905, many members of the Russian Social Democratic Workers' Party declined to wait patiently for the full development of a capitalist system, which, according to an underlying principle of Marxism, would create a truly revolutionary situation, with the proletariat finally becoming ready to take over the means of production, the most fundamental feature of industrial society. Many Social Democrats sought immediate action, and therefore chose to disregard the incompatibility of their behavior with the theoretical principles of the SD organization. For the most part, however, members of local SD groups possessed only a limited notion of and interest in even the most basic of Marxist ideology, and so it was not difficult for young SDs, like one Vasilii Podvysotskii from Odessa, to conclude under the influence of government repressions in 1907: "Our eyes will pop out before we live to see the concentration of capital. No, brothers let's turn to terror instead!" Evidently, Podvysotskii was persuasive: "What is the use of padding out empty theory?" – his comrades concurred – "Our brothers are being hanged, and we are supposed to wait patiently . . . How long are we to wait, until everyone is hanged?"[29] The next step for Podvysotskii and his comrades – as it was for so many other Social Democrats at the time – was to join together in an independent combat group entirely anarchist both in spirit and in its practical activities, devoted primarily to robbing the local wealthy.

Members of the various national factions of the RSDRP throughout the empire also joined in breaking away from the control of their central organizations to form obscure and usually short-lived radical groups. Thus, in the Caucasus, the extremist groups widely known as Terror of the City of Tiflis and Its Surrounding Districts (Terror g. Tiflisa i ego uezdov) was originally part of the local SD organization, but had broken its ties with it for the sake of unrestrained violence.[30]

In addition to the many obscure extremist groups loosely associated with the SR and SD movements, numerous other bands operated throughout the country that chose not to ally themselves with either the socialist or the anarchist camp, despite their persistent, if vague, claims in support of the revolutionary nature of their activities. Their claims were often justified by practical policies, as in the case of a St Petersburg group that by its very name, Death for Death (Smert' za smert'), aimed to strike terror into the hearts of the enemy. Its immediate plan of action was limited to the assassination of a number of prominent statesmen in the capital, including Stolypin, Trepov, and Petr Durnovo.[31] Another such group was a band of some 20 revolutionaries, also operating in St Petersburg, calling themselves the Group of Terrorists-Expropriators (Gruppa terroristov-ekspropriatorov). At their October 1907 triad, members of this band were convicted of attempting "to bring down the existing political regime in Russia by force and to replace it with a democratic republic," starting with an attack on a monastery near the town of Grodno. One of the radicals was sentenced to ten years hard labor for his participation in an attack on another monastery, where the terrorists had planted explosives to destroy the revered icon of the Virgin of Kursk.[32]

Obscure revolutionary groups like these were even more active in the periphery. An underground circle of about a dozen independent extremists operating in the town of Voronezh united themselves in 1907–8 into the League of the Red Fuse (Liga krasnogo shnura), with the ambitious objective of ending the contemporary sociopolitical order in Russia. The fact that they did not even pretend to know what new order was to replace the old oppressive one did not deter the league from developing an immediate plan of action involving a series of political assassinations of public and private figures. All members of the League of the Red Fuse were arrested before they could implement their far-fetched schemes, although they had managed to carry out several armed robberies in Voronezh.[33] In other cities and towns throughout Russia numerous bloody acts of violence were perpetrated by equally obscure groups, such as, for instance, the Black Cloud (Chernaia tucha) revolutionary cell in the Chernigov province, and the Storm (Groza), a combat detachment in the town of Rogachev whose members called themselves "Terrorists-Individualists."[34] Groups like the so-called Avengers (Mstiteli), the Non-Party Union of Terrorists (Bezpartiinyi soiuz terroristov) and Freedom is Inside Us (Svoboda vnutri nas) appeared all too frequently on the pages of periodicals to impress the Russian public in the period after 1905.[35]

There were many extremist groups in the first decade of the twentieth century with such ambiguous ideological foundations that it is often impossible to establish with any degree of certainty the *raison d'être* or political orientation of a particular clandestine circle. Universal rampant violence apparently needed no justification for a group made up of four young men and a girl who plotted the murder of Petr Kropotkin. These extremists *par excellence* seemed to feel that the anarchist guru exerted too moderate an influence over his followers, holding back the forces of revolution, for which he must pay with his life.[36] Another group, the party of the Independent Ones (Nezavisimye), worked out a charter stating that this secret society had been

> organized for the struggle against all sorts of violence, regardless of its source, whether initiated by social organs, political parties, or state institutions. . . . Whatever form violence . . . reveals itself in, whether as terror on the part of extremist parties, or in the form of coercion by bureaucratic organs of the state mechanism . . . any victim will always find most energetic protection from the party against oppression of the individual. The party admits into its ranks people of all ages, without discriminating against any sex, religion, nationality, and profession. A priest, a socialist, and a state official enjoy equal votes in the party.[37]

Judging from the opening section of this charter, the Independent Ones appear to have been a type of vigilante police force, determined to protect indiscriminately all victims of organized violence, whether right- or left-wing. The statement on tactics that follows the discussion of the general goals of the organization vividly demonstrates, however, that the elevated language about defending the innocent and the oppressed was directed against the authorities only, for the party resolved to implement terror "in all cases of aggressive behavior by the government, the police, the inspirators of the bureaucracy, and its spiritual ideologists." The Independent Ones also proclaimed their right to administer justice and implement death sentences four days after a verdict. Because this group included "confiscation of the enemy's material means" among its "punitive measures against persons and institutions that oppress individual freedom" it is evident that, despite the obvious contradiction, the Independent Ones, who claimed to struggle against all sources of violence, promoted their cause primarily by resorting to the very same tactics.[38]

In addition to the obscure extremist organizations that exerted at least minimal efforts to portray themselves as true revolutionaries with the semblance of an ideological profile, there were other radical bands unwilling even to go this far. There is no indication that members of these groups considered themselves anything but common outlaws, regardless of their sometimes bombastic names alluding to their alleged association with the Russian liberation movement. In prison, for example, they did not demand the special treatment usually accorded political convicts, and normally served their sentences among the thieves and murderers.[39] One such group of about a dozen fugitive hard-labor convicts proved obedient tools in the hands of their chief, Grigorii Kotovskii, a proverbial figure in Bessarabia prior to the 1917 Revolution and an equally legendary commander of a Bolshevik cavalry division during the Russian civil war.

Kotovskii came from a noble family, and from his childhood found himself in frequent conflict with his superiors in school and at work (having been fired for embezzlement), and became "fanatically fascinated by the criminal world." A tireless adventurer, Kotovskii became infatuated with the life of the brigand, and as early as 1903 began to take vengeance on the milieu in which he grew up.[40] Although he was said to have occasionally made contributions to the local SR Committee, probably to promote its work among the peasantry, Kotovskii was not formally affiliated with any party. He demonstrated no ideological preferences, directing his activities against the wealthy in general, and expropriating anything he could get his hands on, from currency held by city banks to Persian carpets in private homes. Kotovskii liked to think of himself as a Russian Robin Hood, or "an ideological thief," and although he fully indulged his love of wine, women, and entertainment, he also claimed to have distributed a share of his loot among the poor.[41]

These claims notwithstanding, both the authorities and his criminal acquaintances regarded him as a daring gang leader (*ataman*), and his followers as a band of thieves and vagabonds. In the winter of 1906, after one of his men had betrayed him to the police for the handsome reward of 10,000 rubles, Kotovskii was tried not as a political prisoner, but as a common criminal. Remarkably, many women, among them those in the highest social circles, demonstrated their fascination with this legendary revolutionary rogue by sending him flowers, candies, and admiring notes during his imprisonment.[42] Kotovskii's life-style, manners, and even language (his lexicon was rich in street and prison jargon) suggest that his treatment as a hardened criminal was not inappropriate, a conclusion reinforced by his imprisonment for a while as a common bandit and the chief of a smash-and-grab gang, even after the 1917 February Revolution, when all political prisoners of the late tsarist regime were granted liberty, regardless of their offenses.[43]

On the whole, with the escalation of revolutionary upheaval after 1905, many extremists, even some of those who had formerly determined to prove themselves dedicated freedom-fighters rather than raiders and profiteers, abandoned all efforts to defend their actions with ideological principles. Their only justification for participating in revolutionary banditry was an alleged desire to help their comrades implement vague ideals involving a revolutionary utopia. These obscure radicals openly confessed:

"We are weak in theories and incapable of carrying out party work. We are of no use, except for obtaining money by means of 'exes'."[44]

There were, however, some anarchist and obscure extremist organizations that made a genuine effort to develop a convincing theoretical justification for their policy of expropriations, although none of their explanations were particularly deep or sophisticated in their reasoning. The dominant rationale among these extremists held that instead of humiliating themselves by begging for financial donations from the liberals, or relying upon contributions from the economically deprived proletarians, the revolutionaries must live off the capitalists – the rich merchants, the land and store owners – and other bourgeois exploiters. By expropriating their money and possessions, the radicals were to sustain themselves as full-time professional revolutionaries, and purchase the weapons and explosives required to overthrow the state and the bourgeois establishment.[45]

Within the anarchist camp the radicals could not agree as to how persistent they should be in carrying out their program of "economic terror." Whereas members of the Black Banner organization argued that the workers must continue to labor in the factories and shops despite exploitation and injustice, adherents of the Beznachalie trend declared that a true anarchist must not participate in capitalist production because in so doing he enhanced the strength of the very bourgeoisie that was to be most ruthlessly exterminated. Furthermore, the Beznachalie members insisted that a consistent revolutionary would not support the existing economic system by buying any consumer products; instead, he should satisfy all his needs through the expropriation of private property from the exploiters and oppressors.[46] Other adherents of the Anarchist-Communist trend, as well as some obscure extremist groups, such as the Uncompromising Ones, echoed these themes. Arguing for the necessity of raiding commercial warehouses and stores, they proclaimed thievery as "merely a product of the existing political order, and therefore not a crime."[47]

It is impossible to estimate with precision the total funds expropriated by the anarchists and obscure extremists throughout the Russian Empire after the turn of the century because few of the many autonomous groups engaged in these activities considered it necessary to keep records of incoming resources or expenditures. Still, the amount of damage caused to the state and the public by anarchist "exes" can be appreciated from the large number of newspaper reports describing major robberies at railway stations and state-owned liquor stores, swift attacks on mail coaches carrying large sums of money, or repeated raids on weapon depots and military arsenals. Amid the pervading anarchy after 1905, the radicals proceeded with their expropriations without discriminating among the various institutions and societies that appeared to be potential sources of profit. Indeed, there was no need to recoil from raiding a secondary school, for example, since to many of these extremists, any educational, cultural, or even charitable establishment represented the hated socioeconomic order.[48]

The overwhelming majority of anarchist expropriations, however, were assaults against private individuals and enterprises, largely because these targets tended to be less heavily guarded than financial institutions, and the risk of apprehension was proportionately smaller. At the same time, the profits obtained as a result of acts directed against the personal property of the bourgeoisie were usually also comparatively smaller than the profits from attacks aimed at state banks and other monetary depositories. This is not to suggest that the extremists did not pursue substantial sums of easy money by raiding large private enterprises, such as a sugar factory in the province of Kiev from which they stole 10,000 rubles in cash.[49] For the most part, however, the anarchists and members of obscure extremist groups chose more modest targets for their expropriations, preferring small stores, petty businesses, and private homes, where their chances of escaping safely with at least some reward for their efforts were greater. Since they ran out of funds quickly, these radicals constantly sought new sources of immediate profits, and thus the sheer frequency of their assaults compensated for the relatively small size of the take.

The anarchists directed their primary efforts against members of the bourgeois establishment considered guilty of direct exploitation or "bourgeois oppression," as, for example, in the case of a wealthy elderly widow near Kaluga, whose house a band of extremists broke into, strangled her and her gardener to death, and escaped with a large sum of cash and many valuables.[50] The list of anarchist expropriations of private property continues almost indefinitely; yet this does not mean that these extremists were satisfied merely to "steal what has been stolen," for along with confiscation of property from the rich and the middle-class, they expropriated from petty officials, priests, and virtually anyone who had any possessions. Although such victims usually bore no direct responsibility for the alleged economic exploitation of the proletariat, they were mortal enemies of the extremists by virtue of their position in society. Nor were the poor immune to the extremists' attacks, as was not, for instance, an old woman selling lemons on the streets of Odessa, who was murdered by the anarchists.[51]

An equally common method of revolutionary fund-raising was extortion. In fact, it was the anarchists and obscure extremist group members who most widely practiced blackmail by written demands, notifying individual victims that they were to contribute a specified sum of money to the revolutionary cause by a certain date, or be killed. The demands ranged from as little as 25 to as much as 25,000 rubles.[52] The extremists also employed other forms of extortion: a group calling itself the "Black Falcon Anarchists-Blackmailers" (anarkhisty-shantazhisty Chernyi Sokol) was formed in Odessa in 1906 with the primary objective of propagating, or even forging, compromising information about targeted individuals who were then informed that unless extortion money was paid, the incriminating evidence would be made public.[53] On other occasions, the radicals did not even bother with formal extortion letters, merely showing up in person at the door of a victim, waving their revolvers and yelling, "Your money or your life!" Most targets of extortion chose to capitulate to the demands of the radicals, whereas most refusals resulted in immediate reprisals, frequently in the form of a bomb tossed into the home or office of an obstinate merchant or store owner, as a punishment to him and a warning to others.[54]

Amid the general bloodletting and cruelty fomented by the extremists were occasional humorous incidents associated with the anarchists' practice of unrestrained economic violence, including robberies committed for minimal personal profits. In Kiev, on June 14, 1908, a man and a woman walked into a shoe store, pointed a pistol at the owner, and presented him with a letter of demand from local anarchists. The store owner was most relieved to discover that the total demand amounted to three pairs of boots, which he promptly provided.[55]

The majority of extremists did not limit themselves to such insignificant booty, however. Indeed, the radicals acknowledged that many of their comrades came to consider expropriation a lucrative, if risky, profession, and "turned to the practice . . . as to a trade."[56] These quasi-revolutionaries even began to make mutually profitable deals with their enemies among the bourgeoisie who were sometimes seeking revenge against competitors and therefore willing to provide the expropriators with addresses and precise financial information about potential targets for extortion.[57]

For many extremist groups, revolutionary robbery became a priority, if not their sole objective; other radical activities, such as propaganda, were largely abandoned and only occasionally conducted between "exes," if time permitted. Of all anarchists convicted by the tsarist courts, more than 60 percent were sentenced for armed assaults.[58] Some radical leaders, foremost among them Kropotkin, were very much alarmed by the epidemic of petty robberies which was demoralizing and corrupting the ranks of the revolutionary movement and which attracted "various dregs of society, thieves, and hooligans," operating under the banner of anarchism. In their eyes, the expropriators were "no better than the bandits of southern Italy,"[59] and their behavior discredited the movement in the eyes of the public, which had long since become unable to perceive the difference between common theft and expropriation. The radical leaders therefore sought to limit the avalanche of expropriations, prohibiting small-scale "exes" and threatening abusers with expulsion from extremist groups and even with death.[60]

These measures produced no results, as they were almost universally ignored, and by 1907 the large criminal component of the anarchist and obscure extremist organizations was generally referred to as "the scum of the revolution," submerged in a bacchanalia of debauchery and dissipation."[61] There of course remained "anarchist-fanatics and ascetics," people driven exclusively by their ideological principles, who dressed in rags, ate only enough to avoid starvation, forbade themselves any pleasure or entertainment bearing even a trace of luxury, and determined to preserve "the purity of the revolution."[62] By 1908, however, many extremists admitted that all the lofty ideals of their movement had drowned in a sea of banditry, and that after all the crimes perpetrated by the radicals, nothing remained of the fundamental anarchist slogan that proclaimed expropriation "a great gift from anarchy to the people."[63]

Notes

1   This article is largely based on research material found in ch. 4 of the author's *Thou Shalt Kill: Revolutionary Terrorism in Russia, 1894–1917* (Princeton: Princeton University Press, 1993).

2   Petr Kropotkin, ed., *Russkaia revoliutsiia i anarkhizm: Doklady chitannye na s'ezde Kommunistov-Anarkhistov v oktiabre 1906 goda* (London, 1907), 3; V. Kriven'kii, "Anarkhisty," *Political Parties of Russia: Encyclopedia* (Moscow: Rosspen, 1996), 32.

3   July 11, 1910 police report, Okhrana, XVIb(5)-5B.

4   I. Genkin, "Anarkhisty," *Byloe* 3(31) (1918): 163.

5   Paul Avrich, *The Russian Anarchists* (Princeton, NJ: Princeton University Press, 1967), 34. Avrich's book remains the most thorough scholarly study of anarchism in Russia. See also "Anarkhism" in *Politicheskie partii i politicheskaia politsiia* (Moscow-Minsk-Gomel', 1996), 247. To be fair, the anarchists did contemplate one "creative" project – that special schools be established to educate children as future proponents of independent protest, so that they would be "prepared from childhood to hate all obedience and prejudice" (Kropotkin, *Russkaia revoliutsiia i anarkhizm*, 3. See also "Anarkhizm," 1, Okhrana, XVIb(5)-5A).

6   Kriven'kii, "Anarkhisty," *Political Parties of Russia*, 33.

7   Avrich, *The Russian Anarchists*, 34, 69n.

8   Geifman, *Thou Shalt Kill*, 21.

9   Avrich, *The Russian Anarchists*, 34.

10   Grossman-Roshchin, "Dumy o bylom," *Byloe* 27–8 (1924): 176.

11   Avrich, *The Russian Anarchists*, 43.

12   *Al'manakh. Sbornik po istorii anarkhicheskogo dvizheniia v Rossii* (Paris, 1909), 181.

13   Genkin, "Anarkhisty," *Byloe* 2 (31) (1918): 164; unpublished and undated police brochure, "Anarkhizm i dvizhenie anarkhizma v Rossii," 87–8, Nic. 80–4.

14   *Al'manakh. Sbornik po istorii anarkhicheskogo dvizheniia v Rossii*, 46.

15   Avrich, *The Russian Anarchists*, 34.

16   See, for example, P. Kochetov, "Vologodskaia ssylka 1907–1910 godov," *Katorga i ssylka* 4(89) (1932): 87.

17   Cited in Walter Laqueur, *Terrorism* (Boston-Toronto: Little, Brown, 1977), 42.

18   A. Dobrovol'skii, ed., *Anarkhizm. Sotsializm. Rabochii i agrarnyi voprosy* (St Petersburg, 1908), 14; Kropotkin, *Russkaia revoliutsiia i anarkhizm*, 7, 9, 52.

19   Kropotkin, *Russkaia revoliutsiia i anarkhizm*, 52–4.

20   "Anarkhizm i dvizhenie anarkhizma v Rossii," 55, Nic. 80–4; "Anarkhizm," 55, 92, Okhrana XVIb(5)-5A.

21   Geifman, *Thou Shalt Kill*, 128–9, 131–2.

22   Avrich, *The Russian Anarchists*, 44, 63.

23   Ibid., 51, 63; *Al'manakh. Sbornik po istorii anarkhicheskogo dvizheniia v Rossii*, 45–6.

24   Geifman, *Thou Shalt Kill*, 136–7.

25   Kriven'kii, "Anarkhisty," *Political Parties of Russia*, 33; cited in I. Genkin, "Sredi preemnikov Bakunina," *Krasnaia letopis'* 1(22) (1927): 174.

26   K., "Ivan Timenkov," *Byloe* 14 (1912): 47–9; Beloborodov, "Iz istorii partizanskogo dvizheniia na Urale," *Krasnaia letopis'* 1(16) (1926): 99. Members of local SR organizations occasionally combined forces with defectors from their own ranks for joint ventures (G. Nestroev, *Iz dnevnika Maksimalista* (Paris, 1910), 42).

27   Reference 27, Okhrana, XVIIn-8, p. 1; see also "Anarkhizm," 49, Okhrana, XVIb(5)-5A; and April 22 1904 police report, 4, Okhrana, XIIIc(2)-4A.

28   For a description of terrorist acts and expropriations carried out under the direction of Savitskii see Iagudin, "Na Chernigovshchine," *Katorga i ssylka* 57–8 (1929): 298.

29   S. Sibiriakov, "Pamiati Petra Sheffera," *Katorga i ssylka* 22 (1926): 239.

30   Ultimately, however, as a result of continuous clashes with the nationalist forces in Tiflis, they chose to return to the control and protection of the Social Democrats ("Anarkhizm," 61, Okhrana XVIb(5)-5A).

31   Police report from Paris dated September 14, 1906, Okhrana VIj-15C.

32   "Sudebnaia khronika. Delo o predpolagavshemsia vsryve okhrannogo otdeleniia," newspaper clipping from *Tovarishch* (October 19, 1907), PSR, 8-650.

33   "Sudebnaia khronika," newspaper clipping from *Kolokol* 852 (January 3, 1909), PSR 7-602. For a description of a similar group in Sevastopol' see GAFR, f. 102, op. 1914, d. 340, p. 23.

34   Newspaper clipping from *Tovarishch* 349 (August [1 September] 19, 1907), PSR, 8-650; newspaper clipping from *Rus'* 143 (May 25, 1908), PSR 8-653.

35   Kriven'kii, "Anarkhisty," *Political Parties of Russia*, 33; GARF, f. 102, op. 1912, d. 88, p. 1, 7-7ob; and GARF, f. 102, op. 1914, d. 340, 22ob-23.

36 William J. Fishman, *East End Jewish Radicals, 1875–1914* (London, 1975), 272.

37 "Ustav partii 'Nezavisimykh'," March 1909, Okhrana, XVIa-2.

38 Ibid.

39 See, for example, P. Nikiforov, *Murav'i revoliutsii* (Moscow, 1932), 263.

40 "Vospominaniia byvsh. okhrannika," *Bessarabskoe slovo*, 1930, Nic. 203-25; M. Barsukov, "Kommunist-buntar'," 200-1, Nic. 147-10.

41 Ibid., 202-3; and *G. I. Kotovskii. Dokumenty i materialy* (Kishinev, 1956), 12, 29.

42 *G. I. Kotovskii. Dokumenty i materialy*, 12, 30, 34; "Vospominaniia byvsh. okhrannika," Nic. 203-5.

43 *G. I. Kotovskii. Dokumenty i materialy*, 50; Barsukov, "Kommunist-buntar'," 207, Nic. 747-10.

44 V. Sukhomlin, "Iz tiuremnykh skitanii," *Katorga i ssylka*, 55 (1929): 103.

45 A. D. Kirzhnits, ed., *Evreiskoe rabochee dvizhenie* (Moscow, 1928), 178n; *Al'manakh. Sbornik po istorii anarkhicheskogo dvizheniia v Rossii*, 58.

46 Genkin, "Sredi preemnikov Bakunina," *Krasnaia letopis'*, 193–4.

47 April 22, 1904 police report, 4, Okhrana XIIIc(2)-4A; Reference 27, Okhrana XVIIn-8, 1–2; "K tovarishcham anarkhistam-kommunistam," Nic. 3-3.

48 For numerous examples, see Geifman, *Thou Shalt Kill*, 149, 312 nn. 129–30.

49 Anisimov, "Sud i rasprava," *Katorga i ssylka* 10(95) (1932): 135.

50 P. P. Zavarzin, *Zhandarmy i revoliutsionery* (Paris, 1930), 179.

51 For details see Geifman, *Thou Shalt Kill*, 313 nn. 137–9.

52 See ibid., 313 nn. 144.

53 "Anarkhism" in *Politicheskie partii i politicheskaia politsiia*, 275.

54 For examples see Geifman, *Thou Shalt Kill*, 313–14 nn. 145–6, 148.

55 Newspaper clippings from *Russkoe slovo* (June 15, 1908), PSR 8-653.

56 *Al'manakh. Sbornik po istorii anarkhicheskogo dvizheniia v Rossii*, 104.

57 Ibid.

58 Ibid., 97, 149.

59 Avrich, *The Russian Anarchists*, 50–60; "K tovarishcham anarkhistam-kommunistam" (St Petersburg, September 1906), Nic. 35 3-3.

60 See Geifman, *Thou Shalt Kill*, 314 nn. 155–6.

61 "Anarkhizm," 64, Okhrana XVIb(5)-5A; see a newspaper clipping "Delo anarkhistov-ekspropriatorov," in *Tovarishch* 379 (September 23, 1907), PSR 8-650.

62 Zavarzin, *Zhandarmy i revoliutsionery*, 188.

63 *Al'manakh. Sbornik po istorii anarkhicheskogo dvizheniia v Rossii*, 152; "Anarkhizm," 90, Okhrana XVIb(5)-5A.

CHAPTER SIX

National Minorities in the Russian Empire, 1897–1917

Theodore R. Weeks

The fact that the Russian Empire was a multinational state is crucial for an understanding of the nature and history of that state, at least from the sixteenth to the twentieth century. Indeed, we can hardly relegate this empire and its difficulties with the "national question" to history – the present-day Russian Federation continues to struggle with many of the same issues that baffled tsarist administrators. Unfortunately, the role of national minorities in influencing the course of Russian history has generally been neglected or downplayed. This phenomenon is not so much the result of a conspiracy against the non-Russians but reflects rather the focus of Russian and Western historiography on "big questions" from the perspective of Moscow and St Petersburg. Still, considering that just under half of the population of the former Russian Empire was Russian by ethnicity, it is imperative to include the other half of the population in the study of the pre-revolutionary Russian state.[1]

The present essay does not seek to cover the ethnic diversity of the Russian Empire or state policies toward various ethnic groups, nor does it describe the development of "nationalism" among them during the final two decades of the empire's existence, a period full of great change and revolutionary events. It will start with a quick sketch of the relevant terms and concepts involved, *inter alia*: "national minorities," "Russian," "Russification," "politics" (insofar as that term involved non-Russian groups). This "conceptual" section is followed by a specific discussion of the various nationalities, based mainly on the 1897 census. The next and longest part of this essay consists of "thumbnail sketches" of four dissimilar national groups: Finns, Poles, Armenians, and Tatars. The essay ends with a short discussion of the impact of World War I on the non-Russians, in particular as regards the 1916 Central Asian uprising.[2]

Who were the "non-Russians"? First of all we must recognize the cognitive weaknesses inherent in a category that includes both the highly educated, progressive Finns (who gave the vote to women in 1906, decades before many Western states) and peoples such as the Chukcha and Mari who lacked even a written language before 1917. The least Europeanized and, from the Russian standpoint, least cultured ethnic groups were lumped together in the legal category of *inorodtsy*. This group included small Siberian tribes, semi-nomads such as the Kazakhs, Caucasian mountaineers (such as the Chechens), natives of Turkestan, and Jews. Generally speaking (and Jews, as is so often the case, formed an exception), *inorodtsy* were left alone by the Russian government, did not perform military service, continued to follow their own legal systems and traditions, and were barely touched by the Russian educational and administrative system.

Many "non-Russian" ethnicities had far more in common with the Russians than with each other. They did not present a united front against the Russian administration, as one may see in the conflicts between Armenians and Azerbaijani Turks, Germans and Estonians or Latvians, Poles and Lithuanians, and Jews and Poles. The complexity and importance of these "triangular relationships" (two feuding nationalities and the Russian state) has generally not been adequately taken into account by historians of the Russian Empire.[3]

Lenin spoke of the Russian Empire as a "prisonhouse of nations." Indeed, the lot of non-Russians under the tsar was often unenviable. Many ethnicities, most obviously Poles, Jews, and non-Christians in general, were subject to a variety of legal restrictions and police harassment. And yet we must not forget that most Russians, and in particular Russian peasants, did not enjoy unimpeded civil rights. Certain nationalities, such as the Baltic Germans, enjoyed a quite privileged position within the administrative and military bureaucracies of the Russian Empire. The Russian Empire did not pursue a single, well-defined policy toward "the nationalities" or even against one specific nationality such as the Poles, Armenians, or Jews. Rather, periods of repression and "activism" were often followed by years of bureaucratic inertia and corruption. The single most important aim of the tsarist government and bureaucracy was to keep the empire together and to prevent separatist dangers. Thus the "uncovering" of seditious national circles might often be followed by quite energetic repressions, after which the administration would fall back into its normal lethargy. The

Russian Empire was not a model of bureaucratic efficiency and activism, and the very idea of "total Russification" of all the tsar's subjects was rather alien to the empire's ethos (even if not to the mindset of some of the tsar's servants).

One indication that the Russian Empire, even in the early twentieth century, remained essentially a pre-national state is the lack of any concrete legal definition of the term "Russian." In the Russian Empire (unlike the USSR), there was no legal definition of "Russian" or, for that matter, of any other ethnicity. The Romanov dynasty derived its authority and legitimacy not from the Russian nation but from God and history. And most subjects of Nicholas II probably defined themselves not in "national" terms but as "local" people, in their roles as peasants or townsmen, nomads or sedentary agriculturalists, and – perhaps most importantly – by religion.

The issue of identity and national self-consciousness is further complicated by the existence in the Russian language of two terms that both translate into English as "Russian," but that carry far different emotional and semantic values. The first, and most common, is *russkii*. That adjective is used to describe the language, culture, and even religious faith (i.e., Eastern Orthodoxy) shared by Russians. The other is *rossiiskii*, referring to the entire Russian land (*Rossiia*) and its inhabitants, whether or not ethnically Russian (*russkie*). While *russkii* belongs to a warmer, more intimate sphere, *rossiiskii* tends to be associated with impersonal, bureaucratic institutions. Both the Russian Empire and the present-day Russian Federation are *rossiiskaia*, not *russkaia*. It would, in principle, be possible to speak of a "rossiiskii" German or Tatar (that is, a citizen of the Russian Empire or Federation belonging to the German or Tatar ethnicity), a "russkii" German would seem a contradiction in terms. The key problem of the Russian (*rossiiskaia*) Empire was that it often acted as if it were simply *russkii*.

So what was, then, a Russian (*russkii*)? First of all, we must remember that neither the Russian government, nor most Russians, considered Belorussians and Ukrainians to be nations separate from the Russians. Rather than enunciating differences in culture and language, the Russian government (and, to a lesser extent, society) emphasized similarities and shared history and religion. For the Russian Empire, religion did have a legal reality, because each subject of the tsar had to belong to one religious group or another ("none of the above" was not a possibility). And it was generally accepted that a "real" Russian was of the Orthodox faith. The tsar and his wife had to be Orthodox (foreign princesses were obliged to convert if they wished to marry into the Romanov family), and the Orthodox church enjoyed a special, privileged status within the state. To be sure, by 1900 this rather clear identity of Orthodoxy and "Russian-ness" came increasingly under attack from various sides. Liberal Russians wished to broaden the definition to include "Russian Jews" (but, interestingly, the term "Jewish Russian" (*evreiskii russkii*) sounds very strange to Russian ears) while administrators wished to include Catholic Belorussians and ex-Uniate Ukrainians within the Russian fold. Still, there was an almost overwhelming tendency for the administration to equate "Orthodox" with "Russian."

Even harder to pin down than "Russian" is the term "Russification." If we take it to mean the total assimilation of non-Russians into the Russian nation, then the Russian Empire never pursued such a policy because of the enormous resources it would have required. After all, in 1897 most *Russians* were still illiterate and universal elementary education, while it made important strides before 1914, had still not been introduced in the provinces before the end of the empire. If, however, we define "Russification" in a more modest way, describing the centralizing desire of St Petersburg, it must be conceded that the Russian Empire pursued a policy of Russification in the second half of the nineteenth century and most especially from the 1880s.[4] While the tsar and his bureaucracy were quite unconcerned about the languages spoken at home by the diverse inhabitants of the empire, they did wish that in the long run all of these peoples would acquire a working knowledge of the "governing language," that is, Russian. A career in government service, either civilian or military, demanded an acceptance of Russian language and culture, though there exist many anecdotes from the time about the mangled Russian spoken by Polish aristocrats in the State Council and by Baltic Germans in the Ministries of the Interior and of Foreign Affairs.

Two terms were often used by imperial bureaucrats when they addressed the issue of drawing together the tsar's diverse subjects. One of these was *sblizhenie*, that is, a "drawing closer together" of the non-Russians with the Russian nation. This term could mean a simple adopting of Russian or "European" customs in the areas of personal hygiene, dress, and housing. For Jews, *sblizhenie* would often mean learning the Russian language and casting off traditional Jewish garb and even dietary habits. For Poles, *sblizhenie* could mean abandoning any ingrained hostility toward Russians and dreams of an independent Poland and learning Russian as a language of official use. An even more sweeping kind of "unification" of Russians and non-Russians was described by the term *sliianie* – literally, "merging." This term can be seen as describing a complete coalescence of non-Russian peoples with Russian culture and the nation. However, it must be noted that these terms are used by tsarist administrators at different times in a very imprecise manner and do not necessarily represent specific "policy trends" within the bureaucracy.

Although total Russification was never official policy, the general superiority of Russian culture and the Orthodox church was insisted upon, particularly vis-à-vis non-Christian and Asian peoples. In Central Asia, Russian culture was sometimes touted as a superior civilization that could help lift the local Muslims out of their "medieval stupor." The Russian Empire did establish schools aimed at the native population in Siberia, the Caucasus and Central Asia, but their numbers were too small and methods too unattractive to produce any significant number of bilingual "native intelligentsia" who could serve as a loyal bridge between the Moslem masses and the Russian government. On the whole, the Russians took their role as a "civilizing" force far less seriously than did British, French, or even American colonizers.[5]

Russification was less a cultural weapon than an administrative and political imperative. From its early days, the Russian Empire embraced the form of a centralized state, epitomized by the figure of the tsar, ruling autocratically over all subjects, whatever their ethnicity and religion. Except in times of political weakness and out of practical considerations, the empire never seriously considered any diffusion of this central power at the local level, either in the central Russian provinces or on the periphery. Particularly in the nineteenth and twentieth centuries, when increasing centralization was the order of the day in most developed states (the American Civil War was fought, at least to some extent, over this very issue), Russia's tendency toward centralization and against local privilege was further enhanced and strengthened. Of course, eliminating local privilege very often meant treading on the national toes of non-Russians. Doing away with special institutions and privileges for the Baltic Germans in the 1880s can either be seen as a process of "rationalization" and elimination of local privileges (from the point of view of St Petersburg) or as an attack on national rights (from the Baltic German's perspective). Here the position of Finland, to be considered below in some detail, is particularly important. The tsar and his advisors feared that an autonomous Finland, in many regards beyond the control of St Petersburg, could serve as a launching ground for foreign attacks on the Russian interior. Thus they attempted to justify the highly controversial and from the Finnish point of view quite illegal whittling down of Finnish autonomy in the 1890s and first decade of the twentieth century. For the Russian government, the ideal goal was a centralized state, in which important decisions were reached at the center and then carried out by an efficient bureaucracy throughout the vast reaches of the state. To be sure, this goal was never realized, particularly in respect of efficiency and clear transmission of orders from center to periphery.

Russification could also be used as punishment. The most obvious example of this kind of policy is to be found in the Kingdom of Poland, or the "Vistula country," that is, the provinces of (mainly) ethnic Poland that had been annexed by the Russian Empire at the Congress of Vienna. After the abortive insurrection of 1863 these provinces were administered by

Russian bureaucrats, education (particularly at secondary and higher level, but even in some elementary schools) became Russified, and even shop signs had to be written in both Russian and Polish (furthermore, the Russian inscription could not be smaller or set below the Polish!). St Petersburg justified these harsh measures as a punishment for Polish disloyalty in the two uprisings against Russian authority. After all, Russian Poland constituted an area surrounded on three sides by Prussia and Austria and it was correctly seen as the probable site for a future military clash with these powers. On the other hand, during these years (that is, from the 1860s to 1914) Polish journalism and publishing flourished in Warsaw and other provincial towns, despite the restrictive Russian regime.

The foremost authority on the subject, Edward C. Thaden, speaks of three types of Russification: unplanned, administrative, and cultural.[6] Unplanned Russification refers to intermarriage between Russians and other nationalities that had been taking place at least since the sixteenth century. Administrative Russification is the effort to eliminate local privileges and extend the powers and laws of the center to the periphery. Cultural Russification, finally, entails the teaching of the Russian language and the spread of Russian culture to the national minorities. These three categories are certainly valid, but we must recognize that they overlap and often merge in a practical sense. For example, when after 1863 all Polish administration was obliged to use the Russian language, even in internal documents, this process also entailed a good degree of "cultural" Russification (furthermore, most Poles were forced out of these administrative positions altogether). Suffice it at this point to say that around the turn of the century Russification was taking place on various levels and quite often without specific administrative guidance or interference.

Before we look a bit more closely at the "nationalities" themselves, we must consider the issue of "politics" in the Russian Empire. One may certainly argue that democratic politics did not yet exist in Russia, at least not before 1905. Political parties (even those extolling the virtues of autocracy) were forbidden, neither local nor all-empire parliaments existed, and the press was rather tightly circumscribed by censorship.[7] After 1905 this situation eased somewhat with the creation of the State Duma and a significant easing of censorship, but "democratic politics" in the Russian Empire never passed out of the fledgling stage, even for the most advanced (that is, most literate and urbanized) nationalities such as Finns, Jews, Poles, Armenians, and even Russians. To be sure, some nationalities were under more onerous restrictions than others. Ukrainians, for example, were forbidden to publish either books or periodicals in their native tongue (with the exception of certain ethnographic or folkloric studies) until after 1905. Similarly, Lithuanians could only publish using Cyrillic letters until

1904, which amounted in practice to a ban on printed Lithuanian. Yiddish publishing was also severely restricted, and Yiddish-language dailies (which flourished in the years before World War I) began to appear in the Russian Empire only a year or two before 1905. Since modern politics are unthinkable without literacy, publishing, journals, and newspapers, it is clear that mainly illiterate nationalities, such as Kazakhs and Turkmen, could hardly be expected to participate vigorously in politics except in the most limited, local sense.[8]

Before 1905, "politics" was almost exclusively the preserve of those nationalities that possessed a widely used written language, a literate public, and most often an indigenous noble class. If we look around the empire, we find several nationalities possessing these attributes before 1905: Finns, Baltic Germans, Poles, Georgians, and with certain reservations Volga Tatars, Jews, and Armenians. With the exception of the Jews and to some extent the Volga Tatars, all of these national groups participated in relatively large numbers in administration both in the capital and at home (here the Poles were an exception: they were forbidden after 1863 from holding government positions in the "Vistula provinces" (i.e., the Kingdom of Poland) and Western provinces, but they did figure among government employees in the Russian interior). At the end of the nineteenth century, increasing literacy and prosperity among Lithuanians, Estonians, Latvians, and to some extent Ukrainians meant that these nationalities began to organize themselves to demand such rights as native-language schools. Such demands were usually aimed not against the Russians but against the local "hegemonic nationality," e.g., Germans and Poles. Similar struggles between different nationalities may be observed in the Transcaucasian region where Azerbaijani Turks and Georgians (in different places and ways) came to challenge the financial and social dominance (particularly in the cities) of Armenian merchants and traders. Thus even before 1905 several non-Russian nationalities were on the verge of entering into the political arena and demanding rights not only as citizens, but as members of specific national and cultural groups.

After 1905, this trend continued at an even more rapid rate. Moslems, Poles, Armenians, Jews, Lithuanians, Baltic Germans, Georgians, and members of other nationalities were elected to the State Duma and State Council and, more importantly, formed their own political and cultural groupings, based on ethnicity, shared culture, and perceived common interests. Daily newspapers and political journals appeared in a number of languages ranging from Tatar to Estonian. Political parties representing specific national groups were founded or came out "from underground." Possibly, and most importantly, even *Russians* (especially those of a liberal persuasion, and in particular the Kadets) began to discuss seriously the issue of nationality. The post-1905 Russian-language press is full of articles proposing "solutions" to the burning "national question." Various plans were mooted to divide up the empire into administrative units dominated by one main national group, while guaranteeing the rights of the other nationalities in the area. The experience of Austria-Hungary in bridging the gap between "nations" and "state" was often cited by these Russian liberals as an example of how diverse nationalities could live together under one state organism.[9] Although these appeals may seem naive and even touching, it is clear that in Austria-Hungary (particularly in Austria) national groups *did* participate, and very vigorously, in "politics" – and the national groups in the Russian Empire could learn much from examining the situation in Vienna and Budapest.[10]

A closer and more concrete statistical description of the nationalities may help put some meat on the theoretical bones offered above. The data below is derived from the census of 1897, the first and only modern census of the entire Russian Empire.[11] This census counted 30 national groups (*narodnosti*) having a population of over 200,000, and 16 over 1 million (see Table 1). Almost certainly the statistics were skewed in favor of the

Table 1 Nationalities in the Russian Empire (1897)

Nationality	Population	Percentage total pop.
Great Russians	55,673,000	43.30
Ukrainians	22,415,000	17.41
Poles	7,931,000	6.17
Belorussians	5,886,000	4.57
Jews	5,063,000	3.94
Kazakhs (*Kirgizy*)	4,084,000	3.18
Tatars	3,738,000	2.91
Germans	1,790,000	1.40
Lithuanians	1,658,000	1.29
Bashkirs (incl. *Teptiary*)	1,439,000	1.12
Latvians	1,436,000	1.12
Geogians	1,352,000	1.05
Armenians	1,173,000	0.91
Moldavians	1,122,000	0.87
Mordva	1,024,000	0.79
Estonians	1,003,000	0.78

Russian population. Furthermore, the Russian Empire sometimes divided ethnic groups differently than they would be subsequently in the Soviet Union. To take an obvious example, they distinguished between "Uzbeks" and "Sarts" whereas in present-day parlance both groups would be included under "Uzbek"). Some 4 million Finns were left out of the census entirely.

The four largest nationalities resident in the Russian Empire were all Slavic and Christian nations – Russians, Ukrainians (called "Little Russians" at the time), Poles, and Belorussians. As already mentioned, Russian officialdom (and, indeed, a significant part of Russian society as a whole) considered Ukrainians and Belorussians mere branches of the Russian nation. After all, the Belorussian, Ukrainian, and Russian languages are in many respects similar, and the great majority of all three groups professed the Eastern Orthodox religion. Using this measure, the Russian government could speak of an empire that was mainly Russian – counting some 66 percent of the total population.

The non-Russian nationalities lived mainly on the peripheries of the empire. On the western frontier, there was the autonomous Grand Duchy of Finland to the north, a small mainly Russian area (containing the capital St Petersburg), and the Baltic provinces where the countryside (and, increasingly, the towns) was populated by Estonians and Latvians. Further south, the so-called Western provinces were the home of Lithuanians, Belorussians, and Ukrainians, with a generous number of Polish, Jewish, Russian, and German residents. The ten provinces of the Kingdom of Poland (officially the "Vistula provinces") were dominated by Poles, with significant numbers of Jews and Lithuanians. While the population of Siberia was already by this time (1897) mainly Russian, dozens of smaller and larger ethnicities made their homes in that vast region.[12] Central Asia had only recently (mainly in the 1860s) been added to the Russian Empire, and the native populations – in modern terms – were the Kazakh, Kyrgyz, Turkmen, Uzbek, and Tajik. Increasing Russian (and Ukrainian) settlement in the region was to exacerbate tensions between locals and newly arrived colonists. Finally, the Caucasus and Transcaucasian regions are among the most ethnically diverse in the world, with the numerically largest groups there being Azerbaijani Turks, Armenians, and Georgians.[13]

We must always keep in mind that ethnic groups usually did not live in discrete regions, easily divided off from other, distinct ethnicities. More common is the pattern that one ethnicity would dominate urban areas, and another the countryside. For example, in the Polish provinces, towns and cities often had a higher Jewish than Polish population. Even the two largest cities in the area, Warsaw and Lodz, had very large Jewish populations, numbering over one-third of the total inhabitants. Similarly in the Western provinces, Lithuanian countryside surrounded largely Polish and Jewish towns (such as Vilna), and to the south Ukrainians usually made up the majority of the peasant population while towns and cities had more Jews, Poles, and Russians.[14] This "mixture" of ethnicities would have made any drawing of boundaries along ethnic lines extremely difficult – as would be discovered after World War I.

Furthermore, certain nationalities often dominated a social class or certain economic activities in a given region. The image of the Jew as merchant, trader, and peddler is very well known and did correspond to the social and economic realities of the time. Looking at the Western provinces, we see a very strong link between ethnicity and social and professional standing. The peasant masses were (depending on the locality) Lithuanian, Belorussian, and Ukrainian. Traders, petty merchants, and artisans were more often than not Jews. Landlords, despite the post-1863 restrictions, were very often Poles or sometimes Russians (often absentee) after 1905. The professions (lawyers, doctors, veterinarians, agronomists, engineers) were dominated by Poles, with an increasing number of Russians and Russified Jews by the early twentieth century. This pattern was again common in different areas of the empire: ethnicity had a tendency to carry with it a social component. Some nationalities counted a very high percentage of nobles in their ranks: in particular Poles (4.41 percent), Georgians (5.29 percent), and Tatars (1.60 percent). (For comparison, the figure among Russians was 0.87 percent.)[15] Other nationalities, such as Ukrainians, Lithuanians, or Jews, lacked a noble estate almost entirely.

Some nationalities were more likely to reside on the countryside, others in towns. The most urbanized nationality were the Jews – nearly half of them lived in "cities" as defined by the 1897 census. Other highly urbanized nationalities were Tajiks, Germans, Armenians, Poles, and Uzbeks, all of whom were more likely to live in towns and cities than Russians were. Lithuanians, Ukrainians, Belorussians, Kalmyks, and Kazakhs were seldom town dwellers.[16] In nearly all cases, the majority of a given ethnic group lived off agriculture (either sedentary or, in the case of many Kazakhs, Kyrgyz, and others, as nomadic herders) – here the Jews were the sole exception. Highly urbanized nationalities, however, also tended to be more engaged in industry, services, and the free professions. It is interesting to note that the Poles, in most respects highly restricted in their rights, were actually more likely than Russians to hold administrative jobs (to be sure, these could be in private – as opposed to government – offices, and the percentages are close: 1.2 percent vs. 1.1 percent of the total population) and were nearly as likely to be serving in the military (1.2 percent vs. 1.4 percent).

Literacy rates differed widely among nationalities. Among the most literate were Finns, Estonians, and Latvians, among whom almost universal literacy was achieved before World War I. Germans were also highly literate (nearly 80 percent in 1897), as were Jews and Lithuanians (both around 50 percent). Interestingly, Poles in 1897 could boast of only a 41.8 percent literacy rate, the legacy, no doubt, of anti-Polish measures in education since the 1860s. All of these ethnic groups were more literate than the Russians (29.3 percent literate in 1897). One problem with these statistics is the difficulty in ascertaining whether literacy was determined to mean ability to read Russian or ability to read in any script or language (for example, in Yiddish). It seems clear that more than half of the Jewish population could read Hebrew letters, as this would be necessary for religious reasons, and a well-developed network of Jewish schools (heders, yeshivas, etc.) existed for this purpose. On the whole, literacy diminished as one moved from west to east and always tended to be higher in cities than in the countryside.

Thus at the turn of the century, several "minority nationalities" were more literate, more urbanized, and perhaps even more prosperous as a whole, than the Russians. Obviously within each group there existed large social and economic differences. Furthermore, rates of urbanization and literacy would increase among all groups in the next 20 years, though often at different rates for different ethnicities. In any case, we should not see these "minorities" (the term itself is misleading and inherently Russocentric) as only downtrodden, the mere objects of repression meted out by the Russian government. Rather, as individuals and increasingly as collectives, these ethnicities pursued their own interests in the cultural and economic sphere within the limits placed on any kind of politics and group petitioning within the Russian Empire. Particularly after 1905, with the increased possibilities for publishing (particularly of periodicals, especially dailies) and public discussion of the national issue, non-Russians began to demand more and more vocally, national rights in the fields of education, administration, even politics. As is well known, the Russian government was unable even to neutralize *Russian* discontent, much less that of the non-Russians.

The following section will sketch out the political development of four dissimilar non-Russian ethnicities: Finns, Poles, Armenians, and "Tatars" (mainly Volga Tatars). These four groups cover the western, southern, and eastern borderlands and were undergoing very different cultural, economic, and political development.[17]

The Finns were in a class of their own within the Russian Empire. Since incorporation into the Russian Empire in 1808, the Grand Duchy of Finland had enjoyed a great deal of autonomy, having its own currency, postal service, army, legislature, and civil service. Indeed, many Finnish jurists contended that the Grand Duchy was not "within" but merely "affiliated with" the rest of the empire. While Russian legal scholars tended to dispute this argument, on the practical level Finland was able to run its own affairs to a degree unthinkable in the rest of the empire. Moreover, Russians were restricted in their rights while residing, working, or doing business in the Grand Duchy. Another indication that St Petersburg recognized on a practical level that Finland was "different" is the failure to carry out the 1897 census in the Finnish provinces (of course, the Finnish administration was on the whole far better at gathering statistical data than the rest of the empire). By the late nineteenth century, both Russian nationalists and many administrators in St Petersburg found such a situation intolerable and moved to limit Finnish autonomy in the administrative, military, and political spheres.[18]

The genuine push toward a greater level of unification of Finland with Russia is usually associated with the name of Finland's Russian governor-general of the period, N. I. Bobrikov. From his arrival in Helsinki in 1898, Bobrikov did all he could (sometimes intentionally, sometimes not) to anger Finns and offend their sensibilities. He made it clear that he considered himself, as the tsar's viceroy, the highest power in the land. An imperial manifesto of 3/15 February 1899 set down new guidelines on applying imperial laws to the Grand Duchy. Many Finns feared that this manifesto would give greater power to St Petersburg in replacing Finnish laws with imperial measures. Furthermore, the manifesto was published without proper consultation with the Finnish authorities and Diet, which was widely seen as a violation of Finnish autonomy. While the danger to Finnish autonomy presented by the February Manifesto was only vaguely plausible, Finnish public opinion rallied against the measure, sending to the tsar a "Great Address" signed by over half a million Finns (or more than 10 percent of the entire population of the Grand Duchy). Nicholas II refused to receive the 500-man Finnish delegation that came to St Petersburg to present this address to the monarch.

Worse was to come. Bobrikov referred to the Russian language as the "spiritual banner of Empire" and demanded that all subjects be able to use Russian in the official, governmental sphere. A language manifesto of 1900 set down that henceforth correspondence between the Finnish Senate and the governor-general was to be written in Russian. Bobrikov wanted an even more sweeping measure introduced that would have required *all* official business in the Finnish administration to be carried out in Russian, but the utter impracticability of such a radical measure obliged him to retreat. As it was, the reactions from Finnish society to the language manifesto were extremely negative. Bobrikov also pushed for more teaching of Russian in Finland's schools, though with mixed results.

The measure most offensive to Finns and to Finnish autonomy that Bobrikov pushed through was a new conscription law. Russian officials had long claimed that the Grand Duchy did not shoulder its fair share of the empire's military burden, either in taxes or in manpower. Bobrikov aimed to change this by abolishing Finland's army and extending imperial conscription laws to the Finnish provinces. Some high officials in St Petersburg, including S. Witte, opposed such a measure, fearing that the discontent it would stir up among the Finns would far outweigh any possible military gains. This opposition was overruled, however, by the strong support for military reform in Finland of the minister of internal affairs, D. S. Sipiagin, and the measure passed into law in 1901. Finnish battalions were abolished, and henceforth Finnish youths could be conscripted (though few actually were) to serve in the imperial army. Finnish society severely condemned this newest violation of the Grand Duchy's autonomy.

The level of outrage felt at the 1900 language manifesto, the 1901 conscription law, and Bobrikov's arrogant and offensive treatment (or ignoring) of Finnish institutions made him a hated man in Helsinki and throughout Finland. When the Russo-Japanese War broke out in early 1904, Finns even expressed satisfaction at Japanese victories. One Finn decided to express his anger with Bobrikov's policies in an even more direct manner, and on June 16, 1904 Eugene Schauman, the son of a prominent Finnish public figure and senator, assassinated the governor-general, committing suicide shortly thereafter. A note in Schauman's pocket, addressed to the tsar, soberly explained that Schauman had acted alone, not as a rebel but in order "to convince Your Majesty that great injustice prevails in the Grand Duchy of Finland." Bobrikov's death ended the period of most intensive encroachment on Finnish autonomy, and the revolutionary disturbances of 1905–7 fully occupied St Petersburg for the next few years.

These were important years in Finland. In 1906 Nicholas II acquiesced to a highly democratic reform of the Finnish Diet, giving the vote to all citizens (including women) over the age of 24. Once the revolutionary fever had cooled, however, St Petersburg returned once again to efforts to reduce Finnish autonomy. These efforts culminated in a law passed by the Duma in 1910 that severely restricted the competence of the Finnish Diet, in effect ending Finnish autonomy (while inviting the Finns to send delegates to the State Duma). The main practical result of these measures was to instill an almost unanimous hatred of St Petersburg and all things Russian into the Finnish public, a revulsion that made the declaration of independence in late 1917 all the easier. But looking once again at the practical sphere, we should recall that Finnish autonomy was strong enough in mid-1917 to allow Lenin to seek refuge there after the failed "July days." Hence Russian efforts at repressing Finnish "difference" during the period

1897–1917 had the main effect of strengthening separatist sentiments among the Finns.

Unlike the Finns, by the later nineteenth century the Poles not only enjoyed no official autonomy, but their language and culture were almost universally seen as hostile by official Russia. Reading official documents and reports from the years 1894–1914, one is struck by the constant, unquestioned assumption that Poles were "the enemy" on the western frontier. To be sure, Poles and Russians throughout history have seldom been on the same side, and Poles have not infrequently portrayed themselves as the bulwark of "Europe" (often with the support of the Catholic Church) against semi-barbarian "schismatics" to the east. More concretely, the Poles in the Russian Empire represented a rather unusual case of a historically important nation, with a well-developed and respected (even by Russians!) high culture dating back at least to the Renaissance, but lacking any kind of political or institutional autonomy. Furthermore, Poles were the largest non-Russian nationality after Ukrainians (whom, as we have seen, St Petersburg considered Russians anyway), a nationality with a very large noble class owning significant amounts of land both in the Kingdom of Poland and in the Western provinces (present-day Belarus, Lithuania, and western Ukraine). Despite the high rate of illiteracy among Polish peasants, Poles were on the whole more literate than Russians, and the thriving city of Warsaw – the largest in the empire after the two capitals – possessed a very sophisticated educated class even before 1905. After all, a Pole (Henryk Sienkiewicz) won the Nobel prize for literature in 1905 – decades before any Russian.[19]

After the failed uprising of 1863, Poles were always regarded with a great deal of suspicion by tsarist administrators and Russian Poland's administrative and educational systems were dominated by Russians. Catholics were specifically excluded from most government jobs in the Polish and Western provinces. While the use of Polish in education (especially at the primary level) was not entirely forbidden, Polish history and literature were neglected or totally ignored. The entire system was crowned by the University of Warsaw, an overtly Russifying and generally despised institution. The Polish and Western provinces also lacked even the modest organs of local self-governments in the towns and countryside (City Dumas and zemstvos) that had existed since the 1860s in the interior Russian provinces.

Poles did have certain advantages over other nationalities. As we have seen, their rate of literacy exceeded that of Russians, and while up to 1905 the Polish press operated under censorship even more onerous than that imposed on Russian publications, several sophisticated and highly informative press organs did exist: *Gazeta Warszawska* (Warsaw Gazette), *Kraj*

(Country) (published in St Petersburg), *Przegląd Tygodniowy* (Weekly Review), *Prawda* (Truth), and others. Of course, Polish newspapers and journals published abroad also made their way into the country, often illegally. This variety of press organs reflected a quite well-developed political culture among Russia's Poles.

To simplify somewhat, Polish political opinion at the turn of the century was divided into four broad currents, from right to left: loyalist-conservative, nationalist-conservative, liberal-progressive, and socialist. The "loyalist-conservatives" are usually known in Polish history as *ugodowcy*, or conciliators (i.e., they stressed the necessity of Poles to reconcile themselves to Russian rule), and from 1905 would organize themselves as the "realist" party – though without any electoral success. Generally speaking, this group represented the interests of the conservative Polish landed magnates and plutocracy. Unlike the nationalist-conservatives, this first group would seldom make a political issue out of anti-Semitism. The "nationalist-conservatives," who after 1905 would dominate the Polish representation in the State Duma (as the National Democratic or ND party) were already well organized at the turn of the century. The "Bibles" of the movement, Roman Dmowski's *Thoughts of a Modern Pole* and Zygmunt Balicki's *National Egoism and Ethics* both initially appeared in Austrian-ruled Lvov in the first years of the twentieth century. Dmowski and his National Democratic party were certainly more democratic than the elitist *ugodowcy*, but they also (perhaps inevitably) pursued a far more pernicious policy of overt and consistent anti-Semitism, claiming that Poles must strengthen their own middle class, necessarily at the cost of the Jews in Poland. The refusal of the National Democrats to see Polish Jews as at least potential Poles would bear bitter fruit in the post-1905 years.

The "liberal-progressive" group would coalesce into the various Polish progressive parties from 1905. These are, broadly speaking, the heirs of the philosophy of "Warsaw positivism," best exemplified by the editor of *Prawda*, Aleksander Świętochowski. The progressives exemplified the best hopes for an enlightened, secular, modern Poland, free of class or national conflicts. They were equally antagonistic to the anti-Semites and to the socialists, seeing in each a different kind of threat to the unity of the Polish nation. As is so often the case with middle-class liberals, in Poland after 1905 the progressives were crushed, politically speaking, between the strong nationalists (the NDs) and the activist socialists. Finally, the Polish "socialists" were perhaps the best organized and most popular working-class parties in the Russian Empire. Polish socialism was divided between the more nationalist PPS (Polish Socialist Party) and the more internationalist SDKPiL (Social Democracy of the Kingdom of Poland and Lithuania), whose cumbersome name reflects a desire to avoid identification with any one ethnic group. Naturally, both of these parties were illegal, and both played a very important role in the events of 1905.[20] The Jewish Bund was also very active in the Polish provinces, where around 14 percent of the total population was Jewish.

Hence the Polish nationality in the Russian Empire presents a unique, diverse, and even contradictory picture. Most Poles were peasants, and many of these were illiterate. At the other end of the social order there were immensely rich magnates such as the Radziwiłł, Zamoyski, and Potocki families. In the middle we find a well-educated (often with doctorates from German universities) professional class and a lively press which became all the more interesting, even rambunctious, after 1905. Several Poles served in the imperial State Council in St Petersburg both before and after 1905. Polish officers were also no rarity in the Russian army. At the same time, Poles could not receive higher education in their native tongue, faced restrictions on land purchases in the Western provinces (and various other disabilities), and were governed in a highly bureaucratic manner by imported Russian administrators. These contradictions were only to be "solved" after the massive blood-letting of World War I.

Moving from the western borderlands to the distant south, beyond the Caucasus Mountains, along the Russo-Turkish frontier, we find the Armenians. Armenians lived on both sides of the border, numbering just over 1 million in the Russian Empire. Armenians are Christians and were among the first ethnic groups to embrace Christianity. Armenia's neighbors to the east and south are Moslems, and herein lies the greatest difficulty, and tragedy, of Armenian history. While Turkish–Armenian relations lie outside the limits of this essay, the relations between Armenians and Azerbaijani Turks (in the Russian Empire simply called, like most settled Moslems, "Tatars") can hardly be understood without some examination of each group's relations with the Russian imperial administration. As Christians, Armenians generally felt more comfortable (and safe) in the Russian Empire than under Ottoman rule. Many Armenians served in the Russian army and bureaucracy, most notably the minister of internal affairs under Alexander II, Count Michael Loris-Melikov. By the early twentieth century, however, many young Armenians – like young Russians, Poles, Jews, and others – wanted more. The well-organized national and social movements among the Armenians showed that they, too, were ready to play a far greater political role in the Russian Empire than present institutions allowed.[21]

Sociologically speaking, the Armenians in the Russian Empire may be divided into two main groups: urban middle-class and rural peasants. Armenian peasants made up some three-quarters of the total nationality in the 1897 census, with 15 percent registered as townspeople (*meshchane*

– a rather flexible and non-specific legal category). It is important to remember that these figures refer to legal *estates*, not classes. It would be quite possible to find an Armenian "peasant" actually living in a town and engaging in trade. Still, these figures give us a general idea of their socio-logical make-up. In comparison, the percentage of Armenians in the townspeople category exceeded that of any other national group in the empire except, predictably, Jews, Germans, and – just barely – Poles. Most Armenian peasants lived in Erevan province, where Armenians made up some 55 percent of the total population. Armenian peasants also lived in small communities throughout Transcaucasia, making for them the idea of national territorial autonomy a very problematic one.

Armenians also made up the largest single nationality in the largest cities of Transcaucasia, not only in Erevan (the present capital of the Republic of Armenia) but in Tiflis (now Tbilisi, capital of Georgia), and Baku (now capital of Azerbaijan). Nearly a quarter of all Armenians lived in towns and cities, a level of urbanization exceeded in the empire only by Jews, Tajiks, and Germans. Many of these Armenian town-dwellers were quite prosperous, holding a position in the region somewhat akin to that of the Jews in Poland. And, it must be said, attitudes of the local Moslem peasantry and, to a lesser extent, Georgians often paralleled the antago-nisms expressed by Poles about Jewish merchants and traders. Azerbaijani and Georgian nationalists, like their Polish counterparts, often bewailed the weakness of their native middle classes and accused the Armenians of usurping the rightful place of the Azerbaijani or Georgian bourgeoisie.

Before the mid-1860s, Armenians did not present any kind of political danger to the Russian authorities. Only from the 1880s were efforts made to "integrate" (read: Russify) Armenian schools into the Russian system. These attempts led to a confrontation with the Armenian church (here, as in many other areas, including Poland before 1863 and Central Asia for the Moslems, religion and education went hand in hand). Rather like its bungling restrictions on the Lithuanians two decades earlier, the Russian attack on Armenian education simply fanned the fires of nationalism. Partly in response to these aggressive anti-Armenian measures, the Armenian Revolutionary Federation (best known as the Dashnaktsutiun) was formed in 1890. The Dashnaktsutiun would call for cultural and polit-ical rights for Armenians in the Ottoman and Russian Empires, and would develop into the single most important nationalist party among the Armenians. The decade before 1905 was a dark one, particularly as a result of the rapidly anti-Armenian head of the civil administration in the Caucasus, Prince Grigorii Golitsyn. Golitsyn holds a place in Armenian history rather like that of the detested M. N. Murav'ev ("the hangman") or Warsaw governor-general I. V. Gurko in Polish annals. With the revolu-tionary events of 1905, Golitsyn was recognized by St Petersburg as more of a liability than an asset and was replaced by the more reconciliatory Count I. I. Dashkov-Vorontsov, who would remain at his post until 1915.

As for the Armenians themselves, by the post-1905 period they had come to be seen (in part correctly) by the Russian administration as a "rebellious" nationality. The reality, of course, was more complex. Armenian society was torn between the older, more prosperous fathers who remained on the whole indifferent to national and social struggles and their more radical sons, passionately engaged in both nationalist and socialist parties. Suny puts the matter very strongly: "In time, the Armenian middle class would have to be forced by terror to become part of the national struggle."[22] Politically the Armenians were divided between nationalists and Marxists, but during the post-1905 period Armenian nationalists recognized the situation across the border in Ottoman Turkey as far more threatening and hence limited their national demands within the Russian Empire. This truce between Armenians and the Russian authorities was also helped by the generally enlightened policy of the local viceroy, Count I. I. Dashkov-Vorontsov. Many Armenians probably also recognized their vulnerable position in the region and did not wish to further exacerbate nationalist feelings. Still, the spread of Marxist and nationalist ideologies continued, particularly among the younger generation, and would bear fruit in 1917 and after.[23]

For all the social and ideological differences among them, Armenians with their distinctive language, script, and religion at least recognized each other as members of the same nation. The same could not be said about the Russian Empire's "Tatars." At the present time, the term "Tatar" is used to describe two related but distinct ethnic groups: Volga Tatars and Crimean Tatars. At the turn of the century, however, "Tatar" was often used to refer to nearly any settled (i.e. not nomadic) Moslem, particularly those living in European Russia. We must note here that of the Moslems living in the Empire, the great majority spoke a Turkic language, with the major exception being the Tajiks. The differences between these various languages (in present terms, Kazakh, Tatar, Azerbaijani Turkish, Uzbek, and Kyrgyz) are apparently seldom greater than those existing between Slavic languages. All are, of course, closely related to the Turkish language. At the turn of the century, when education for these peoples was still dominated by Islamic schools (in which the primary language of learning was Arabic or Persian), the idea of one "Panturanian" language for all Turkic peoples seemed a distinct possibility. On the practical level, however, national identity was weak; religious and (in Central Asia) tribal affiliations continued to play a far greater role.

Because Russian statistics tend to lump together various groups under the rubric "Tatar," exact figures on these peoples are difficult to come by.

Still, one thing seems clear: Volga Tatars were the most educated, most urbanized, and most "politicized" group among the Empire's Muslims. Their culture was centered in the city of Kazan on the upper Volga, where they made up around one-quarter of the total population, according to official figures. Publishing in Tatar (still using the Arabic script) flourished in Kazan, particularly after 1905, and S. Zenkovsky even calls turn-of-the-century Kazan "one of the four cultural capitals of the Moslem world." Tatars also dominated Moslem education, not only in the Volga region but in many parts of Central Asia. The "new method" (*usul u jadid*, often known as jadidism) in education proposed by the Crimean Tatar Ismail Bey Gasprali (known in Russian as Gasprinskii) attempted to modernize Moslem education – rather like the Jewish Haskalah movement of some half-century earlier.[24]

The Russian government's policy toward the Tatars (and toward Moslems in general) was, as we have come to expect, rather contradictory. The Volga Tatars were, after all, the first major non-Russian group to be incorporated into the empire (by Ivan the Terrible's conquest of Kazan in 1552). In general, the Russians did not attempt forcible conversion of the Muslim Tatars but, on the other hand, they did offer special incentives to converts. According to official figures, nearly 5 percent of the empire's Tatars were Orthodox believers in 1897. This low figure attests to the general lack of success of conversion efforts. Attempts to bring Russian culture to the Tatars were only somewhat more successful. From 1870, the Russian government embarked on an educational experiment usually known after its creator, N. I. Ilminskii, a professor of Turkic languages in Kazan. Ilminskii advocated a system of state schools which would offer instruction both in Russian and in the local language and would avoid any attempts at overt Christian proselytizing. On the whole, these schools probably did more to educate modern Tatar nationalists than to "fuse" the Tatar nation with the Russian.[25]

In 1905–6, three Moslem Congresses were held, bringing together Muslims from the whole Empire under Tatar leadership. One of the direct results of these congresses was the creation of the Ittifak (Muslim unity party), which was closely affiliated with the liberal Russian Kadet (Constitutional Democrat) party. Muslims were represented in all four Dumas, though their representation was severely reduced (by more than two-thirds) by the electoral law of July 3, 1907. Even in the conservative Third Duma, however, Muslim delegates banded together in their own parliamentary grouping, rather like the Poles in the so-called *Koło*. But probably more important than the Duma for the development of Tatar politics were the modernizing trends among both religious and secular thinkers and educators. As Rorlich points out, even religious schools were caught up in the spirit of social change, most notoriously in the case of the Bobi *medrese* whose teachers were arrested and brought to trial in 1911. Fledgling Marxist groupings among the Tatars were also developing, alongside religious and national groups. In 1917, when the Romanov Empire passed into history, Tatar intellectuals and politicians were ready to seize the reins of political power.

The outbreak of World War I augured major changes for the Russian Empire's nationalities. The tsar held out to Poles the possibility of a postwar restoration of Poland under the scepter of the Romanovs; Baltic Germans kept their heads down as much as possible, and the empire's Jewish community feared for the worst. Already by the end of 1915 German troops had taken Warsaw and most of Russian Poland, and were threatening to advance further still. Jews underwent terrible hardships, accused of spying for the Germans and often summarily evacuated from their homes near the front line. The "temporary" lifting of the Pale of Settlement did little to ease their sufferings. In general it must be said that the empire did little to win the support of the non-Russians for the war effort, but it is likely that no amount of propaganda could have won over Poles or Jews, or made Tatar mothers understand why they should send their sons to fight the Germans. On the other hand, Russian defeats on the battlefield raised the hope that the oppressive tsarist regime's days were numbered and that a new, more liberal regime would soon replace it. It should be remembered that with rare exceptions (the Polish Socialist Party being one), no significant movement among *any* of the Russian Empire's major ethnicities called for outright independence before the empire's collapse in 1917.

The war affected all subjects of the tsar, even those who were not subject to military conscription. As manpower shortages became acute, the Russian administration hit on the idea of recruiting Central Asian men (hitherto exempt from the draft) to serve in labor battalions in the rear. This decision precipitated a major uprising of Central Asian Muslims in 1916. For several years earlier, relations between local peoples and Russians had become increasingly strained by the large numbers of Slavic (especially Russian and Ukrainian) agricultural colonists in the region. Kazakhs and Kyrgyz in particular found more and more that the best pasturelands for their flocks were being settled by Slavic peasants. This threat to their way of life considerably exacerbated their relations with Russian authorities, and this anger burst out into the open in reaction to the *ukaz* of June 25, 1916, which called up the native male population of Turkestan to perform labor duties for the army.

At first the Russian administration and colonists were caught unaware, and the native rebellion spread quickly in the Central Asian Steppe, Turkestan, and Semirechie. Once the Russians realized the extent of the revolt and called in military forces, however, the natives were doomed. Some 3,500 Russians and an undetermined but far higher number of Muslims lost their lives in the revolt and its aftermath. In a sense, the Central Asian revolt of 1916 can be seen as the last attempt by a semi-nomadic, traditional people to protect itself against the colonialist incursions of European "modernization."[26]

Looking over the two decades between 1897 and the collapse of the Romanov Empire in 1917, we see many important changes in the political structure of the Empire but far more significantly in the political mobilization of all subjects of the tsar. For non-Russians, this was a period of increasing political and national consciousness, growing levels of literacy, and a burgeoning press culture. To be sure, already before 1897 political parties of various sorts had existed among the Finns, Poles, Jews, Armenians, and Baltic peoples. But by 1917 the number of political organizations had grown enormously and, more importantly, the politically conscious segment of each nationality was gaining in significance. Still, a very high level of illiteracy and widespread poverty precluded or at least complicated broad political participation in most regions of the empire. Nor did national restrictions disappear; indeed, to cite only two cases, they increased in regard to Jews in these decades and Poles received only minor concessions after 1905.

Despite its ambiguous impact on non-Russians, the revolution of 1905 did form a watershed for them, as for all subjects of Nicholas II. After 1905, with the easing of censorship, the permitting of private schools and the formation of private organizations, and the opening of the Duma, the possibilities for political participation greatly increased. On the other hand, the scope or liberality of these reforms should not be exaggerated. Censorship had been eased, but remained very potent all the same. Schools could be opened, say, using Polish as the main language of instruction, but they lacked the privileges (and funding) of government schools and remained under intense scrutiny from local authorities who, in many cases, had the schools harassed or even shut down. The Duma did provide a tribune for very frank criticism of local authorities but was a rather frail institution upon which to build a vigorous political culture. All things considered, during the years before 1914, the seeds of political participation among the non-Russian nationalities had been planted, had germinated, and in some cases were already beginning to bear fruit in the form of well-organized political parties and the development of a relatively well-informed and politically active proto-electorate. Despite the battering of the world war and civil war, the political lessons learned before 1914 would, for better and for worse, play a very significant role in shaping post-1917 East-Central Europe and Eurasia.

Notes

1 For a general overview of the nationalities and their place in the Russian Empire at this time, see Hans Rogger, "Empire at home: the Non-Russians," in *Russia in the Age of Modernisation and Revolution 1881–1917* (London: Longman, 1983), 182–207; and Raymond Pearson, "Privileges, Rights, and Russification," in Olga Crisp and Linda Edmondson, eds, *Civil Rights in Imperial Russia* (Oxford: Clarendon Press, 1989), 85–102. Much useful information on the topic is to be found in S. Frederick Starr, ed., *The Legacy of History in Russia and the New States of Eurasia* (Armonk, NY: M. E. Sharpe, 1994).

2 On the national question in general during the imperial period, see Marc Raeff, "Patterns of Russian Imperial Policy Toward the Nationalities," in Edward Allworth, ed., *Soviet Nationality Problems* (New York: Columbia University Press, 1971), 22–42; and Leonid I. Strakhovsky, "Constitutional Aspects of the Imperial Russian Government's Policy Toward National Minorities," *Journal of Modern History*, 13 (December 1941): 467–92.

3 But see, for example, John Klier, "The Polish Revolt of 1863 and the Birth of Russification: Bad for the Jews?" *Polin: A Journal of Polish-Jewish Studies*, 1 (1986): 96–110.

4 This is not to say that Russificatory tendencies, defined broadly, are not at work considerably earlier. See, for example, Marc Raeff, "Patterns of Russian Imperial Policy Toward the Nationalities," in Edward Allworth, ed., *Soviet Nationality Problems*, 22–42; and for a very detailed and rich case-study of the Volga region, Andreas Kappeler, *Rußlands erste Nationalitäten: Das Zarenreich und die Völker der Mittleren Wolga vom 16. bis 19. Jahrhundert* (Cologne: BECK, 1982).

5 Instead of singling out the Russian Empire for its admittedly retrograde and discriminatory policies toward non-Russians, we should remember that Theodore Roosevelt, president of that most progressive political entity, the United States of America, denounced the practice of immigrants of speaking "foreign" languages, insisting that all must learn and use English, that a "boarding house of languages" would not be tolerated. The German Empire in these years took concerted (though ineffective) measures to weaken the hold of Polish and Catholic culture in its eastern regions. Even more ambitiously, the Hungarians (Magyars) in Austria-Hungary aimed to spread their language throughout their half of the Dual Monarchy and severely limited the number of schools giving instruction in other languages. The assumption, shared by most nationalists, of one state – one nation – one culture (and even language) was enormously strong and pervasive.

6 Edward C. Thaden, "Introduction," in E. Thaden, ed., *Russification in the Baltic Provinces and Finland, 1855–1914* (Princeton: Princeton University Press, 1981). This collected work is recommended to anyone interested in the dynamics of nationalism and nationality policy in the Russian Empire.

7 Even the arch-conservative Holy Brotherhood, dedicated to upholding the values of autocracy, was looked upon with great suspicion and was rather quickly disbanded. See Stephen Lukashevich, "The Holy Brotherhood:

1881–1883," *American Slavic and East European Review*, 18(4) (December 1959): 491–509.

8 An excellent introduction to this region is provided by Edward Allworth, ed., *Central Asia: 130 Years of Russian Dominance, A Historical Overview*, 3rd edn (Durham: Duke University Press, 1994).

9 An extremely interesting example of this kind of argumentation is found in A. I. Kastelianskii, ed., *Formy natsional'nogo dvizheniia v sovremennykh gosudarstvakh* (St Petersburg: Obshchestvennaia pol'za, 1910). The essays collected in this tome compare the situations in Russia, Austria-Hungary, and the German Empire.

10 Two classic works on nationality and politics in the Habsburg Empire are Robert A. Kann, *The Multinational Empire: Nationalism and National Reform in the Habsburg Empire, 1848–1918* (New York: Columbia University Press, 1950); and Hans Mommsen, *Die Sozialdemokratie und die Nationalitätenfrage im habsburgischen Vielvölkerreich* (Vienna: Europa-Verlag, 1963).

11 The census results were published in 89 volumes (organized generally by province) under the general title *Pervaia vseobshchaia perepis' naseleniia Rossiiskoi Imperii* (St Petersburg, 1899–1904). A handy compendium of the most important data is *Pervaia vseobshchaia perepis' naseleniia Rossiiskoi Imperii: Obshchii svod*, 2 vols (St Petersburg, 1905).

12 An excellent recent treatment of the so-called "small peoples of the North" which gives much new information about the difficulties faced by both tsarist and Soviet administrators in this region is Yuri Slezkine, *Arctic Mirrors* (Ithaca: Cornell University Press, 1994).

13 For insight into the ethnic complexities of the Caucasian region, see Ronald Suny, *Transcaucasia: Nationalism and Social Change: Essays in the History of Armenia, Azerbaijan and Georgia* (Ann Arbor: University of Michigan Press, 1983); idem., *The Making of the Georgian Nation*, 2nd edn (Bloomington: Indiana University Press, 1994); and Audrey L. Altstadt, *The Azerbaijani Turks: Power and Identity under Russian Rule* (Standford: Hoover Institution Press, 1992).

14 On Kiev and its ethnic diversity – and conflict – during this period, see Michael F. Hamm, *Kiev: A Portrait, 1800–1917* (Princeton: Princeton University Press, 1993).

15 Noble is here defined as "hereditary noble." These figures and those that follow are taken from the very helpful statistics on the nationalities (based on the 1897 census) compiled and published in two volumes: Henning Bauer, Andreas Kappeler, and Brigitte Roth, eds, *Die Nationalitäten des Russischen Reiches in der Volkszählung von 1897* (Stuttgart: Franz Steiner, 1991), esp. vol. 2. See also the simplified tables in A. Kappeler, *Rußland als Vielvölkerreich* (Munich: C. H. Beck, 1992).

16 To be sure, Tajiks and Uzbeks lived in "towns" that were very different from those inhabited by, say, Jews or Armenians – what do Bukhara and Riga have in common, aside from the designation "urban area"? This fact should further alert us to look beyond bare statistical categories (including those of "ethnicity") to the often maddeningly complex reality that lies, so to speak, "beneath" these seemingly precise and "objective" categories.

17   The Jews, who were arguably the single most politicized ethnic/national group in the Empire, are considered in a separate chapter of this collection.
18   On the situation of the Finns in the Russian Empire during this period, see C. Leonard Lundin, "Finland," in Thaden, ed., *Russification*. A detailed account of the most severe period of attempted Russification is Tuomo Polvinen, *Imperial Borderland: Bobrikov and the Attempted Russification of Finland 1898–1914*, trans. Steven Huxley (Durham: Duke University Press, 1995).
19   On the "Polish question" in the Russian Empire see: Edward Chmielewski, *The Polish Question in the Russian State Duma* (Knoxville: University of Tennessee Press, 1970); T. Weeks, "Defining Us and Them: Poles and Russians in the 'Western Provinces,' 1863–1914," *Slavic Review*, 53(1) (Spring 1994): 26–40; and the appropriate sections in Piotr S. Wandycz, *The Lands of Partitioned Poland 1795–1918*, 2nd edn (Seattle: University of Washington Press, 1984); and T. Weeks, *Nation and State in Late Imperial Russia: Nationalism and Russification on the Western Frontier, 1863–1914* (DeKalb: Northern Illinois University Press, 1996).
20   On these events, see Robert E. Blobaum, *Rewolucja: Russian Poland, 1904–1907* (Ithaca: Cornell University Press, 1995).
21   An excellent introduction to modern Armenian history in English is Ronald G. Suny, *Looking toward Ararat: Armenia in Modern History* (Bloomington: Indiana University Press, 1993). See also R. Suny, ed., *Transcaucasia, Nationalism and Social Change.*
22   R. Suny, "Populism, Nationalism, and Marxism among Russia's Armenians," in *Looking Toward Ararat*, 70.
23   An excellent "case-study" of national, social, and ideological factors at work in the city of Baku is Ronald Suny, *The Baku Commune, 1917–1918: Class and Revolution in the Russian Revolution* (Princeton: Princeton University Press, 1972).
24   On the Tatars and Muslims in the Russian Empire, see, for example, Azade-Ayşe Rorlich, *The Volga Tatars* (Stanford: Hoover Institution Press, 1986); Alan Fisher, *The Crimean Tatars* (Stanford: Hoover Institution Press, 1978); and Serge A. Zenkovsky, *Pan-Turkism and Islam in Russia* (Cambridge, Mass.: Harvard University Press, 1960).
25   On the Il'minskii "system," see Isabelle Kreindler, "Educational Policies toward the Eastern Nationalities in Tsarist Russia: A Study of the Il'minskii System" (PhD diss., Columbia University, 1969).
26   On the 1916 revolt, which was probably doomed to failure from the start, see Pierce, *Russian Central Asia*, 265–97; Martha B. Olcott, *The Kazakhs*, 2nd edn (Stanford: Hoover Institution Press, 1995), 118–27; and Edward D. Sokol, *The Revolt of 1916 in Russian Central Asia* (Baltimore: Johns Hopkins University Press, 1954).

PART III

"The Loyal Opposition" and the Russian Right

CHAPTER SEVEN

The State Duma:
A Political Experiment

John Morison

The Duma was not a sudden inspiration – a panic reaction to the crisis of the general strike in the fall of 1905 and to mounting anarchy. Rather, it came as the successful culmination to a long process of debate and argument within the social and bureaucratic elite of Russia. One should perhaps discount the Boyars' Duma of early medieval Rus' and Muscovy as a precedent, and also the Zemskii Sobor, or Assembly of the Land of the seventeenth century, as they were essentially advisory bodies which died a natural death rather than developing into legislatures. The crisis of 1730 was of a different order. The Supreme Privy Council attempted unsuccessfully to limit the powers of the new ruler, the Empress Anna, by reserving to itself the power of decision in all important matters of state. But the Council was dominated by members of two aristocratic families who were motivated by self-interest rather than by the wish to establish a constitutional order in Russia.[1]

Genuinely modern constitutional ideas had begun to penetrate Russia's educated social elite on a serious scale by the end of the eighteenth century, in part as a consequence of Catherine the Great's flirtation with the ideas of the *philosophes*, but mainly in response to the proclamations of liberty and of equality of rights and opportunities by the French and American Revolutions. At the beginning of the nineteenth century it seemed for a time that the emperor, Alexander I, was going voluntarily to cede a constitution to his people. He certainly had a genuine interest in constitutions and was willing to grant one to the Finns and to the Poles, but not to the

Russians. He allowed and even commissioned subordinates to prepare serious projects, but in reality interpreted the word "constitution" to mean merely an orderly system of government and administration. The consequent frustration of those who wished to limit the power of the autocrat found expression in the futile Decembrists' revolt in 1825, when the Northern Society demanded a constitutional monarch checked by an executive legislature and the Southern Society a republic. The new ruler, Nicholas I, drove such aspirations firmly underground, where they nevertheless survived in secret discussion circles. Humiliating military defeat in the Crimean War led his successor, Alexander II, to go along with an extensive reform program, ranging from emancipation of the serfs through greater freedom of opinion, an independent judiciary, equality before the law, and greater access to education to elected institutions of local self-government. These measures could certainly be seen as laying the foundations for a constitutional order, but Alexander II resolutely refused to "crown the edifice," and curtly rejected modest proposals by his brother, by his minister of the interior, and by his gendarme chief to introduce an elective element into central government. Like Alexander I, he was prepared to grant constitutions to foreigners, in his case the Bulgarians, but not to his own people. A revolutionary bomb under his dining room helped to persuade him to make modest gestures of conciliation towards moderate opinion in society only hours before his assassination on March 1, 1881, but this was very far from being a genuine move towards representative government. The new ruler, Alexander III, was unyielding in his defense of autocracy and is credibly reported to have said: "Constitution? That a Russian tsar would swear allegiance to some sort of herd of cattle?"[2] But even his bluff resolution could not hold in check the development of a constitutional movement in which educated society was provoked rather than intimidated by his far from successful attempts to unpick his father's reforms. His untimely death in 1894 should have made no difference, since his inexperienced son, Nicholas II, promised to uphold autocracy as firmly and unflinchingly as his unforgettable father, and rejected all constitutional aspirations as "senseless dreams." These brave, or perhaps foolhardy words, certainly represented Nicholas's genuine and instinctive convictions, but he was to be persuaded to betray his instincts by forces beyond his control and by pressures from within the ruling circles.

By the turn of the century, there was a developing sense of crisis which was detectable even to foreign diplomats. Industrial unrest, as yet localized peasant disturbances, a general student strike in 1899, and growing demands for self-rule from the non-Russian majority of the empire's population showed how wide-based this crisis was. But perhaps the most dangerous threat of all came from the political articulation of social discontent by a rapidly growing constitutional movement. This was based on the elected members of the zemstvos, the local government bodies which were becoming increasingly frustrated by the checks on their activities, on those of the zemstvos' professional employees such as teachers and doctors, and on professional associations which were increasingly and illegally drawing political conclusions from discussions of professional issues. For Russia to survive as a great power, the regime had had to develop industry and commerce and to expand educational facilities at a rapid pace, thereby expanding the size of the professional groups which now joined the progressive element of the gentry in providing leadership and foot soldiers for the liberal movement. The process had become more radical by the eve of the 1905 Revolution, with those prepared to settle for a consultative assembly now in a decided minority. The majority was prepared to join with some of the revolutionary parties in demanding a legislative assembly with real powers, elected by universal, free, direct, and equal suffrage. A feeling of crisis was transformed into a real crisis by the unsuccessful war against Japan into which the regime had most unwisely stumbled. Military failure yet again in Russian history was to lead directly to significant reform as a way out of crisis.

The crucial turning point in the descent into the anarchic disorder of 1905 was the assassination by terrorist bomb of the firm and unyielding minister of the interior, V. K. von Plehve, on July 15, 1904. Plehve's instinct had always been to shoot his way out of trouble, and to stand resolutely against the revolutionary and constitutional challenge from within Russian society. The choice as his successor of Prince P. D. Sviatopolk-Mirskii was a surprise to everyone, with the exception of the tsar's mother who had pressed his candidature on her son. His appointment on August 25, 1904 effectively marked a radical change of direction at the heart of government, and dramatized the extent to which the ruling elite was divided between those who rejected any change to the autocratic structure of government, and those who believed that concessions to society were needed, including the involvement in law-making of elected representatives of society. The constitutional virus had infected not solely gentry and professional groups in society at large, but also significant numbers of the central bureaucracy, including ministers, and important members of aristocratic and court society. Sviatopolk-Mirskii, a straightforward and honest man, had made sure that the tsar was under no illusions in appointing him. He pointed out that his views were radically different from those of his two predecessors, that he was a "zemstvo man," and that he considered it to be necessary to seek a reconciliation between the government and Russian society. The press should be granted more freedom, police abuses curbed, self-government extended, elected delegates summoned to St Petersburg, and policies towards the non-Russians of the borderlands changed. The tsar appeared to agree with all of this, only expressing some doubt about the wisdom of allowing workers to hold meetings undisturbed and remarking that the borderlands would have to wait some years for zemstvos.[3]

Nicholas II was a rather more complex, calculating and politically intelligent individual than has sometimes been supposed. He was determined at all costs to preserve the essence of his autocratic powers, but realized that tensions in society were now so great that some concessions to moderate liberal opinion were necessary in order to widen his social base of support. By appointing Sviatopolk-Mirskii he had indicated his willingness to listen to these opinions, even if expressed by elected representatives, but clearly expected them in return to leave him with the unchallenged right of decision. He preferred to deal personally with moderates of high social standing, particularly if, like Sviatopolk-Mirskii, they also had a military background. For all his idealization of his relations with the ordinary people, Nicholas had no real understanding of, or sympathy towards the aspirations and grievances of simple peasants and workers.

True to his word, Sviatopolk-Mirskii tried to conciliate society. By so doing, he raised expectations which he could not satisfy since the tsar was unwilling to approve of any measure which might be construed as actually limiting his supreme authority. The word "constitution" aroused in him the same hostile reaction as it had in his immediate predecessors. Although he was prepared to listen to advice from representatives of the people, their ultimate duty was to obey, and certainly not to dispute his authority or, worse still, to share his powers. By allowing the holding of a zemstvo congress in 1904 and also the organization of reform banquets which turned effectively into political meetings, Sviatopolk-Mirskii permitted the constitutional opposition to organize itself and so raised the political temperature to a level which it proved impossible to control. As the threat to the regime from society mounted, the ruling circles were deeply divided on what to do. Many, including some ministers and members of the tsar's family, urgently pressed for dramatic concessions and the involvement of popularly elected representatives in the business of law-making. Others, such as his uncle Sergei Aleksandrovich and the trusted new governor of St Petersburg, D. F. Trepov, urged firmness and repression. By contrast, the influential chairman of the Committee of Ministers, S. Iu. Witte, argued for the reforming role of an enlightened bureaucracy. As the crisis mounted and the carnage of Bloody Sunday failed to quieten the unrest, the tsar ducked and weaved. On the one hand, he dispensed with the services of Sviatopolk-Mirskii and issued an imperial manifesto on February 18, 1905, reasserting the principle of autocracy and denouncing sedition. On the other hand, he made it clear that he was going to establish a consultation process whereby his subjects would be able to make their opinions known to him, and agreed to issue a rescript promising a national consultative assembly.[4] The mild and well-meaning new minister of the interior, A. G. Bulygin, was given the job of working out the details. This concession came too late to calm public opinion. The new professional associations, the liberal press, public meetings and progressive opinion in general made it clear that it would accept nothing less than a real constitution, with a legislative assembly elected on the widest possible franchise and effective checks placed on the absolute powers of the autocrat. By the time that Bulygin had finished his work, it was clear that his consultative Duma, or assembly, had no future. Tired and dispirited, he finally persuaded the tsar to allow him to retire. With a general strike looming, and mounting disorder, the situation seemed to be getting completely out of the government's control. His advisors and entourage faced Nicholas II with a stark choice: either to use military force to restore order, or to make serious constitutional concessions in order to buy off a significant part of the opposition. In the end, he adopted both courses of action. His October Manifesto offered the prospect of civil liberties and a legislative assembly with real powers of control over the executive. This was to be followed by the widespread imposition of martial law, and a savage campaign of repression accompanied by field courts martial to inflict immediate and arbitrary retribution on those judged to be rebels.

The new political order that emerged out of the crisis of 1905 was riddled with contradictions which were rooted in the vastly different conceptions of its nature held by its major players. So far as the tsar was concerned, he had not granted a constitution. In making this assertion, he was probably technically correct. The October Manifesto had made promises in a far from precise form which were subsequently implemented by amendments to the Fundamental Laws. His interpretation of events harked back to the seventeenth century, and to the Zemskii Sobor which had been summoned by the autocrat to give him the benefit of advice from representatives of different sections of society. Hence the October Manifesto insisted that the changes would come about as a result of a decision by the autocrat, by "Our inflexible will." What had been given could presumably also be altered or removed by that same will. The "newly established legislative order" did not, in the ruler's view, terminate or in any real sense modify the supreme authority of the autocrat in Russia.

In sharp contrast, revolutionaries and constitutionalists celebrated the October Manifesto as heralding a new era in Russian history, and as the dawn of a constitutional order. It is true that some Social Democrats were skeptical, but most revolutionaries were eager to believe that the new legislative body would be transformed into a constitutent assembly which would create a socialist utopia in Russia. The deep-rooted constitutionalist movement contained within it a wide spectrum of views, but the revolutionary events of 1905 had radicalized its core within society. It would be satisfied by nothing less than a legislative assembly with full powers and

elected by universal franchise, or in other words by a democracy in advance
of anything then achieved in the rest of Europe. To believe that such a
change could be achieved overnight by a society that was still relatively
backward was to display that lack of realism characteristic of the Russian
intelligentsia. Others in the constitutional movement were less ambitious.
Even if the numbers of those who would have been satisfied by a merely
consultative assembly had shrunk significantly, there were many who were
prepared to cooperate in trying to make a quasi-constitutional order work,
in which the autocrat would retain real powers but would have to work
with elected national representatives in a parliamentary assembly. Count
Witte, the driving force behind the October Manifesto, had his own distinctive statist vision. He aspired to achieve a well-ordered state, directed
by an efficient and coordinated executive. The autocrat would thus cede
authority, in practice if not in theory, to his ministers and the bureaucracy
who, in the interests of efficiency, would enlist the cooperation of an elected
legislative assembly, thereby healing the destructive breach between the
regime and society.[5]

The new system which emerged as promises were transformed into legal
enactments could be interpreted as a victory by all of the parties concerned, a measure of the contradictions which it contained or failed to
resolve. Thus, on the one hand, fundamental civil liberties, the bulwark of
any constitutional order, were granted and discriminatory regulations
which oppressed various groups in society, such as the Old Believers, were
withdrawn or modified. Freedom of conscience, speech, assembly, and
association were at least notionally granted, as was inviolability of the
person. On the other hand, some elements of discrimination were retained,
particularly against the Jews, and large areas of the country continued to
be placed under martial law or a state of extraordinary security. In these
areas, citizens' rights were curtailed and exceptional powers were granted
to local officials. This state of affairs continued long after the 1905
Revolution had been repressed.[6] Witte had aspired to replace the previous
system of government, under which ministers were individually appointed
by and were responsible to the tsar and had no collective responsibility or
coherent general policy, by one in which a cabinet of ministers would
operate together in a disciplined manner to produce an agreed coordinated
policy under a chairman, or prime minister, who would have powers of
appointment and discipline. Witte achieved the title, which he coveted, but
little of the reality of cabinet government. The tsar insisted on retaining
the right of ultimate decision (often exercised), control over the appointment of ministers (sometimes delegated), and of dismissals, and the practice of receiving individual reports from ministers. Notwithstanding all
this, something like a coordinated government policy was achieved, at least
until 1912, but the tsar insisted on his prerogative to behave as an auto-

crat in practice as well as in theory, and no prime minister, not even the powerful Petr A. Stolypin, could feel secure. Witte himself, whose ability was exceeded only by his ego, was incapable of playing the part of fawning courtier and did not last long in the post.

The change to which the constitutionalists attached most importance was the establishment of a national Duma, or parliament, which was to have legislative powers. The October Manifesto seemed, on an optimistic reading, to be offering elections under a wide franchise, with universal suffrage soon to follow, and a Duma with unbreakable control over all legislation, and supervisory powers over the legality of the actions of the executive. If the manifesto had been implemented in the positive spirit in which it seemed to have been issued, Russia would have been blessed with a constitution in some ways reminiscent of that of the USA. A powerful executive, headed by a prime minister responsible to an hereditary ruler rather than to an elected president, would have been checked and balanced by an elected legislature, which would have the final say in matters of law-making. However, the function of checking the legality of the operations of the executive would be left, in a vague manner, to the legislature rather than to a Supreme Court. The hereditary ruler would check the activities of the legislature, but by his own will rather than by reference to a written constitution. Moreover, Russia was to remain a unitary state rather than a federation. However, as was soon to be revealed, the tsar was moved in issuing the manifesto not by a generous desire to embrace constitutionalism but by devious tactical considerations. He was bending with the wind in order to save as much as possible of the autocracy. As soon as conditions were more propitious, he hoped that the twigs of autocracy would spring back into place, ready to smother the new constitutional growths.

The continuing crisis meant that the tsar could not revert to a consultative assembly, a move which would have further provoked rather than conciliated Russian society. All future laws should therefore pass through the Duma, which would also have the right of legislative initiative. However, as the new order evolved, the powers of the new Duma were clipped. The tsar retained the right of veto. Laws also had to pas through the State Council, which served as an upper chamber. Since up to half of its members were appointed by the tsar, it was to be receptive to his influence and a very effective check to the lower house. The tsar could prorogue the Duma at will. Even its control over the legislative process was subverted by Article 87 of the Fundamental Laws which allowed the Council of Ministers to submit a legislative proposal directly to the emperor when the State Duma was in recess.[7] The built-in safeguards were to prove on occasions to be inadequate. The October Manifesto had promised the Duma "the possibility of a genuine participation in supervising the conformity with law of actions [pursued] by the authorities established by Us."[8] This grudging concession was deliberately couched in vague language and its implementation was to be a source of much friction between executive and legislature. Ministers were appointed by the emperor and were responsible to him for all their political and administrative activity, even if the new prime minister was allowed on many occasions to act as intermediary. But ministers also had to deal with the elected Duma. Legislation for which they were responsible had to go to the elected chamber for frequently detailed scrutiny and for approval. Most ministers could also be subjected to "interpellations" on the legality of their administrative actions. If the Duma was dissatisfied, it could, by a two-thirds majority, refer the matter to the tsar for his decision. The Duma could also question ministers, a power which was used extensively and vigorously and which proved to be much more effective in practice than that of interpellation. It even succeeded in extending this practice to foreign and military affairs which were formally the exclusive preserve of the tsar. But interpellations and questions could in reality only harass or embarrass ministers and not subject them to real control. The Duma's most effective weapon was the financial one: the state's annual budget had to be approved by it. This was to give the Duma considerable leverage over the executive, which could be used to influence its policies. Moreover, the rule that an annual recruitment law was to decide the size of the armed forces allowed indirect pressure to be exerted in the field of military policy, an area theoretically excluded from the purview of the Duma.[9]

The new political order which emerged from the 1905 Revolution thus retained a strong executive and bureaucracy, responsible in a very real sense to the emperor in person. However, the creation of the post of prime minister and the concession of the principle of a unified government notionally loosened this direct, personal control from on high without removing it, thereby leaving the path open for intrigue and arbitrary intervention. Civil liberties had been introduced or extended. However, the ability of independent courts to protect these liberties was weak, and the freedoms themselves were to be suspended in many regions as the right of the autocrat and executive to employ extraordinary measures to combat disorder and sedition was widely used. The main innovation was the creation of an elected national legislative body. This had the potential to develop as the driving force in the new political order, and as the basis of a new and genuinely constitutional structure. As already mentioned, however, ambiguities and contradictions abounded. A key uncertainty was the basis on which the Duma was to be elected. The October Manifesto had promised an extension of the franchise already agreed for the Bulygin Duma so as to include "those classes of the population who at present are totally deprived of the franchise," and specifically held out the prospect of universal suffrage in the future.[10] A battle royal developed over the extent to which this promise should be implemented. True to his devotion to the seventeenth-century concept of an assembly of all the land, Nicholas II made it clear that he wanted all sections of society to be represented. He was sufficiently astute to realize that nothing less would pacify society at this particular juncture. So strongly had constitutional notions entered the consciousness of sections of Russia's ruling elite that the principle of universal suffrage received strong support from surprising quarters, including some ministers and some hitherto conservative members of the provincial nobility. The special conference called to decide the issue was divided, and Prime Minister Witte wavered from side to side. In the end, the tsar decided the issue. Universal suffrage was rejected as the immediate precursor of a democratic republic which would be "unthinkable and criminal."[11] Nevertheless, the electoral system which he did approve was radical enough. A complex system of predominantly indirect election via curias of electors meant that the vote of an urban worker was worth far less than that of a member of the gentry.

The peasantry were treated relatively generously, not only electing their own deputies but also, if they met the property qualification as significant numbers now did, participating in the landowner's curia. Witte, and ruling circles in general, retained a startling faith in the innate loyalty and conservatism of the peasantry, but S. E. Kryzhanovskii, a high official at the heart of the fray, was to prove closer to the mark: "a peasant would sell out both the Tsar and God for a desiatina of land."[12]

For the new system to work, a spirit of conciliation and cooperation was necessary from both sides. This was to be notably absent from the First and Second Dumas. The tsar had already made it clear to Witte that in his view the Duma would be an enemy.[13] Both Witte and then Goremykin as prime ministers would have liked to establish good working relationships with the Duma, but were bound to give priority to resolute and often harsh measures to restore law and order, including the use of arbitrary courts martial and martial law. An unbridgeable gap opened between the governments and the Dumas when the former, notwithstanding the radical nature of much of their programs, were unable to satisfy the Dumas on the land issue, not least because of the tsar's unyielding position. The first two Dumas were elected before peace and order had been restored to the country. The political right had been stung into outraged protest by the October Manifesto but had been slow to organize itself politically and to adjust to the new political order, to which it was totally opposed. The way was thus open, thanks also to the wide franchise, for the first two Dumas to be dominated by those to the left of centre to whom the new order was just a temporary staging point en route to the institution of a fully constitutional (or in some cases revolutionary) political structure.[14] The clash was made obvious at the opening of the First Duma. The tsar and his entourage came dressed in all their finery to be confronted by V. D. Nabokov lounging in the front row with his hands in his pockets and openly smirking at Nicholas II's speech, and by serried ranks of unshaven and even unwashed peasants in their rough working clothes. According to Kryzhanovskii, it seemed as if the Russian land had sent to Petersburg "all that was savage in it, full of hate and malice." The intelligentsia in these Dumas was swamped by the "boiling energy" of the "black masses," who were ruled by their instincts. Members became drunk and disorderly in taverns and then pleaded parliamentary immunity when policemen came to arrest them. A couple of peasant members were caught selling "entry tickets" to the Duma. Perhaps more seriously, some were using their parliamentary immunity shamelessly to carry on revolutionary agitation. Sessions became disorderly as ministers were shouted down.[15] Encouraged by a flood of petitions from peasants, a majority insisted that private land should be expropriated and redistributed to the peasantry. The landed gentry had been alarmed by the attacks on their persons and their properties in 1905–6 and so soon forgot their earlier grievances against the government and rallied to the support of the status quo. The tsar took their side and made it clear that inviolability of private property was to him an immutable principle. Deadlock ensued, and the only way out was to prorogue the First Duma and hold new elections. These only made matters worse as the revolutionary parties made large gains and the short-lived Second Duma was even more intransigent and obstreperous than the First.

Even before the Second Duma met, Nicholas II had found a hard-headed and resolute new prime minister, Stolypin, the former Saratov provincial governor. He it was who used Article 87 of the Fundamental Laws to pass his own version of radical agrarian reform, minus land expropriations. He also substantially revised the electoral system so as to narrow the franchise and thereby change the political complexion of the Duma. The law of June 3, 1907 aimed to do precisely that, to ensure a victory in the next elections to "the more cultivated layers of society," whilst seeing that the tsar's wish that all layers of society should be represented was honored at least to a certain extent. But the rules were manipulated to ensure that significant estate owners, or in other words the 30,000 members of the landed gentry, would dominate the electoral assemblies.[16] The desired results were achieved. In the Third Duma, the numbers of revolutionary and radical liberal, or Kadet, deputies were greatly reduced. The leading role now passed to the Octobrists, to the right of center, and to gentry groups further to the right. The far right had become better organized and had increased its representation, but was nevertheless little more than an irritant. The far left, in the shape of the revolutionary parties, was still represented, but on a sharply reduced scale, and could realistically hope only to make propaganda rather than influence events.

This revision of the electoral law is often presented as a "constitutional coup," with the implication that the Duma had been so emasculated that it was now effectively no more than a harmless talking shop. If that had been the overriding intention of Stolypin and the emperor, it is difficult to understand why they did not abolish the Duma. Perhaps, as Peter Gatrell has recently hinted, this is the real question one should ask about the "coup."[17] A resort to dictatorial administration and an end to electoral representation was certainly on the agenda for discussion at the time, but the ruler and his prime minister decided against such a drastic act.[18] As has already been noted, constitutional notions had taken deep root in Russian educated society, and now found considerable support even at the highest level. To have destroyed the Duma would have rendered the task of bridging the gap between regime and society impossible, and would have seriously damaged Russia's international reputation with her allies, and with the financiers whose loans were indispensable. But to have continued with an unchanged electoral law would have rendered the achievement of a productive working relationship between regime and Duma unachievable. Social hatreds would have intensified, and the volcano would probably have erupted again long in advance of 1917. Thus Stolypin was ironically trying to achieve a democratic end by non-democratic means.

This tactic worked, and under the "June 3 system" Russia's political structure was altered to incorporate the Duma as a meaningful partner. Nicholas II was able to convince himself that the autocracy remained intact. To him, the modified Duma was a means whereby he could maintain direct contact with loyal Russian society. It could serve as a useful check on the newly unified government and on the pretensions of the bureaucracy, whilst itself being controlled by the State Council and by his own substantial remaining prerogatives. Stolypin himself believed in the need for the primacy of an efficient, reforming administration and bureaucracy. The Duma could serve as an important source of pressure against opponents of reform and as a useful counterweight to the obstructive tendencies of the autocrat. Moreover, he believed that progress depended on social stability. The Duma could play a key role in achieving this by furthering the process of reconciliation between regime and society.

For Stolypin's tactic to succeed, he had to establish a working partnership with the centrist forces of the Duma. This he achieved by cooperating first with the Octobrists and then, further to the right, with the Nationalists. The Octobrists were heavily dependent on landed interests, but Stolypin's defence of the principle of the inviolability of private property secured their support for his continued agrarian legislation and other reform measures. This productive relationship was put under strain by the dispute over the Naval General Staff bill of 1909. Guchkov, the Octobrists' forceful leader, had made military reform one of his key ambitions. In this specific instance, control over naval personnel was the issue in question. However, this was seen by many conservatives in the State Council, and not without justification, as an intrusion into an area reserved for the emperor. Stolypin had cooperated in this attempt to extend the authority of the Duma and the Council of Ministers. Nicholas II was not amused. He dismissed the war minister and rejected the bill. Stolypin was curtly ordered to "end the present unclarity in the examination of military and naval bills," or in other words to restrict the Duma's rights and to abandon his support of the Octobrists on this issue.[19] The partnership with the Octobrists finally collapsed in 1911. Stolypin was a dedicated reformer of local government, which for him was the basis for a soundly administered state. He saw the zemstvos, the local elected assemblies, as essential allies in this process, and in 1910 introduced a bill to extend these bodies into six south-western provinces from which they had hitherto been excluded because of the doubtful loyalty of the local, largely Polish gentry. To ensure Russian domination of these new zemstvos, curias based on nationality were introduced into the local electoral procedures, and property qualifications were lowered. The latter provision antagonized many gentry supporters of the new bodies. The tsar advised leaders of the right to vote "according to their conscience." Encouraged by this intervention from on high, the State Council decisively rejected the bill, which had already been amended in the Duma. In a rage, Stolypin bullied Nicholas II into closing both chambers and passing the bill under Article 87. The Octobrists and others were incensed by this scorn for constitutional procedures. Both houses brought interpellations against the prime minister, and the Duma decisively rejected his explanations. Stolypin's alliance with the Octobrists was killed by this conflict, but the fissures and conflicts within the Octobrist fraction had long before made it an unreliable partner.[20] Realizing this, Stolypin had as early as 1909 begun to stress the Russian nationalist aspects of his policies and to seek a new partnership with the Russian Nationalist Party. For Stolypin, the crisis over the Western Zemstvo bill did not mark the end of his "constitutional experiment," but rather the opening of a new chapter based on a move to the right and a new alliance with a fresh political force in the Duma which was based on the self-interested defense of the interests of the landed gentry.[21] Stolypin's assassination on September 1, 1911 cut short this relationship. His successor, V. N. Kokovtsov, was a far less forceful character, less able and willing to impose his will on his ministerial colleagues. This changed the balance of the new political order, weakening the position of the executive vis-à-vis the emperor. The elections to the Fourth Duma returned a motley assortment of deputies, with no working majority. The disunified government now lacked a partner in the Duma with which to build a constructive relationship. The initiative had returned to the autocrat. It took the crisis engendered by World War I to bring oppositional deputies together in a Progressive Bloc which was able to extract some concessions from the ruler, but in the end it was fatally rejected by Nicholas II. The Duma had shown that it still had the will and ability to play a constructive role. The February Revolution was to give the forces it represented their opportunity, but too late for constitutionalism to have a fair chance of success.

From the preceding analysis, it will have become apparent that no mature party political system had emerged in the Duma, although the formation of the Progressive Bloc from six groups provided hopeful signs that the lessons of coalition politics were being learned. With the exception of the main revolutionary parties and, to some extent at least, the Kadets, there was a general lack of national political organizations and party discipline. Many deputies represented specific non-Russian groups and so were sectional by definition. Other major groupings such as the Octobrists were fractions rather than parties. The electoral curias tended to choose well-known local personalities without fixed party labels. The deputies, on arrival in St Petersburg, would then gravitate towards the "fraction" most compatible with their general views. Affiliations were thus weak, and proper party discipline well nigh impossible to achieve. A workable system of coalition politics was also impeded by the profusion of represented political groups, from extreme left to extreme right. Moreover, the nature of the "June 3 system" gave little incentive for the development of disciplined party politics. The executive was at a distance from the legislature, which was essentially a reactive body, able to criticize and perhaps amend, but without real responsibility. Nor was there the lure of office to provide a stimulus to the development of party discipline.[22]

An early breed of exiled Russian liberal historians tended to see the history of the Duma as one of a tragically missed opportunity, of an evolving constitutional order shattered by the disaster of the Bolsheviks' seizure of power. More recent historical writing on the subject has been dominated by the impact of Leopold Haimson's seminal article in which he argued that groups and classes in Russian society had become increasingly polarized, that the labor movement posed a dangerous threat by 1913–14, and that the country, far from evolving towards a socially stable parliamentary democracy, was sliding towards a revolutionary crisis.[23] Much of the debate which has followed has been tangential to the issue of Duma politics as such.[24] Nevertheless, the implication of much that has been written is clear: the Duma was a dead cause well before 1914, at best a political irrelevance and with little real prospect of meaningful development. A case along these lines can certainly be made. After June 3, 1907, the Duma effectively represented the interests of 30,000 or so landed gentry. Other social groups were represented, but generally at a derisively low level. Peasants and workers, the huge majority of the population, could hope for little from its deliberations. Political parties, from the Kadets leftwards, were illegal. The political scene in the Duma was fragmented and ill-disciplined, leading to ineffectiveness. The development of a civil society was necessary as a precondition for an effective parliamentary system, but this was being frustrated at every corner as the civil rights promised in 1905 were hedged around with restrictions and became only partially operative.

And yet, such a negative appraisal is perhaps based on the typical expectation of members of the radical Russian intelligentsia that new political systems and radical social transformations could be achieved almost overnight. The "June 3 system" was intended to make a considerably modified political system actually work, and to a significant extent it succeeded. A unified executive to a degree was balanced by a national elected legislature, and both provided counterforces to the still notionally unlimited powers of the autocrat.

The function of the Duma in this new system was not to govern, but to improve and approve legislative projects and to exert some measure of control over the executive. The possibility of legislative initiatives added some bite to this real, if limited role. The Duma fairly quickly developed effective procedures and powerful committees, in no small part thanks to the work of Kadet deputies. The State Council was very mistrustful of reforming initiatives from below. Consequently, the Duma was generally ineffective in generating and promoting its own legislation. Its initiatives, however (for instance in the field of universal primary education), could act as a goad and stimulus to the government to take over these measures. Where it was often very effective was in revising and improving legislation presented to it by ministers. The knowledge that a bill would be carefully and effectively scrutinized by a body which had the power to reject it was in itself an effective instrument of control by the Duma over the executive. This function of supervision or control was strengthened by the Duma's right of interpellation, and of putting questions of enquiry. These could be powerful means of calling ministers to account for their actions. No longer could ministers act in a vacuum, responsible to the will of the autocrat alone. They now had to justify their bills and their actions before an active political body which had sufficient teeth to make life very awkward for those whom it judged to be incompetent or recalcitrant. Some areas were defined as being outside the competence of the Duma. These reserved areas were military and naval legislation, and matters relating to the imperial family, to the administration of the Orthodox Church and other religious bodies, and to foreign affairs. It has already been noted how the Duma succeeded to some extent in intruding in military and foreign affairs, and in giving considerable momentum to military reform. Finance was the lever by which this was achieved. When extra sums were required for such purposes, the Duma was able to question and to seek improvements and modifications in return for its consent to new credits. In other areas, the Duma's budgetary control was more extensive and allowed a greater degree of influence to be exerted. Bureaucrats from the relevant ministries often worked together with Duma committees in a constructive spirit. The help of the Duma in securing financial discipline in such areas as railway construction could be of positive benefit to the government.

For all its vicissitudes and the presence within it of extremes to left and right intent above all on nuisance-making, and notwithstanding the lack of a properly functioning party system, the Duma had carved out for itself a distinctive and real political role and was, on a day-to-day basis, gaining rather than losing influence, notwithstanding the autocrat's underlying deep hostility. This was understood by some important groups in society. Thus, a group of Moscow industrialists led amongst others by the Riabushinskii brothers formed a new party, the Progressists, which made some impact in the elections to the Fourth Duma.[25] However, the bulk of the population had good grounds for alienation, an alienation which was a fundamental source of weakness for the Duma. Not without good reason, the peasants saw the Third and Fourth Dumas as the "landlords' Dumas," whilst industrial workers responded to their virtual exclusion by electing Social Democrats where possible, thereby signaling clearly their hostility. The free speech and immunities granted to Duma deputies contributed to the independence and variety of opinion fundamental to a civil society, but were used by the workers' representatives in a spirit hostile to and contemptuous of the development of parliamentarianism in Russia.

The verdict on the "June 3 system" thus has to be a mixed one. The Duma developed a distinctive and increasing role as a partner in legislation, and as a controller of efficiency and legality in government. Notwithstanding the irresponsibility of some of its extremist members, it stood out as a beacon of free speech and independence of thought. The hostility of the autocrat might remain undimmed, but bounds had effectively been put on his notionally limitless powers. However, despite the rapid spread of literacy and the development of a mass culture, a yawning divide still separated those dominating the Duma from the bulk of the population who had yet to become citizens in the full sense of the word. The Duma was still a very shallow-rooted creation, and therefore vulnerable and liable to upheaval in any period of social turmoil.

Notes

1   For a good discussion of the crisis, see David L. Ransel, "The government crisis of 1730," in Robert O. Crummey, ed., *Reform in Russia and the USSR* (Urbana and Chicago: University of Illinois Press, 1989), 45–71.

2   V. N. Chernukha and B. V. Anan'ich , "Russia Falls Back, Russia Catches Up: Three Generations of Russian Reformers," in Theodore Taranovskii, ed., *Reform in Russian History* (New York and Cambridge: Woodrow Wilson Center and Cambridge University Press, 1995), 77.

3   "Dnevnik kn. Ekateriny Alekseevny Sviatopolk Mirskoi za 1904–1905 gg.," *Istoricheskie Zapiski*, 77 (1965): 241–2.

4   For a good discussion of the debate, see Andrew M. Verner, *The Crisis of Russian Autocracy. Nicholas II and the 1905 Revolution* (Princeton, NJ: Princeton University Press, 1990), ch. 5.

5   Ibid., chs 6–7.

6   Jonathan W. Daly, "On the Significance of Emergency Legislation in Late Imperial Russia," *Slavic Review*, 54(3) (1995): 621–7; Peter Waldron, "States of Emergency: Autocracy and Extraordinary Legislation," *Revolutionary Russia*, 8(1) (1995): 19–21.

7   For the full text, see Marc Szeftel, *The Russian Constitution of April 23, 1906*, Studies presented to the International Commission for the History of Representation and Parliamentary Institutions, XLI (Brussels: Les éditions de la Libraire Encyclopédique, 1976), 99.

8   Ibid., 216.

9   Ibid., 218–24, 310–13.

10 Verner, *Crisis*, 242.

11 Ibid., 288.

12 Ibid., 281–91; S. E. Kryzhanovskii, *Vospominaniia* (Petropolis, n.d.), 60–74.

13 Kryzhanovskii, *Vospominaniia*, 66.

14 For a full analysis of the elections to the First Duma, see Terence Emmons, *The Formation of Political Parties and the First National Elections in Russia* (Cambridge, Mass. and London: Harvard University Press, 1983).

15 Kryzhanovskii, *Vospominaniia*, 80–7.

16 Ibid., 107–13.

17 Peter Gatrell, " 'Constitutional Russia': A response," *Revolutionary Russia*, 9(1) (1996): 91.

18 Kryzhanovskii, *Vospominaniia*, 115–16.

19 Geoffrey A. Hosking, *The Russian Constitutional Experiment* (Cambridge: Cambridge University Press, 1973), 80–5, 92–7.

20 Ibid., 116–46; Alexandra Shecket Korros, "The Landed Nobility, the State Council, and P. A. Stolypin (1907–11)," in Leopold Haimson, ed., *The Politics of Rural Russia 1905–1914* (Bloomington and London: Indiana University Press, 1979), 134–8.

21 Robert Edelman, "The Russian Nationalist Party and the Political Crisis of 1909," *The Russian Review*, 34(1) (1975): 1–54.

22 Szeftel, *The Russian Constitution*, 448–52.

23 Leopold Haimson, "The Problem of Social Stability in Urban Russia, 1905–1917," *Slavic Review*, 23(4) (1964): 619–42, and 24(1) (1965): 1–22.

24 For an excellent historiographical discussion of the debate, see Edward Acton, *Rethinking the Russian Revolution* (London: Edward Arnold, 1990), 55–82.

25 Michael C. Brainerd, "The Octobrists and the Gentry in the Russian Social Crisis of 1913–1914," *Russian Review*, 38(2) (1979): 168–9.

CHAPTER EIGHT

Liberalism and Democracy: The Constitutional Democratic Party*

Melissa Stockdale

The Constitutional Democratic Party, or Party of People's Freedom (nicknamed the Kadets), was the largest political party in imperial Russia prior to 1917 and also the only self-avowedly liberal one. It was formed in 1905 from the left wing of the zemstvo constitutionalist movement and the more moderate half of the Union of Liberation, espousing a constitutional and democratic form of government for Russia and far-reaching social reforms. By spring 1906 the party had approximately 100,000 members and in the national elections won the most seats to the short-lived First Duma, which it dominated. From 1907, revisions to the electoral law and government persecution drastically reduced the party's size and influence, but the Constitutional Democrats nonetheless managed to remain politically active and intact, even as more moderate constitutional parties split or ceased to exist. In February–March 1917, Kadets experienced a return of influence and popularity, playing a leading role in the creation and composition of the Provisional Government. Less than ten months later the Provisional Government had been overthrown, and the Kadet party declared illegal;

* I wish to thank the International Research and Exchanges Board, the Fulbright-Hays Foundation, the John M. Olin Foundation, the Research Council of the University of Oklahoma, and the Russian and East European Summer Laboratory of the University of Illinois for support that made possible the research and writing of this paper.

most of the leadership joined anti-Bolshevik groups during the civil war and eventually emigrated.

Although there is no full study of the Constitutional Democratic Party for its entire existence, nor of the history of Russian liberalism, numerous articles and books examine Kadet views, values, or tactics for given periods in the life of the party or in relation to specific issues.[1] Since the party failed to achieve any of its goals, it is perhaps not surprising that the great majority of these studies are highly critical, even in those instances where the author is sympathetic to the Kadet program.[2] Scholars have faulted the Kadets for excessive radicalism in both theory and tactics; for an insufficiently developed respect for law and a corresponding inability to condemn political violence; for a failure to distinguish between the Russian government and the Russian state, and to appreciate the fragility of the latter.[3] Conversely, some scholars have found the Kadets wanting in both vision and resolve, noting their tactical ambivalence or timidity, their increasingly bourgeois or elitist perspectives, and their preocccupation with statist and even great power concerns at the expense of social betterment.[4]

The disparity of these appraisals stems not only from the differing perspectives of their authors, but also from the focus of study. The Constitutional Democrats were more radical in 1906 than in 1917. The party was also far from homogenous, and had, for most of its history, right and left wings. Finally, there was a tension, even a dichotomy, in the very conception of the party, one reflected in its name. In a country lacking traditions of respect for law and the individual, the commitment to constitutionalism – by which Kadets meant political and personal liberties and a rule-of-law state – was not easily joined to a commitment to democracy. Kadets' recognition that constitutionalism was a concept alien to most of the population was signaled by their decision, in January 1906, to give themselves an additional name, the "Party of People's Freedom." They were also painfully aware of the problems posed by the "double visage" of the party. That they nonetheless tried to retain both faces had as much to do with their conception of what Russian liberalism should be as it did with tactical considerations.

Liberalism

The Kadet party grew out of the liberation movement, the initiators of which were liberal zemstvo activists, or *zemtsy*, such as Ivan Petrunkevich and Dmitrii Shakhovskoi.[5] These were men with real experience of rural Russia and the problems bedeviling it. They believed passionately in the importance of human liberty and a rule-of-law state that would protect citizens from the arbitrariness and illegality of Russian government. But they were also deeply concerned by the plight of Russia's poor peasants, so that from the start the kind of liberalism they had in mind was one that would promote and improve the welfare of Russia's peasant masses as well as secure the liberties, rights, and participation in politics desired by more educated and privileged groups of which they were representatives.

Zemtsy began discussing the problems of rural Russia in the early 1890s. By the end of the decade growing frustration provided the impetus for discussion of ways and means to organize like-minded people to persuade the government to enact social reforms, broaden civil liberties, and grant some political participation. In June 1902 they began publishing a journal abroad, *Osvobozhdenie* (Liberation), that would help organize such groups and disseminate their ideas. Its appearance marked, as George Fischer has noted, the transformation of Russian liberalism from a "state of mind" into a movement.[6]

The effort to establish the paper and organize groups around it also meant attracting intellectuals and urban professionals. Most notable of these were the young Marxist economist Petr Struve and the historian Pavel Miliukov. What intellectuals like Struve and Miliukov brought to the burgeoning liberal movement was not so much radicalism as the theoretical underpinnings that helped articulate what twentieth-century Russian liberalism was, as well as the publicistic skills necessary to disseminate its ideals and program. Struve, with his background in Marxism and growing interest in neo-idealism, contributed a powerful theoretical articulation of human liberty as an end in itself. He also helped connect the commitment to freedom to social reformism.[7] Miliukov brought a rich knowledge of Russia's past, as well as of European history which could provide the background against which to evaluate Russia's experience.

In 1902 Miliukov began to investigate the history of Russian liberalism and socialism, coming to the conclusion that the two had a great deal in common. The most important features flowed from their common origin in the Westernized nobility: Russian liberalism, no less than socialism, grew out of the intelligentsia tradition. It had always been more intellectual, more humanitarian, and less class-based than classical European liberalism; over time, it became more "democratic" in its social composition as well. It differed from Russian socialism in being more practical in its immediate goals, and above all in its awareness that political liberty had to be secured before social issues could be justly resolved.[8]

By 1903 Russian liberals were ready to insist that one of the distinguishing characteristics of Russian liberalism was a commitment to constitutionalism. Both Miliukov and Struve agreed in the pages of *Osvobozhdenie* that reform-minded *zemtsy* who did not recognize Russia's need for institutionalization, popular representation, and a written constitution that would make the government subject to law had no place in the future liberal party.

A second principle that liberals pledged themselves to was that of democracy. They believed that liberalism could not represent the interests of a single class, but must stand "above" classes and work for the whole nation, an orientation they called *nad-klassnost'*. This was both a principled and a pragmatic stand. They believed Russia's population was becoming more politicized, and would demand a voice in determining its own fate and the fate of the nation. They envisioned forming a political party, and that party would have to attract popular support and win votes. But their commitment to democracy also reflected their very notion of what progressive politics meant in the twentieth century. It was not a matter of the enlightened few acting for the many, but of all the population being represented equally. Not every liberal was wholly supportive of the principle of universal, equal, direct suffrage – some felt Russia was not as yet ready for that step – but Russian liberals were by 1903 committed to the principle of general franchise.

The third component of liberalism worked out by these individuals was social reform. They believed that liberalism could no longer be understood as simply the extension of political liberty and civil rights: *every* citizen had to have the opportunity to exercise liberty, and that could not happen as long as huge portions of the population lived in great poverty and lacked equal access to education.

Perhaps one of the most eloquent expressions of these views was made by Prince Dmitrii Shakhovskoi. Since he was a zemstvo man, it helps underscore the fact that Russian liberalism was not radicalized by the intelligentsia, who had moved away from the more modest, pragmatic zemstvo set of goals appropriate to Russian conditions, as Vasilii Maklakov would later charge.[9] This was how Shakhovskoi defined Russian liberalism for the founding congress of the Union of Liberation in January 1904:

> It consists in the affirmation of liberty as the fundamental demand of life. In this foundation we see . . . not only the wisest, most practical means for our contemporary policy, but also the basic good of social life which we value for itself independently of its practical results . . . No less than other political parties we have in mind economic and social reforms. In our time a liberal program is unthinkable and impossible without a broad plan of social improvements in which and through which freedom finds its concrete realization. Agrarian reform, factory and labor legislation, the whole aggregate of tasks of economic and social policy must find a place in our program, but all on the grounds of and in connection with our basic foundation – freedom of the individual. . . . Freedom, as the genuine and universal principle of politics, is the freedom of all and not only of some. The democratic principle is the logical and moral consequence of the liberal program, and however

unclear the distant prospects of democracy, we must say: we accept the consequences together with the foundation . . . In the development of Russian liberalism the democratic tendency is both a firm historical tradition and an urgent practical necessity. Any liberalism other than a democratic one would lack soil in Russian society and would not find in it a response.[10]

Some conservatives would later charge (and some scholars would agree) that this form of Russian liberalism was not really liberalism at all. It was too radical, too interventionist, too little concerned with strict legality, the suggestion being that it was a not quite genuine offspring of true liberalism, being somehow distorted through the Russian prism. The substance of such a charge is undermined by putting "Kadet" liberalism in the context of the reorientation of European liberalism at the turn of the century. In Britain and France liberal parties were embracing the principle of broad social legislation, and not only in order to compete with socialist parties for the mass vote. Liberals were also responding to the moral and economic issues raised by the very phenomenon of modern, industrial society, which entailed rethinking classical liberal ideas about the nature of liberty and the relationship of the individual and the community.[11]

Looked at in this way, it is clear that the mainstream of Russian liberalism, as espoused by the Kadets, was not illiberal. Miliukov could in fact assert that it was *easier* for Russians to embrace the new liberalism than for west Europeans, since Russians lacked the distrust of state intervention and of limits on the enjoyment of individual rights that hampered older liberal traditions in Europe from accommodating state-directed social reform.[12]

The party program, affirmed at the 1905 founding congress and only slightly amended before 1917, reflected these values. A good part of the program embodied a traditionally liberal emphasis on liberty and individual rights, separation of church and state, a rule-of-law government and independent courts. Articles in the first four sections of the program set out the party's commitment to personal inviolability, freedom of speech, conscience, and assembly, equality of all before the law without distinction on the basis of religion, nationality, or social origin, and elimination of special courts. Liberal values which also reflected distinctively Russian conditions were embodied in the section extending rights of local self-government, and in the general emphasis on decentralization and extension to communities of greater control over local affairs, including education, as well as in the article guaranteeing citizens freedom of movement and abolishing the internal passport system.[13]

The program also dealt extensively, however, with social issues, including provisions for social welfare and protection of labor that would not become part of liberal programs in other countries for some time to come. The nine articles dealing specifically with labor guaranteed the right to unionize and strike; the extension of protective labor legislation and of an independent overview of labor conditions, along with criminal sanctions for violation of labor laws; introduction of the eight-hour working day – immediately where possible, gradually elsewhere – and introduction of mandatory health insurance, contributed to by employers, and state old age security and disability allowances. Also of material interest to the laboring population were the articles in the section on financial policy calling for the introduction of a progressive income tax and progressive tax on inheritance, a general lowering of indirect taxes, and a gradual repeal of indirect taxes on items of general consumption.

The agrarian section of the party's program was the most controversial, particularly the two articles addressing the land hunger of the peasantry.[14] These articles provided for the creation of a state land fund, whose holdings would be transferred to peasants in need of arable land, with the type of tenure dependent upon customs of land ownership and usage in any given region. The major sticking point was the source of lands in the reserve fund, since it would include not only state, crown, and monastery lands but also, in some cases, expropriated private holdings; the state was to bear the cost of reimbursing owners for their land, and at a "just" rather than market price.

The agrarian platform was a compromise, meant to strike a balance between party members who favored more sweeping expropriations and others who insisted, on both ideological and pragmatic grounds, that respect for rights of private property was a critical component of a liberal program. This balance was a workable one in the initial phase of the party's existence: while the agrarian platform undoubtedly alienated some landowners who might otherwise have voted for Kadet candidates in local and national elections, it was apparently an attractive feature for those peasants who did vote for the Kadet ticket in elections to the First and Second Dumas.

At the party's founding congress in October 1905, Miliukov justifiably declared that by virtue of their program the Constitutional Democrats were "the most left of any group analogous to us in western Europe." Some critics of the party have suggested that this was a fundamental political miscalculation: a liberal party organizing itself in a backward country should not set out to achieve social reforms more far-reaching than those advanced by liberal parties in the most progressive states of the time. To do so was to risk alienating the party's "natural" constituency – urban middle classes and professionals, and the progressive gentry – in hopes of attracting a mass following for whom socialist platforms would be more attractive anyway.

Kadets were in fact determined to build a mass party, a consideration which necessitated inclusion of social reform measures if they were to hope to compete with socialist parties. But as has been noted, inclusion of those measures owed as much to conviction as to political calculation. Protection of the interests of the laboring population was thus not only good politics but the right thing to do, a conviction which explains why the Kadets did not alter their program until 1917, despite changes in the electoral laws and the political climate which seemingly made programmatic changes politically expedient.

Organization and Social Composition

According to party statutes adopted at the 1905 founding congress, the party's affairs would be run by an elected central committee which would also have the right to co-opt additional members. The most authoritative body of the party was its national congress, to be held annually; the party congress elected the central committee and only the congress had the power to change the party program. The central committee had approximately 40 to 45 members at any given time; particularly heavily represented were professors and scholars (Miliukov, Struve, A. Kizevetter, A. Kornilov, V. Vernadskii, L. Petrazhitskii), lawyers and jurists (M. Vinaver, V. Nabokov, Maklakov, F. Kokoshkin, S. Muromtsev, M. Mandelshtam, V. and I. Gessen), and liberal zemstvo activists (A. Koliubakin, Petrunkevich, F. Rodichev, Shakhovskoi, and P. D. and P. D. Dolgorukov).[15]

From its founding, the party energetically set about building a national organization, often making use of existing liberation groups. In one respect, the pattern of Constitutional Democrats' organization mirrored that of *all* political parties in the empire, legal or otherwise, in that it followed lines of transportation. As V. V. Shelokhaev has noted, most political organizations were to be found in cities and towns; the further one went from railway lines and developed roads, the less one encountered any sort of organized political activity. More specifically, a strong correlation existed between areas of zemstvo activity and Kadet activity. Of a total of 346 Kadet organizations established between 1905 and 1907, 307 were located in European Russia; of these, 247 were located in the 34 provinces with zemstvos.[16]

As Terence Emmons has demonstrated, the Kadets tended to be strongest in bigger cities.[17] The two capitals, far and away the most populous cities of the empire, were Kadet strongholds. Moscow had more than 8,500 party members and 17 district party committees, in addition to the city- and province-level committees. Petersburg had approximately 9,000 party members and 12 district committees. Outside the capitals, important areas for the Kadets included Kiev province, with more than 3,400 registered party members; Astrakhan, with 1,600; the Don oblast, with 2,450; Kherson province, including the city of Odessa, with more than 1,700; and Lifland province, with 1,200. Bessarabia, Vladimir, Kostroma, Perm, Saratov, Tauride, Tver, Tiflis, Tula, Kharkov, and Iaroslavl provinces had 500 or more members, as did the Siberian provinces of Tomsk and Einisei. Kazan, which boasted a university, had 400 members in its city organization.[18]

Explaining why Kadets were able to build strong organizations in some areas but not in others is frequently difficult, given the near absence of studies of the party outside the capital cities. One exception to this is a fascinating study by I. V. Narskii of political parties in the four Urals provinces of Perm, Ufa, Orenburg, and Viatka in the years 1901–16. Narskii found that extremist parties of the left and right flourished in the Urals: only in Orenburg did liberal and moderate political groups account for more than 13 percent of political organizations (although Kadets and Octobrists were well-represented in each provincial capital city). He also found that only the largest cities had more than one party's organization, suggesting how far removed Urals residents were from pluralistic perspectives. Despite the numerical inferiority of the liberals, both the extreme right and left directed most of their political polemics against the Kadets rather than against each other, both sides fearing liberals' potential attractiveness to voters they hoped to claim for their own organizations. Narskii suggests that the polarization and intolerance of Urals politics may have been paradigmatic of conditions in other, equally less-developed areas on the fringes or outside of European Russia; the political center on the "periphery" was small and frequently embattled.[19]

Determining the social composition of the party is also difficult. Data is incomplete and is frequently available only for 1905–6, and its use is complicated by the inconsistent terminology or categories employed by local Kadet groups in identifying the occupation or social estate of their members. What is clear, however, is that the make-up of the party was diverse, and that Kadet groups in various regions could have very different social and occupational profiles. The Vasileostrov district party organization in St Petersburg, for example, included 142 workers, 36 artisans, 57 clerks and shop assistants – all people of decidedly humble status – as well as 49 traders and merchants, 27 state servants (*chinovniki*), 38 office workers (*sluzhashchie*), 12 teachers, 16 engineers, 31 university faculty and 43 students, a factory owner, and a justice of the peace. In contrast, the composite data for five provincial city organizations of the party, amounting to over 1,000 individuals, show nine workers, 111 artisans and shop clerks, 143 "petty bourgeoisie" (*meshchane*), 163 peasants, 92 traders and merchants, 232 *chinovniki*, 224 members of the intelligentsia, seven students, 18 large landowners, eight urban property owners, nine factory owners, and three clerics, as well as 25 people of unknown occupation. Still another picture is presented by the Estonian national group of the Kadet party in Narva, which was composed of 55 workers, 30 artisans and shop clerks, 30 merchants, and 15 members of the intelligentsia.[20]

The number of women in the party is also difficult to gage, since few Kadet groups gave specific information on gender. The party leadership was certainly male-dominated – only one woman, Ariadna Tyrkova, was on the central committee before 1917. The party program included several provisions of interest to women, but Kadets' commitment to equality for women was rather ambivalent; the program's extension of the suffrage to women, for example, passed by the barest minimum of votes, and the best-known fracas of the party's founding congress was between Pavel Miliukov and his wife over this issue.[21] At the same time, the Kadets were the only non-socialist party promising the vote and full civil rights to all citizens irrespective of gender.[22]

The data we have available thus shows that by social composition the Kadets were what they claimed to be, a socially diverse and "non-class" party, and not a "bourgeois" party as their rivals and critics charged. In the formative first seven months of its existence the party attracted not insignificant numbers of peasants and workers (though not so many as they hoped), large numbers of the so-called "petty bourgeois" – artisans, shop clerks and retail workers, and small traders – and large numbers of schoolteachers and low-salary white collar employees, that is, the lower middle classes. The Kadets had relatively small numbers of the "big bourgeoisie" – bankers, capitalists and large-scale businessmen, prosperous urban property owners, industrialists; these people were more attracted to the Octobrists or, after 1909, to the pro-business Progressive Party. Even if the term "bourgeoisie" is employed more elastically to include members of the liberal professions and the intelligentsia – that is, *any* non-noble individual enjoying a middling income or better, and not engaged in manual labor – more than half the party membership was not bourgeois.

Left-wing critics of the party nonetheless labeled the Kadets "bourgeois." They did so on the grounds that the goals the Kadets worked for were, at bottom, bourgeois, and that the effect of a Kadet victory would be to deliver power into the hands of the bourgeoisie. In their view, Kadets cynically included in their program popular provisions that they would not or could not implement; pressuring the liberals to adopt more radical postures and at the same time "unmasking" their real nature and predicting their inevitable betrayal of the working masses were staples of extreme left political polemics.[23] The "bourgeois" label was a genuinely damaging one for a party seeking a broad social base; Shmuel Galai has argued that over the long term it significantly undermined the Kadets' credibility in the eyes of the working classes.[24]

The drawback to diversity was the difficulty it entailed for the party in trying to act consistently without pulling it apart. The principal fault line was not so much the oft repeated one of intellectuals versus *zemtsy* – some *zemtsy* were radical and some intellectuals were, or became, more conservative, Petr Struve being a prime example. But there were very real and deep-seated divisions, which reflected not only social and occupational differences, but also the different experiences of provincials and those living in major cities: the former group was much more exposed to unbridled arbitrariness and persecution by local authorities. This came up clearly, for example, at a 1908 regional conference organized by the party's Duma deputies in order to meet with representatives of provincial groups. One delegate reacted strongly to Struve's contention that sharp critiques of the party's cautious tactics in the Third Duma reflected Russians' political ignorance. Provincial dissatisfaction was to be explained not by political immaturity, he insisted, but by the fact that "in the provinces people often find themselves in a situation it is impossible to bear patiently." Fiery speeches in the Duma denouncing provincial conditions and government behavior were, for them, "balsam to our wounds."[25] Throughout the history of the party, the central committee tended to be more moderate and cautious in proposals than provincial representatives taken as a whole. Trying to assuage provincial concerns and win support for central committee positions was a perennial concern, one often necessitating concessions or compromises.

There were also significant differences on the issue of nationality policy. Minorities, most especially Ukrainians, Jews, Armenians, and to a certain degree Muslims, could be a crucial liberal constituency, attracted by the Kadet programmatic commitment to equality of all before the law, religious freedom, and national cultural self-determination. But representatives of those minority groups would increasingly feel that the party was not doing enough in the Duma to protect and advance their interests. At the fall 1909 party conference, for example, Ukrainian delegates charged that Kadets were only paying lip service to the principles of national minority rights.[26] These delegates warned that faith in liberal good intentions was being undermined, which would translate into loss of votes if the party did not change its behavior.

On the other hand, there was a balancing act going on. For example, provincials reporting in 1906 on their progress in organizing a Kadet group in Briansk noted hostility to the Polish autonomy called for in the party program, adding that few individuals really understood what autonomy was; they were also running up against the problem of anti-Semitism.[27] Pursuing a mass electorate, while espousing equal rights for

Jews and other national groups, could pose problems. Even the Kadets' somewhat tepid support for women's suffrage created difficulties. At the second party congress, in January 1906, the Tatar delegate I. Akchurin strenuously opposed women's suffrage, claiming that it ran contrary to Muslim religious principles and warning that if Kadets insisted on making this a binding part of their program "3 million Muslim votes will be lost."

What all this meant was that Constitutional Democrats sometimes had to employ highly ambiguous language or less than perfect compromise tactics in order to satisfy all their disparate groups. The heterogeneous party could not always be clear cut, consistent, and decisive in its positions, which could translate into loss of votes and heightened suspicions about the party's nature and intentions. As Vasilii Maklakov later insisted, the quest for unity caused the party to vacillate, to appear "insincere."[28] This problem of course raises the important question of why Kadets did not cease trying to accommodate so many, why they did not split into several smaller, more cohesive and ideologically united groups. It was frequently rumored that the liberals were on the verge of splitting into different parties, and in 1913–14 it even appeared that such a split was imminent; so why did the leadership work assiduously to prevent it?

Purely practical considerations played a role. Virtually all the Kadet leadership, even those most dissatisfied with the party and Miliukov's tactical lines, believed that the only hope for effecting change lay in being a large party. For instance, Petr Struve declined offers to come over to the tiny Party of Peaceful Renovation in 1907, despite his ideological affinities with that group, because, as he explained, only a mass party could hope to have political influence. Similarly, although Maklakov in 1912 told a friend of his admiration for "Octobrism as liberalism," he went on to express his conviction that should the Kadets draw any closer to the Octobrists they would simply forfeit their voters to the Social Democrats.[29]

October 1905 to June 1907

The first ten months of the party's existence, from its founding in October 1905 through the dissolution of the First Duma, is the best-studied period of the party and also the one most frequently criticized. It was then that Kadets were at the height of their influence, but it was also their most militant phase, during which the liberals continued working with the radical socialists even after promulgation of the October Manifesto – the policy known as "no enemies on the left." This policy was a considered but costly one, reflecting a basic dilemma confronting liberals: while experience showed that moderates acting in isolation were ignored by the government, continued liberal cooperation with the left reinforced the government's disinclination to distinguish between those desiring peaceful change and genuine revolutionaries.

In 1906 in Russia's first-ever national elections, Kadets garnered over 37 percent of the urban vote and nearly one-third of the seats in the Duma, making them the largest single party in the lower house. The party's excellently organized electoral campaign and the revolutionary parties' boycott of the elections contributed to this victory, but liberals were also right to interpret it as popular approval of their program. They thus entered the Duma feeling empowered to fight for its implementation. The Duma's first formal declaration of legislative intent basically embodied the Kadet program; when the government simply rejected it as "inadmissible," Kadets joined in a unanimous Duma vote demanding the resignation of the entire cabinet. The possibility for constructive work all but disappeared a mere three weeks into the Duma's term; much of its time would now be given over to denunciation of both government actions and policy. Although the Kadets did work to forestall the most provocative and procedurally illegal proposals emanating from the large Trudovik group to their left, on whose support they depended in order to form a voting majority, speeches by Kadet deputies were often as fiery and intemperate as those of any radical. In short, Kadets made a number of politically unsound moves in what was admittedly a novel and difficult situation. For the new legislature to have had any chance of functioning successfully, both the government and the Duma's largest party needed to demonstrate more patience, good will, and ability to compromise than either side seemingly possessed.[30]

On July 9, 1906, having decided it was impossible to work with the First Duma, the government issued an order dissolving it. The Kadet response to this act was one of the greatest miscalculations in the party's history. Outraged by the dissolution and certain that it would provoke full-scale disorder, party leaders decided the Duma should respond by calling upon the population to protest the act through passive resistance, refusing to pay taxes or furnish army recruits. One hundred and twenty Kadet Duma deputies, along with 80 Trudovik and Social Democratic deputies, converged on Vyborg, Finland where they could discuss the text of the appeal – drafted by Miliukov – beyond the reach of the Russian police. Although many Kadet deputies questioned the efficacy of this form of protest, all those present signed the appeal.[31]

The Kadets had seriously misread the country's mood. The few disorders which broke out on behalf of the Duma were easily quelled by the authorities, and the "Vyborg Appeal," as it came to be known, evoked little popular response. Its signatories, however, were prosecuted for their illegal act; in one fell swoop the majority of the Kadets' most prominent figures, including Petrunkevich, Shakhovskoi, Nabokov, Vinaver, and Kokoshkin, became ineligible to participate in future Dumas. The party's sponsorship of an appeal to citizens to break the law also stained its reputation, calling into doubt its political responsibility and the credibility of its liberalism. If it is too much to say that the Kadets developed what one scholar has termed a "Vyborg complex," an enduring "distrust of the masses," the ignominious end to the First Duma did have a lasting impact on their views.[32] The majority of the leadership were resolved, in future, not to underestimate the power of the government, not to count too heavily on the militancy of the population, and not to act outside the law.

The Second Duma was convened February 20, 1907 and dissolved just 94 days later; this time, the legislature's brief life span owed relatively little to Kadet mistakes. The Kadets were determined to devote themselves to constructive legislation, making their slogan "Preserve the Duma." However, the loss of support from more conservative *zemtsy* and electoral competition from the revolutionary parties (who decided not to boycott the elections), reduced their contingent to approximately 100 seats; while still the largest single party in the Duma, their position was not dominant. In addition, the greatly expanded representation of radical parties of both right and left, most of whom regarded the parliamentary process with contempt, meant Kadets could do little to moderate the behavior of a deeply polarized body. With hindsight, some Kadet leaders felt the Duma might have lasted longer had the liberals forthrightly condemned political violence when this issue came up for debate in May, as Prime Minister P. A. Stolypin desired; reluctance to sever ties with the left and repugnance at governmental resort to violence prevented them from doing so. But given the unruliness and radicalism of the Second Duma, such a step would likely not have changed the authorities' decision to obtain a more cooperative legislature by simultaneously dissolving the Second Duma and promulgating a new, much more restrictive electoral law.[33]

The Third of June System

From the dissolution of the Second Duma the Kadets had to operate under new and difficult conditions. The electoral law of June 3, 1907, by sharply curtailing the representation of national minorities and less prosperous urban dwellers, cut deeply into the liberals' constituency, while government obstruction hampered their efforts to campaign. The Kadets were reduced to a minority opposition group in the Third Duma, initially holding 54 seats. The Octobrists were now the largest party and the political "center," with 120 seats; to their right were some 200 more conservative deputies as well as nearly 50 proponents of the radical right.[34] The Kadets found themselves shut out of the most important committees, heckled when they gave speeches, and denounced as seditious, unpatriotic, and dis-honorable in the speeches of others. In these conditions the Kadet deputies in the Duma – led by Miliukov, who had finally been eligible for election – adopted a defensive strategy intended to restore their reputation and bring with it some ability to influence the legislature. They worked conscien-tiously in committees, eschewed provocative gestures, and offered a reso-lution condemning all forms of political violence, terror included.[35]

The Kadet's position was now, as Miliukov put it in 1909, that of "the opposition *of* His Majesty, not opposition *to* His Majesty." The controversy generated by this remark, within the party as well as on the left, showed that many Kadets were not entirely comfortable with the role of "loyal opposition."[36] Yet most of the leadership considered this role the only tenable one for a party committed to parliamentary government and peaceful change, and the fraction's careful conduct did mitigate much of the majority's initial hostility. By spring 1909, with order restored in the countryside, Octobrists were ready to cooperate with the Kadets and the Progressive fraction in pressing for promised reforms. The Kadets worked with Octobrists to pass generously amended versions of government bills on religious faith, and interpellations on government persecution of the press and of trade unions. Kadets also secured minor modifications in other bills, such as one extending to two years the provision for teaching non-Russian elementary-school children in their native language.[37]

These were exceedingly modest accomplishments when weighed against the enormous expectations Kadets brought to the First Duma. But had these measures been realized in law they would at least have proved that the Duma could accomplish *some* progressive reform, and therefore might have helped check mounting public indifference toward the Duma and "politics" in general. Unfortunately, most of these efforts did not become law, as reform bills passed by the Duma were gutted or killed in the State Council, the conservative upper chamber of the legislature, or failed to win the tsar's approval. Successful right-wing obstruction of other components of Stolypin's reform program had the further consequence of shifting his energies to projects less likely to provoke conservative ire, most especially nationality policy.

Kadets watched with dismay the development of the "nationalist cam-paign" in 1910–11, for the various bills intended to tighten national bonds in the empire and bolster the "genuinely Russian" unleashed a wave of Great Russian chauvinism that took even Stolypin by surprise. Kadets would have to try to oppose discriminatory legislation which flew in the face of their liberal values and whose results would be, they believed, dan-gerously divisive. They were also experiencing strong pressure from national minorities, who felt Kadets needed to do more to advance or protect the rights of minority citizens. But liberals realized it would be difficult to deflect strong passions without finding themselves again isolated and powerless in the Duma. Their position was further complicated by differences within the leadership. A minority on the right, ideologically inspired by Petr Struve, felt that the Kadets were indeed insufficiently nationally minded, that the party did not give enough thought to preservation of the empire and promotion of a Russian national identity that could meld the peoples of the empire into a genuine nation.[38] Small wonder that Fedor Kokoshkin, one of the party's experts on nationality issues, warned in fall 1909 that "the nationality question could become the rock on which the party smashes."[39]

The most contentious nationality bills were those concerning Finland. Ostensibly intended to integrate Finland into the empire's post-1905 institutional order, they in effect deprived the Finns of the last remnants of self-government Russia had granted them in their 1809 Constitution. With support from the left wing of the Octobrists the Kadets fought these measures in Duma committees and in strong speeches on the Duma floor, as well as in press campaigns, but were powerless to prevent their passage. They found it equally impossible to staunch the torrent of anti-Semitic vituperation issuing from the Duma's extreme right. And, as feared, they were pilloried for their efforts. The liberal paper *Rech'* was accused of accepting a 250,000 ruble bribe from the Finns, and Miliukov even received death threats from the Union of Russian People.[40] The Third Duma completed its five-year term, in the opinion of Miliukov, discredited in the eyes of the country and "the whole civilized world," while the Kadets had almost nothing to show for their tactics of compromise and restraint.[41] Nor did the results of the 1912 elections to the Fourth Duma promise any improvement: while massive government interference in the elections only augmented slightly the number of conservative deputies, it did prevent the Kadets and other opposition parties from making significant gains.[42]

The mood of the country was at the same time becoming more confrontational, as the strike movement resumed and spread, disorders occurred again at universities, and the government appeared to be settling into a consistently reactionary course. Kadets faced the prospect of becoming completely irrelevant politically if they failed to respond to new conditions. There were some Kadet leaders, in fact, such as Nikolai Nekrasov, who believed the Kadets must finally shed their "illusions" about the Duma, and regard it strictly as a podium for denouncing the regime's policies rather than as an institution capable of achieving meaningful reform. They urged a new turn leftward and a focus on organizational work outside the Duma, with the moderate socialists and popular masses.[43]

Most of the leadership considered such an orientation politically unrealistic as well as an abandonment of constitutionalism. As a sort of half measure the party would instead adopt more confrontational and demonstrative tactics in the Duma. What this meant in practice was the reintroduction of old liberal bills which had no real prospect of passage, such as that on universal suffrage, greater use of interpellations into government illegality, and voting with the left to reject the entire budget appropriations of the most objectionable ministries.

These tactics exacerbated the frustrations of more conservative party notables, who saw in them an ill-considered return to former tactics that had not worked the first time around. Individuals such as Maklakov, Chelnokov, Gredeskul, and Tyrkova desired a fundamental reorientation in a different direction. Kadets should not only be *more* moderate, but should also rethink some of their program, most especially the agrarian provisions. Their natural allies were not the socialists, who never ceased abusing the Kadets, but rather the Progressives and left Octobrists, groups committed to reform by strictly legal means and more sensitive to Russia's state interests. In spring 1914 divisions between these two orientations were so pronounced that observers predicted the Kadets would formally split into their "two constituent parts," forming a national liberal party and a radical-democratic one.[44]

The condition of the party outside the major cities was also cause for concern. The government never formally legalized the Constitutional Democratic party, which meant individuals in state service were prohibited from belonging to it. Government harassment, growing public indifference to politics, and the party's chronically poor finances all contributed to the melting away of membership. Where there had been 346 Kadet organizations in 1906, by 1909 this figure had shrunk to 100; by 1913–14 there were only 80. Surveying this state of affairs at a party meeting of 1913, Ariadna Tyrkova exclaimed, "The central committee is a fiction. Who are we? Imposters? Last Mohicans? Kadet diehards?"[45]

Given these circumstances, some scholars have suggested that the outbreak of World War I came as something of a relief to the Kadet party.[46] Disagreements over orientation and tactics could be shelved as Kadet liberals directed all their energies to the war effort. The government's tolerance of public organization in support of the war, however grudging and uneven, created new outlets for those energies, while the unambiguous patriotism of the party finally persuaded its conservative critics that Kadets were not lacking in national feeling.

At the outbreak of the war, the great majority of party members shared the conviction that differences within the party, within society at large, and between society and the government must all be temporarily suspended in the interests of national unity. A small minority on the left wing of the party agreed with Aleksandr Kerensky and the Trudoviks that the opposition should attempt to extract concessions from the government in exchange for its declarations of support, but most supported fully

Miliukov's declaration in the Duma, during the extraordinary one-day session called for on July 26, 1914, that the Constitutional Democrats "are united in this struggle. We set no conditions and demand nothing; on the scales of war we simply place our firm will for victory." The Kadet commitment to the "sacred union" between the people and its government was in fact so strong that the party persisted in refusing publicly to criticize the government well into 1915, despite the pointlessly repressive actions of civil and military authorities.[47]

As might be expected, the sort of language in which Kadets couched patriotic exhortations and disquisitions on the goals of the war differed from the more traditional and nationalistic language of parties to their right. The Kadets feared German militarism and also shared, to varying degrees, both the common enthusiasm for liberation of "our Slavic brothers" and less romantic great power considerations, particularly acquisition of Constantinople and control of the Dardanelles. However, Kadet publicists were equally likely to stress that the war would win greater freedom and justice within Russia: the loyal sacrifices of the Russian people *and* the need for enormous reconstruction loans from the democratic allies would ensure the far-reaching democratization of postwar Russia.[48]

Kadets threw themselves into war work of all kinds, including organization of relief for soldiers' families, the wounded, POWs, and refugees. They took active part in the two most influential national societies for war work, the All-Russian Union of Zemstvos and the All-Russian Union of Cities, dominating the latter from its founding in September 1914.[49] This activity corresponded to their patriotic sentiments and notions of civic duty, but liberals were also conscious of its future political potential. Natalia Dumova suggests that Kadets realized war work in public organizations could serve as a surrogate for the political activity that had long been impossible in the provinces, allowing them to reanimate ties with each other and reestablish their influence in local society.[50] The speed with which some 169 local Kadet groups sprang into being after the February Revolution probably owed a good deal to the war work of the preceding years.

From late spring 1915, however, differences within the party resurfaced in response to military setbacks and government repression. Anger towards the government and the demand for a ministry responsible to the Duma grew. The gravity of the military threat finally enabled Kadets, Progressives, Octobrists and a portion of the Nationalist fraction in the Duma to bury their differences and form a coalition, the Progressive Bloc, whose moving spirit was Miliukov. The bloc's program was intentionally moderate, in order that it build a truly broad base in the Duma and appear as reasonable as possible to the government. It demanded, for instance, a ministry enjoying popular confidence, rather than one responsible to the

Duma, and its proposed changes – including an end to religious persecution, easing of censorship, and restoration of labor unions – were not sys-
temic ones. A number of Kadets, in fact, considered these demands scarcely
adequate to the bloc's goal of restoring public confidence in the government and its ability to win the war; they also worried that it entailed too
much compromise of the party program.[51] Had the bloc's program been
accepted by the tsar – and the chances for this appeared good in August
1915 – Kadets would no doubt have swallowed their reservations and
swung solidly behind it.

But Nicholas instead ignored the bloc and prorogued the Duma until
February 1916. Despite this blow Miliukov and the other "centrists" on the
party central committee made preservation of the bloc, in hopes of its eventual acceptance by the government, their tactical lodestar. This decision
necessitated extreme restraint on issues such as Jewish equality, in order
to retain the more conservative wing of the bloc. From that point tensions
within the party mounted unchecked. At party conferences and meetings
increasing numbers of provincial delegates and members of the central
committee lashed out at these tactics as ineffectual and dangerous. In fall
1916, as apprehensions about the country's revolutionary mood grew
more widespread, the growing left wing of the party warned that if the
Kadets did not make common cause with the people and help organize new,
radical organizations outside the Duma, they would lose whatever popular
influence they still enjoyed – and with it the hope of channeling an out-
burst into constructive channels. Other Kadets countered that such steps
were too likely to fan revolutionary passions, with potentially disastrous
consequences for the war effort.[52] The tsarist secret police observed these
disputes with satisfaction, reporting that the Kadets were too internally
divided to the able to agree on any line of tactics at all.[53]

However, in the first few months following the revolutionary upheaval
in 1917 Kadets had tried to avert, the party displayed both unity and
dynamism. Gripped by the general euphoria over the nearly "bloodless"
overthrow of tsarism, most Kadets could persuade themselves that political freedom and a more competent administration would unify the country
for victory. Miliukov and other Kadets played a prominent role in the organization of the new regime and assumed five ministerial portfolios in the
Provisional Government – those of foreign affairs, transport, education,
agriculture, and Finland. At the local level, in cities all over Russia, Kadets
frequently took the initiative in forming "Committees of Public
Organizations" which brought together representatives from a wide variety
of groups for the maintenance of law and order.[54]

Some Kadets on the left suggested at the Seventh Party Congress in late
March 1917 that in the new conditions of truly democratic, republican
Russia the party must promptly reach out to the masses, cooperating

closely with socialists and articulating a program of broad social reform. The great majority of the 300 delegates to the congress, however, strongly endorsed the central committee's insistence that in order not to exacerbate social tensions and political polarization, thereby threatening the war effort, the party should instead preserve its "non-class" orientation, working for the interests of the nation as a whole. It must defer discussion of fundamental social and economic reforms until convocation of a democratically elected constituent assembly, which alone would have the legitimacy to chart the country's future course.[55]

Meanwhile, the Kadets marshaled their considerable organizational and publicistic skills to build support for the new government and the party's positions. Dozens of brochures were produced in huge editions of up to 700,000 copies and distributed nationally, Kadet newspapers began appearing in 25 provincial cities, and special efforts were made to bring the party's message to peasants and to soldiers' groups.[56]

These efforts could not staunch the ebb in party popularity that commenced in the spring. Problems stemmed primarily from the war. Although differences existed over war aims, virtually all Kadets believed Russia must continue the fight until total victory. Even after Foreign Minister Miliukov's refusal to heed the soviet's pressure for modification of war aims triggered massive street demonstrations in late April, resulting in organization of a coalition cabinet and his own ousting from office, the official Kadet position on the war remained unchanged. This position – with its concomitant insistence on the need for self-discipline and elevation of national interests over class ones – was increasingly unpopular with a war-weary population hungry for social reform. Looking back, several Kadets who pressed for a negotiated peace identified their party's equation of the revolution with the war effort as a fateful mistake. As Vladimir Nabokov put it, "[I]f it had been clearly realized in the first weeks that for Russia the war was hopelessly lost and that all attempts to continue it would lead nowhere . . . catastrophe would perhaps have been successfully avoided."[57]

As order in the country disintegrated and class and national antagonisms deepened, the party leadership became still less inclined to seek compromise. In the opinion of most of the central committee, the pressures and demagoguery of the extreme left were enough to guarantee that popular demands would keep escalating and moderate socialists keep lurching leftward. Care for the nation as it fought a terrible war required more statemindedness than either the people or socialists were displaying.

While there was ample cause for the majority to think as it did, it is hard to dispute William Rosenberg's suggestion that the Kadet decision to pursue the "politics of state rather than popular consciousness" was tactically disastrous. Elections in May and June to the Petrograd and Moscow city councils demonstrated graphically the Kadets' declining popularity; in the two cities that had always been their strongest centers of support they could not capture so much as 22 percent of the vote.[58] The party was hurt still more by the popular perception that it had conspired with General Lavr Kornilov, in late August, to overthrow the Provisional Government and suppress the Petrograd Soviet (the so-called "Kornilov Affair.") The Kadets most likely did not engage in any conspiracy, but their repeated insistence on the need for strong government and their refusal to condemn unequivocally Kornilov's actions created grounds for the belief that they had taken sides against "democracy."[59] They found themselves discredited and politically isolated at the time of the Bolsheviks' successful October coup; their party was outlawed before the year was out.

Notes

1 Full-length studies devoted to the Kadets include Nathan Smith, "The Constitutional-Democratic Movement in Russia, 1902–1906" (PhD diss., University of Illinois, 1958); Judith Zimmerman, "Between Revolution and Reaction. The Constitutional Democratic Party, October 1905 to June 1907" (PhD diss., Columbia University, 1967); V. V. Shelokhaev, *Kadety – glavnaia partiia liberal'noi burzhuazii v bor'be s revoliutsiei, 1905–1907 gg.* (Moscow: Nauka, 1988); William G. Rosenberg, *Liberals in the Russian Revolution. The Constitutional Democratic Party, 1917–1921* (Princeton, NJ: Princeton University Press, 1974); Natalia G. Dumova, *Kadetskaia partiia v period pervoi mirovoi voiny i Fevral'skoi revoliutsii* (Moscow: Nauka, 1988). There is still no comprehensive history of liberalism in Russia. George Fischer's *Russian Liberalism* (Cambridge, Mass.: Harvard University Press, 1958), does not go beyond 1905; Victor Leontovitsch, *Geschichte des Liberalismus in Russland* (Frankfurt am Main: Vittorio Klostermann, 1957), excludes Kadets from his history of liberalism in Russia on the grounds that they were more properly radicals than liberals. Andrzej Walicki, *Legal Philosophies of Russian Liberalism* (Oxford: Oxford University Press, 1987), distinguishes between the developed legal consciousness of several Kadet jurists and that of most of the Kadet leadership.

2 The most notable exceptions are Shmuel Galai, particularly "The Tragic Dilemma of Russian Liberalism as Reflected in Ivan Il'ich Petrunkevich's Letters to His Son," *Jahrbucher für Geschichte Osteuropas* 29 (1981): 1–29 and Michael Karpovich, "Two Types of Russian Liberalism: Maklakov and Miliukov," in Ernest J. Simmons, ed., *Continuity and Change in Russian and Soviet Thought* (Cambridge, Mass.: Harvard University Press, 1955), 129–43.

3 See for example Leonard Schapiro, "The Vekhi Group and the Mystique of Revolution," *Slavonic and East European Review*, 34 (December 1955), reproduced in his *Russian Studies* (New York: Viking, 1986), 68–92; Richard Pipes, *Struve: Liberal on the Right, 1905–1944* (Cambridge, Mass.: Harvard University Press, 1980); Donald Treadgold, *Lenin and His Rivals* (New York,

1955); Anna Geifman, "The Kadets and Terrorism, 1905–1907," *Jahrbucher für Geschichte Osteuropas* 36 H. 2 (1988): 248–67.

4   See, for example, William Rosenberg, "Kadets and the Politics of Ambivalence," in Charles Timberlake, ed., *Essays on Russian Liberalism* (Columbia, Mo.: University of Missouri Press, 1972), 139–63 in addition to his *Liberals in the Russian Revolution*; Raymond Pearson, *The Russian Moderates and the Crisis of Tsarism, 1914–1917* (New York: Barnes and Noble, 1977) and his introduction to *Vtoroi vserossiiskii s'ezd Konstitutsionno-demokraticheskoi partii 5–11 yanvarya 1906 g.* (White Plains, NY: Kraus International, 1986). Soviet scholars, of course, had no choice but to condemn the Kadets as hypocritical enemies of working-class interests, an interpretation many revised under glasnost; a good illustration of the former view is the first monograph by Natalia G. Dumova, *Kadetskaia kontrrevoliutsiia i ee razgrom (Oktiabr' 1917–1920 gg.)* (Moscow: Nauka, 1982), which bears little resemblance to the views expressed in her 1988 monograph referred to above.

5   The literature on the liberation movement is extensive. The most important account of the Union of Liberation by a participant is Shakhovskoi's, "Soiuz osvobozhdeniia," in *Zarnitsy*, 2 (1909): 81–171. Studies particularly helpful for understanding constitutional democracy's outgrowth from the liberation movement are Klaus Frolich, *The Emergence of Russian Constitutionalism, 1900–1904: The Relationship between Social Mobility and Political Group Formation in Pre-revolutionary Russia*, trans. Suzanne M. Read (The Hague: M. Nijhoff, 1981); Shmuel Galai, *The Liberation Movement in Russia, 1900–1905* (Cambridge: Cambridge University Press, 1973); and K. F. Shatsillo, *Russkii liberalizm nakanune revoliutsii 1905–1907 gg.* (Moscow: Nauka, 1985).

6   Fischer, *Russian Liberalism*, 119.

7   Struve's role as a founder of the liberation movement, his signal contributions to early twentieth-century Russian liberal thought, and his gradual disenchantment with "Kadet" liberalism and the party he helped found, are explored in Richard Pipes, *Struve: Liberal on the Left, 1870–1905* and *Struve: Liberal on the Right, 1905–1944* (Cambridge, Mass.: Harvard University Press, 1970 and 1980).

8   Miliukov's most extensive treatment of the history of Russian liberalism and socialism, based on lectures he gave in the United States in 1903 and 1904, is *Russia and Its Crisis* (Chicago: University of Chicago Press, 1905), especially 281–2, 321–2, 398–9, 424–8.

9   Maklakov, a lawyer and founding member of the Constitutional Democratic party, was one of the most prominent representatives of its more conservative wing; in emigration, he wrote extensive critiques of the party's behavior, focusing on its radicalism in the years 1905–6; see V. A. Maklakov, *Vlast' i obshchestvennost' na zakate staroi Rossii (vospominaniia)* 3 vols. (Paris: Biblioteka "Illustrirovanāia Rossiia," 1936). The classic treatment of his polemic with Miliukov on this theme is Michael Karpovich, "Two Types of Russian Liberalism: Maklakov and Miliukov," in Ernest J. Simmons, ed., *Continuity and Change in Russian and Soviet Thought* (Cambridge, Mass.: Harvard University Press, 1955), 129–43.

10 "Pq" [Dmitrii Shakhovskoi], "Politika liberal'noi partii," *Osvobozhdenie*, 20 (March 19/April 1, 1904): 346.

11 On the origins and nature of the "new liberalism" in Great Britain and France, see Michael Freeden, *The New Liberalism: An Ideology of Social Reform* (Oxford: Clarendon Press, 1978), H. V. Emy, *Liberals, Radicals, and Social Politics, 1892–1914* (Cambridge: Cambridge University Press, 1973) and William Logue, *From Philosophy to Sociology* (DeKalb, Ill.: Northern Illinois University Press, 1983).

12 Miliukov, *Russia and Its Crisis*, 335–7.

13 The program as adopted by the founding congress is contained in *Konstitutsionno-demokraticheskaia partiia. S'ezd 12–18 oktiabria 1905 g.* (St Petersburg: Tipografiia tovarishchestva "Obshchestvennaia pol'za," 1905); an English translation of the slightly revised program issued by the second congress is in Basil Dmytryshyn, *Imperial Russia: A Source Book, 1700–1917*, 3rd edn (Fort Worth, Tex., 1990), 438–44.

14 The party's most extensive treatment of its agrarian program is the popular brochure by M. Ia. Gertsenshtein, *Zemel'naia reforma v programme partii narodnoi svobody (konstitutsionno-demokraticheskoi)* (Moscow: Tipografiia G. Lissnera i D. Sobko, 1906).

15 Composition of the central committee during its first two years is provided in the *Otchet tsentral'nogo komiteta K. D. partii za dva goda s 18 oktiabria 1905 g. po oktiabr' 1907 g.* (St Petersburg: Obshchestvennaia pol'za, 1907), 3–5. From January 1906 through April 1907 the central committee coopted another 25 individuals, including ten provincial representatives, members of national minorities, and Duma and State Council deputies. Only five central committee members resigned, three on the basis of disagreements over party policy or tactics (N. L'vov, M. Mandelshtam, N. Shchepkin).

16 Shelokhaev, *Kadety*, 61–3.

17 Terence Emmons, *The Formation of Political Parties and the First National Elections in Russia* (Cambridge, Mass.: Harvard University Press, 1983), 277.

18 Figures come from the first appendix in Shelokhaev, *Kadety*, 297–309; Shelokhaev has at least partial data for 56 of the 64 provinces which he shows as having Kadet organizations; he has some data for six of the 11 oblasts which he identifies as having Kadet organizations.

19 I. V. Narskii, *Politicheskie partii na urale (1901–1916): Avtoreferat* (Cheliabinsk: Cheliabinskii gos. universitet, 1995), 31–3, 36.

20 Shelokhaev, *Kadety*, 67–9. The figures listed all come from records of the Kadet central committee, in GARF; the city organizations in the composite are for Vladimir, Vologda, Kovensk, Orlov, and Sestrorechie provinces.

21 P. N. Miliukov, *Vospominaniia* (Moscow: Izd. Politicheskoi literatury, 1991), 208–9 and Ariadna Tyrkova–Vil'iams, *Na putiakh k svobode* (New York: Izdatel'stroimeni Chekhova, 1952), 240–3.

22 On the relationship of organized women's groups and the Kadets see Linda Edmondson, *Feminism in Russia, 1900–1917* (Stanford: Stanford University Press, 1984), 49–50, 60–3, 66–70.

23 A good example is the book by Lunacharskii, *Tri kadety* (St Petersburg, 1908?), dedicated to proving that Miliukov, Struve, and Rodichev were the

"servants of the bourgeoisie," for all their seeming support for popular needs.

24 Shmuel Galai, "The Kadet Quest for the Masses," in Robert B. McKean, ed., *New Perspectives in Modern Russian History* (New York: Macmillan, 1992), 93.

25 Meeting of Third Duma fraction of Kadet party with representatives of regional party groups, June 1 and 2, 1908, in GARF f. 523, op. 1, d. 6, ll. 87, 92.

26 Studies devoting considerable attention to Kadet relationships with national minorities are Olga Andriewsky, "The Politics of National Identity: The Ukrainian Question in Russia, 1904–1912" (PhD diss, Harvard, 1991), esp. 325–420, and Christopher Gassenschmidt, *Jewish Liberal Politics in Tsarist Russia, 1900–1914: The Modernization of Modern Jewry* (New York: New York University Press, 1995), who makes clear that several founding Kadets, including Vinaver and Sliozberg, had been initiators of the Jewish rights movement a decade earlier.

27 Report of the Briansk group, Orel gubernaia, to the central committee, in GARF f. 523, op. 1, d. 33, l. 1; this group also complained of harassment from the governor, financial difficulties, and even the aloofness of another Kadet group in the same uezd.

28 Maklakov, *Vlast i obshchestvennost'*, 484–7.

29 Pipes, *Struve: Liberal on the Right*, 44–5, and letter of Maklakov to A. V. Bobrishchev-Pushkin of October 30, 1912, quoted in Avrekh, *Tsarizm i IV duma*, 220–1.

30 For election results see Emmons, *Political Parties*, 351–6. Important Kadet accounts of the First Duma include M. M. Vinaver, *Konflikty v Pervoi dume* (St Petersburg: Tipografiia Obshchestvennaia pol'za, 1907), and Vasilii Maklakov's highly critical *Pervaia gosudarstvennaia duma* (Paris: YMCA Press, 1939); a Kadet justification of party behavior up to the elections to the Second Duma is A. A. Kizevetter, *Napadki na partii Narodnoi svobody i vozrazheniia na nikh* (Moscow: Tipografiia G. Lissnera i D. Sobko, 1906). The best English-language account of the First Duma is Abraham Ascher's excellent *The Revolution of 1905, Authority Restored* (Stanford: Stanford University Press, 1992), 81–110, 162–201.

31 The Kadets' account of the Vyborg Appeal, composed in 1910, is by M. M. Vinaver, *Istoriia vyborgskogo vozzvaniia (Vospominaniia)* (Petrograd: Izd. Partii narodnoi svobody, 1917; see also Miliukov, *Vospominaniia* 266–8. An account suggesting that Kadets were not so concerned to forestall disorders as they later claimed is Ascher, *The Revolution of 1905*, II, 201–10.

32 Raymond Pearson suggests that the experience of Vyborg intensified Kadet "distrust of the masses," leading to debasement of the party's policies and even betrayal of its ideals: "The Vyborg Complex," *Irish Slavonic Studies* (1980): 81.

33 On the elections, see Emmons, *Political Parties*, 365–71; on the issue of violence, see Melissa K. Stockdale, "Politics, Morality, and Violence: Kadet Liberals and the Question of Terror, 1902–1911," *Russian History*, 4 (Winter 1995), 455–80. The fullest Kadet appraisal of the Second Duma is Vasilii Maklakov, *Vtoraia gosudarstvennaia duma* (Paris: La Renaissance, 1948); the

best scholarly account is Ascher, *The Revolution of 1905: Authority Restored*, 292–329.

34   For an analysis of the Third Duma elections and of the composition of the Kadet and opposition fractions in the Third Duma, see Alfred Levin, *The Third Duma, Election and Profile* (Hamden, Conn.: Archon Books, 1973), esp. 29–36, 59–69, 95–111, 133–6.

35   The fullest studies of the Third Duma are Geoffrey Hosking, *The Russian Constitutional Experiment: Government and Duma, 1907–1914* (Cambridge: Cambridge University Press, 1974) and A. Ia. Avrekh, *Stolypin i tret'ia duma* (Moscow: Nauka, 1968); Kadet behavior in the Third Duma is examined in Thomas Riha, *A Russian European: Paul Miliukov in Russian Politics* (Notre Dame: University of Notre Dame Press, 1969), 153–93 and Melissa Kirschke Stockdale, *Paul Miliukov and the Quest for a Liberal Russia, 1880–1918* (Ithaca, NY: Cornell University Press, 1996), 173–97.

36   Miliukov made the remark at the London Lord Mayor's banquet, in summer 1909, as part of a Duma delegation to the British parliament; on the negative response see Riha, *A Russian European*, 178–9.

37   An overview of the party's legislative efforts in the Third Duma is L. Nemanov, "Itogi deiatel' nosti tret'ei gosudarstvennoi dumy," in *Ezhegodnik gazety Rech', 1912 g.* (St Petersburg, 1912), 97–117; more extended treatment is provided in the annual account of the fraction's activity, *Konstitutsionno-demokraticheskaia partiia: III gosudarstvennaia duma: Otchet fraktsii narodnoi svobody*, 5 vols (St Petersburg, 1908–12), which also contains the texts of the principal Kadet speeches in the Duma. On Kadet cooperation with the Octobrists see Ben-Cion Pinchuk, *The Octobrists in the First Duma, 1907–1912* (Seattle: University of Washington Press, 1974), 84–6.

38   For the views on nationality of the dissenting Kadets on the right see, esp., Richard Pipes, *Struve: Liberal on the Right*, 88–96, 174–86; Judith Zimmerman, "Russian Liberal Theory, 1900–1917," *Canadian-American Slavic Studies* I (Spring 1980): 1–20.

39   Meeting of Moscow branch of Kadet central committee, Nov. 27, 1909, in GARF f. 523, op. 1, d. 245. ll. 12–13.

40   For accounts of the Finnish legislation and debate surrounding it see Hosking, *Constitutional Experiment*, 106–16 and Stockdale, *Paul Miliukov*, 190–2. The charges of bribe-taking and the Kadets' unsuccessful suit for libel are reviewed in *Rech'* April 19, 1914.

41   P. N. Miliukov, "Politicheskie partii v Gosudarstvennoi dume za piat' let," in *Ezhegodnik gazety Rech', 1911 g.* (St Petersburg, 1911), 86.

42   Statistics for deputies to the Fourth Duma were reported in *Rech'*, December 12, 1914. Miliukov calculated that Kadets gained six seats in the Fourth Duma, as compared to the 53 they held at the end of the Third; P. Miliukov, "The Representative System in Russia," in J. Duff, ed., *Russian Realities and Problems* (Cambridge: Cambridge University Press, 1917), 32.

43   By 1912 a number of Kadets, including Petrunkevich, Shakhovskoi, and the generally moderate Aleksandr Kizevetter, were urging a more militant stance on the party. The most radical proposals, calling for illegal oppositional work with the masses outside the Duma, were put forward by left Kadet Nikolai

Nekrasov at the 1914 party conference. His proposals are reproduced in *Rech'*
March 2, 1914; records of the debate are contained in the party archive,
GARF f. 523, op. 1, d. 16, ll. 8–26. The fullest discussion of the debates
between right and left flanks of the party is in A. Ia. Avrekh, *Tsarizm i IV duma,
1912–1914 gg.* (Moscow: Nauka, 1981).

44   Conservative Kadets' critiques of the more provocative tactics adopted by
the party in the Fourth Duma took various forms. One was joint publication
with the Progressives of a newspaper, *Russkaia molva,* critical of the official
Kadet line. Maklakov and Chelnokov made the case for a turn rightward
in central committee meetings of March 1914; see GARF f. 523, op. 1, d.
245, ll. 179–81. For a detailed evaluation of the conservative critique and
Struve's role in its formulation, see Pipes, *Struve: Liberal on the Right,* 174–
86.

45   Quoted in Riha, *A Russian European,* 197. The figures come from V. V.
Shelokhaev, *Ideologiia i politicheskaia organizatsiia rossiiskoi liberal'noi
burzhuazii, 1907–1912 gg.* (Moscow: Nauka, 1991), 10.

46   Pearson, *Russian Moderates,* 16–19.

47   Miliukov, *Vospominaniia,* 395–402.

48   Miliukov was the most prolific Kadet writer on the war; see especially his "Tseli
voiny," in *Ezhegodnik gazety Rech' na 1916 g.* (Petrograd, 1916), 1–196. Many
Kadets contributed pieces on war aims to the liberal journal *Vestnik Evropy,*
Strvue's "national liberal" journal *Russkaia mysl',* and to wartime collections;
among the latter see especially N. N. Mikhailov, ed., *Chego zhdet Rossiia ot
voiny: sbornik statei* (Petrograd: Prometei, 1915); M. I. Tugan-Baranovskii,
ed., *Voprosy mirovoi voiny* (Petrograd: Pravo, 1915); and *Grazhdanin-voin. A.
M. Koliubakin, 1868–1915* (Moscow: Tipo-lit tovarishchestva I. N. Kushnerev,
1915).

49   Kadets M. L. Chelnokov and N. M. Kishkin were president and vice-president
of the organization, five of ten members of the central committee were
Kadets, and party members were prominent in its special committee on "War
and Culture."

50   Dumova, *Kadetskaia partiia,* 36–42; Pearson argues, in contrast, that the war
only worsened the Kadets' situation in the provinces: *Russian Moderates,*
79–80.

51   The most thorough treatments of Kadet attitudes toward the Progressive Bloc
are Thomas Riha, "Miliukov and the Progressive Bloc in 1915," *Journal of
Modern History,* 23 (1960): 16–24; Dumova, *Kadetskaia partiia,* 55–91; and
Pearson, *Russian Moderates,* 42–71, 90–7, 107–14.

52   The February 1916 Sixth Party Congress is discussed in detail in A. Ia.
Avrekh, *Raspad tret'eiiunskoi sistemy* (Moscow: Nauka, 1985), 221–32 and
Raymond Pearson, "Miliukov and the Sixth Kadet Congress," *Slavonic and
East European Review* 52 (April 1975): 210–29; on the fall 1916 conference,
see *Rech'* October 27, 1916 and the report by the secret police (Okhrana), contained in B. B. Graves, ed., *Burzhuaziia nakanune Fevral'skoi revoliutsii* (Moscow,
1927), 145–8.

53   Okhrana reports of December 1916 and January 1917, cited in Pearson,
Russian Moderates, 125, 132–3.

54   The most detailed account in English of Kadet activities in the provinces in March 1917 is Rosenberg *Liberals in the Russian Revolution*, 59–66.

55   The Seventh Party Congress was covered extensively in *Rech'*, March 26, 27, and 28, 1917.

56   The best source on the party's activities and membership is its official journal *Vestnik partii narodnoi svobody*, which resumed publication May 11, 1917 after a nine-year hiatus. For discussion of Kadet efforts to reach out to a mass audience see Dumova, *Kadetskaia partiia*, 122–7.

57   Baron B. E. Nolde, "V. D. Nabokov in 1917," and V. D. Nabokov, "The Provisional Government," in Virgil D. Medlin and Steven L. Parson, eds, *V. D. Nabokov and the Russian Provisional Government* (New Haven, Conn: Yale University Press, 1976), 24–7 and 87, respectively.

58   For a detailed analysis of the elections see Rosenberg, *Liberals in the Russian Revolution*, 157–67.

59   On Kadet involvement in the Kornilov affair see Dumova, *Kadetskaia partiia*, 170–98; Rosenberg, *Liberals in the Russian Revolution*, 196–233; and Stockdale, *Paul Miliukov*, 259–61, 353–4.

CHAPTER NINE

The Union of October 17

Dmitrii B. Pavlov[1]

The "Union of October 17," along with several parties and organizations closely linked to it, represented the right flank of the Russian liberal camp; in the country's political spectrum it occupied the position between the Constitutional Democrats and the rightists. Yet the line separating the Octobrists from adjacent political groups was quite unstable and fluctuating. Some small organizations that were tied to the Octobrists by historical origins – such as the "Party of Peaceful Renovation" – were also very closely linked to the Constitutional Democrats, who stood to the left of the Union. At the same time, a whole range of secondary political formations of Octobrist type (including the "Party of Legal Order," "People's Party of the Union of October 17" in Ekaterinoslav, "Society of Legal Order and the Manifesto of October 17" in Kolomna, "Party for Tsar and Order" in Kaluga, the "Anchor" society of Baku, and a few others) in their practical activity often differed from extreme monarchists only nominally. This situation allowed the leftist opponents of the Octobrists to relate them to the Black Hundreds, while the Black Hundreds accused the Union members of "hidden constitutional democratism." As time went on and the party gradually slipped to the right, the boundaries between the Octobrists and conservative monarchists were becoming increasingly shrouded.

As a political trend, the Octobrist movement appeared and began to define its organizational structure on the basis of "the minority position," which was formulated at the time of the zemstvo-urban congresses in 1905. Yet, formation of various parties within the liberal camp was completed for the most part only after the publication of the Manifesto of October 17, 1905. Believing that the essential preconditions for the development of the constitutional monarchy had been created, the would-be Octobrists undertook to form a party of the new order, adopting the date of the imperial manifesto as part of the Union's title. Although in subsequent years many Octobrists urged the party's leadership to change the cumbersome "nametag" of the party, throughout its entire life span it existed under this original title.

The structural formation of the Union of October 17 derived from several meetings which took place in Moscow and St Petersburg in late October 1905 between liberal zemstvo activists and representatives of the bourgeoisie at large. Along with developing the party's program, participants initiated a process aimed at establishing the Union's leading organs, i.e. Moscow and St Petersburg sections of the central committee. By November, the would-be Octobrists represented a more or less cohesive group, playing an active role at the zemstvo-urban congress in Moscow. The congress adopted their "special opinion" in a resolution on general politics, in which they advocated the support of the government in its attempts to "establish order for the sake of the most speedy convocation of the State Duma." They also expressed their disapproval of direct elections to the Duma and of turning the Duma into a constituent assembly. In addition, the resolution of "the minority" decisively rejected prospects for Poland's autonomy. Nor did they find it possible immediately to abolish the "extraordinary measures and emergency military conditions" that the authorities had declared throughout the empire in response to the revolutionary upheaval in the country. This "special opinion" laid the basis for the Octobrist program, whose first version was published in the newspaper *Slovo* (Word) on November 9, 1905.

The November zemstvo-urban congress also gave the forming party its future leader, one of the three Guchkov brothers, Aleksandr. A hereditary honorary citizen, Aleksandr Guchkov (1862–1936) came from a family of well-known Moscow entrepreneurs and had been the director of the Moscow Discount Bank since 1902. He gained celebrity and the reputation of a fearless and determined patriot in the years of the Russo-Japanese war, in which he took part as the chief emissary of the Russian Society of the Red Cross. Guchkov's debut as a politician occurred in the fall of 1905 during the September zemstvo-urban congress, where he declared that his criteria for determining political allies and foes were the issues of Polish autonomy and "the decentralization of legislation" (needless to say, he opposed both). At the November zemstvo-urban congress Guchkov persisted in this nationalistic manner, soon finding himself in the position of vice-chairman of the Moscow Central Committee of the Union of October

17. By 1906 he was an indisputable leader of the Octobrists, remaining in this capacity for the entire period of the party's existence.

Aleksandr Guchkov's elder brothers – Fedor and Nikolai – also came to play important roles in the Union. Fedor Guchkov (1860–1913) entered the Octobrist central committee in 1907, where he occupied a key position as treasurer. In December of the same year he was elected to be executive director of the Moscow Cooperative for Book and Newspaper Publishing, thus emerging as *de facto* head of the party's central newspaper, *Golos Moskvy* (The Moscow Voice). For his part, Moscow city mayor and director of a tea trade cooperative "Botkin and Sons," Nikolai Guchkov (1860–1935), like his younger brother Aleksandr was a member of the Moscow section of the Octobrists' central committee since its very formation.

A patriarch of the zemstvo movement, Dmitrii Shipov (a large-scale landowner), and the Guchkov brothers (entrepreneurs), represented the two social strata which largely shaped the formation process of the Octobrist movement: landed nobility on the one hand, and trade and industrial circles on the other. Very soon a third social influence appeared to complement the first two – a bureaucratic one. Its heralds in the Union of October 17 were a whole group of Octobrists in the capital headed by Baron P. L. Korf, the first Secretary of the St Petersburg section of the central committee, and by M. V. Krasovskii, his deputy.

Altogether there emerged 260 sections of the Union of October 17 in 1905–7, and the vast majority (approximately 200) came to life during the period of the elections to the First Duma. The largest Octobrist organizations throughout the entire party's existence were in Moscow and St Petersburg, with the one in the capital consisting of 5,000 people by late December of 1905.[2] The total number of party members in the years of the 1905–7 Revolution can be estimated as 75,000–78,000 people. Local Octobrist sections tended to die out and disappear easily, but, by the same token, they also resurrected their activity in the time of elections with similar ease. Taking into consideration the passiveness of the majority of Union members, it is important to note that the real influence of the Octobrists upon the country's political life was not at all proportionate to the party's impressive size.

In terms of geographical location the vast majority of local sections of the Union of October 17 came into existence in zemstvo provinces of European Russia with its relatively developed system of land ownership by the gentry. In non-zemstvo provinces and in the "national outskirts" of the empire the number of the Octobrist organizations was small. The quantity of rural sections was slightly larger – about 30 in all. Along with the Union's sections, there appeared in some cities a few Octobrist student factions and some Octobrist German groups. Finally, in 1905–6 some 23 political organizations whose programs and tactics were similar to those of the Octobrists joined the party, though retaining their autonomous rights.

The Union of October 17 was structurally planned as "a union of all parties of the center regardless of secondary differences and nuances,"[3] and was from the outset a rather amorphous formation, since the very beginning the Union's charter allowed parallel membership in other parties and organizations, and this indeed became common. Membership in the Union of October 17 did not lead to obligatory execution of any special party tasks or even to paying membership dues (the latter – a nominal amount – were introduced in the Union charter only as an obligatory condition of its official legalization). Despite the fact that from 1906 the Octobrist leaders had tried to exercise strictly party-like methods of administering the Union, many of its members continued to view it as a debating society rather than an organization with rigid discipline and hierarchy. Paradoxically, this spirit of broad-mindedness went hand in hand with the glorification of the person of Aleksandr Guchkov; hailing his merits and toasts in his honor became essential attributes of all the party forums from 1907.

Both at times of election campaigns and in the course of everyday activity local sections of the Union of October 17 exercised wide autonomy, which included independent choice of temporary political allies. According to the by-laws adopted at the Union's Second Congress, the rights of local organizations became even more extensive. "We are implacable monarchists, but in our interparty regime we are incorrigible republicans even with a certain penchant toward anarchism," Guchkov complained bitterly.

Such a characteristic feature of revolutionary mentality as the readiness to sacrifice everything for party goals was absolutely alien to the Octobrists. And this was the precise cause of the Union's permanent financial hardships, despite the fact that its membership consisted of rather well-to-do and sometimes very wealthy people. As a rule, the Union attracted individuals of mature age and of high educational level, people of fully established and very respectable social position. The majority of the Octobrists belonged to the age-group that had given the Russian liberation movement a whole generation of revolutionaries in the 1880s. But very few of them had paid tribute to radicalism, preferring to serve Russia in ways sanctioned by law.

The Union of October 17 included numerous representatives of enlightened officialdom, who, according to Ariadna Tyrkova-Williams, a leading member of the Kadet party, were very much unlike "those ugly creatures of prereform Russia described by Gogol and Shchedrin."[4] The Octobrists certainly could not boast a "flower garden" of personalities similar to that of the Constitutional Democrats, which, incidentally, was a constant concern of the Octobrist leadership, especially prior to elections. Nevertheless, we find among the Octobrists such outstanding and remarkable people as zemstvo and political activists Count P. A. Geiden, M. A. Stakhovich, and Count N. S. Volkonskii; such well-known lawyers, university professors, scientists and artists as L. N. Benua, V. I. Ger'e, G. E. Grum-Grzhimailo, P. P. Marsero, F. N. Plevako, V. I. Sergeevich, and N. S. Tagantsev; and such prominent publishers and journalists as N. N. Pertsov, A. A. Stolypin, and B. A. Suvorin. Other members of the Union included leading representatives of merchant and industrial circles: N. S. Avdakov, A. F. Mukhin, E. L. Nobel', Ia. I. Utin, and the brothers V. P. and P. P. Riabushinskii. There were also celebrated representatives of other professions, among them the head of world-famous jewelry firm, Karl Fabergé.

Were we to attempt to draw a "social portrait" of the "generic Octobrist," it would include the following features: a male aged 47–8, a descendant of a noble family (less often, a merchant, who would be a hereditary honorary citizen), a beneficiary of higher education (often with a law or general humanities degree). He would be an official of rank V-VIII, a city resident of one of the zemstvo provinces, a board member of a bank or stock company, land or real estate owner. Thus, to generalize about its social composition, the Union was a party of the service nobility and a large-scale industrial and financial bourgeoisie, which had assumed some traits of the gentry.

Contrary to all the Union's leaders' expectations of attracting to their organizations representatives of the "democratic segments" of the population, particularly workers and peasants, these efforts were to no avail; among members of the Union workers and peasants could be counted in single figures. The Workers' Party of the Union of October 17 and the Peasant Union, both created in late 1905, never turned into mass organizations. In fact, the Workers' Party ceased to exist as early as the first pre-election period. It took a little over a year after the party's formation for the Octobrists finally to appreciate that their attempts to obtain widespread support of the worker and peasant constituencies were hopeless. For its part, the Union's gentry majority, which brought to the party its spirit of the nobility and its corporate mentality, was suspicious and contemptuous of political parties of the "scum," be they revolutionary organizations or those on the extreme right. "We are the party of the masters," a member of the Union's central committee stated in February 1907.[5]

The development of the Union's program underwent several stages. The first stage corresponded to the period of October 1905, when its rather general version was published along with a programmatic appeal signed by 33 members of the central committee. The second period covers 1906 and the first half of 1907 after the expanded and revised program was adopted at the First Congress of the Union in February 1906. At the Second Congress in May 1907 the program was subject to further editing. Finally, the third version of the program incorporated the labors of two party conferences (October 1907 and November 1913), as well as the Union's Third Congress (October 1909). A peculiarity of this third version was the fact that statements of the program were formulated in concrete terms and elaborated on with the purpose of turning them over to the Duma as legislative propositions.

The central place in the program of the Union of October 17 was the issue of state power structure in Russia. "The Russian Empire," stated the first paragraph, "is a hereditary constitutional monarchy, in which the emperor as the bearer of the supreme authority is restrained by stipulations of the Fundamental Laws."[6] The Octobrists thus pronounced themselves to be opponents of the unrestricted power of a monarch.

Advocating the abolition of unlimited autocracy, the Octobrists categorically rejected the idea of introducing a parliamentary regime in Russia, considering it unsuitable from both the historical and the political points of view. The party leadership considered the monarchical form of government to be essential for preserving Russia's "ties with the past," as "a guarantee for the right course" of the state ship, which would be protected from hopeless storms and waverings, or, to put it simply, a vouch for appropriate (and organic) development of Russia on the basis of its 1,000-year-long tradition. Characteristically, the Octobrists judged, albeit with certain reservations, that it was suitable for a constitutional monarch to keep the title of "autocrat," believing it to be part of Russia's heritage.[7]

According to the blueprint developed by the Octobrists, the structure of supreme power in Russia was to include a reigning (and actively governing) monarch and a two-chamber "people's representation." Of these, the State Duma, was to be formed on the basis of direct elections in cities and two-staged ones in "other areas." The Octobrists envisaged the Duma as the lower chamber, whereas the upper legislative chamber – the State Council – would serve the purpose of correcting and adjusting the Duma's decisions. Half of the State Council's members were to be appointed by the monarch. Thus, the only serious discrepancy between that part of the Octobrists' program and the Statement on the State Council of February 20, 1906, was the equilibrium in authority of the State Council and the State Duma (in the official version the State Council received a decisive vote).

In the question of distributing authority between "representatives of the people" and the monarch, the Octobrists were clearly in favor of the latter. In their opinion, not a single law could be introduced or revoked without the emperor's sanction; the tsar also had the right to appoint and dismiss ministers, whose responsibility was theoretically divided equally between the monarch and the "people's representatives." In order to achieve a minister's dismissal, however, the Duma had to initiate an official judicial procedure against him. Under such conditions, the control of the legislative chambers "over the lawfulness and legitimacy of governmental organs," proclaimed in the program of the Union of October 17, was but an illusion. In reality, these chambers, the upper and the lower ones, received the rights of legislative initiative, interpellation, and confirmation of state budget.

The second part of the Octobrists' program was devoted to the party's demands in the sphere of civil rights. It contained a list of propositions typical for a liberal party, including the freedom of conscience and confession, personal immunity and the inviolability of one's home, as well as freedom of speech, assembly, unions, travel, etc. This part of the party's program appeared to be the most democratic. The trouble was that in practice the Octobrists often violated these propositions of their own program. This was especially true in cases dealing with the equality of civil rights in general and the rights of Jews in particular. Under the pressure of their western and south-western sections, which opposed granting equal rights to Jews, the Octobrist leaders did everything to defer the solution of the problem even inside the party itself.

As to the nationality issue in general, the Octobrists took for granted the necessity to preserve the "one and indivisible" Russia (these words were cited in the first paragraph of the party's program in accordance with a decision of the Second Congress). They found it necessary to resist "any proposal that directly or indirectly aimed at dismemberment of the empire and the idea of federalism."[8] Exception was made only for Finland, which was to be given "the right to a certain autonomous state structure," but on the condition of "governmental connection with the empire." In formulating the rights of national minorities, the Octobrists declared their readiness to satisfy and defend their cultural, but not political needs. Moreover, the Octobrists stressed that "the limits of these rights" would be defined by what was for the Union a self-evident priority, the imperial unity. It may be concluded, therefore, that as far as the nationality issue was concerned, the Octobrists remained staunch advocates of conservative nationalist and empire-oriented principles. It is revealing that the nationality issue was not even mentioned in the official program of the Union of October 17; the Octobrist leaders limited themselves to very general appeal statements when dealing with nationality rights.

Conversely, the program paid much attention to socioeconomic problems, the most critical of them being the agrarian one, in the eyes of the Octobrists "the most acute and important question throughout almost the entire territory of great Russia." The Octobrists clearly appreciated that the difficulty of the existing situation was that of the peasantry, who were suffering from lack of land; they found the peasants' demand for additional land plots to be quite legitimate. The Octobrists proposed to satisfy these demands, firstly, at the expense of the state – by setting up special land committes, which would then distribute unused state lands among the peasants. Secondly, the Octobrists also planned to help the peasants by way of establishing a so-called Peasant Bank, which would assist the peasants in purchasing land from private owners. As the most radical measure, the program of the Union of October 17 presupposed compulsory confiscation of designated land allotments from private landlords, who were always to be compensated for the loss of property. In their appeals to the peasants, the Octobrists argued that the land must be purchased after "a fair assessment and without ruining landed estates. It is not appropriate to confiscate the land without paying for it; it is unjust and will not end well."[9]

The major emphasis of the Octobrist agrarian program, however, was not on the land issue, but on economic and legal ones. The Octobrists considered it expedient to equalize the peasants in their rights with the rest of the country's citizens by abolishing all laws that diminished the legal status of the tax-paying layers of society. Even more important was to eradicate the administrative supervision over the peasants, to liquidate the *obshchina* (peasant commune), and to introduce a number of measures to improve the economic conditions in the countryside, such as to develop a system of agricultural credits, actively to promote agronomy, and expand trades.

It may thus be assumed that in their approach to the agrarian problem, the Octobrists remained in concert with Stolypin's policies in the countryside. Yet, unlike Stolypin, who counted primarily on a rather thin layer of "solid and vigorous" peasants, the Octobrists hoped that by destroying the commune they would be able in a relatively short time to create a large populace of well-to-do peasantry, which *en masse* would support the tsarist regime.

An emphasis on practicality and the stress on secondary issues were characteristic features not only of the agrarian part of the Union's program, but also of that regarding workers. The first two paragraphs were devoted to the problem of raising cultural and educational levels and improving the living conditions of the proletariat. Only after this did the program describe a system of measures to regulate the relationship between workers and entrepreneurs and also depict the Union's attitude toward mass proletarian organizations and movements. The Octobrists were prepared to recognize the freedom of worker organizations, unions, assemblies, and even strikes, but only those related to the laborers' economic, professional, and cultural needs. Strikes were to be altogether prohibited in the industries where "stoppage could harm primary state and social interests." Regarding the sensitive issue of the duration of the

working day, the Octobrists took the side of the Russian industrial establishment. Treatment of this question in the Union's program was rather
schematic, referring to the necessity to standardize the maximum length
of working hours and regulate overtime labor. The Octobrist press sought
to clarify this point in the party program; in one of his brochures, V. M.
Petrovo-Solovovo wrote: "Our Union will, of course, welcome the shortening of the working day as long as this will cause no loss for industry or
trade, but it does not insist . . . categorically . . . on the eight-hour working
day."[10] In their attempts to substantiate this position, the Octobrists reasonably noted that under the conditions of Russia's technical backward-
ness, and given the great number of religious holidays (in comparison with
western Europe), the shortening of the working day down to the European
level would lead to an abrupt escalation of prices and very tough competition for Russian goods.

The Octobrists' unwillingness to agree to any radical concessions to
the workers became evident also at a later period, in particular during
the 1907 Union conference. While designing a strategy for their Duma
activity, the Octobrists rejected the expansion of social insurance, which
was guaranteed in their program to all categories of hired labor.
Nonetheless, in their propagandistic literature the Octobrists asserted that
as far as workers were concerned, the Union pursued the same goals as did
the Social Democrats, and the only difference was that the Union preferred
a path which was "calm and peaceful," yet marked by "definite and determined creative work." "We call you to the struggle for free labor," wrote the
Octobrists in their appeal to "comrade workers," but this struggle would be
"for labor, not an escape from work."[11]

The final sections of the Octobrist program were devoted to the issues of
public education, judicial reform, and the system of local administration,
as well as measures in the sphere of economy and finance, and problems
of church reform. In the afterword to the Octobrist program we read:
"Political and civil freedom proclaimed in the Manifesto of October 17 must
revive the torpid strength of the people, bring up the spirit of brave energy
and enterprise, the spirit of independent action and self-assertion, and thus
create a strong foundation and the best precondition for moral resuscita-
tion."[12] Such unconcealed optimism was in sharp incongruity with the
Octobrists' timid and moderate attempts to solve any key practical problems of Russian daily life.

The Octobrists did not hide their hostility toward the revolution and
even provided the government with practical assistance in suppressing it,
though never becoming thoughtless and ruthless executors of official decisions, as was the case with the Black Hundreds. Because of their attempts
to adjust their party tactics to the official policies of the government, which
as time went on increasingly departed from the basic principles of the

Manifesto of October 17, the Octobrists were nicknamed (not entirely appropriately) "the party of the latest government directive" or even "the party of the vanished document." "The Union hates revolution as the greatest evil and the greatest obstacle to establishing order in Russia," declared a St Petersburg Octobrist group in its leaflet.[13]

The immediate impetus for the formation of many Octobrist branches was the aspiration "to fight the disarray." Of the 29 sections of the Union that in one way or another declared the purpose of their formation (be it in their leaflets, appeals, or letters to the central committee) 25 formulated their primary task exactly so. Significantly, owing to their rejection of extremist politics, some Octobrist branches, such as those in Tver and Tikhvin, at their inauguration meetings ordered special church services to be held, during which they prayed for the end of the civil strife – a special gesture against political violence. Another major cause of the formation of local Octobrist organizations was the desire to cooperate closely with the government – something which the Octobrists in Samara formulated most precisely: "The goal of the party is to create a closely knit circle of people around the government for the purpose of united, fruitful, and creative work."[14]

Guided by this principle from the very period of preliminary work on formation of the Union, the leaders of the emerging party, Dmitrii Shipov, Aleksandr Guchkov, and Mikhail Stakhovich, began to negotiate with Prime Minister Sergei Witte the possibility of joining his cabinet. As a result, although the Octobrists proclaimed their "approval of Count Witte's program in principle and their complete trust in the government," they refused to accept the "inconvenient burdens" of ministerial portfolios, justifying their unwillingness to enter the cabinet with lack of experience. The real reason for their refusal was probably twofold: personal distrust of the prime minister which was widespread in liberal circles, and the instability of his cabinet at the time of escalating revolutionary storm. The Octobrists were also scared away by the possibility of occupying neighboring ministry positions with P. N. Durnovo; Witte particularly insisted on giving the portfolio of interior minister to this extreme reactionary, and gossip in the capital even designated him as a potential candidate for the post of Russia's prime minister. On the whole, despite their fruitlessness, the negotiations nevertheless represented a definite intention from both sides to proceed toward "united and productive work" in the future.

The events of November and December 1905 were marked by a perceptible slipping of the Octobrists to the right. They reacted to the November postal and telegraph strike by a series of angry articles in the newspaper *Slovo*, in which they demanded the most resolute measures from the government "to restore order." Revolutionary disturbances in the army and navy were met with the same harsh disapproval on the part of the Octobrists. In December 1905, Guchkov made a personal donation to Moscow's municipal administration for the benefit of the families of soldiers who had fallen victims during the suppression of the November naval uprising in Sebastopol. Simultaneously, the Octobrists were most generous in expressing their loyal sentiments to the tsar. For example, the participants of the first joint meeting of St Petersburg members of the Union on December 4 sent a telegram to Nicholas II, cheering "the constitutional tsar of the free people with a loud hurrah."[15]

In December 1905, the Octobrists turned from words to actions in assisting the authorities in suppression of the armed uprising. Besides issuing a number of appeals, in which they disapproved of the activities of the revolutionaries and fully justified the punitive actions of the government, the Octobrists secretly financed the operations undertaken by the governor-general of Moscow, who received 165,000 rubles for the purpose of suppressing the disturbances.

It may appear that by the end of 1905 there was a complete mutual understanding between the government and the Octobrists, but in fact the first serious disagreements between them date back to that very period. The December instructions of several administrative organs prohibiting the officials to enter political parties were rather painful for the Union of October 17, since these sanctions substantially reduced the inflow of new members. The prohibition by the government of St Petersburg of the organization of "any public and private meetings of a political or economic kind"[16] in the city and its suburbs elicited an even greater negative reaction in Octobrist circles, because the order paralyzed the activity of the law-abiding Octobrists in the capital for a month-and-a-half. The Octobrists were not so much stricken by the narrow-mindedness and hostility of the decision as by the ease with which the government abrogated one of the main principles of the October Manifesto, which, in the tsar's words, was supposedly "the complete and convinced expression" of his "uncompromising will." The Octobrists were surprised to find out that the government, which had certainly carried out the first task of the Octobrist tactical plan, i.e. had suppressed "the sedition," was not at all eager to proceed to the second stage – the convocation of the Duma. And the New Year's Eve interview of Count Witte, in which he declared that even after the manifesto the tsar remained the unrestricted autocrat, produced confusion among the Octobrists, and for the first time forced them to criticize the prime minister and – soon – the entire official political course.

After intensive central committee discussions of the Union's position vis-à-vis the government, the issue was included in the agenda of the First Congress of the party. The Congress's resolution regarding the government's policies was written in a tone unusually harsh for the Octobrists. They demanded the "instantaneous" issue of temporary rules "to guarantee the freedom given by the Manifesto of October 17." The Octobrists also insisted on the abolition of the intensified extraordinary security and other measures, considering them unlawful, responsible for discontent in the country, and falling short of reaching their goals. The major emphasis was placed on the necessity to speed up the Duma elections by all means and to determine the exact date of its convocation.[17]

The Octobrists in fact started their election campaign as early as November 1905, when "the joint Committee of Moderate Parties" was constituted in St Petersburg on their initiative. The committee united representatives of ten constitutional-monarchist organizations and gave birth to an election coalition of the four of them: the Union of October 17 itself, the Party of Legal Order, Progressive Economic Party, and the Trade and Industrial Union. The Bloc of Four existed only in Moscow and St Petersburg. In the periphery (in Kazan, Tambov, Iaroslavl, and other provinces) the Octobrists more often made coalitions with another organization of the bourgeoisie at large, the Trade and Industrial Party.

As a rule, at pre-election meetings the Union of October 17 lost to its competitors on the left, the Constitutional Democrats: the Octobrists' moderate views differed sharply from the radical trends prevalent in society at the time, and the party's position was additionally weakened by lack of effective speakers. Therefore, in their agitation efforts the Octobrists counted particularly on the press – something which they indeed had the means to develop into a reliable tool. Almost every fifth section of the Union of October 17 was involved in publishing. Fifteen sections had periodicals at their disposal, not to mention the means to print leaflets, pamphlets, and brochures. Some branches (for example, the one in Iaroslavl) even had two periodicals. In 1906, the Octobrists published over 50 newspapers altogether, in Russian, German, and Latvian. According to the Union's control committee, about 80 brochures were issued in 1905–7, and some of them were published in millions of copies. Moreover, some Octobrist brochures were republished and circulated by government agencies, such as the Synod and the War Ministry. During the first Duma election campaign the enormous figure of 3 million copies of Octobrist publications propagated in St Petersburg alone represented twice the number of residents of the capital. By the end of February 1906, the circulation of a single appeal, entitled "On the State Duma," was 5 million copies.

All these efforts, however, proved to be fruitless, since the "democratic voter" did not support the Octobrists. In St Petersburg, for example, none of the 160 candidates of the parties of the "bloc" were elected even to candidate status, despite the fact that among them were such renowned people as the mayor N. A. Reztsov, writer N. L. Klado, leader of provincial nobility Count V. V. Gudovich, and architect P. I. Shestov. In the end, the "bloc" parties managed to send only 16 deputies to the Duma, and their voice in the Russian parliament could barely be heard. The fact that the Octobrists turned out to be the rightmost faction of the Duma did not promote the party's popularity either. The faction's leaders P. A. Geiden, M. A. Stakhovich, and N. S. Volkonskii gained fame as the initiators of the thwarted Duma disapproval of "political murders" or terrorist assassinations. They also acquired a reputation as politicians who opposed forced expropriations of land from the nobility and the immediate abolition of class limitations. Still, the Octobrist deputies could not exert serious influence upon the work of the First Duma owing to their numerical insignificance.

The bitter pill of the First Duma experience was somewhat sweetened by a new proposal to the Octobrist leaders to occupy certain ministerial positions. Negotiations on this matter started on Stolypin's initiative and continued from May to July 1906. They ended, however, just like the talks in the fall of 1905. After the break-up of the First Duma and the suppression of uprisings in Sviaborg and Kronshtadt, the tsarist regime no longer needed the assistance of the liberals, and the negotiations discontinued. On August 24, 1906, the government published a statement announcing the new policy of military field courts martial for the prosecution of radicals on the one hand, and a forthcoming series of social and political reforms in line with the October Manifesto on the other. This official declaration became a milestone in the history of the Union of October 17.

An interview given by Aleksandr Guchkov concerning the August 24 declaration initiated a new turn in the Octobrist political course. In that interview he justified the dissolution of the Duma and expressed full support for Stolypin's actions. The majority of the party members were entirely behind Guchkov, who was elected chairman of the Union on October 29, 1906.[18] At the same time, there were some Octobrists who did not expect this step, which signified for them a departure from the party's original principles. In the fall of 1906 the Union's founders, Dmitrii Shipov and Mikhail Stankevich, left its central committee to join the Party of Peaceful Renovation, which served as a buffer between the Constitutional Democrats and the Octobrists. Consequently, the plan of uniting the Party of Peaceful Renovation with the Union – something which had seemed to Guchkov quite feasible and even inevitable in the summer of 1906 – became irrelevant.

The failure of the first election campaign and internal conflicts in the higher echelons of the Union of October 17 that followed exacerbated its disorganization and the backslide of the local Octobrist sections. At least 60 of them ceased to exist as early as the summer of 1906. By the beginning of 1907 the number of the Union's local organizations was reduced by half – down to 128 in all – and the number of adjoining factions fell from 23 to 13. The number of branch representatives at the Union's congresses decreased drastically; whereas delegates from 95 organizations took part in the party's first congress, only 22 of them sent delegates to the second one.

Gradually, the entire political image of the Union began to change. According to the memoirs of a Constitutional Democrat Vasilii Maklakov, "the Octobrist ranks began to be joined by people who were indifferent to the manifesto and criticized not only Guchkov's policy, but Stolypin's as well. They entered the party not because of their sympathy for its liberal program, but because it was a more respectable firm than the rightists." On the whole, the Octobrists entered the Second Duma election campaign weaker than and not as numerous as they had been at the time of the elections to the First Duma.

The Union's next turn to the right was evident from its election tactics. It was the extreme rightists who took the place of the constitutional-monarchist parties as the Octobrists' allies. While formulating the party's tasks for the election period in November 1906, Guchkov pointed at a coalition with the right as the only possible way forward for the Union of October 17. Coalitions between the Octobrists and the Black Hundreds had been rather rare previously, but during the elections to the Second Duma they became a rule. Under the conditions of the party's drifting to the right from the fall of 1906, the Octobrist leaders were increasingly convinced of the necessity to give up the most "vulnerable" aspects of their program. Among these principles the primary ones were support for the granting of equal rights to Jews and the confiscation of privately owned land.

Despite having the advantages of being a legal party which was not usually subject to governmental persecution, as was the case with the leftists, the Octobrists managed to get only 43 of their deputies elected to the Second Duma. The faction's growth to more than twice the size that it had been in the First Duma was still a relatively modest success. The type and direction of Octobrist activities in the new Duma were very little different from their experience a year earlier. The Octobrist faction insisted on formal parliamentary disapproval of revolutionary terror, criticized the agrarian bills of the Trudoviki (Laborists) and the Constitutional Democrats (yet without proposing any bills of their own), and supported the government's point of view of the issue of helping the starving. The only new trend was that the Octobrists' main objective in Duma activities was the formation of "a stable constitutional center," which was to consist of representatives of the moderate parties and the right wing of the Constitutional Democratic faction. The idea, however, was never realized and throughout the entire session of the Second Duma the Octobrists were isolated and not supported by either the right or the left.

During the final stage of the Second Duma, the Octobrists, together with the rightists, supported Stolypin's demand to deprive some members of the

Social-Democratic faction of their parliamentary deputy immunity after they had been accused of plotting a coup d'état. Octobrist circles also approved of the dismissal of the Second Duma which they called "a deplorable necessity," and of new electoral legislation, which gave them hopes for success during the next election campaign.

The notorious "coup of June 3, 1907," which altered the country's electoral laws, was, in the eyes of many contemporaries and latter-day historians, a result of Stolypin's effort to create a more acquiescent and cooperative Duma, upon which he could rely for the imposition of his legislative agenda. Be that as it may, the inauguration of the "June 3 system" forced the Octobrist leadership to adjust their tactics. The Octobrists assigned responsibility for the shaking up of legal order in the empire not to Stolypin's administration, but to the revolutionaries, who even after October 17, 1905 continued to wage "senseless fratricidal warfare." As far as they were concerned, the monarch had the right to change the electoral legislation "in the interest of the state and the nation," since even after October 17, 1905 the tsar still preserved his "free will" and "exclusive prerogatives."

The new electoral law allowed the Octobrists to occupy the leading position in the Third Duma, where they managed to form a powerful faction consisting of 154 deputies. This was 112 more deputies than they had had in the Second Duma, and thus was an unquestionable victory. The Octobrists owed their success to the widespread support of the bourgeoisie that had joined their camp. At the same time, the Union's position in the upper chamber of the Russian parliament, the State Council, was also rather impressive; there, a dominating "group of the center" was Octobrist in spirit. Yet the large Octobrist Duma faction was never a monolithic formation; its vacillating tendencies were clearly the stronger. For this reason the parliamentary course of the party was subject to constant oscillations and frequent changes of the faction's decisions. All this, in conjunction with the government's actions, eventually led to the failure of the Union's strategies in the Duma, which had been worked out at the first all-party conference in October 1907.

Despite the party's resounding success during the Third Duma elections, the disintegration of the Octobrist forces in the periphery continued under the "June 3 system." Although in 1909 the total number of the Union's provincial sections remained practically the same as it had been in 1907 (127 in all), membership in local factions declined significantly. Moreover, many peripheral committees existed in name only and were totally inactive. The formation of any new branch of the Union was regarded as something of an event, worthy of being mentioned in the annual central committee report.

The activities of the central committee itself began to change in character and intensity: its sessions were held no more often than two or three times a month, and its members began to be preoccupied with issues far removed from mainstream politics, such as charitable work and the temperance movement. Thus, in April of 1908 the central committee initiated the collection of donations and the purchase of clothing and food to assist those Muscovites who had suffered as a result of an unusually high flood. The emphasis on economic and financial matters became a characteristic feature of the central committee's activity in the years following the end of the revolutionary crisis. As time went on, the activity of the Union's central committee began considerably to resemble the style of the "June 3 system" of Russian parliament, which contemporaries labeled "the Duma vermicelli."

The Octobrists counted mostly on Stolypin's government in their attempts to carry out their Duma program. According to Guchkov, they concluded a tacit "treaty" on "mutual loyalty" with the government. This deal provided for a mutual agreement to pass a broad program of reforms in the Duma – reforms which were to ensure further development of the "fundamentals of the constitutional order." As long as Stolypin at least made it look as if he was fulfilling his end of the unspoken agreement, the Octobrists followed him unfailingly and were in fact the government's party.

From the very first session of the Third Duma, the Octobrists supported all repressive measures of the government against the revolutionary movement. They voted for the allocation of increased funds for police, the Gendarme Corps, and the establishment of investigative organs; they also advocated the continuance of administrative exile. The majority in the Octobrist fraction also supported nationalistic laws with regard to Finland and western zemstvos. In their Duma speeches the Octobrists maintained that the authorities had the right to declare not only extraordinary conditions throughout the empire, but, in exceptional cases, even a state of war, because, as the Octobrists argued, during the struggle against "open rebellion," the "violation of rights of certain individuals" was acceptable. Needless to say, statements of this sort were contradictory to the general political program of the Union of October 17.

In the Third Duma, the Octobrists aligned themselves primarily with the moderate right. For a long time they rejected all proposals from the Kadets to join forces in order to form "an efficient constitutional center" in the Duma. Under pressure from the right, the Octobrists refused to allow representatives of the Kadet faction to enter the Duma's presidium and also prevented them from joining the committee on state defense.

As the crisis of the "June 3 system" deepened, and the reactionaries consolidated their strength, the mass of the trade and industrial bourgeoisie (which had previously provided the Octobrists with so much social and material support) began to leave the Union of October 17. As Guchkov was forced to acknowledge in one of his speeches, the Octobrists felt more and more isolated in the Duma and elsewhere. This compelled the Octobrist leadership to look for opportunities for maneuver in order to take the party out of this dead-end situation.

After their defeat during supplementary elections in Moscow, at their Third Party Congress the Octobrists resolved to use their right for legislative initiative in the Duma more actively. The congress devised a series of legislatures in order to introduce them for discussion in the Duma. The proposed laws were very much in line with Stolypin's reform program, with zemstvo and judicial reforms receiving primary attention.

Yet the persistent official steering to the right was depleting even the Octobrists' patience, their "supplicatory stance" notwithstanding. From 1910 onwards, the Duma faction of the Union of October 17 increased its criticism of what it considered to be inappropriate actions by the central administration and its local representatives. Thus, beginning on February 22, 1910, amidst discussions of the Interior Ministry's budget, Guchkov declared: "Under the present conditions my colleagues and I no longer see any former obstacles justifying the slackening in implementing civil liberties, those liberties that . . . have been endorsed by the October 17 Manifesto along with political freedoms. We do not see any impediments to a more speedy realization . . . of a firm lawful order on every level of our state and social life." Appealing to the government, Guchkov insisted on the expediency of eliminating those obstacles which the Duma legislatures continuously encountered in the State Council. He also called on the local administration to intensify the "preparatory course of instruction on the fundamentals of constitutional law" and urged the officials in the periphery to retain their independence from the extreme right. Guchkov ended his speech with a sentence full of intent: "Gentlemen, we are waiting."

The timid dissent of the Octobrists had no effect on the government, however. In March 1911, Guchkov was compelled to leave the post of chairman of the Third Duma in protest against the unconstitutional action of the government. Simultaneously, the party leadership abruptly changed its attitude toward the parties on the Duma's left: the Octobrists began to seek agreements with the progressives and Kadets. One negative and quite painful consequence of this step for the Octobrists was the sharpening of tensions within their parliamentary faction, which by the end of the Third Duma session was on the verge of a schism.

The assassination of Stolypin in September 1911 caused shock among the ranks of the Octobrists. Their precarious hope for a chance to carry liberal reforms through the Duma, propped up by their "agreement" with the central administration, had resulted in a fiasco. For their part, after Stolypin's assassination even the moderate Octobrists were no longer welcome in government circles. Party members on the periphery, in accordance with their bureaucratic habit of reacting keenly to mood swings in the center, did not hesitate to respond with a mass exodus from the Union of October 17. According to police department information, in most provinces sections of the Union disappeared in 1912; where Octobrist organizations continued to exist, they survived as numerically insignificant groups and usually did not distinguish themselves with any conspicuous activity.

During elections to the Fourth Duma, the Octobrists received only 98 deputy mandates; it is particularly noteworthy that the leader of the Union himself was disenfranchised. Taking into account the fruitless experiment in collaboration with Stolypin in the Third Duma, the Octobrist leadership made certain corrections in the political course pursued by its Duma faction. Still hoping for the government's "sensibility" and "moral authority," as well as for its reformist potentials, the Octobrists intensified the tone of their Duma speeches somewhat and, together with the progressives, began to insist more firmly on the fundamental aspects of the October 17 Manifesto. The unwillingness of V. N. Kokovtsev's administration to give concessions to the liberals forced the Octobrists to sharpen their criticism of government activities not only as far as local affairs were concerned, but also on the central level of administration, including the Interior Ministry. Elements of Octobrist dissent could also be seen in what turned out to be the annual commemorative ceremonies by the party's central committee on the day of Stolypin's death. Finally, during the November 1913 conference of the Union of October 17 the party bitterly criticized the government's political course.

Now of the view that the Russian domestic situation was heading for crisis, during central committee meetings and on the pages of the *Moskovskii Golos* (Moscow Voice), the Octobrists ardently debated the question of how "major upheavals" in politics could be avoided. In the course of the discussion left Octobrists insisted on the necessity to form a bloc with the progressives and the Kadets for the purpose of creating "an oppositionist center" in the Duma and carrying out constitutional reforms. Conversely, the right wing of the party considered such a coalition unacceptable and protested sharply against the left Octobrists' suggestion of turning down the government's request for the Duma to approve credits. As a result, despite all appeals for unity expressed at the November 1913 conference, in December the Duma faction split into three components: the zemstvo-Octobrists, which included 65 members; the very core of the Union, numbering 22; and a group of 15 former members of the fraction, who had declared themselves non-party activists, but who in reality had formed a coalition with the Duma's extreme right.

The split in the fraction and then the party as a whole brought the Union of October 17 to the verge of catastrophe. The local sections of the party, whose fragile existence was in its death throes, in essence ceased to be involved in any activities. Contrary to all assertions on the part of the Octobrist leaders to the effect that the schism in the party would not lead to a weakening of its position in the Duma, the remnants of the formerly powerful Octobrist faction in the Tauride Palace appeared quite impotent: the zemstvo-Octobrists were like a pendulum, swinging from right to left as circumstances dictated; the left Octobrists persisted in their efforts to create a progressive bloc in the Duma, not daring, however, to finalize its break with the government. Torn by internal controversies and squabbles, the Octobrists oscillated between the right wing of the Duma and representatives of the liberal opposition. On the one hand, they supported (albeit with serious reservations) official domestic policies; voted for large financial allocations to the government's military programs; and continued their polemics with the Duma's left. On the other hand, however, the Octobrists constantly doubted the validity of their own political course. To the end they remained unable to break this vicious circle.

World War I led to the final disintegration of the Union of October 17. On July 1, 1915 the *Moscow Voice* ceased to exist, and soon all activities of the central committee of the party died out. The attempts on the part of the police department to discover the party's active peripheral branches at the time produced no results. Some local Octobrist groups, deficient in members, isolated from one another, and busy with organizing assistance to the wounded and to civilian refugees, did not pursue any political activity during the war. For all practical purposes, the Union of October 17 ceased to exist as a party, although such eminent Octobrist leaders as A. I. Guchkov, M. V. Rodzianko, and I. V. Godnev continued to play prominent roles in the political life of the country until the summer of 1917.

Notes

1   This essay has been translated from the Russian by Eugene Budnitsky.
2   "Programma Soiuza 17 oktiabria," *Slovo*, November 9, 1905.
3   "Ustav Soiuza 17 oktiabria," Rossiiskii Gosudarstvennyi Istoricheskii Arkhiv (further cited as RGIA), f. 869, op. 1, d. 1283, p. 96.
4   A. V. Tyrkova-Vil'iams, *Na putiakh k svobode* (London: Overseas Publicaitons Interchange, 1990), 50.
5   "Protokol zasedaniia TsK 13 febralia 1907 g.," in D. B. Pavlov, ed., *Partiia "Soiuz 17 oktiabria": Protokoly s'ezdov i zasedanii TsK*, vol. 1 (Moscow, 1996), 300.
6   "Programma 'Soiuza 17 oktiabria.'" RGIA, f. 869, op. 1, d. 1283, p. 58.
7   "Partiia 'Soiuz 17 oktiabria.' Protokoly s'ezdov i zasedanii TsK. 8 i 9 ianvaria 1906," *Zhurnal soedinennogo soveshchaniia Peterburskogo i Moskovskogo otdelenii TsK*, 1: 49–50.

8　"Postateinoe izlozhenie 'Vozzvaniia Soiuza 17 oktiabria,'" RGIA, f. 869, op. 1, d. 1283, p. 28ob.

9　"V chem sostoit pozhelaniia 'Soiuza 17 oktiabria,' ili ego programma," Izdanie Narvskogo i Iamburgskogo komitetov Soiuza 17 oktiabria (14 febralia 1906 g.), GARF, f. 115, op. 1, d. 91, p. 13.

10　V. M. Petrovo-Solovovo, "'Soiuz 17 oktiabria,' ego zadachi i tseli, ego polozhenie sredi drugikh politicheskikh partii. Rech, proiznesennaia 30 dekabria 1905 g. na obshchem sobranii Tambovskogo otdeleniia Soiuza" (Moscow, 1906), 29.

11　"Ot 'Soiuza 17 oktiabria' k rabochim," GARF, f. 115, op. 1, d. 8, p. 56.

12　GRIA, f. 869, op. 1, d. 1283, p. 59ob.

13　"Vozzvanie komiteta 'Soiuza 17 oktiabria' po Kazanskoi chasti g. S.-Peterburga 'K izbirateliam'," GARF, f. 115, op. 1, d. 8, p. 67ob.

14　"Otchet ob obshchem sobranii Partii poriadka na osnovaniiakh Manifesta 17 oktiabria," *Golos Samary* (January 1, 1906).

15　"Partiia 'Soiuz 17 oktiabria.' Protokoly s'ezdov i zasedanii TsK. 4 dekabria 1905," *Zhurnal pervogo obshchego sobraniia "Soiuza 17 oktiabria,"* 1: 30.

16　*Slovo*, December 12, 1905.

17　"Rezoliutsiia 1-ogo s'ezda 'Soiuza 17 oktiabria po voprosu ob otnoshenii 'Soiuza 17 oktiabria' k vnutrennei politike pravitel'stva," *Partiia "Soiuz 17 oktiabria,"* vol. 1, 154–5.

18　"Protokol zasedaniia TsK 29 oktiabria 1906 g.," ibid., 237.

CHAPTER TEN

Hopeless Symbiosis: Power and Right-Wing Radicalism at the Beginning of the Twentieth Century

Aleksandr Bokhanov[1]

An event occurred in Russia in the fall of 1905 which significantly changed both the social situation within the enormous empire and the political conditions of Russian state power. On October 17 Tsar Nicholas II signed a manifesto "On Improvement of State Order" which spoke about "bestowing on the people" the unshakeable foundations of civic freedom: personal inviolability, freedom of conscience, speech, assembly, and organization. It also promised to involve all the sections of the population in elections to a legislative assembly, the State Duma, and to recognize the Russian parliament as an organ without which "no law could come into force." The country's traditional leadership thus embarked on the road of constitutional change. The last chapter in the history of tsarist Russia had begun: it was the period of the "constitutional experiment."

The October Manifesto appeared at a time of acute sociopolitical upheaval, when revolutionary passions raged throughout the country. The government no longer faced the issue of whether or not to agree to introduce fundamental changes. The leaders of the state now had to decide *which* measures should be taken to establish the new and inevitably more liberal order, while retaining the traditional social and political institutions and structures. It was not an easy step for the Russian tsar to take. In a situation where the sociopolitical crisis had reached its apogee, where the very existence of the traditional system was threatened, and where the emperor found himself virtually alone, he approved something that he had always believed to be useless for Russia – the great historical anomaly, which consisted simply of imitating Western European norms and patterns, and which, in Nicholas II's opinion, could bring no positive results.

A great deal has been said about the political innovations of October 1905 being the result of revolutionary pressure on Nicholas II, who, it has been suggested, was driven only by fear of anarchy. It has also been frequently suggested that the tsar only used the October 17 Manifesto as an involuntary tactical move intended to divert attention from the weakened central administration at any cost, in order to return to the old political practices after the revolutionary wave abated.[2] This viewpoint, however, seems to be historically incorrect. It appears that the tsar made up his mind to grant the manifesto following a deliberate, painstaking and fraught decision-making process. Two days after the fateful ruling, on October 19, 1905, the tsar wrote to his mother the Dowager Empress Mariia Fedorovna in Denmark:

> My dear Mother, you can't imagine how much I suffered before making the decision! . . . All over Russia they did nothing but scream, and write, and ask for it. Around me, I heard the same thing from many, very many; I could rely on no one except honest Trepov [governor-general of St Petersburg]. There was no other way out but to make the sign of the cross and to give what everybody was asking for. The only consolation was the hope that it was God's will, that this difficult decision would lead dear Russia out of this intolerable situation, in which it has been for nearly a year.[3]

Both Russian and Western historiography have reached the conclusion that Nicholas II was a person whose practical decisions in domestic policies hinged strictly on his reactionary views. In the period following October 1905, Russia's supreme ruler was said to have dreamed of nothing better than returning to the good old days of unrestricted power. This impression is yet another historical inaccuracy. Of course, the revolution was instrumental in influencing the state political course. But as far as the tsar's intentions were concerned, his personal outlook, sympathies, and preferences have often been erroneously interpreted as the impulse behind his real political actions. Nicholas II did not belong among the reformers. Nor is it conceivable to imagine him as a sage. But he had one important trait for a politician: he was capable of accepting new realities and finding the strength to step over what he had been accustomed to for the sake of state interests. This was what happened during the state and legal reforms of 1905–6.

In October 1905 the tsar made a decision which was contrary to his views concerning the country's welfare, contrary to his convictions that authoritarian rule was beneficial for Russia; his decision contradicted his 1894 coronation pledge, which obliged him to preserve, unaltered, the prerogatives of the autocratic monarch. But the time had come to make a sacrifice and Nicholas II made it, disregarding his personal principles at a time when the revolutionary wave had nearly engulfed the country, and he could no longer await support from elsewhere. A few years after this turning point, Nicholas II wrote sadly to his mother recalling the events of fall 1905: "Now, when everything is quiet, the gentry have started to complain about various innovations and reforms, but I would like to know how, in what way, did they help the government during that terrible fall of 1905. In no way. They all hid and kept silent, thinking that the end had come."[4]

Why was it that at crucial moments the imperial government lacked strong social support, that it did not have defenders ready to stand up for the principles and traditions they had pledged allegiance to, praised, and admired? This question concerned not only the tsar. A great deal was written about this issue at the time, and many discussions took place; different arguments were offered by both advocates and opponents of unlimited monarchy. Everyone involved in contemporary affairs of state justified himself and his behavior. But less than 12 years later, in early March 1917, the situation was repeated. Once again the tsar was abandoned and, under pressure of circumstances, accepted what everyone around him was "writing about, screaming about and asking for": he abdicated.

Did the traditional monarchic system have public support at all, or was it lost irretrievably by the beginning of the twentieth century? There were, of course, monarchists in Russia, and many of them. But they were a motley crowd, of different forces, groups, and factions which never had a single organizational center, a single program for action, or an ideological and political platform rooted in the needs of the moment. It is therefore possible to begin to understand the role and nature of Russian right-wing activists by outlining some of the essential elements of the traditional national political consciousness. The problem is directly linked to the issue of the Russian national character and "outlook," which is defined by modern political science and sociology as the "national mentality."

Russian monarchism and conservatism was based on a patriarchal foundation, on the ideas and norms which had been shaped in ancient times and which for centuries remained unchanged. To be a monarchist was to be a convinced Orthodox Christian, to revere "the Sovereign anointed by God," to obey unconditionally the authority of the state manifested in its institutions and the orders issued by its officials. In theory at least these ideas were founded on "Love and Faith" and were not subject to critical analysis or intellectual revision. The sacral nature of the tsar's power and his charisma were the axis of the monarchist political outlook.

Since olden times the tsar had personified power and law in Russia. Inevitably, these traditional and archaic principles were to clash with the pragmatic approaches and rational ideas of modernity, with European egalitarian theories and liberal teaching on social order and the transformation of political life. For the sake of self-preservation Russian monarchism and conservatism had to adapt to the new requirements of the political game; there was an urgent need to develop up-to-date political mechanisms and ideas adequate to the new times and capable of resisting the liberal challenge and radical demands.

In the Russian context, the concepts "monarchist" and "conservative" were of the same order, but in reality they were not identical. The Russian conservative was sure to be a monarchist. But far from all monarchists were conservative, that is adherents of the established outlook, capable of justifying their support for the traditional sociopolitical system.

As an attitude of mind and a system of state-oriented political convictions, Russian conservatism assumed well-defined forms in the nineteenth century. The "ideological niche" of Russian monarchism included elite members of society: high-ranking officials, members of the aristocracy and the church hierarchy. During various historical eras and particularly at crucial turning points, Russian conservatives, while bemoaning the irretrievable passing of former days, never in fact intended to put the clock back or reverse the course of events in some way. Herein lies the fundamental difference between conservatives proper and out-and-out reactionaries, seeking to turn the future into the past at any price.

The conservative milieu (with its variety of trends, opinions, and attitudes) yielded several major statesmen who designed measures and took steps with the goal of adapting the autocratic system to the new conditions. These were the initiators and implementers of a series of reforms during the nineteenth and early twentieth centuries, the most notable figures being Sergei Witte and Petr Stolypin. The former was associated with the policy of rapid industrial modernization which began at the end of the nineteenth century; the latter made his contribution with a series of effective measures early in the twentieth century aimed at reorganizing land ownership and utilization – based on the general principles and laws of the market economy.

Russian conservatism was a phenomenon of political culture, but it coexisted with, and frequently exploited for its own purposes, that fundamental aspect of Russia's domestic make-up – the "dark spontaneity" (*temnye impul'sy*) of its people – those numberless "grey masses" (*serye massy*) who clung to their centuries-old and unquestioned assumptions about the nature of political power, embodied in the tsar as Divine Providence.

Inert and primitive popular monarchism had no ideological rationale; it was an irrational manifestation of the popular mentality, the focus of the social passion of the crowd and the energy of the masses. It was also the breeding ground for extreme right-wing forces which emerged as an active political factor in the twentieth century. (And perhaps it may be noted at this point: when communist power was established in the country, these spontaneous forces, having lost their original orientation, as well as their former religious and secular monarchist leaders, frequently replicated the behavioral patterns typical of the extreme right, only now under a red flag – by inciting violence against undesirables and initiating Bolshevik social pogroms.)

The Manifesto of October 17, 1905, unexpected as it was for all of Russia's unofficial political activists, was a real blow for the rightists. Conservative-monarchic circles perceived it as an act of violence against the monarch perpetrated by his own entourage, as a betrayal of historical traditions and the indispensable foundations of the state. At the top of their voices, the rightists began to hurl accusations of an anti-Russian conspiracy, allegedly inspired and plotted by the cosmopolitan bureaucracy, Europeanized liberals, mad socialists and nihilists of all brands, corrupt journalists, and Jews. Confusion, bewilderment, shock, and despair led to anger manifested in extreme forms of social confrontation.

At the turn of 1906 the streets of cities, towns, and Jewish settlements in virtually all parts of Russia became the scene of vicious clashes, often involving bloodshed, between those who welcomed the manifesto, regarding it as the dawn of the age of freedom and democracy in the country, and those who saw it as the beginning of the end of the real Russia, a mortal threat to the entire centuries-old order. Monarchists-traditionalists believed that everything was not yet lost, but only by rallying all "healthy national forces" around the tsar and the Orthodox Church was it possible to resist the devastating onslaught of liberal ideas and extremist acts by the radical socialists and anarchists. Numerous right-wing political groups appeared in the political arena during this period on the wave of spontaneous efforts to defend Russia and the tsar against sedition.

The first political formation of the right was the so-called "Russian Assembly," which came into being in St Petersburg in 1900. Originally it pursued only educational purposes, and its charter indicated that its main task was to "acquaint society with everything important and original done by the Russian people in all spheres of scholarship and the arts."[5] Very soon, however, all other issues became overshadowed by acute social and political concerns; as a result, it was no longer possible for the "Russian Assembly" to restrict its pursuits merely to the sphere of national culture and education.

The first right-wing activists suddenly found themselves among friends – a large number of rightist groups and alliances which came into existence at the end of 1905: these included the Monarchist Party, the Union of the Russian People (URP), the Party of Order, the Double-Headed Eagle, the Union of St Michael Archangel, and others. By that time, neither educational nor cultural, but political slogans and aims prevailed in the programs of these organizations. Among their goals the most important were to preserve a united and indivisible empire, and to defend the prerogatives of the absolute autocrat as well as the rights and privileges of the Orthodox Church and Orthodox citizens.

A party which in November 1905 emerged under the name of the Union of the Russian People became the largest and most influential right-wing organization in the empire (its charter was officially registered in August 1906). Aleksandr Dubrovin, hitherto an obscure doctor, became the chairman of its board. The most notable extreme right-wing politicians who were its sympathizers or officials at different times were Vladimir Purishkevich, Nikolai Markov, Vladimir Gringmut, and Aleksandr Nikol' skii. Among its leading activists were people of rather diverse backgrounds, ranging from Ivan Vostorgov, an Orthodox clergyman (*protoierei*), to Lev Tikhomirov, a revolutionary renegade, who had been a member of the Executive Committee of the notorious People's Will.

The Union of the Russian People published a newspaper *Russkoe Znamia* (Russian Banner), for several years the most widely distributed mouthpiece of the extreme right; its maximum circulation ranged between 12,000 and 15,000 copies. Still, it is difficult to establish with any degree of precision the number of members in the URP; there was no registration in the party. Moreover, the URP allowed for collective membership, and in some places all the village inhabitants "from the youngest to the oldest" joined the party in a single collective act. Leaders of monarchist organizations estimated the number of their followers as at least 3 million in 1905–6. Yet, according to the Police Department, there were 358,758 members of the Union of Russian People and 47,794 activists of other monarchist organizations in 78 provinces throughout the empire at the beginning of 1908.[6] If the police figures were to be considered adequate (and the source is quite reliable, it seems), the URP emerged as the largest widespread political organization in Russia at the time.

Called the "Black Hundreds" by opponents, the extreme right-wingers become active in late 1905, and before long their powerful political influence was only too obvious. Crowds of many thousands at meetings and demonstrations made a strong impression and seemed to convince the Orthodox monarchists that the popular support for old Russian values had not disappeared. "For the Tsar, the Motherland, and our Faith" was an unsophisticated emotional appeal which brought people into the streets. And although the right-wing movement was headed by educated and politically aware individuals, the common "dark folk" (*temnyi narod*) was its driving force, for which any well-worded demands for a constitutional and law-based state would be idle talk.

The right-wing monarchist leaders had no illusions about the intellectual or psychological sophistication of their constituency, and their strategy and tactics were thus intended chiefly for people with a primitive mindset and a very narrow political horizon. The first clauses of the charter of the Union of the Russian People indicated that the organization set itself "the unswerving aim of developing national Russian self-awareness and of firmly uniting Russian people of all estates and wealth in the common effort for the benefit of our dear Fatherland, Russia, united and indivisible. The benefit of the Motherland lies in the unshakeable preservation of the Orthodoxy, the unrestricted Russian autocracy and nationality."[7]

These declarations were made at a time when national representative and legislative institutions were being established in the form of the State Duma; when the Fundamental Laws of the Russian Empire had already been revised; and the provision that the tsar had unlimited rights had already been excluded from them. At the same time, under the new system "no new law could be enacted without the approval of the State Council and the State Duma or come into force without being upheld by the Tsar Emperor."[8] Although the concept of "autocrat" was retained with regard to the monarch, it lost its odious ring after the changes were made, now being simply an historical title, a tribute to tradition.

Intense political debates on the nature of the new Russian state system and the legal underpinnings of power broke out after the appearance of the revised edition of the Fundamental Laws in April 1906. Some believed that the newly introduced separation of powers signified the establishment of democratic rule; others, mostly from among the opponents of the regime, regarded all the constitutional changes as "a fig-leaf for autocracy" and thought that at the first opportunity the authorities would take away any concession that the dissenters had managed to extract from the government by way of the liberation struggle.

In this controversy the right-wingers benefited from an unwavering intellectual certainty with regard to their own position. They were convinced that democratic freedoms, the parliamentary system, and the executive power's responsibility before a legislative chamber might be fine for Europe, but, as far as Russia was concerned, were completely inappropriate to the country's peculiar social conditions. "Simple Russian people" (the "dark folk") were too remote from Western political norms and ideas; their traditions and mentality had been shaped in a totally different historical context, and for that reason "alien flowers would not grow" in Russia. A prominent conservative, Prince Vladimir Meshcherskii wrote in early 1906 on the pages of his newspaper *Grazhdanin* (Citizen): "The autocratic Russian tsar is incomparably more restricted by his responsibility before God and his conscience than the president of the French Republic."[9]

The principle of the separation of powers and the idea of representative institutions based on popular elections were thus completely unacceptable to the right-wingers; they contradicted their main assumption that intrinsically Russia was "an autocratic and Orthodox country."

The leaders of the right-wing movement were perfectly aware that they could not count on support among the educated sections of the population, and that their main adherents, their primary ground swell of support, were the inert and largely irrational masses capable of understanding only emotional and easily accessible political slogans and appeals. At the monarchist congress in Kiev at the end of 1906, Baron N. A. Engel'gardt urged clear and simple words to be written on the Black Hundreds' banner: "Russia for Russians! For Faith, Tsar, and Fatherland! For the basics: Orthodoxy, Autocracy, and the Popular Spirit! Down with the revolution! No need for the constitution! For autocracy not restricted by anything!"[10] All right-wing parties included these formulae in their programs in one form or another.

Russian monarchists-traditionalists were strongly encouraged by the fact that Nicholas II received representatives of their cause after the issuing of the October Manifesto. During audiences held on December 23, 1905 and February 16, 1906, he used words that were music to the ear of any one of those who declared themselves to be "truly Russian people":

> My autocracy remains the same as it was in olden times . . . I believe that with your help the Russian people and I will manage to defeat Russia's enemies . . . I myself shall carry the burden of power levied on me in the Moscow Kremlin, and I am certain that the Russian people will help me. I shall account for my power before God . . . Unite, Russian people, I am counting on you.[11]

It thus seemed that the monarch was fully in accord with the right-wingers regarding the rejection of all political innovations declared in the October Manifesto. Indeed, the tsar also believed that changing the principles and structures of power was harmful and inadmissible. Deep in his heart he was with those who urged that "the native origins and foundations" should be preserved. But the words had been said, and the decision to take the road of liberal reform was irreversible. Up until his abdication, Nicholas II did not once have the desire to renege on what had been announced in 1905, although the right-wingers repeatedly urged him both in public and through various private channels to abandon these "dangerous experiments." This chiefly concerned the loathsome Duma, which the monarchists-traditionalists accused from the very first day of being responsible for virtually all of Russia's troubles.

On the eve of the issuing of the October Manifesto, the tsar wrote to the governor-general of St Petersburg Dmitrii Trepov:

Yes, Russia is receiving a constitution. There were not many of us who resisted it. But support for the struggle was not forthcoming from anywhere, a growing number of people turned away from us, and finally the inevitable happened. Nevertheless, honestly, I prefer to yield everything at once, instead of being forced to give in on minor points in the near future and in the end to come to the same thing.[12]

The monarchists-traditionalists could not dispute the monarch's will, which at least in theory was an incontrovertible law for them. At the same time, however, they could not accept the constitutional innovations or acknowledge the new center of legislative power in the form of the state-wide representative organ elected by the population, whose membership and activities were not regulated by the supreme power. They regarded the emerging parliament as a consultative council under the emperor. The charter of the Union of the Russian People declared that "the State Duma, alien to any limitation of the tsar's power, must be Russian in its national character." It ought to be "obliged to report truthfully the genuine needs of the people and the state in order to assist the legislature in implementing imperative reforms."[13]

When in early 1906 it became clear that elections to the Duma would indeed be held, the right-wingers were forced to accept the new political conditions and to join the campaign for electing deputies. This was an undesirable change in their tactics, but it was inevitable. With difficulty, lacking relevant skills and interest, the monarchists-traditionalists set out on the precarious path of overt factional struggle, the struggle of socio-economic and political ideas, as well as party tactics. Yet, the ultra-conservatives had no doubts: the majority would say "no" to trends alien to the "Russian spirit."

On the eve of the elections the rightists distributed printed materials throughout Russia urging voters not to follow "Russia's enemies." A leaflet issued in a mass printing under the characteristic title "Autocracy or Constitution?" stated:

The tsar decided to summon individuals elected by the population to provide regular counsel on affairs of state and to indicate people's needs . . . Only those persons who desire to take state power into their own hands might interpret the law on the State Duma and the October 17 Manifesto as the introduction of a constitution (parliamentary system) in Russia and the Tsar's rejection of the Autocracy.[14]

The results of the elections to the First State Duma, however, did not fulfill the hopes of the right. The winners were those who based their election campaigns on fierce criticism of the authorities and the country's sociopolitical and economic conditions in general. Nikolai Markov, formerly one of the most prominent right-wing statesmen and, after the fall of monarchy in Russia, a political émigré, wrote:

> The body of common people, whose opinions were brilliantly expressed by the Union of the Russian People, perceived the restricting of the Autocrat's rights as the worst disaster for Russia and for that reason refused to hear anything about a constitution, did not want to allow the thought that the Tsar was no longer an autocrat, that the Tsar's will was restricted from then on, and that the Tsar's conscience was no longer free. On the other hand, the Tsar-Autocrat himself had ordered recognition of the State Duma and the laws of 1906, even though they contained obvious signs of restricting and belittling the autocratic power.

But, according to Markov, the monarch's will forced the URP "to enter the struggle against the subversives . . . under the most unfavorable conditions for the organization of the common folk [the USP], that is, under the conditions of party parliamentarism." As he saw it, the idea of the constitution, represented by the State Duma, defeated the idea of autocracy, represented by the Union of the Russian People.[15]

It is of major significance that Markov should express these thoughts in the 1920s, when all of Europe's right-wingers observed the establishment of fascism in Italy – the triumph of strong national authoritarian power – with sentiment and admiration. The surviving Russian radical conservatives were no exception in this regard. "Yes, we are specific fascists, Russian fascists, and frankly we envy the Italian fascists since we have not been able to defeat the enemy yet," declared one of the monarchist spokesmen.[16] For his part, Markov argued with bitterness that

> if the Russian government at the time had been able to understand what Mussolini subsequently realized in Italy, and instead of stubbornly opposing the tsar and the monarchist group leaders had supported and implemented the appropriate, salvaging idea of the need for the Supreme Power to rely on the best sections of the population organized in strong unions, Russia's history would have been entirely different.[17]

The Orthodox autocratic tsardom, where the wise monarch would rule in "indissoluble union" with the simple, "pious folk," in an atmosphere of peace, agreement, and prosperity, was an old dream of the Russian traditionalists. The desire to realize it in practice could yield nothing but disappointment and resentment. Inevitably the obdurate pursuit of the illusion would result in domestic destabilization. And it did. In the last stage of Russia's imperial history, the right-wingers turned into "breachers of the peace" and did a great deal to discredit the tsar and the general notion of supreme power in Russia.

From 1906 on the right-wingers had to adapt to parliamentary forms of political negotiation. A paradoxical situation evolved in which the "orthodox monarchists" advocated defending the tsar and the monarchy in the spirit of traditional rule, while the supreme ruler supported a course which contradicted the principles and purpose of the right-wingers. Needless to say, the monarchists, while zealously defying the governments of Sergei Witte (October 1905 to April 1906) and Petr Stolypin (July 1906 to September 1911), could not pretend that the new political course was not the result of a conspiracy to thwart the will of the tsar; they were perfectly aware of the fact that the "constitutional experiment" had been sanctioned by Nicholas II and was being implemented with his explicit approval.

Nevertheless, the radical monarchists persistently directed their assaults against the "bureaucracy," the government, and high officials, and in doing so, they besieged and eventually attacked the very epicenter of power, the monarch himself. In December 1906, during his audience with members of monarchist organizations who demanded that the unbending power of the autocrat be confirmed, Nicholas II stated: "The manifesto I granted on October 17 is the full and assured expression of My steadfast and incontestable will, and an act that is not subject to change."[18] The right-wingers, however, did not seem to attach particular importance to these words. In the years that followed, they never ceased to repeat that "the tsar was a prisoner."

Such was their public position, but privately, inside the extreme monarchist group, in reality a completely different and occasionally anti-tsarist mood prevailed. Lev Tikhomirov reiterated an opinion widespread among the right-wing leadership when he wrote in his diary on October 28, 1905:

> Various conservative circles decided to set up their "Union of unions." What sense is there in it, if the tsar destroys everything and does not allow anything to be built? Of course, all these associations, whoever they belong to, are useful for the future because Russia is disintegrating, and the most important thing for its population is to get together in unions. But so long as such a person is at the head of the state, nothing but destruction can occur.[19]

Gradually, the rightists began to advocate and popularize ideas which undermined the very "fundamental principles" to which they always gave lip service. On the eve of the collapse of the monarchy in 1917, most rightist leaders had no doubts that the tsar was "weak" and "bad." Although the right-wingers had never proposed a coherent system of social reforms or even social reorganization, they castigated government policies with truly maniacal obsession, denouncing absolutely everything and everyone associated with the central administration. Even the tsar did not escape their attacks. It was the rightists who purposely exaggerated the Rasputin affair, turning Grigorii Rasputin into a problematic figure of paramount political importance.

The rightists awaited "strong decisions" and "firm words" from the monarch; they craved for "social restitution" which never came about, and, as far as they were concerned, the "state ship was heading in the wrong direction." In the rightists' eyes, the tsar's chief fault lay in his failure to head a public movement to turn back the course of events.

Indeed, there is no evidence to demonstrate that the tsar ever sought to return to the past, to the pre-October 1905 situation. Yet the opportunities to do so existed, such as at the time of the disbanding of the First Duma in the summer of 1906 and at the pivotal point of the Second Duma dissolution in June 1907, as well as in the following years. Even though momentous changes were indeed introduced in the country's electoral law in 1907, the representative legislative chamber – at the core of Russia's new constitutional arrangement – was not abolished. If Nicholas II had really "wished to turn back the wheel of history," as the radical monarchists always demanded (and as many historians subsequently suggested), he could have attempted to do so and most likely would have encountered little or no resistance in the postrevolutionary period. Yet he did nothing of the sort, although his "ideological sympathizers" cursed his "indecisiveness" and urged him to go ahead.

After the elections to the First and the Second Dumas produced a socialist and left-liberal parliamentary majority, many rightists openly appealed to the tsar to do away with such a hotbed of revolution. But the central administration adopted a different course. It could but did not postpone the convocation of the Third Duma indefinitely (as the monarchists-traditionalists beseeched the tsar); new elections were to be held at the time specified by law. Moreover, when the parliament resumed its work, the ruling power did not reject the practice of interacting with elected representatives. Until the fall of the monarchy, cabinet chairmen and ministers regularly appeared before the Duma deputies, discussed their programs, and provided explanations. All major bills passed through the "purgatory of the Duma."

Under the circumstances, the looming falling-out of the tsar with the politically active rightists became virtually unavoidable; this was particularly evident in their attitude with regard to Stolypin's administration. Initially, Nicholas II and his prime minister hoped that "true monarchists" would become the social mainstay of Stolypin's course of reform. After the dissolution of the Second Duma, the Union of the Russian People sent the tsar an enthusiastic telegram, supporting the action entirely. Still assuming that the organization's goals reflected the interests and hopes of the common folk – an illusion that he continued to live under – Nicholas II replied: "Let the Union of the Russian People be my reliable support, serving for everyone as a model" in defending law and order.[20]

Intense political polemics broke out as a result of this statement. Some regarded such public expression of sympathies inappropriate; others saw this as self-exposure on the part of the central administration; still others concluded that the tsar had finally "become enlightened." Indeed, the tsar *was* about to see the light, but in a way hardly welcome to the right-wingers: soon he was to realize that the monarchist parties were rather dubious organizations, which were obviously unable to provide any genuine support for the government. As a result, in the summer of 1907 Nicholas II effectively dissociated himself from those who defined themselves as "the loyal monarchists." The involvement of the Union of the Russian People in political assassinations, several sensational trials in which members of the Black Hundreds were the accused, scandals inside the right-wing parties – all led to this estrangement.

As far as Stolypin was concerned, he too was originally well disposed to the rightist organizations. As one of his distinguished colleagues later recalled, after coming to power the prime minister sought to create a mass social movement that was nationalist and socially controlling in character, similar to the one that would be founded by Mussolini.[21] In line with this objective, in 1906–7 the rightist organizations received government subsidies estimated at 3 million rubles (about 1.5 million dollars).

When it became obvious that the "allies," always eager to take advantage of concessions and financial allowances, were unable to engage in constructive activity and could not conduct daily political work within the framework of the law, Stolypin was forced to reconsider his attitude vis-à-vis the ultra-conservatives. For their part, Dubrovin and his supporters gradually became sworn opponents of Stolypin and his reform course. And the prime minister became the object of vicious and often abusive criticism on the pages of the *Russkoe Znamia* (Russian Banner), which was recurrently subject to fines and other punishments for "inadmissible assaults" against state officials.

Although the Union of the Russian People, along with some other smaller right-wing parties which had repudiated the October Manifesto, succeeded in having several deputies elected to the Duma, they had very little influence on political life and official domestic policies. The rightists' influence on the central administration was more apparent not at the political hub, but at a social level, primarily among the nobility, with its corporate interests, who were represented by the Council of United Gentry Societies (the "United Gentry"). This was an organization of landowning nobility which was founded in May 1906 and headed by some of the most prominent Russian aristocrats, such as Count A. A. Bobrinskii, Prince

N. F. Kasatkin-Rostovskii, and A. A. Naryshkin. The United Gentry proclaimed as its credo that the "supreme autocratic power is the unchanging
belief of the Russian people," and that it must "be guarded from any
encroachments."

The United Gentry, whose membership consisted of the country's aristocratic elite, had broad and varied contacts at the very top of the power
pyramid. Narrow corporate egoism turned the Russian aristocracy into a
hostage to its own landed interests, depriving it of long-term historical
vision. Members of the United Gentry thus became irreconcilable enemies
of Stolypin's policy. In their attacks against the prime minister and his government the organized gentry and the aristocrats hardly differed from the
"people of the streets," the Black Hundreds.

In 1908, a well-informed correspondent of the *Daily Telegraph* conveyed
in most precise terms the mood of the upper echelons of the gentry, which
"profoundly loathed the results of Stolypin's tenure" as the head of the
cabinet. In their view, "the loyal Duma and the equally loyal prime minister took up the cause inherited from the insurgent assemblies and political
incendiaries."[22] If it were up to them, Stolypin would not occupy his post
for a single day, but he remained prime minister and minister of internal
affairs for more than five years, and his activities were broken off not by
forced retirement (which the rightists dreamed of for years, regularly generating "reliable rumors" concerning his imminent fall), but by death as a
result of terrorist assassination on September 1, 1911.

Needless to say, the government course underwent fluctuations, and
many of the official resolutions were not accomplished in their entirety or
were changed during the implementation process. This was due to a variety
of reasons, not the least among them being the influence of the older generation of high-ranking bureaucrats, the "people of yesterday," whose traditional primary goal – the new political setting notwithstanding – was to
secure leading government posts for members of their own social and professional circles. Still, it is significant that during more than ten years of its
existence, the Duma monarchy did not allow a single prominent right-wing
politician to gain access to state power.

After 1905 the government retained most of the main features of the
modernization course. Stolypin's farmer-oriented transformation of agriculture continued, and in spite of the right-wing press, which waged a
bitter campaign against "foreign predators," the policy of encouraging free
enterprise and attracting foreign investments remained unchanged. The
independent judiciary survived. Although censorship was not abolished,
those in charge of it did their job "with velvet gloves." The right to form
various associations, as well as numerous other civil rights were preserved,
and the right-wing program thus seems to have failed miserably on most
counts as far as domestic issues were concerned. Nor did the rightists

achieve their goals in international affairs; for better or worse, Russia developed an alliance with liberal France and Britain and avoided diplomatic partnership with the kaiser's Germany. More importantly, perhaps, the State Duma retained its prime position in the country's political life; the tsar did not abolish it even after the beginning of World War I. On the whole, all the principal changes that were implemented after October 1905 and that drastically altered the face of imperial Russia were accomplished in spite of the desires, attitudes, and political efforts of the extreme right.

Notes

1   This article has been translated from the Russian by Sergei Sossinsky.
2   See, for example, Alexandra S. Korros, "The Legislative Chamber History Overlooked: The State Council of the Russian Empire, 1906–1917" in this volume.
3   GARF, f. 642, op. 1, d. 2328, p. 14.
4   "Perepiska Nikolaia II i Marii Fedorovny," *Krasnyi arkhiv*, vols 1–2 (50–1) (Moscow–Leningrad, 1932), 184.
5   V. Ostretsov, *Chernaia sotnia i krasnaia sotnia* (Moscow: "Voenizdat," 1991), 7.
6   S. A. Stepanov, *Chernaia sotnia v Rossii (1905–1914 gg.)* (Moscow: "Rosvuznauka", 1992), 105.
7   Ostretsov, *Chernaia sotnia i krasnaia sotnia*, 41.
8   *Svod Zakonov Rossiiskoi Imperii*, vol. 1, part 1 (St Petersburg, 1906), Article 4.
9   *Grazhdanin*, 7 (St Petersburg, 1906): 9.
10 *Tretii Vserossiiskii s'ezd russkikh liudei* (Kiev, 1906), 62.
11 GAEF, f. 116, op. 2, d. 1, p. 1.
12 R. Sh. Ganelin, *Rossiiskoe samoderzhavie v 1905 godu: Reformy i revoliutsiia* (St Petersburg: "Nauka", 1991), 214.
13 The right-wingers extended the concept of "Russianness" not only to ethnic Russians but also to the Ukrainians and the Belorussians ("Ustav Obshchestva 'Soiuz Russkogo Naroda'" in Ostretsov, *Chernaia sotnia i krasnaia sotnia*, 42).
14 GARF, f. 116, op. 1, d. 76, p. 1ob.
15 N. E. Markov, *Voiny temnykh sil* (Moscow: "Moskvitianin", 1993), 117–18, 120.
16 *Ezhenedel'nik vysshego monarkhicheskogo soveta* (Berlin, July 2, 1923). For additional details see Hans Rogger, *Jewish Policies and Right-Wing Politics in Imperial Russia* (London: Macmillan, 1986).
17 Markov, *Voiny temnykh sil*, 118.
18 S. S. Ol'denburg, *Tsarstvovanie imperatora Nikolaia II* (St Petersburg: "Petropol", 1991), 329.
19 "25 Let nazad. (Iz dnevnika L. Tikhomirova)," *Krasnyi arkhiv*, 3 (1930): 93.
20 *Slovo*, St Petersburg (June 6, 1907).
21 S. E. Kryzhanovskii, *Vospominaniia* (Berlin, 1938), 152.
22 Article reprinted in Russian conservative newspaper *Kievlianin*, June 10–11, 1908.

PART IV

The Establishment

CHAPTER ELEVEN

The Security Police and Politics in Late Imperial Russia[1]

Jonathan Daly

As revolutionary conspiracies and mass opposition movements gathered strength during the last four decades of the Russian Empire, the imperial security police developed and expanded in an attempt to meet the challenge. This essay tells that story by drawing upon a wide range of published and unpublished official documents, many of them only recently declassified in the Russian archives. As the story unfolds, it becomes clear that the imperial security police grew more sophisticated and professional, especially from the mid-1890s to the end of the monarchy in 1917. They also affected politics in two ways. First, the security police maintained a thorough and continuous watchfulness over many aspects of social and political life. The point here, in principle at least, was to provide objective, detailed information permitting senior officials to take timely steps to avert outbursts of popular discontent and to undertake such reforms as were necessary to preserve public tranquility and state security. Second, they aimed to thwart plots to overthrow the existing state order. In this regard, the bulk of the security police's energy was devoted to matching wits with members of the terrorist "People's Will" from the late 1870s to the mid-1890s and with Social Democrats and Socialists-Revolutionaries after the turn of the century.

The assiduous terrorist campaign against the emperor and his officials waged in 1878–81 was a watershed in the development of the security police in Russia. During this period, the People's Will essentially forced the imperial regime to develop modern methods of covert operation. When broad opposition movements arose in the 1890s, the imperial security police refined and expanded these methods and subsequently were able to hold most revolutionary leaders at bay. Yet they proved powerless to combat the kind of mass popular agitation which nearly put an end to the imperial order in 1905. The granting of some civil liberties to the emperor's subjects and the establishment of a semiconstitutional order beginning in 1906 partially isolated the radical opposition. Moreover, major improvements in security police technique and organization introduced during the interrevolutionary years permitted the security police both to respect legal procedure and to neutralize the "professional revolutionaries." Popular discontent deepened again beginning in 1916 amidst the rigors of World War I. Opposition to the regime gradually overwhelmed the security police, whose main activities were the surgical removal of revolutionary leaders and the provision of sophisticated domestic intelligence on the "popular mood." By late February 1917, only the army could have saved the monarchy.

The People's Will

Until the rise of the People's Will, the imperial regime had devoted little attention to the development of a security police apparatus. Immediately after the Decembrist Uprising, Nicholas I established his famous Third Section and Gendarme Corps in 1826, and Alexander II, having survived an assassination attempt in April 1866, instituted in St Petersburg the empire's first security police bureau (*Okhrannoe otdelenie*). No further improvements were undertaken until late 1880. Indeed, when the People's Will declared "open season" on the emperor (August 26, 1879), his security police were, in the words of one member of the terrorist organization, "weak and disorganized . . . lamentable."[2] The disarray in the security service was due in no small measure to the fact that the People's Will had their own spy within the security police system. Nikolai Kletochnikov, whom Vera Figner called "utterly invaluable," undermined the efforts to combat the People's Will from January 1879 till December 1880.[3] The least that can be said is that the security police were manifestly less efficient and sophisticated in this period than were the revolutionary adversaries of the imperial order.

The government tried to compensate for this deficiency by expanding the powers of administrative officialdom.[4] This was, of course, practically useless for combating a small, highly conspiratorial terrorist organization, such as the People's Will. It was as if the government had declared war on the entire country in retaliation for the damage inflicted by a few dozen revolutionaries. The struggle against conspirators required a highly sophisticated security police, yet no efforts were made to reform police institutions until August and October 1880 when a new police institution, the Police Department, replaced the Third Section and a security bureau (the second one in the empire) was established in Moscow.[5] Grigorii Sudeikin, chief of the security bureau in St Petersburg and one of a rare breed of professionally sophisticated gendarme officers, penetrated the People's Will with informers and arrested several of its members by early 1881. Although he failed to prevent the murder of Alexander II on March 1, 1881, over the next two years Sudeikin, his assistant Peter Rachkovskii, and their key informer, Sergei Degaev, arrested the remaining members of the People's Will. The revolutionaries exacted their revenge – Degaev turned traitor and helped them to murder Sudeikin in December 1883 – but the People's Will never returned to its former strength.

It had been impossible for the imperial regime to combat the People's Will without resorting to informers. To do so was to emulate the conspirators, for Kletochnikov demonstrated that one well-placed individual could nearly incapacitate an apparently formidable, secretive organization. Degaev and other police informers revealed that the imperial security police could learn the same game, a game that played itself out in kaleidoscopic variety until the fall of the imperial order. As Sudeikin's demise plainly shows, however, this powerful weapon was double-edged. Its inherent dangers were hidden for almost two decades because during those years the regime faced almost no conspiratorial threats and the few active conspirators were inept. The plot of 1887 was the only serious exception and it was foiled thanks to the police's system of mail interception.[6] The relative absence of such dangers lulled senior police officials into complacency and few advances were made in security police methods before the 1890s. In practical terms informers were considered expendable and few of them survived longer than a year or so before they were unmasked. If this policy of neglect was bad for the struggle against anti-government groups, however, it was a great boon for the security police in general, for a few unmasked informers went on to play an extremely important role as directors of security police operations until the revolution of 1905.

Most gendarme officers were men with military training and an abiding sense of hierarchy and authority, occasionally men of talent, but lacking a subtle understanding of the forces imperiling the regime. Those who reformed the security police system over the next two decades, by contrast, were men like Peter Rachkovskii and especially Sergei Zubatov. Rachkovskii had worked briefly as an informer in 1879 (until Kletochnikov blew his cover), then virtually created the Paris Security Bureau which he headed from 1884 to 1902. Zubatov, an informer for the Moscow Security Bureau in 1886–7, was appointed chief of that bureau in 1896. He appropriated

and further developed the methods of Sudeikin and by the end
of the decade, according to an official police report, the Moscow bureau
had become the heart and soul of the empire's security system.[7] Zubatov,
Rachkovskii, and several others introduced into the system an inventive-
ness, a vitality, an enthusiasm, and a spirit of adventure and iconoclasm
previously absent from Russia's security service. More importantly, they
sought to professionalize the service by training police personnel and
by establishing precise methods of operation. Working primarily in the
Moscow and Paris bureaus, they essentially created imperial Russia's
mature security system, what some outsiders called the *okhrana* or, pejo-
ratively, *okhranka*.

Zubatov's New Security Police

Beginning in the 1890s, a broad antigovernment ferment developed
throughout the Russian empire, in response to the government's apparent
inability to deal with the terrible famine of 1890–1. Radical youths trav-
eled to the famine-stricken areas and agitated for a revolutionary uprising.
Out of their experience several underground organizations developed in
the People's Will tradition.[8] In addition, from the early years of Nicholas
II's reign, his government faced a steadily growing, continually diversifying oppositional movement within the population. The number of gendarme inquests into political crimes rose from 56 cases involving 559
people in 1894 to 1,522 cases involving 6,405 people in 1903, an increase
of 1,259 percent and 608 percent, respectively.[9] The multiplication of such
cases continued through the 1905–7 Revolution, nearly overwhelming the
capacity of the regime's police and military forces to deal with them, before
subsiding in 1908.

Still, until the turn of the century, the security police had revolutionary
conspirators well under control. Rachkovskii, in Paris with a dozen informers, kept abreast of developments among the radical émigrés and
occasionally arranged their arrest in collaboration with European police
forces.[10] The Police Department coordinated the information sent in from
provincial gendarme stations, mail interception offices, and the security
bureaus in the imperial capitals and in Paris. It also recruited informers on
an irregular basis. Often this was done without much genuine effort on the
police's part. For example, in 1893 the would-be notorious spy Evno Azef
voluntarily offered his services.[11] Meanwhile, the most important active
war against subversion was being waged in Moscow by Zubatov, who did
more than anyone to systematize and render more sophisticated the standard methods of security policing.[12] Indeed, one senior police official later
described the Moscow bureau as the "quasi-official central investigatory

[*rozysknoe*] agency of the Police Department. In a word, Moscow in those days [*c.*1894–1902] was considered a school for informers and surveillants."[13] Zubatov questioned political suspects as though leading a radical discussion circle, showering them with attention, offering them food and drink, and arguing passionately that the people never profit from revolutionary violence, that only the emperor was capable of implementing needed reforms in Russia. His enthusiasm and energy were extremely attractive to revolutionaries lacking deep convictions and permitted him to turn some of them away from the paths of political opposition. Professing a "profound love for and faith in his cause," like a radical activist, Zubatov imparted to several of his protégés in the security bureau an ardent commitment and dedication rarely encountered in gendarme officers.[14]

Zubatov's closest assistant, Evstratii Mednikov, a clever Old Believer of peasant stock, refined the deployment of plain-clothes police agents, called surveillants (*filery*). The gendarmes' easily recognizable blue uniform made them utterly incapable of conducting covert surveillance, yet before the early 1880s they were allowed to undertake plain-clothes operations only in exceptional cases. At the Moscow Security Bureau, surveillants memorized the city's physical layout, including restaurants, bars, factories, taxi stations and tramway routes, as well as streets, alleys and courtyards, to enable them to maneuver freely around suspects. During training, experienced agents accompanied fresh recruits on their rounds after teaching them to recognize and commit to memory facial features through systematic study of physiognomy and by poring over photographs of revolutionaries. Finally, the novices learned to employ make-up and disguises, of which the security bureau kept an abundant supply. Surveillants jotted down their observations in diaries, tens of thousands of which are preserved in the police archives. They are generally little more than a dull catalogue of pedestrian occurrences in the life of persons under surveillance, yet security bureau clerks used them to prepare a welter of "finding aids," including weighty name and place registers and complex diagrams of relations among opponents of the regime. The number of such trained surveillants in Moscow rose from 17 in 1881 to 50 in 1902, after which the number fluctuated between 50 and 100. (After the turn of the century, the St Petersburg bureau's staff of surveillants modestly exceeded these figures.)[15]

More important than surveillants were informers, without whom "the political police are blind," in the words of one security chief.[16] The Third Section had employed secret informers since its creation, yet once again Zubatov devised systematic methods for their use. He was a master at questioning them, winning their confidence, and maximizing their usefulness. Zubatov emphasized that case officers must win their agents' trust, protect them from discovery, assist them in adversity, and increase their faith in the Russian monarchy.[17] He urged his officers, according to one of them, to treat their informer as

> a beloved woman with whom you have entered into illicit relations. Look after her like the apple of your eye. One careless move and you will dishonor her . . . Take this to heart: treat these people as I am advising, and they will understand your needs, will trust you, and will work with you honestly and selflessly.[18]

The number of informers was never great, and before Zubatov they were very few indeed. Kletochnikov, who had access to the security police's most sensitive files in 1879–80, found a record of only 115 permanent informers in the whole empire – this at the height of terrorist attacks against the emperor and his officials.[19] Later, there were part-time police informers within nearly every major social group and profession, although even the security bureaus in the imperial capitals never employed more than 50 permanent informers. Most important informers were students in the 1880s and 1890s, and members of the two principal revolutionary parties (the SRs and the SDs) after the turn of the century. People became informers for a variety of reasons. Some agreed to inform in order to take revenge upon their erstwhile comrades (Zubatov claimed this of himself), some sought adventure or took a liking to their case officers; probably all feared punishment and desired material benefits. A few earnestly wished to serve their government in its struggle against the onslaught of revolutionary sedition. Wages ranged from 5–10 rubles to 100–200 rubles monthly. (By contrast, surveillants and skilled metalworkers earned 50 rubles per month.)[20] Valuable, long-time informers could hope to receive a solid pension (up to 3,000 rubles or even more for the stars) or a one-time lump-sum subsidy (as much as 5,000 rubles).[21] Zubatov defined informers as the security police's principal and most valuable means of surveillance, and therefore considered his main task to acquire and supervise them. Sometimes he used chance meetings with industrial workers or personnel of important public organizations as opportunities to recruit them as agents. A certain number of informers simply proposed their own services. The majority of agents began to work for the police after arrest – and under interrogation. It was natural to desire a pardon, perhaps even to repent, amid the fear and loneliness that accompanied arrest. With this in mind, security bureau chiefs often sought to persuade political detainees to serve the state by bullying some of them and by promising leniency to others, depending on each individual's character. The informers infiltrated legal and illegal groups and organizations, providing inside information which security bureau officers verified by deploying more than one informer per target organization along with per-lustration and external surveillance.[22]

The rise of broad-based opposition movements in the 1890s pre-sented the government with a new menace. The relatively efficient security bureaus in the imperial capitals drove radical activists out into the provinces,[23] where the majority of provincial gendarme authorities were, by the admission of the Police Department itself, "unsuited for tracking down plotters in clandestine fashion . . . [each] struggling with the [revo-lutionary] movement in a haphazard manner."[24] Therefore, the Moscow Security Bureau was authorized in 1894 to create a special detachment of highly experienced surveillants as a mobile force capable of traveling quickly to localities with a high incidence of antigovernment activity. The mobile surveillance brigade (*Letuchii otriad filerov*) was headquartered in Moscow because of its central location in European Russia and because Moscow's security bureau had already acquired its reputation as the nerve center of the Russian security police, a reputation it owed to Zubatov (who was still deputy director).[25] As a sort of moveable security bureau, the mobile brigade was designed to uncover distribution networks of rev-olutionary literature, illegal printing presses, and propaganda rings. It per-mitted Zubatov to extend his reach throughout the empire: to neighboring provinces, to St Petersburg and, equipped with translators, as far afield as Belorussia, Ukraine or the Baltic region. As such, it virtually became an executive arm of the entire security police system, of which Zubatov there-fore became *de facto* co-director. From his headquarters in Moscow, and in constant contact with the Police Department, Zubatov coordinated major operations across the empire – from surveillance to mass arrests. The key to its success was its mobility: those under surveillance were less likely to recognize a surveillant constantly on the move than one permanently stationed in one place. The brigade achieved its success with a staff of only 30 surveillants in 1894 and 50 in January 1901.[26]

Zubatov's development of new police methods, especially the systematic and extensive employment of informers, was undoubtedly the most significant advance in Russian political policing since the creation of the Third Section. It also set him at odds with the majority of Russian security policemen, the gendarmes, especially such venerable war horses as General V. D. Novitskii, gendarme chief in Kiev. Such policemen, even when lacking precise information about criminal activity, sometimes arrested dozens of people in order to discover a few political criminals: that is, not on the basis of evidence of political wrongdoing, but in order to obtain evidence.[27] Zubatov argued, by contrast, that suspects should be arrested or exiled administratively only upon discovery of strong evidence of their involve-ment in political crime, to avoid creating victims and alienating the popu-lation from the government.[28] Zubatov preferred to wait patiently for an underground group to come into possession of incriminating evidence (illegal literature, forged passports, explosives, or weapons) or for the arrival of a major revolutionary leader from abroad, before arresting its members. The point was to let the group reveal its purposes in order both to learn more about the broader movement of which it was a part and to catch it *in flagrante delicto*.[29]

Mass Opposition and the Security Police under Zubatov

If Zubatov's methods were more effective and fruitful in the long run, however, they were also more dangerous. By allowing the revolutionaries room to maneuver, the police risked letting them perpetrate crimes. Likewise, informers were obliged to participate more fully in the work of the illegal organizations, laying them open to charges of provocation. Given the difficulties and dangers inherent in the new approach, it is hardly surprising that many gendarmes continued to prefer the older, more heavy-handed methods.[30] Yet Zubatov was surely right that by the mid-1890s the security police had to ascend to a higher level of professional sophistication. Whereas the opposition "movement" had comprised a few dozen members under Nicholas I and only a few thousand under Alexanders II and III, it fell to Nicholas II's lot to rule over an empire in which social discontent gradually became a mass phenomenon. Zubatov realized that the police could no longer gather vague information about the existence or activity of a revolutionary group, and then proceed to liquidate it; the security system was not equipped to punish or otherwise neutralize all such "suspicious" people in Russia. Furthermore, as a former radical himself, he was convinced that much popular discontent was justified. In any event, he felt that the government could not afford to alienate the hordes of people caught in the gendarmes' nets.[31] A radical activist, V. V. Vodovozov, explicitly contrasted the two types of political policeman:

> He [Novitskii] was menacing to individual persons who fell into his hands, he was menacing for the peaceful inhabitants of Kiev, perhaps [also] for moderate liberalism, but the revolutionary movement flowed right past him, suffering from him much less than from the more refined heroes of political policing [*sysk*], like Zubatov.[32]

Also unlike the Novitskiis (and indeed most senior government officials), Zubatov recognized in the labor movement the regime's most formidable potential opposition in the 1890s. If the police had been physically able to arrest a large portion of the revolutionaries of the 1870s and 1880s, it would prove impossible to arrest 10,000 (or 100,000) striking workers.

The massive strikes of 1896–7 underscored this point. Moreover, the SDs were enjoying considerable success in spreading their revolutionary theories and agitation among the ranks of the industrial workers. In this context, Zubatov conceived of an astonishing program: to organize industrial workers on behalf of the government and to strive to improve the material conditions of their life in order to win them away from the revolutionary opposition. He argued that only the absolutist monarchy, an institution above classes and estates, could advance the industrial workers' interests. The revolutionaries, he asserted, wished to use them only to further their own political goals. Zubatov was here responding to Marxism's growing hegemony among the radical intelligentsia in the second half of the 1890s. The patronage of Moscow's powerful governor general, the emperor's uncle, Grand Duke Sergei Aleksandrovich, permitted him to implement this bold policy. Of course, Zubatov's security bureau gave radical labor organizers no quarter and, consequently, Moscow acquired the reputation among experienced SD activists as a dangerous place to work.[33]

Apparently in response to a coalescing of revolutionary organizations in the late 1890s, in January 1898 the Police Department created a Special Section for coordinating security policing operations throughout the empire. The Special Section's staff of five assistants, seven clerks and three typists (1900) were nearly all civilians until 1905, when a few gendarme officers took important positions. The new institution was so secretive that one entered it by passing through Chief Leonid Rataev's office on the top (fourth) floor of the Police Department building at 16 Fontanka Quay in St Petersburg, whilst the chief and his assistants concealed the true nature of their work, claiming to be professors, writers, or merchants. Some of them were accustomed to exercising the rules of secrecy, having formerly plied the trade of secret informer. While the actual fighting against the revolutionary opposition was left to Zubatov in Moscow, the Special Section in St Petersburg analyzed, classified, and interpreted data furnished by police institutions, informers, and perlustration; surveyed the various opposition groups and movements and prepared assessments of their strength and significance; compiled, organized, and indexed information on social disorders, students, workers, and the general mood of the Russian population; and coordinated the search for political criminals.[34]

The SDs held their first congress in Minsk on March 1–2, 1898, but the police immediately arrested every delegate – save three whom Zubatov deliberately left at liberty, in the hope that they would lead him to their colleagues in revolution.[35] Both police repression (Lenin, Martov, and Potresov were exiled to Siberia) and philosophical and programmatic differences among SDs delayed the convocation of a Second Party Congress until 1903. In the meantime, there erupted in 1899 student disorders which an insightful gendarme officer described as "the commencement of that public [*obshchestvennoe*] movement, which, growing steadily thereafter, won over an ever broader range of people, merged with the revolutionaries and flowed into the revolution of 1905."[36] Student disorders broke out again in 1901, the year in which the SR party began to cohere. The party's program of political terror began on February 14, 1901 with the murder of the minister of education, N. P. Bogolepov. That summer, Zubatov admitted that "despite a whole series of successful arrests the revolutionary movement . . . [is] growing and consolidating itself."[37] Indeed, although his men seized the SR press and arrested most of the activists connected with it in fall 1901, those who fled abroad reestablished the newspaper in Switzerland in early 1902 and worked with greater urgency than ever to bring together the SRs at large.[38] By late 1901 and early 1902, industrial workers and university students participated jointly in major demonstrations, which prompted Zubatov to propose to organize a countermovement among students designed to divide radicals and moderates (official sanction was not forthcoming). The government itself first overreacted to the demonstrations, then relented: it conscripted into the army and expelled hundreds of students from the universities (on the authority of the law penned in part by Bogolepov in 1899), only to readmit them in the fall.[39] The message was clear: the government is arbitrary and repressive, but not overly to be feared by committed radicals. It was precisely at this moment that Lenin argued that the revolutionary movement would triumph only if a "few professionals, *as highly trained and experienced as the imperial security police*, were allowed to organize it."[40] It seems, however, that the greatest threat to the regime was less the revolutionary conspirators, whom the Russian security police generally managed to control, but mass opposition movements.

Indeed, neither the provincial gendarme stations, nor the security bureaus, nor even Zubatov's mobile brigade could cope with the growing and diversifying opposition.[41] Few gendarmes were prepared to match wits with antigovernment activists, and the mobile brigade, which had been created to make lightning strikes in specific localities, was now stretched to the limit of its resources, its agents almost permanently based in more than a dozen places.[42] Zubatov persuaded the interior minister, V. K. Plehve (who replaced the assassinated D. S. Sipiagin in April 1902), to authorize the creation of a network of provincial security bureaus staffed by dynamic gendarme officers and surveillants transferred from the mobile brigade. Zubatov was named Special Section chief in August and 20 bureaus were created from then until June 1903.[43] The new institutions occupied an ambiguous position within the imperial bureaucracy. In matters affecting "state security" they were independent and authoritative, but in all other affairs they were partially subordinated to the provincial gendarme station chiefs. It is unclear what this "subordination" meant, since the bureau chiefs were empowered, "in extreme circumstances," to launch searches or arrests outside their provinces without contacting either local authorities or the Police Department. This was a prescription for disastrous intra-bureaucratic relations and many gendarme chiefs were justifiably furious.[44] Be that as it may, the new bureaus, especially in Kiev, Odessa, Kharkov, and Ekaterinoslav, delivered impressive results. Most notably, Aleksandr Spiridovich in Kiev arrested two key terrorist organizers of the SR "combat organization," M. M. Mel'nikov and G. A. Gershuni, in January and May 1903, respectively. When May Day demonstrations did not take place in 1903 almost anywhere in the empire except in the Caucasus region, senior police and Interior Ministry authorities exulted and ascribed the good news to the efforts of the new security bureaus.[45]

Within a few months, however, with Zubatov's unexpected dismissal, the security system lost its source of inspiration. In July 1903, massive strikes swept the Black Sea littoral and the Caucasus: a foretaste of the October 1905 general strike. Zubatov urged moderation in dealing with the unrest, the more so as his labor experiment was well entrenched in Odessa. Yet on Plehve's orders, the general strike in that city was brutally crushed in mid-July.[46] Zubatov waxed indignant, treated Plehve with great disre-spect, and, it has beeen argued, may have worked with Witte and others to oust him. Such a conspiracy by itself would surely have given Plehve grounds to dismiss Zubatov and to banish him from the major cities of Russia (which he did on August 19), but it seems that the alleged com-plicity of Zubatov's labor activists in the Odessa strikes gave Plehve as well as Zubatov's other enemies in the government sufficient grounds to denounce him as "an enemy of order" and therefore to punish him for this severely.[47] In any event, the security system was deprived of its most tal-ented director. He had introduced into it hallmarks of professionalization and bureaucratization, most notably in the establishment of precise rules of operation and specialized training, which together fostered the replace-ability of individual office-holders. Unfortunately, however, there had been too little time for these reforms to take hold and in November 1904 Mednikov lamented that the entire system was crumbling before his eyes.[48]

1905 and the Post-Zubatov Security Police

It could not have happened at a worse time. Plehve had been assassinated in July 1904. The conciliatory attitude of his successor, P. D. Sviatopolk-Mirskii, merely encouraged oppositional sentiment, which had been build-ing under the pressure of government repression, to burst forth into a fever of social militancy which was exacerbated by Russia's sagging fortunes in its war with Japan. Bloody Sunday (January 9, 1905) ignited massive popular unrest and throughout the year the opposition movements grew into a mighty phalanx of antigovernment forces – agrarian and urban, educated and illiterate, left-liberal and revolutionary. Officials were continuously threatened by terrorist attacks. From February 1905 to May 1906, 1,075 of them were killed or wounded.[49] Since the security police, by their very nature, were powerless to forestall spontaneous, disorganized outbursts of mass popular discontent, the regime would have been less endangered had the regular police apparatus held firm.[50] Yet it did not: under A. G. Bulygin, the entire Interior Ministry was in "complete disorganization [*razval*]" by late summer.[51]

As is well known, the crisis peaked in October with a general strike that immobilized much of urban Russia and prompted the emperor to agree to diminish the power of officialdom and to reinforce the rights of his subjects.[52] In this new context, many officials had no idea how to act or react, to the extent that in early November the Police Department considered it necessary to deny rumors that the security bureaus and gendarme stations would shut down.[53] To make matters worse, terrible agrarian violence broke out in nearly every province of European Russia from late October through December and an armed uprising took place in Moscow in mid-December. The entire imperial order might have collapsed had not the hardline Peter Nikolaevich Durnovo been appointed interior minister in late October by a fearful Premier Sergei Witte over the indignant protests of nearly all the public figures in Russia.[54] The new interior minister and other proponents of law and order drew three conclusions from the anarchy of late 1905. First, signs of weakness and concessions to the opposition tended to undermine the regime. Second, only decisive leadership and timely repression had a prayer of holding the system together. Third, the peasantry and petty urban dwellers could not be relied upon to oppose the radicals. In a word, only a harshly authoritarian state could survive in Russia given the strength of the opposition and the complexity of the social and economic problems facing the country. By January 1906, this view held sway within a large portion of officialdom.[55]

The confrontation between regime and revolutionaries for another two years remained bloody. The regular and especially military courts heard thousands of state-crime cases beginning in 1906. Whereas 308 alleged political criminals had passed before military judges in 1905, 4,698 did so in 1906.[56] "Punitive expeditions" restored order along the trans-Siberian railroad, in Ukraine, in the Caucasus, and, most notoriously, in the Baltic region (where between December 1905 and May 1906 some 1,170 people were killed). All told, 14,000 people may have lost their lives in the government's attempt in 1905–6 to preserve the regime and restore order.[57] Even so, the revolutionary terror did not abate. As many as 1,126 government officials were also killed, and another 1,506 wounded, in 1906. These figures more than doubled the following year; non-official casualties were just as gruesome.[58] Moreover revolutionaries and common bandits carried out 4,138 armed robberies in 1906 (up from 3,219 in 1905).[59] To improve control of all kinds, thousands of additional regular policemen were recruited in 1906 (at a cost of 18 million rubles).[60]

At the same time, state and opposition confronted one another uneasily in the State Duma, the new parliament of the Russian Empire. On April 26, the less despised Peter Stolypin replaced Durnovo as interior minister and was appointed premier on July 8, the day before the Duma's sudden dissolution. During the interparliamentary period that followed, Stolypin intended to implement a whole raft of reforms, but his notorious first major act (one week after a terrorist attempt on his life which left 27 people dead) was to institute military field courts for trying persons alleged to have committed violent attacks on state officials or institutions. The field courts, which were obliged to pass judgment in no more than two days and to carry out the sentence (usually death) within one day, operated until April 1907, and executed as many as 1,000 alleged terrorists.[61]

Stolypin is perhaps best known for this official campaign of counter-terror and for his land reforms or "wager on the strong" peasants, but his administration also reformed the security police system. From December 1906 to January 1907, Stolypin's protégé and director of the Police Department, M. I. Trusevich, created eight regional security bureaus, each comprising six to 12 provinces and corresponding roughly to the spheres of activity of the SR party.[62] Their directors were the security bureau chiefs in St Petersburg, Moscow, Kharkov, Kiev, Odessa, Vilna, Riga, and the gendarme station chief in Samara.[63] The directors were supposed to coordinate and improve the operations and information-gathering of the several gendarme stations and security bureaus within their jurisdictions, but also had the right to order arrest and search operations. This angered gendarme station chiefs who were nearly all of higher rank.[64] To alleviate these tensions and improve operations, Trusevich issued numerous directives and manuals on security police methods and organized periodic summit meetings.[65]

The acrimony between regime and public was even more bitter in the Second Duma than in the first, and on June 3, 1907 the emperor again peremptorily dissolved the assembly. Expecting massive popular disorder, Stolypin ordered administrative and police authorities to preserve public order at any cost.[66]

Overall, however, a spirit of moderation prevailed among senior police officials. A series of directives rebuked lower administrative and police authorities for taking indiscriminate recourse to administrative exile and for insufficiently strict observance of legal procedure.[67] These strictures were directed primarily at provincial gendarme and security chiefs who often found it difficult to penetrate the revolutionaries' conspiratorial defenses. The major security bureaus, by contrast, disposed of well-placed informers permitting them to focus their attention on genuine subversion. This was an extremely important distinction. The police system was able to function within the framework of a legal, semi-constitutional order only insofar as its security police apparatus possessed a reasonably effective intelligence-gathering capability. The efficiency of the bureaus in the imperial capitals and a few provincial cities permitted them to undermine revolutionary organizations without harassing large numbers of innocent people. Only a really sophisticated police system can distinguish between mere malcontents and genuine subversives.

But perhaps Russia's security men were too sophisticated. Novitskii and other ordinary police officials surely thought so, as did the Social Democrat, Osip Ermanskii. In his experience, the security men who employed Zubatov's tactic often gave wider latitude than did ordinary gendarme officers to revolutionary activists in the hope that they would incriminate themselves further. Yet, asked Ermanskii,

> who gained more from this policy, the government or the revolutionaries? . . . While the Police Department carefully gathered material and then subjected it to scientific analysis, we were permitted to place a mine beneath the very edifice of absolutism and capitalism whose safeguard and perpetuation that clever [police] system had been designed to ensure.[68]

The Calm Before the Storm

Of course, Ermanskii was viewing the system from the point of view of the collapse of the monarchy, an event far from inevitable. Beginning in late 1907 and early 1908, the regime gained the upper hand in its struggle against the radicals, of whose activity the Police Department reported a significant diminution.[69] One senior official reported in early 1908 that "everywhere revolutionary newspapers bitterly complain about the intensification of the 'reaction' and about the indifference of the population to the activity of revolutionaries, and this is a good sign of the return to tranquility of the country."[70] Indeed, the first issue of a new Socialist Revolutionary party journal declared in April that "the autocracy has reestablished itself."[71] Many radical activists remained, but they were driven largely underground, and senior police officials felt sufficiently confident over the next two years to return most of the empire to normal law, to issue fewer death sentences, and to seek to prevent excessive use of administrative punishments.[72] The regime seemed very much in control, the revolutionaries had been routed, and constitutionalism and the rule of law were not entirely jettisoned to accomplish this.

On January 7, 1909, the SR party repudiated one of its most celebrated terrorist leaders, Evno Azef, as a police informer. The perfect "double agent," both police and party had considered him utterly loyal. Azef's exposure severely damaged the SR party by engendering within it "an obsessive preoccupation with accusations and mutual suspicions."[73] The unmasking of almost two dozen more informers over the next four years merely exacerbated this problem.[74] By January 1913, the security police could report that, although the SR party's program of terror and broad social base made it potentially the most dangerous political organization in Russia, it then existed only in emigration and even there most party activists "consider their future, in the sense of continued revolutionary work, finished."[75] Senior police officials, in their response to the Azef affair, worried that it would become harder to recruit new informers. A police directive urged gendarme and security chiefs to reassure their informers that the Police Department had been able to protect Azef for 16 years, but also to warn them that all provocation would be punished severely. It seems, in fact, that the recruitment of police informers did not suffer much from the Azef affair; most of the 94 informers employed by the St Petersburg Security Bureau in 1913 – it had never employed a larger number – had been hired during the previous three years.[76]

The Police Department's success in devastating the revolutionary organizations did not cause it to become complacent. The Special Section cajoled, provoked, rebuked, encouraged, and criticized both the regional and provincial security bureaus and the gendarme stations with great frequency and vigor. A steady stream of directives urged them to acquire more informers, to study the revolutionary organizations, to train more surveillants, to use conspiratorial methods, to send agents deep into the countryside, to cooperate more effectively, to provide more precise information, and to use good judgment before searching suspects. Experienced gendarme officers were sent out to the provinces on inspection tours, a serious training course for gendarme officers was instituted in 1910, and for this purpose Special Section clerks drew up large, multi-colored diagrams of the major revolutionary parties.[77]

The security system was definitely becoming more professional and productive, but its reputation suffered a further blow on September 1, 1911 when an erstwhile police informer, Dmitrii Bogrov, fatally shot Prime Minister Stolypin in Kiev. Public opinion waxed indignant at the thought that the security police were still relying on such unsavory elements as Bogrov, that is, like Azef, a police informer out of control. The reactionary Prince V. P. Meshcherskii called the Okhrana "the most harmful, immoral, and dangerous invention in the Russian bureaucratic system," a sort of

"Spanish Inquisition with a slight softening of manners." N. A. Gredeskul, a well-known Kadet jurist, admitted that in the face of massive political terror the government had had to adopt secret and underhanded methods, but he added that this had led inevitably to the Azef and Bogrov affairs. Since political terrorism had by 1911 come largely to an end, the government, he argued, should put an end to its own covert operations.[78] Curiously, the Kadet was more sympathetic to the regime's predicament than was the monarchist. Gredeskul was right: it is essentially impossible to combat a conspiracy without resorting to conspiratorial methods. This was true in the case of both People's Will and the SR terrorists. But once the latter had been disorganized, was it not possible for the police to renounce such methods as Gredeskul urged? Unfortunately, the SRs never officially repudiated the use of terror, and many SD leaders continued to lay plans to orchestrate the violent overthrow of the imperial order. Thus, in the interest of state security, the imperial security police continued to deploy secret informers among them, and quite successfully: the major revolutionary parties in 1912 were so disorganized that they could not much turn to their benefit the deep popular outrage provoked by the massacre of 172 striking workers in the Lena goldfields on April 4, 1912.[79]

Vladimir Fedorovich Dzhunkovskii, appointed deputy interior minister in January 1913, launched a series of reforms of the security police aimed at cutting costs and restricting police reliance on informers. In March he prohibited the recruitment of informers in the military, despite a growing perception among senior police officials, expressed at two security conferences in late 1912, that the use of informers should be increased to combat the spread of sedition among enlisted personnel. In May, Dzhunkovskii also banned maintaining informers in secondary schools, which appears not to have been a widely developed practice anyway.[80] It might have seemed that he had in mind an all-out assault on the security system, for between May 1913 and February 1914 he abolished most of the provincial and regional security bureaus and transferred their functions to the provincial gendarme chiefs. At the very least this was a strange policy, given the incessant criticism of most gendarme officers by senior police officials and in view of the fact that a police report of December 1912 had attributed the annihilation of the revolutionary movement to the efficiency of the regional bureaus.[81] In the short term, nevertheless, Dzhunkovskii's reforms seem not to have gravely weakened the security system, and for two reasons: the security bureaus in the imperial capitals remained strong (although Dzhunkovskii dismissed the very able St Petersburg bureau chief, Mikhail von Koten); the regional bureaus were not abolished until January 1914 when the revolutionary organizations had already been severely weakened.[82]

The logical response to this situation for many revolutionaries lay in developing legal methods of protest and agitation. The SDs founded *Pravda* in April 1912 and *Luch* (Ray of Light) in September, Bolshevik and Menshevik newspapers, respectively. The police watched them, naturally, seized individual issues, and occasionally closed them down, but they repeatedly reopened under different names, a ruse which the police were legally powerless to prevent. *Pravda*, for example, was closed down eight times during its two-year prerevolutionary existence. The police's only recourse was to maintain informers within the editorial board. One informer, Miron Chernomazov, edited *Pravda* from May 1913 to February 1914.[83] Similarly, the Bolsheviks participated eagerly in the Fourth Duma, elected in late summer and early autumn 1912. Of one of the six Bolshevik deputies, Lenin wrote in 1912: "For the *first* time we have an *outstanding leader* (Malinovskii) from among the workers representing us in the Duma." Malinovskii was, in fact, a police informer. In May 1914, Dzhunkovskii ordered his dismissal. The rumors attending this event stunned the Bolshevik leadership, as Azef's exposure had disconcerted SR leaders, to the extent that Lenin, still dumbfounded, barely reacted to the major political strikes of industrial workers in Petersburg and Moscow in June 1914.[84]

War and Revolution

Historians disagree on whether the incidence of labor unrest between April 1912 and June 1914, which was greater than during the previous years, proves that the regime was unstable.[85] All agree, however, that the declaration of war against Germany on July 17, 1914 at least temporarily put an end to this and other popular unrest in Russia. The maintenance of public tranquility was facilitated by the immediate imposition on every corner of the empire of a state of either extraordinary security or martial law, which permitted the suppression of legal newspapers, trade unions, and educational societies linked to revolutionary groups.[86] The security police also arrested many remaining underground activists and worked to keep Bolsheviks and Mensheviks from uniting. By early 1916 the prospects for revolution seemed to many revolutionary activists very dim.[87]

Yet the imperial system was on the eve of collapse. In September 1916, A. D. Protopopov, a favorite of Rasputin and an incompetent administrator, became the fifth interior minister in 13 months. The economic situation also began rapidly to deteriorate in late 1915 and worsened throughout 1916; price inflation of basic necessities increased dramatically while wages failed to keep pace, and necessary goods disappeared sporadically from shops. By the fall of 1916, even skilled workers began to suffer as prices continued to rise. Already in February 1916 the Moscow Security Bureau reported that as a cause of acute discontent inflation "is playing an all but decisive role." By late November, a court security police report spoke of a "food crisis," and on February 5, 1917 the Petrograd Security Bureau predicted that hunger riots (*golodnyi bunt*) would be the "first step on the path of . . . the most horrible kind of anarchistic revolution." Two days later, the same bureau predicted that massive popular disorders could be expected on February 10 and 14.[88] Large-scale strikes did, in fact, take place on February 14, but efficient police crowd control prevented their getting out of hand. As late as the night of February 25, the Petrograd Security Bureau arrested 100 radical activists. The bureau's last report was prepared on the 27th amid a general strike, massive troop mutinies, and the formation of the Duma's Provisional Committee and the Soviet. That evening crowds sacked and burned the security bureau headquarters in Petrograd.[89] Although Moscow and much of the rest of the empire temporarily remained calm,[90] this concatenation of events marked the end of the imperial regime.

On March 4 and 10, the Provisional Government abolished the security bureaus, the Police Department, and the Gendarme Corps (transferring gendarme officers and enlisted men to the regular army), and dismissed all governors and vice-governors. On March 18 it created a bureau for counterespionage, but against domestic threats to state security the new regime left itself nearly defenseless.[91] This was because Russia's new leaders seem to have naively imagined that the collapse of the monarchy would usher in a new form of politics without internal threats to state security. In fact, the dismantling of the imperial police apparatus, as odious as its institutions may have been to many educated Russians, was an invitation to takeover by political conspirators. The imperial security police could not forestall the February Revolution, because it was driven purely by mass discontent; a reasonably sophisticated security police almost certainly could have saved the Provisional Government from the October Bolshevik overthrow, which lacked the sort of mass participation that brought down the imperial dynasty and regime in February.

Notes

1   This essay, which is part of a larger study currently in preparation, owes much to thoughtful criticism by James Cracraft and Scott Lyden and to grants from the Campus Research Board of the University of Illinois at Chicago and from the International Research & Exchanges Board (IREX), with funds provided by the National Endowment for the Humanities and the United States Information Agency. None of these persons or organizations is responsible for the views expressed.

2   "Iz arkhiva L. Tikhomirova," *Krasnyi arkhiv* 6 (1924): 155.
3   V. P. Leikina and N. L. Pivovarskaia, eds, *Arkhiv "Zemli i voli" i "Narodnoi voli"* (Moscow: Izd. vsesoiuznogo obshchestva politkatorzhan i ssyl'no-pereselentsev, 1930), 20–9.
4   See Jonathan W. Daly, "On the Significance of Emergency Legislation in Late Imperial Russia," *Slavic Review* 54 (Fall 1995): 606–8.
5   *PSZ*, series 2, vol. 55, part 1, no. 61279; Iu. F. Ovchenko, "Moskovskaia 'Okhranka' na rubezhe vekov," *Otechestvennaia istoriia*, 1993, 3: 195–6. On the Police Department, which, unlike the Third Section, was subordinated to the Interior Ministry, see L. I. Tiutiunnik, "Department politsii v bor'be s revoliutsionnym dvizheniem v Rossii na rubezhe XIX–XX vekov (1880–1904 gg.)" (Kand. diss., Moskovskii gosudarstvennyi istoriko-arkhivnyi institut (hereafter: MGIAI), 1986).
6   D. C. B. Lieven, "The Security Police, Civil Rights, and the fate of the Russian Empire, 1855–1917," in Olga Crisp and Linda Edmondson, eds, *Civil Rights in Imperial Russia* (Oxford: Clarendon Press, 1989), 244; Alexandre Spiridovitch, *Histoire du terrorisme russe, 1886–1917* (Paris: Payot, 1930), 10, 20–1. Spiridovich was a top gendarme officer who wrote several important historical works on late imperial Russia as well as valuable memoirs.
7   "Obzor deiatel'nosti Moskovskogo okhrannogo otdeleniia," April 25, 1895, GARF, f. 102, op. 316, 1906, d. 215, l. 1–8.
8   See Allan K. Wildman, "The Russian Intelligentsia of the 1890's," *American Slavic and East European Review* 19 (April 1960): 157–79; Spiridovitch, *Histoire du terrorisme russe*, 46–8, 52–3.
9   A. F. Vovchik, *Politika tsarizma po rabochemu voprosu v predrevoliutsionnyi period (1895–1904)* (Lvov: Izd. L'vovskogo universiteta, 1964), 262.
10 See, for example, "Nalet P. I. Rachkovskogo na narodovol'cheskuiu tipografiiu," *Byloe*, 23 (July 1917): 277–83.
11 *Pis'ma Azefa, 1893–1917* (Moscow: "Terra"–"Terra," 1994), 14–15.
12 These methods are neatly delineated in Lieven, "Security Police," 243–7.
13 "Evno Azef: Istoriia ego predatel'stva," *Byloe* 24 (August 1917): 195. See also S. Mel'gunov, ed., "Iz perepiski okhrannikov: Pis'ma L. A. Rataev–S. V. Zubatov, *Golos minuvshego* 10 (January 1922): 51.
14 Zubatov to Rataev, July 26, 1901, GARF, f. 102, OO, d. 2, ch. 1, lit. g, l. 75. On Zubatov's approach and successes, see Jeremiah Schneiderman, *Sergei Zubatov and Revolutionary Marxism: The Struggle for the Working Class in Tsarist Russia* (Ithaca, NY: Cornell University Press, 1976), 79–82.
15 On Mednikov, see Spiridovich, *Zapiski*, 40–1; Mednikov service record, GARF, f. 63, op. 53, d. 32. On the first uses of surveillants, see Komissiia dlia obsuzhdeniia voprosa o reforme naruzhnogo nabliudeniia, "Zhurnal," ibid., f. 102, op. 316, 1909, d. 361, l. 23. On their development in Moscow, see Iurii F. Ovchenko, "Moskovskoe okhrannoe otdelenie v bor'be s revoliutsionnym dvizheniem v 1880–1904 gg." (Kand. diss., Moskovskii gosudarstvennyi universitet, 1989), 69. For surveillance diaries, see GARF, f. 63, op. 45, dd. 1–391. One such diary was published: I. P. Belokonskii, ed., "'Grokhovoe pal'to' (Pamiatnaia knizhka prefessional'nogo shpiona)," *Minuvshie gody* 9 (September 1908): 290–312. For police reference guides, see GARF, f. 63,

op. 45, dd. 493–7, 501–11, 531. For personnel statistics, see "Shtat," October 1880, ibid., op. 1, d. 340, t. 1, l. 375; Moscow Security Bureau (hereafter: MOO) to Police Department (hereafter: DP), October 30, 1902, ibid., f. 102, OO, 1906, otd. 1, d. 125, l. 35; "Spisok filerov," 1913, ibid., op. 316, 1913, d. 200, ll. 8–12: security police budget, December 31, 1902, ibid., OO, 1902, d. 825, l. 167 ob.

16   A. V. Gerasimov, *Na lezvii s terroristami* (Paris: YMCA Press, 1985), 56. See also, Rachkovskii, "Kratkaia zapiska," May 27, 1902, GARF, f. 5802, op. 1, d. 214, ll., 18–22.

17   A. A. Bukhbinder, "Zubatovshchina v Moskve," *Katorga i ssylka* 1 (1925): 96–7.

18   A. Spiridovich, *Zapiski zhandarma* (Moscow: Izd. "Proletarii," 1930), 50.

19   See I. V. Orzhekhovskii, *Samoderzhavie protiv revoliutsionnoi Rossii (1826–1880)* (Moscow: Mysl', 1982), 122.

20   Security police budget, December 31, 1902, ibid., OO, 1902, d. 825, l. 167 ob.; Gerald D. Surh, *1905 in St Petersburg: Labor, Society, and Revolution* (Stanford: Stanford University Press, 1989), 24.

21   DP dossier, GARF, f. 102, op. 316, 1906, d. 1019, ll. 20–20 ob., 79, 98, 103, 125; "Spisok sekretnykh sotrudnikov," 1912, GARF, f. 102, op. 316, 1912, d. 202, t. 2, l. 26–26 ob.; Spisok sekretnykh sotrudnikov," 1912, ibid., 1913, d. 200, l. 14–17 ob.

22   Spiridovich, *Zapiski*, 48–9, 193–5; Gerasimov, *Na lezvii*, 57–8; Pavel P. Zavarzin, *Rabota tainoi politsii* (Paris: Izd. avtora, 1924) 16–20; Biographical report, 1917 (Provisional Government), GARF, f. 504, op. 1, d. 369, ll, 65–6. The best place to start exploring the lives of informers is Leonid Men'shchikov, *Okhrana i revoliutsiia. K istorii tainykh politicheskikh organizatsii v Rossii*, 3 vols (Moscow: Izd. politkatorzhan, 1925–8).

23   Wildman, "Russian Intelligentsia of the 1890s," 176–7; Spiridovitch, *Histoire du terrorisme russe*, 46–8, 52–3.

24   G. M. Trutkov to DP director, September 22, 1903, GARF, f. 102, OO, 1902, d. 825 (hereafter: Trutkov report), ll. 202 ob., 206 ob.

25   DP to gendarme chiefs, August 13, 1902, GARF, f. 102, OO, 1902, d. 825, l. 25; DP circ., May 15, 1913, ibid., 1913, d. 119, l. 186. Trutkov report, 202–3 ob.

26   Deputy MVD to MVD, October 20, 1909, GARF, f. 102, OO, 1909, d. 50, ch. 2, ll. 91v–d. For reports on these operations, see GARF, f. 102, OO, 1902, d. 825, ll. 202–15; ibid., 1901, d. 825, t. 6; ibid., f. 63, op. 53, d. 216, ll. 1–33. On the brigade's methods, see "K rukovodstvu filerami letuchego otriada," ibid., f. 102, OO, 1898, d. 1, ch. 1, lit. v, ll. 189–90; Menshchikov, *Okhrana i revoliutsiia*, 1: 282.

27   Trutkov report, l. 207.

28   MOO report, October 14, 1900, GARF, f. 102, op. 316, 1908, d. 538, ll. 279–80.

29   As reported by Spiridovich, *Zapiski*, 133.

30   Novitskii charged that Zubatov's system led inevitably to provocation ("Zapiska gen. Novitskogo," *Sotsialist-Revoliutsioner* 2 (1910): 62).

31   On Zubatov's labor program, see "Professional'naia organizatsiia rabochikh" (written not earlier than 1900 by Lev Tikhomirov): GARF, f. 1723, op. 2, d.

31, ll. 55–66; Zubatov to Rataev, September 1900 ("Dva dokumenta iz istorii Zubatovshchiny," *KA* 19 (1926): 211); Schneiderman, *Zubatov*, 73–6.

32 V. D. Novitskii, *Iz vospominaniia zhandarma* (Moscow: Priboi, 1929), 24.

33 On Zubatov's labor program, see note 31; on his antirevolutionary activities, see Ovchenko, "Moskovskoe okhrannoe otdelenie," 161–3, 170–2.

34 On the creation, staffing, and operations of the Special Section, see Tiutiunnik, "Department politsii," 53–8; Rataev, "Zapiska dlia pamiati," July 8, 1902, GARF, f. 102, OO, 1902, d. 444, lit. A, ll. 12–14; Rataev to Zvolianskii, February 1902, ibid., l. 1 ob. Its measures to preserve its secrecy are discussed in S. G. Svatikov, *Russkii politicheskii sysk za-granitseiu (Po dokumentam Parizhskogo Arkhiva Zagranichnoi agentury Departamenta Politsii)* (Rostov-na-Donu: Pervoe paevoe rabochee tovarishchestvo, 1918), 6; as well as by a former security policeman who defected to the revolutionary camp, M. E. Bakai, in his unpublished memoir, "Pri politsii," GARF, f. 5881, op. 1, d. 221, l. 154. On Rataev, consult Spiridovich, *Zapiski*, 81; Ovchenko, "Moskovskoe okhrannoe otdelenie," 160–1.

35 Ovchenko, "Moskovskoe okhrannoe otdelenie," 160–1.

36 Spiridovich, *Zapiski*, 81–2.

37 Cited from an archival source in Madhavan K. Palat, "Police Socialism in Tsarist Russia, 1900–1905," *Studies in History* 2 (January–June 1986): 76.

38 Spiridovitch, *Histoire du terrorisme russe*, 59, 69–74, 91–8; Trutkov report, l. 209; Ovchenko, "Moskovskoe okhrannoe otdelenie," 108.

39 Ovchenko, "Moskovskoe okhrannoe otdelenie," 141–2; Samuel D. Kassow, *Students, Professors, and the State in Tsarist Russia* (Berkeley and Los Angeles: University of California Press, 1989), 110–16, 129–31, 147, 159–72.

40 Lenin, *Chto delat'?*, in *Polnoe sobranie sochinenii*, 5th edn (Moscow: Gos. izd. politicheskoi literatury, 1959), 6: 126–7. Italics supplied.

41 Trutkov report, l. 210.

42 DP to gendarme chiefs, May 4, 1902, GARF, f. 102, OO, otd. 1, 1906, d. 125, l. 28–28 ob.

43 Mednikov to Spiridovich, May 6, 1902, "Pis'ma Mednikova Spiridovichu," *Krasnyi arkhiv* 17 (1926): 193. Bureaus were created in Vilna, Ekaterinoslav, Kazan, Kiev, Odessa, Saratov, Tiflis, Kharkov, Simferopol, Nizhnyi-Novgorod, Perm, Rostov-on-Don, Poltava, Kishinev, Zhitomir, Vyborg, Ufa, Tomsk, Irkutsk, and Krasnoiarsk (Tiutiunnik, "Department politsii," 282).

44 "Polozhenie o nachal'nikakh Rozysknykh otdelenii," GARF, f. 102, op. 262, 1902, d. 10, ll. 1–4; "Svod pravil, vyrabotannykh v razavitie utverzhdennogo Gospodinom Ministrom Vnutrennikh Del 12 Avgusta tekushchego goda Polozheniia o Nachal'nikakh Rozysknykh Otdelenii," October 21, 1902, ibid., ll. 5–8. Novitskii's "Zapiska," cited above, literally heaps vituperation upon Zubatov. Novitskii submitted his resignation on June 1, 1903: Novitskii, *Iz vospominaniia zhandarma*, 187–8. Yet some provincial and city governors, as well as numerous public prosecutors and even some gendarme chiefs, welcomed the new bureaus (see Spiridovich, *Zapiski*, 112–13; N. N. Ansimov, "Okhrannye otdeleniia i mestnaia vlast' tsarskoi Rossii v nachale XX v.," *Sovetskoe gosudarstvo i pravo*, 1991, no. 5: 120; Trutkov report, ll. 221 ob.–222, 223).

45 Trutkov report, ll. 214, 220 ob.–221; Mednikov to Spiridovich, January 30, 1903 ("Pis'ma Mednikova Spiridovichu," 197).

46 See "K istorii vseobshchei stachki na iuge Rossii v 1903 g.," *Krasnyi arkhiv* 88 (1938): 76–122; "Istoriia 'legalizatsii' rabochego dvizheniia: Spravka Osobogo otdela Departamenta Politsii," *Byloe* 23 (July 1917): 86–93; Schneiderman, *Zubatov*, 312–32.

47 The best exposition of the conspiracy thesis is Schneiderman, *Zubatov*, 354–7. My forthcoming book on the security police will challenge that argument along the lines here indicated, but the issue seems too complicated ever to be resolved to complete satisfaction.

48 Mednikov to Spiridovich, February 8, 1904 and November 7, 1904 ("Pis'ma Mednikova Spiridovichu," 207, 211).

49 A. M. Zaionchkovskii, "V gody reaktsii," *Krasnyi arkhiv* 8 (1925): 242.

50 A police report of September 22, 1903 admitted as much: GARF, f. 102, OO, 1902, d. 825, ll. 210 ob., 221–221 ob.

51 As reported by Bulygin's administrative secretary, D. N. Liubimov: "Russkaia smuta nachala deviatisotykh godov, 1902–1906. Po vospominaniiam, lichnym zapiskam i dokumentam" (Bakhmetev Archive, Columbia University), 298–9.

52 The standard work on this is Abraham Ascher, *The Revolution of 1905*, 2 vols, (Stanford, Calif.: Stanford University Press, 1988–1992).

53 Police circular, November 5, 1905, GARF, f. 102, OO, 1902, d. 825, l. 237.

54 So argues D. C. B. Lieven, "Bureaucratic Authoritarianism in Late Imperial Russia: The Personality, Career and Opinions of P. N. Durnovo," *The Historical Journal*, 26 (1983): 394.

55 Ascher, *The Revolution of 1905*, 2: 13–15.

56 L. I. Gol'dman, ed., *Politicheskie protsessy v Rossii: 1901–1917* (Moscow: Izd. vsesoiuznogo obshchestva politkatorzhan i ssyl'no-poselentsev, 1932), 1: 6, 19, 50, 52, 61, 85, 86; N. N. Polianskii, *Tsarskie voennye sudy v bor'be s revoliutsiei, 1905–1907 gg.* (Moscow: Moscow University Press, 1958), 33.

57 Ascher, *Revolution of 1905*, 1: 333–5; Viktor Obninskii, *Polgoda Russkoi Revoliutsii. Sbornik materialov i dokumentov k istorii russkoi revoliutsii. Oktiabr' 1905–aprel' 1906* (Moscow, 1906), 173. Obninskii was a well-known Kadet activist.

58 Robert W. Thurston, *Liberal City, Conservative State: Moscow and Russia's Urban Crisis, 1906–1914* (New York: Oxford University Press, 1987), 95; Anna Geifman, *Thou Shalt Kill: Revolutionary Terrorism in Russia, 1894–1917* (Princeton: Princeton University Press, 1993), 21.

59 The number fell to 3,305 in 1907 (Geifman, *Thou shalt Kill*, 21–31, 43).

60 *PSZ*, series 3, vol. 25, part 1, nos. 27162, 27165, 27166, and subsequent numbers; Witte to Nicholas II, December 24, 1905 (*Sovet ministrov rossiiskoi imperii, 1905–1906 gg. Dokumenty i materialy* (Leningrad: "Nauka," 1990), 118, 146).

61 N. I. Faleev, "Shest' mesiatsev voenno-polevoi iustitsii," *Byloe* 2 (February 1907): 43–81.

62 DP report, November 15, 1913, GARF, f. 102, op. 316, 1914, d. 366, ll. 1–3.

63 Peregudova, "Departament politsii," 191–2.

64 "Polozhenie o Raionnykh okhrannykh otdeleniiakh," reproduced in *Istoriia politsii dorevoliutsionnoi Rossii (Sbornik dokumentov i materialov po istorii gosudarstva i prava). Uchebnoe posobie* (Moscow: MVD SSSR, 1981), 69–71; DP circular, January 8, 1907, GARF, f. 102, op. 260, d. 17, l. 1; DP report, July 17, 1909, ibid., op. 316, 1909, d. 194, l. 10 ob.

65 DP circular, September 6, 1907, GARF, f. 102, op. 260, d. 17, ll. 108–108 ob.; DP circular, 14 June, 1908, ibid., f. 280, op. 5, d. 5000, ch. 3, t. 1, l. 3; DP to governors, January 8, 1907, ibid., f. 102, op. 260, d. 17, ll. 1a–1a ob.; "Otchet zasedanii pervogo s'ezda Nachal'nikov Raionnykh Okhrannykh Otdelenii," in Soviet Union, Glavarkhiv, *Sbornik materialov i statei* (Moscow: Gos. izd., 1921), 196. The most important new manuals were: "Polozhenie ob okhrannykh otdeleniiakh," February 9, 1907, GARF, f. 102, op. 262, 1907, d. 23, ll. 7–12 ob.; "Instruktsiia Departamenta politsii po organizatsii i vedeniiu vnutrennego (agenturnogo) nabliudeniia," February 10, 1907, ibid., op. 308a, d. 236, ll. 1–7.

66 A. M. Pankratova, ed., *Revoliutsiia 1905–1907 gg. v Rossii: Dokumenty i materialy* (Moscow: Izd. Akademii nauk SSSR), part 2, book 1, pp. 85–6, 89.

67 DP circular, June 23, 1907, GARF, f. 102, OO, 1911, d. 101, ll. 2–3; DP circ., June 27, 1907, ibid., op. 260, d. 17, l. 63.

68 O. A. Ermanskii, *Iz perezhitogo (1887–1921)* (Moscow: Gos. izd., 1927), 47–9.

69 DP circular, September 3, 1907, GARF, f. 102, op. 260, d. 17, ll. 99–105 ob. MOO to DP, September 10, 1907, ibid., f. 280, op. 1, d. 3000, t. 2, ll. 76–83; DP circular October 4, 1907, ibid., f. 102, op. 260, d. 17, ll. 189b–189b ob.

70 Ansimov, "Okhrannye otdeleniia i mestnaia vlast'," 123.

71 *Revoliutsionnaia mysl'* 1 (April 1908): 1.

72 By September 1912 only Voronezh, Ekaterinoslav, Kursk, Moscow, St Petersburg, Samara, Saratov, Kharkov and Chernigov Provinces (plus four provinces of Poland) remained under reinforced security: Daly, "Emergency Legislation," 626.

73 Nurit Schleifman, *Undercover Agents in The Russian Revolutionary Movement. The SR Party, 1902–1914* (London: Macmillan, 1988), 174. See also V. Burtsev, *V pogone za provokatorami* (Moscow: Molodaia gvardia, 1928), 118–51; B. Nikolaevskii, *Istoriia odnogo predatelia. Terroristy i politicheskaia politsiia* (Moscow: Izd. politicheskoi literatury, 1991), 264–73. Anna Geifman is preparing a major study on Azef.

74 Schleifman, *Undercover Agents*, 81.

75 MOO to DP, January 27, 1913, GARF, f. 102, OO, 1913, d. 9, l. 82–5 ob.

76 DP circular, January 1909, GARF, f. 102, op. 316, 1907, d. 721, ll. 56–7; Police report, November 10, 1911, ibid., 1911, d. 148, ll. 6 ob.-7; list of informers, 1913, ibid., d. 1, ch. 57, lit. D, ll. 168–9; see also ibid., f. 4888, op. 5.

77 Statistical table on directives, December 1912, GARF, f. 102, OO, 1912, d. 248, l. 48; Gerasimov inspection report, July 17, 1909, ibid., op. 316, 1909, d. 194, ll. 6–60 ob.; DP circulars and reports on inspections, April and December 1912, ibid., OO, 1912, d. 248, ll. 7–10, 14 ob.–23 ob., 46–8; "Konspekt lektsii," ibid., op. 253, d. 243, ll. 1–146; diagrams, ibid., d. 387; ibid., op. 316, 1911, d. 1, ch. 69, lit. d, ll. 25–9.

78 *Grazhdanin*, no. 36, September 18, 1911, p. 15–16; N. A. Gredeskul, *Terror i okhrana* (St Petersburg: Tip. "Obshchestvennaia pol'za," 1912), 28–9.

79 A. P. Koznov, "Bor'ba bolshevikov s podryvnymi aktsiiami tsarskoi okhranki v 1910–1914 gg.," *Voprosy istorii KPSS*, 1988, 9: 60–2; Robert B. McKean, *St Petersburg Between the Revolutions: Workers and Revolutionaries, June 1907–February 1917* (New Haven and London: Yale University Press, 1990), 88–97.

80 DP circular, March 13, 1913, GARF, f. 280, op. 5, d. 5000, ch. 12, l. 103; conference reports, December 1912, ibid., f. 102, op. 261, d. 21, ll. 5–8; DP circular, May 1, 1913, Okhrana Collection, Hoover Institution Archives, XIIId(1), 11.

81 MVD circular, May 15, 1913, GARF, f. 102, OO, 1913, d. 119, ll. 185–8; DP report, November 15, 1913, ibid., op. 316, 1914, d. 366, ll. 4–6 ob.; MVD circular, February 22, 1914, ibid., f. 280, op. 5, d. 5000, ch. 10, ll. 19–20 ob.; DP report, December 1912, ibid., f. 102, OO, 1912, d. 248, l. 40 ob.

82 "Uchet Departamenta politsii opyta 1905 goda," *Krasnyi arkhiv* 18 (1926): 221–3.

83 "Zhandarmy o 'Pravde'," *Proletarskaia revoliutsiia* 2(14) (1923): 460–1; Ralph Carter Elwood, "Lenin and Pravda, 1912–1914," *Slavic Review* 31 (June 1972): 375–9.

84 Ralph Carter Elwood, *Roman Malinovskii: A Life without a Cause* (Newtonville, Mass.: Oriental Research Partners, 1977), 28, 43, 56; I. S. Rozental', "Stranitsy zhizni generala Dzhunkovskogo," *Kentavr*, 1994, 1: 94.

85 Leopold Haimson, "The Problem of Social Stability in Urban Russia, 1905–1917," *Slavic Review* 23–24 (December 1964 and March 1965); McKean, *St Petersburg*, 192, 226–7.

86 Daly, "Emergency Legislation," 626; Ivan Menitskii, *Revoliutsionnye dvizheniia voennykh godov (1914–1917): Ocherki i materialy* (Moscow: Izd. Kommunisticheskoi akademii, 1925), 126–7, 244–6.

87 DP circular, September 16, 1914, reproduced in V. K. Agafonov, *Zagranichnaia okhranka* (Moscow: Izd kniga, 1918), 205; MOO report, December 21, 1915, GARF, f. 102, op. 316, 1916, d. 186, l. 158; MOO report, June 1, 1916, ibid., f. 63, OO, 1916, d. 68; McKean, *St Petersburg*, 380, 385–90, 401–3.

88 MOO report, September 30, 1916, GARF, f. 102, OO, 1916, d. 48, ch. 46, ll. 53–4; Special Section of Court Commandant report, November 26, 1916, ibid., f. 97, op. 4, d. 117, ll. 93–5; Petrograd Security Bureau report, February 5, 1917, ibid., ll. 124–124 ob.; Petrograd Security Bureau report, February 7, 1917, ibid., f. 1467, op. 1, d. 582, ll. 44–5 ob.

89 McKean, *St Petersburg*, 399–400; Tsuyoshi Hasegawa, *The February Revolution: Petrograd, 1917* (Seattle and London: University of Washington Press, 1981), 204; POO report, February 26, 1917, GARF, f. 102, OO, 1917, d. 341, ll. 43–5, 48–9; "Fevral'skaia revoliutsiia i okhrannoe otdelenie," *Byloe* 29 (January 1918): 175–6.

90 B. F. Livchak, "Krakh planov 'okhrany' Moskvy ot revoliutsii," *Voprosy istorii* (April 1974): 116–24.

91 Zhurnal zasedanii Vremennogo pravitel'stva, March 4, 10, and 18, 1917, GARF, f. 1779, op. 2, d. 3, ll. 2, 3 ob., 25, 70.

CHAPTER TWELVE

Legislative Chamber History Overlooked: The State Council of the Russian Empire, 1906–1917[1]

Alexandra S. Korros

Introduction

In convincing Nicholas II to issue the manifesto of October 17, 1905, the chairman of the Council of Ministers Sergei Witte hoped that the promise of a popularly elected legislature would bring an end to the general strike and the other widespread revolutionary disturbances that had so paralyzed the Russian Empire. Like the Egyptian pharaoh who regretted his decision to release the Israelites, the tsar and his closest advisors soon had second thoughts about making this enormous concession to the revolutionaries and tried to find ways to prevent the promised constitutional order from taking hold. As the disorders abated, and the government's troops and police began to regain their hold over society, the tsar's senior bureaucrats and closest advisors met in a series of secret meetings, called Special Conferences or Crown Councils, to work out the details of the new constitutional order.[2]

The task before these men was a daunting one. They had to create the rules for the new legislative body promised by Nicholas II while they simultaneously tried to figure out how to prevent the emperor from losing his absolute power to the new legislature. The October Manifesto had not specified the exact shape of the new legislative institutions, although most Russians interested in the subject were under the impression that the new legislature would be a unicameral body. Therefore, following one of Witte's suggestions, the Special Conference decided to transform the tsar's Russian

Imperial State Council from an appointed body of retired bureaucrats whose job it was to advise the emperor on legislative matters into the upper chamber of a bicameral legislature. To ensure the State Council's conservative character, the Special Conference decided that unlike the Duma which was elected by popular male suffrage, the State Council would be composed half of appointed and half of elected representatives. Following the example of other "upper chambers" of bicameral legislatures, the elected members of the State Council would come from limited and reliable constituencies including the Assemblies of Nobility, the provincial zemstvos, the landowners of non-zemstvo provinces, the clergy, Trade and Industry Councils, and the Academy of Sciences and universities. In this manner the State Council would act as a conservative "buffer" to the anticipated radicalism of the State Duma.

As Abraham Ascher and other historians who have closely studied the period tell us, the liberal public was stunned and angered by the news that the Duma would have an unanticipated legislative partner. Conservatives were also surprised, but pleased by the idea that Russia would not be plunged into an orgy of constitutionalism and reform.[3]

By examining the political structure and activities of the State Council in some detail, we will discover that even within the more conservative strata of Russian society, there were many who saw the new era of legislative activity as an opportunity to introduce reform. Others, fearful of losing their positions of influence, tried to use the State Council as it had been intended – to stop the new legislative assemblies. These conflicting viewpoints were played out in the State Council itself, revealing how deeply politicized even the most conservative strata of Russian society had become and would remain during the "constitutional period" preceding the 1917 Revolutions.

Like the State Duma, the State Council existed for only eleven years, 1906–17, as a legislative institution.[4] While the political issues facing the upper chamber were relatively few during the first two sessions, particularly because of the short duration of the First and Second Dumas, the political configuration and operations of the upper chamber developed patterns that would hold true during later and longer sessions. During the Stolypin era, which corresponds to the second through sixth sessions of the State Council, the Chairman of the Council of Ministers strove to create a working majority in the upper chamber to complement the pro-government majority in the State Duma fostered by the electoral law of June 3, 1907. Following his assassination in September 1911, Stolypin's successors were less interested in pursuing an aggressive reform agenda in conjunction with the Duma and State Council. Consequently, the legislative assemblies diminished in their importance as policy-making institutions, thereby making the debates and politics of the State Council more a reflection of the developments in Russian society than a creator of those developments. In this essay we shall examine in some detail the State Council's political structure during its first two sessions, discuss how Stolypin sought to configure a reliable majority in the upper chamber to pass his legislative reform, and determine how the State Council's role changed in the years immediately preceding World War I and the 1917 Revolution.

The New Legislative Order

While the inclusion of a reformed State Council in the legislative system may have surprised many political observers, they all agreed that it would be a very conservative body inclined to support the tsar and his government. The new upper chamber was composed of 98 appointed retired bureaucrats and military men, the majority of whom were already members of the prereform body.[5] Seventy-four of them were noble landowners.[6] Of the remaining State Council representatives, six came from the clergy, six were professors from the Academy of Sciences and universities; and 12 were elected from among representatives of trade and industry.

While each provincial zemstvo elected one representative to the new upper chamber, in contrast, all the other elections took place in electoral assemblies. Some groups such as the Trade and Industry representatives decided immediately to organize themselves as a bloc of votes, fearing that as non-nobles they would be ignored by most of the other members. Most of the clerical representatives were high-ranking and very conservative churchmen. In contrast, the Academy of Sciences and the universities elected the Constitutional Democrats and unaffiliated liberals to represent their interests in the new chamber.[7]

By the time the members of the State Council assembled for the first time, it was apparent that the elected members would not be quite as conservative as those in Nicholas II's entourage had hoped. Numerous zemstvo and noble delegates considered themselves "moderates" and occasionally even "liberals," and quite a few were affiliated with the new political parties that had sprung up as a result of the events of 1905.[8]

Many of the members were leaders of the nobility in their provinces and had come to know one another through periodic meetings of gentry or zemstvo activists.[9] In his memoirs, V. M. Andreevskii of Tambov, one of the noble representatives, recalled that while many nobles had been frightened by the peasant disturbances the previous summer and fall and had abandoned some of their ideas about universal suffrage and popular sovereignty, not everyone had moved all the way to the right. And although he differed with his friend, political moderate and Octobrist, P. N. Trubetskoi, a supporter of the new constitutional order, Andreevskii, a self-proclaimed conservative, nevertheless worked to elect him as a noble representative to the State Council.[10] Among both the elected and appointed representatives, political affiliations may have been important, but personal ties often overrode political differences. These differences, however, became evident immediately, when the State Council met for the first time to consider its reply to the tsar's Address from the Throne which opened the legislative chambers on April 23, 1906.

In the highly politicized aftermath of the 1905 crisis, even what should have been a proforma response to the tsar was an opportunity to make a political statement. Therefore, the most liberal deputies to the State Council, the members of the Academic group and other elected Kadets from the zemstvos and landowner assemblies, met prior to the first official meeting to develop a unified strategy to exert influence on the State Council's statement. In doing so, they effectively organized themselves as the upper chamber's first political faction. At the council's first working meeting, Ufa zemstvo representative Prince V. A. Kugushev, a Kadet, proposed an amendment to the Address to the Throne requesting amnesty for political prisoners who had not engaged in any violent acts. The Chairman of the State Council, Count D. A. Sol'skii, immediately dismissed the chamber, to prevent the differences over the Address to the Throne from disrupting decorum. Seeking to avoid any embarrassing confrontation, Sol'skii suggested a series of private meetings to compose an Address to the Throne with which all could agree. Gathering in private residences over the next few days, the State Council members became more thoroughly acquainted with one another's political views, and began to coalesce into political groups.

Those unconditionally opposed to the Council's liberals on the questions of amnesty emerged as the assembly's right wing, who were generally determined to maintain the tsar's position as an autocrat regardless of the October Manifesto, which they viewed as a mistaken concession. They were equally resolute in holding on to their own privilege and property against the onslaught of the radical forces represented in the lower chamber.

The bulk of the council deputies did not fit into either the liberal or the right-wing coalition and sought compromise. These seekers of consensus on the Address to the Throne became the nucleus of the State Council's largest political bloc, the Center. Many gravitating toward the Center group were from the zemstvo assemblies. Others included almost all the Polish noblemen representing the Western provinces and Poland, the members of the Trade and Industry group, most of the Baltic German, and several noble representatives who had been active in the zemstvo movement. In addition, several appointed members rapidly accepted leadership positions in the Center, including former minister of agriculture and state domains A. S. Ermolov. Many of these appointed members came from the justice and finance ministries, or the Senate. Like Ermolov, they considered themselves politically progressive and were anxious to test out the new constitutional order. The bureaucrats who joined the Center thought it was their duty to implement the new constitution in an orderly and responsible manner and to find ways to cooperate with the new State Duma.

The debate over the Address to the Throne reveals a great deal about the character of the nascent Center group. When the State Council reconvened, three versions of the Address were brought to the floor. The Left's version demanded amnesty for those arrested for political activities during 1905; the Right's proposal rejected the concept entirely; whereas the Center, after affirming the State Council's complete loyalty to the empire, sought amnesty for those charged exclusively with non-violent political activities. The following week, at the Address's second reading, the right-wing leader F. D. Samarin offered an amendment to include in the amnesty all those arrested for protecting the tsar (including those who had taken part in the pogroms and similar acts of violence). Despite the conspicuous temerity of the proposal, Samarin's version of the compromise passed by a vote of 88 to 48.[11]

In early June the Center produced a Statement of Principles affirming the constitutional order. It read in part: "We maintain that the first concern of the government must be the establishment and maintenance of the defense of internal peace and order in Russia, based on law and respect for individual freedom and the right to property of each citizen."[12] Released on June 9, the Statement of Principles concluded with an invitation to all members who shared similar views to join the Center in working to support the State Council's important role in the new constitutional order. Apparently, the statement was an effective recruiting tool since a number of new members joined, raising the group's size to over 100 members – a "majority" of the State Council.[13]

Not everyone joining the Center was willing to go along with its policies automatically. One member asserted: "I must state that belonging to the Group cannot deprive me of my freedom of opinion in those cases where I may feel obligated to express a view contrary to that accepted by the Group."[14] Other members of the State Council strongly disapproved of the Center's position. In declining the Center's invitation, Samarin noted that he disagreed with the group's affirmation of the constitutional-monarchical principle. "I hold the conviction," he wrote, "that the constitutional form of government does not have a strong basis in our reality."[15]

During the course of the first session, the State Council had few opportunities to determine its place in the parliamentary system since only two bills arrived from the Duma. Yet even the fate of these two pieces of legislation can be instructive. The first bill abolishing capital punishment came to the floor in late June. Just as with the Address to the Throne, the Right vehemently opposed the legislation while the Left supported it. Rumors had it that the committee considering the bill was trying to draft a compromise version outlawing capital punishment except in cases of regicide, treason, and armed uprising. While the bill was still in committee, the first Duma was dismissed, and when the bill came up for consideration in the State Council during its second session, it voted not to consider it since the bill had been passed by a discredited Duma.[16]

The fate of the second bill – for emergency food allocations to famine-stricken provinces – was more interesting. The government proposed a sum of 50 million rubles for famine relief, but declined to specify a timetable for disbursement or the source of the funds. The Duma's amendment was to decrease the amount to 15 million rubles, which was to be spent immediately in July, reducing the State Budget by the same amount. In the State Council, the Right supported the government's proposal, but the Left and most of the Center group supported the Duma's amended version. Eventually, the Center-Left coalition prevailed, passing the Duma's bill. A British observer commented that the State Council's vote constituted "a great moral victory for the Duma" and even speculated that it could be considered a vote of no confidence in the Goremykin government.[17] In this particular instance, the Center and Left of the State Council clearly took their constitutional responsibilities seriously.

The Stolypin Era, 1906–11

On July 9, Nicholas II dismissed the State Duma. Many of its Kadet leaders repaired to Vyborg, Finland in an effort to reinvigorate the spirit of 1905 and to press for the tsar's adherence to the constitutional system. Arrested and prevented from running for office in the legislature, the Kadet party's fortunes in the upcoming Second Duma seemed to be on the wane. Moreover, Nicholas II named a new and dynamic Chairman of the Council of Ministers to replace the ineffectual Goremykin – Petr A. Stolypin.

Unlike his predecessor, Stolypin (an outside to St Petersburg politics, having served as the governor of Saratov where during 1905 he successfully suppressed local unrest) had an agenda, an extensive list of reforms that he wished to enact. One of his primary goals was to transform the Russian peasantry into a law-abiding and responsible sector of the population. He preferred to use the legislative chambers in order to achieve his ends, but he did not scruple to manipulate the new constitution to introduce new laws without legislative approval.

Upon taking office, Stolypin acted unhesitatingly to restore order by using field courts martial to put down revolutionary disturbances. At the same time, he replaced some of the most unpopular reactionaries in the Goremykin government with moderates.[18] In November 1906, using the emergency provisions of Article 87 of the Fundamental Laws, Stolypin enacted his land reform statute which permitted peasants to withdraw from the repartitional commune, consolidate their strips into contiguous land holdings and establish private farms.[19]

With such a vigorous leader at the helm of government, the position of the political groups in the State Council was bound to change substantially. Whereas during the first session, the Right had defended the government, while the Center had found itself in opposition on several occasions, now there would be a shift with the Center having the opportunity to play a crucial role in enabling Stolypin to enact his reforms. For its part, the Right faced a threat far more serious than revolutionary disorders.

At first it seemed that Stolypin should be relatively successful in the State Council, since the Center's resolutions at its first meeting in October 1906 reflected support for a broad range of what would become Stolypin's major programmatic goals. Having convened on the first anniversary of the October Manifesto, the Center proclaimed itself in favor of restoring order to Russia and reaffirmed the existence of a constitution, calling for reforms of local government and peasant land-holding that bore remarkable similarity to the land reform of November and the proposals for local government reform that Stolypin would put forth in March 1907.[20]

By the time the State Council reconvened in February 1907, its internal operating structure was an accomplished fact: the Left composed mostly of the academic representatives and the five or six elected members allied with the Kadet party; the nearly 100-member Center; and the Right with a rather indeterminate number of supporters. During the Council's first session, the Right had been almost unwilling to organize itself, as if fearing that creating an infrastructure would amount to a tacit recognition of the legitimacy of the constitutional order. By the outset of the second session, the group's leaders had apparently changed their minds: the Right had aggressively reorganized for the new session, adding a new nonvoting bureau in order to mobilize more effectively.[21]

Appearing before the State Council in March, Stolypin spoke about his plans for local government reform as a means of continuing the transformation of Russian society – the process that had begun in the peasant land reforms introduced under Article 87.[22] The response of the Council's three groups revealed much about their political attitudes. While the Right endorsed the government's intention to restore order, it purposely omitted comment on the other projects.[23] The Left called for a return to the regular order of business, choosing to ignore Stolypin's proposals because of his violations of the October Manifesto and his use of field courts martial. In contrast, the Center's motion expressed the group's full readiness to cooperate with the government's bills and measures "directed at the welfare of the people and the establishment of order and law." The Center's resolution carried unanimously.[24]

Yet the moderates did not prevail during the remainder of the session. Although nominally a majority of the State Council, many of the Center's problems revealed themselves during the second session, and despite numerous efforts to remedy them, were to linger on through the entire Stolypin era.

The Right discovered quickly that the Center was not as powerful as it seemed when the conservatives moved for an interpellation against the minister of education, P. M. von Kaufman, questioning his handling of revolutionary disorders at Moscow and St Petersburg Universities. In response, the Center sought to defend the government through a tactical maneuver, calling for a return to the regular order of business, effectively canceling the interpellation. Their move barely passed on the first reading, getting less than 80 votes. That meant that the Center could not muster the nominal 100 votes its lists promised.[25]

The death of State Council chairman, E. B. Frish on March 31, further pinpointed the Center's weakness. The position vacated by Frish had been held by a senior bureaucrat of extensive and distinguished service background who could easily be admired by all State Council members. However, when the upper chamber convened after Easter recess, members of the Center and the Left discovered to their dismay that the newly appointed chairman of the State Council was the conspicuously right-wing former minister of justice M. G. Akimov, who was likely to act in a highly partisan manner. Akimov was the brother-in-law of P. N. Durnovo, one of the State Council's most outspoken supporters of a return to the old order. While the veteran bureaucrats puzzled over this strange appointment, the liberal press envisioned an "anti-government cabal."[26]

In what seemed almost a desperate move, the leaders of the Center group tried to act as an independent political party by introducing a proposal to reform the First Department of the Senate. The effort to initiate legislation, as well as the nature of the legislation itself, illustrate both the dilemma and the strength of the Center. Its strength lay in the expertise of several of its members, both elected and appointed, in the intricacies of government affairs. It is significant that these expert bureaucrats obviously envisioned the State Council as the place to address the problem of overlap between the justice ministry and the Senate. Had they succeeded in their effort to introduce legislation in the upper chamber, they might have transformed the State Council into an initiator rather than a responder to the

Duma's legislative agenda. Unfortunately, not only did their bill fail to gain approval in the upper chamber, but its support was limited to the 39 members of the Center who had introduced it along with 12 members of the Left. When the government declared the proposal premature, and the Right accused the bill's initiators of trying to change the nature of the State Council, no other Center members wanted to support their colleagues. Instead of enjoying a triumph, the group suffered a humiliating defeat.[27]

The Center's leaders tried to remedy this almost insoluble problem by proposing a series of measures requiring Center members to inform the bureau prior to a vote on the Council floor if they planned to deviate from group tactics and discipline. P. V. Dicheskul, a zemstvo representative from Bessarabia who had often gone his own way, responded that when the Center group had formed, it had purposely avoided any clear-cut political position. Moreover, it had "never occupied itself with elaborating some kind of . . . discipline," for to do so without declaring itself a political party outright was meaningless.[28]

Immediately prior to the abrupt conclusion of the second session, the State Council passed a major change in its composition which made it impossible for the Center to impose effective discipline. The upper chamber voted to use proportional representation by lists to determine the composition of the State Council's permanent committees where all the actual legislative work occurred.[29] This change meant that the Center had no choice but to retain as many of its members as possible, or there would be too few members on the various commissions and committees that determined the Council's agenda. As a consequence, the Center which itself was already split into several sub-groups had to tolerate a total lack of group discipline – or lose most of its members.

Furthermore, the Center now acknowledged its own "group organization" more openly, carefully preparing its lists proportionally by allocating specific places to its "basic group," "the Poles," the "Trade and Industry" representatives to ensure that each had a fair share of its members on all committees. It is through this process that we learn about the most important of the Center's subgroups, one that would eventually play a very important role in determining the Center's success or failure. It was called the Neidgardt group, named after Nizhni Novgorod zemstvo representative, A. B. Neidgardt, Stolypin's brother-in-law.[30] Composed of elected representatives from the zemstvo and Assemblies of Nobility, the subgroup appeared on Center rosters as early as 1906. Neidgardt and his 18 or so followers tended to be more conservative than many of their colleagues, but were reluctant to join the Right.

On June 3, 1907, the tsar, acting on Stolypin's request, prorogued the Second Duma and announced a new electoral legislation promulgated under Article 87 of the Fundamental Laws. While Stolypin's move was clearly a violation of Russia's weak constitutional system, the State Council representatives who had proclaimed themselves satisfied with the October Manifesto did not cry foul. Instead, they sought to extract benefits from the new Duma configuration. The new Duma was sufficiently conservative to work effectively with the State Council's nominal "majority." Ironically, Stolypin's coup d'état provided the first real opportunity to create a working bicameral legislature, albeit a highly conservative, property-based one.[31]

The off-chance that such cooperation would result in a bicameral legislative majority for Stolypin forced the Right to develop strategies to discredit Stolypin and his supporters. Using the lessons learned from the previous two sessions, the Right exploited the divisions in the Center group, and used connections with court circles to bolster its position in the State Council at the Center's and Stolypin's expense. The rightists exerted their influence at court to appoint new members to the upper chamber opposed to a viable parliamentary-style regime. Simultaneously, they mobilized the nobility to oppose Stolypin's local government reform.

By 1908 Stolypin must have known that conservative noble groups such as the United Nobility were deeply opposed to his proposals for local government reform.[32] Among the issues discussed at the group's congress was the fear that such reform would result in diminished representation of the gentry in the State Council at the very time they wished to increase the number of members from the nobility.[33] Democratization of the zemstvo meant the eventual democratization of the State Council, which they wished to maintain as "a conservative institution, restraining those impulses which are beyond the strength of the State." Prominent leaders of the United Nobility, as well as members of the State Council Right, attempted to disparage Stolypin in the tsar's eyes by accusing the prime minister of opposing naval rearmament and thus usurping the imperial prerogative on funding of battleships for the imperial Russian navy – a touchy issue with the tsar.[34]

Opposition to local government reform was not limited to the State Council Right; members of the Center active in the zemstvo and United Nobility were also deeply concerned about losing their primacy in the district while extending the zemstvo down to the village level.[35] There was no question that the Right's tactics had put Stolypin into a difficult position in the State Council.

Yet the major crisis for Stolypin did not occur until March 1909 during the Council's fourth session. By then, the Right's tactics were quite obvious. Because the Center had consistently failed to provide Stolypin with a reliable majority in the upper chamber, the issue on which the Right sought to discredit the prime minister was to accuse him of usurping impe-

rial prerogative on military matters. Indeed, this was a weak area for
Stolypin whose primary allies in the Duma – the Union of October 17 and
its leader Alexander Guchkov – wanted to play a key role in determining
the military budget. In the State Council those who opposed any legislative
intervention in the military budget were also the chief opponents of local
government reform. All this placed Stolypin in a continuing dilemma –
how far could he go in backing his Duma allies when they voted on military budgets, when many of his State Council supporters feared going too
far and risking their places in the Council by incurring the tsar's (or
Akimov's) displeasure. During the third session, Stolypin successfully
finessed this dilemma over a bill allocating funds to the navy for building
four battleships. In a speech in the State Council, he assailed his Duma
allies, the Octobrists, for holding the ships hostage to naval restructuring,
successfully asked the upper chamber to restore the credits for the ships
and approve the budget, thus escaping a trap the Right group had tried to
lay for him. It was still a narrow victory with a much smaller showing of
Center votes than their lists vouched for.[36]

The question of the creation of a naval general staff and the Duma's
approval of credits for its formation engendered the first of Stolypin's parliamentary crises. In late May 1908 the Duma passed a series of naval
credits, including allocations for the Naval General Staff.[37] When the State
Council's Finance Committee took up the matter in late June, members of
the Right, especially Durnovo and P. Kh. von Schwanebach, the former
state comptroller, accused the government of usurping rights belonging
exclusively to the tsar.[38] Despite State Comptroller Kharitonov's protests,
the State Council, with support from the Right and Center, rejected the
credits at the conclusion of the third session.[39]

The Naval General Staff bill, reintroduced and approved by the Duma in
early 1909, came up for consideration in the State Council in March. This
time the bill was a crucial test for the Stolypin administration. The government bill was identical to its predecessor, partly because the general
staff had now become a necessity for the navy and this was the only way
to obtain the required Duma majority.

The day the State Council convened to consider the bill, its galleries were
filled with journalists and spectators, including many Duma deputies.
More members than usual attended the meeting, and even the seven ministers who were also members of the State Council sat in their loges.[40] After
various government spokesmen made the case for the bill, the leaders of
the Right, Stolypin's permanent antagonists, spoke in opposition to the bill,
stressing that it was inconceivable to pass such legislation if only because
it violated the Fundamental Laws and the tsar's prerogatives.[41]

The crucial vote on the bill considered adopting the minority report that
advocated deleting the section of the bill which included the lists and

appropriations for the General Staff. In a secret ballot the minority view went down to defeat 75 (for) to 87 (against). Subsequently, the Naval General Staff bill passed the State Council with only 50 members in opposition.[42]

The real crisis had just begun. Although they had lost the vote in the State Council, Stolypin's enemies to the Right continued to press their attack by criticizing the government for allying itself with a "left" coalition to pass a bill compromising the tsar's prerogatives.[43] Further, Stolypin and his allies were blamed for having betrayed the State Council's purpose of protecting the throne from the Duma's encroachments.[44] As if in response, on April 1, Nicholas issued an official prescript complimenting the prime minister on his service to Russia and awarding him the Order of the White Eagle. Not everyone was reassured, however, and the Kadet *Rech'* asserted that the tsar's actions had not stopped those anxious to oust Stolypin.[45]

Indeed, the Right managed to convince the tsar that approval of the Naval General Staff bill would mean relinquishing imperial prerogatives. Stolypin journeyed to Tsarskoe Selo and, according to the British ambassador, "has seen the Emperor, and has explained to His Majesty that his sanction of the Bill would entail no such consequences; his Excellency added, however, that if the Imperial sanction were refused, resignation would be the only course left open to the Government."[46] Regardless of this, the tsar rejected the Naval General Staff bill, ordering Stolypin and the ministers of war and marine to decide exactly which legislation of military concern came under the tsar's discretion and which should be handled by the legislative chambers. In the same prescript, however, Nicholas II also emphasized his full approval of the government's actions. When the tsar's actions were announced in the State Council, the Right applauded, causing observers to conclude that the group thought that it had won an important victory.[47]

The consensus of opinion was that the Right would continue to seek pretexts similar to the Naval General Staff bill to force Stolypin's resignation. Although the tsar had not signed the bill, he continued to support his prime minister. Stolypin, in turn, was forced to recognize that he was vulnerable to defeat in the State Council because the Right enjoyed particularly good access to the court. Although Stolypin had called the tsar's bluff by threatening to resign his position, such threats would eventually become ineffective if used too often.

Having been stymied in its effort to discredit Stolypin in the eyes of the emperor, the Right group now turned to its other tactic to alter the balance of power in the State Council against the prime minister – the actual membership of the chamber. Despite the Right's apparent success in controlling the appointments list, modifying elected representation was crucial to both sides in configuring the upper chamber. Stolypin's success in passing the

Naval Staff bill was partially attributable to the Polish *Koło* whose 15 members tended to take positions diminishing imperial prerogatives. The Poles in the State Council were mostly landowners from the nine Western provinces, as well as representatives of the Kingdom of Poland. There was little that could be done about the latter group, but there were many Russians in the Western provinces who resented the fact that because Polish nobles were the largest landowners in the Western provinces, they were to represent them in St Petersburg.[48] Among the most outspoken proponents of this view, D. I. Pikhno, publisher of the newspaper *Kievlianin* (The Kievan), had joined the State Council as an appointed member in 1907. Pikhno, an ardent Russian nationalist, was a strong advocate for increasing Russian membership from the Western provinces in the State Council. At the end of March 1909 Pikhno proposed changing the electoral procedure to the State Council from the nine Western provinces by introducing separation of nationalities into the electoral law. Elections would take place in separate assemblies of Polish and Russian landowners, so that in the end, instead of nine Poles, there would be six Russians and three Poles representing the region.[49]

To everyone's surprise, when the bill came up in the State Council, Stolypin spoke out strongly in support. He stated that the government had always understood the inadequacy of the electoral law for the Western provinces, but the introduction of the zemstvo would solve this problem. He therefore announced that the government would introduce legislation to extend the mandates of the existing members for a year, thus delaying the State Council elections in these provinces while the legislation for the new zemstvo proceeded through the legislative chambers. In short, the Stolypin government sought to integrate the proposal into its general program of local government reform that included extending the zemstvo into all the provinces of the Russian empire. The vote was lopsided. By 94 to 64 the State Council moved to send the Pikhno proposal to a special committee, thus creating a new majority in the upper chamber consisting of Nationalists, the Right and a part of the Center. All could see that the Center group clearly had no control over its own members, and therefore could no longer claim a majority in the upper chamber.[50] *Birzhevye vedomosti* (Stock-Exchange News) recognized the new reality with a page one editorial entitled "*Na Pravo!*" (To the Right!), commenting that while during the Naval Staff's crisis, the government had been decisive in its rejection of the Right, the meeting of May 8 had produced a turn of the government to the right.[51]

During the following session, the State Council's fifth, Stolypin exploited his new nationalist majority. By following this policy, he continued to control not only most of the Center's votes (though by no means all of them),[52] but also the votes of the Right who were sympathetic to Great

Russian nationalism. The issue, of course, was how long such a policy could persist. Nationalists, who had been among Stolypin's strongest critics prior to the government's turnabout in May 1909, were now among his staunchest supporters. In the Western provinces, the Nationalist party backed Stolypin in almost all his policies, not merely those touching directly on their specific interests.[53] Yet the less than committed nationalists among the right-wing members of the State Council followed the new course with skepticism and unwillingness at best. If anything, they tried to find new ways to discredit the prime minister, but found it difficult to argue that his policies in the legislative chambers exceeded his prerogatives.

Stolypin appeared to be gaining full control of the State Council. The new year's list for 1910 reflected his victory the previous spring, since all the new members were either government ministers or individuals who joined the Center. Yet, despite the optimism regarding new appointments, the overall impression was that legislation was hopelessly stalled in the upper chamber. There were even rumors that Nicholas II had personally berated Akimov for the lack of progress of bills through the State Council, resulting in an enormous increase in activity that spring for a wide variety of legislation including Stolypin's 1906 Land Reform bill.

In the meantime, the Center found itself caught even more firmly on the horns of the dilemma it had been faced with since the second session. It had no meaningful means to curb the independent ways of its members; nor did it have a policy to which all could agree. The flurry of legislation sharpened divisions, pitting trade and industry representatives against the landowners who predominated in the group, making it clear just how tenuous the Center coalition had become. Stolypin knew that only his nationalist majority could provide a pro-government bloc, but it depended on his ability to keep his right-wing opponents in line. Thus, the new nationalist policy peaked in spring 1910 with the gutting of a bill to change the status of Old Believers, and the passage of a bill curtailing Finnish autonomy. These projects broke the unity of the Right against Stolypin and united the Nationalists, Right, and parts of the Center pitting them against the Left, the Polish Koło, most Baltic Germans, and some members of the fractured Center's "basic" group.

Historians always point to the Western Zemstvo Act as the moment when Stolypin took his greatest gamble and failed to win in the State Council.[54] This particular piece of legislation turned out to be the center-piece of Stolypin's new nationalist policy because it combined his effort to create a new majority in both legislative chambers with his commitment to alter local government in the Russian Empire. The proposal to introduce the zemstvo in the Western provinces was not a simple extension of the institution under the law of 1890, since the property qualifications contained in the law ensured landlord domination, which would mean continued control by the Poles. After the Polish insurrection of 1863, despite major efforts by the government to encourage Russian landholding in the west, many Russians were absentee proprietors with voting privileges in other provinces. Peasants working the land, officially classified as Russian, were mostly White Russian or Ukrainian, and often Catholics or Uniates. Frequently, they were extremely dependent on their landlords. Nevertheless, in the south-west provinces, there were a number of nationally conscious Russian peasant proprietors who would have been excluded under the 1890 Law.[55]

The government bill sought to remedy these problems by introducing the zemstvo only in the six south-west provinces where there were sufficient numbers of Russian landowners. The idea was to modify the 1890 law in two ways: there would be created two separate curiae – one for Russians and one for Poles – at the province and district levels, and there would be established an artificial number of members of Polish and Russian nationality. The creation of the curiae would undermine a primary characteristic of the zemstvo – election by social group. In fact, the zemstvo would become a Russian national unit.[56]

Other rules were added to prevent creation of a peasant majority by restricting the number of communal peasants in each district to one-third the total and prohibiting their membership in the provincial zemstvo. The bill provided for increased clerical representation and restricted the number of non-Russians who could be employed by the zemstvo. Finally, recognizing the unique population configuration of the area, the bill specifically prohibited Jews from zemstvo participation.[57]

After numerous delays the Western Zemstvo bill came up for approval in the State Council in January 1911. Stolypin's speeches before the upper chamber emphasized the importance he placed on the national curiae, which he claimed would simply legitimize an already existing situation. It would give the less experienced Russian element the opportunity to control the western region, but in a manner separating them from the "clever" Poles. Stolypin stressed the need to recognize national differences and deal with them to prevent danger to the sovereignty of the Empire.[58]

Opponents of the bill included the Poles who of course affirmed their loyalty to the empire. The Left group in the State Council claimed that the national curiae deprived the zemstvo of its non-political status. Others maintained that creating a zemstvo with national curiae violated the idea of a multinational empire; while still others argued that all zemstvos had to be structured identically, and that the precedent in the west might undermine the very idea of the zemstvo in the rest of Russia.[59] The most ominous statement against the bill came from V. F. Trepov, who had close connections with court circles through his brother, the Police

Commandant D. F. Trepov, and who likened it to a move in a governmental card game designed to undermine the tsar's power. Nevertheless, the State Council voted 103 to 56 to move to a second, article-by-article, reading of the Western Zemstvo bill with most of the Right, and Center voting in favor – apparently, Stolypin's majority held.[60]

Yet, when the Western Zemstvo bill came up for its second reading in early March, the debate focused on the national curiae provision and the results were decidedly different. The minority of the State Council's special committee with P. N. Trubetskoi as its spokesman, suggested that introduction of the zemstvo be delayed until such a time when national curiae would be unnecessary.[61] To this Stolypin responded with an ultimatum: "The government," he proclaimed, "considers the question of national divisions . . . a question of state importance, the central question of the present legislation." He explained that should any other methods be adopted, the Poles would remain the predominant element and wreak havoc in the electoral assemblies.[62] Unfortunately for him, the State Council decided to ignore Stolypin's words and voted 69 to 90 to reject Article Six of the Western Zemstvo Act. In defeating the national curiae, the upper chamber handed Stolypin a devastating and unexpected setback.[63]

As we piece together the causes of Stolypin's defeat, his reaction, and the ministerial crisis that followed, it appears that the failure of the Western Zemstvo Act proved an acid test for Stolypin's "constitutionalism," leading to his defeat in both legislative chambers. Once he lost the tsar's confidence and his residual support outside the Nationalist camp, he had no way of retaining power or completing his reform agenda.

Stolypin's minister of finance and successor V. N. Kokovtsov remembered that the prime minister had been entirely sure of his success in securing the vote for the Western Zemstvo Act at the State Council. So unexpected was the result that "Stolypin immediately fled the meeting room and everyone understood that something out of the ordinary had occurred."[64] But in analyzing the vote, it is clear that although the Center group made every effort to support the prime minister, the provisions of the Western Zemstvo Act had forced some previously reliable members to desert. For some of the zemstvo men, the idea of lowering the property qualification to admit Russians was intolerable.[65]

The Right group split as well. Nationalists like A. S. Stishinskii and Pikhno, who had been Stolypin's fiercest critics in 1909, stuck by the prime minister, supporting the curiae, while other Rightists, like Trepov, remained irrevocably opposed to Stolypin's policies and tried their best to use all their influence against the bill. The extreme Right understood that passing the Western Zemstvo Act with national curiae would strengthen Stolypin's position: in 1913 he would surely gain six additional supporters from the Russian State Council representatives from the Western provinces. This would be accompanied by a similar increase in the number of Nationalist Duma deputies, giving Stolypin a much stronger basis in both chambers. In order to stop him, the Right fixed on the national curiae because without them the introduction of the zemstvo would alter very little.[66]

Within a week of the defeat, the papers gave more details of what had transpired. Stolypin had informed Akimov prior to the debate on the curiae that the "highest circles" fully supported the Western Zemstvo Act. In transmitting Stolypin's message to Durnovo, Akimov passed it on to his colleagues in such a way as to make it seem insulting. Kokovtsov tells us that Durnovo sent a letter to the tsar criticizing the national curiae for alienating loyal Polish landowners from the government, inspiring anti-Russian aspirations in those leaning towards Austria, and pushing the "cultured" class out of zemstvo work.[67] In a March 3 audience with the tsar, Trepov convinced Nicholas that the project was really a "revolutionary concoction," obtaining permission for the Right to vote "according to conscience," thus releasing 53 members of the group to vote against the national curiae if they so chose.[68]

After the vote, Stolypin informed the Council of Ministers that he wished to resign, but that the tsar had not been willing to permit him to do so. According to Kokovtsov's account, Nicholas II was surprised that Stolypin placed such importance on the national curiae issue. He suggested that Stolypin resubmit the Western Zemstvo bill, and that he would use his influence to secure its passage this time. Stolypin explained to the emperor that no second review was possible because the Duma would never accept the bill without the national curiae. Since the tsar would not let him resign, Stolypin proposed that Nicholas II prorogue the legislative chambers for three days and ratify the Western Zemstvo Act, complete with national curiae, under the provisions of Article 87 of the Fundamental Laws. The prime minister asserted that the Duma would have no reason to refuse to reenact the bill later on and by the time it was resubmitted to the State Council, it would have already proved how effective it was. Finally, Stolypin asked the tsar to banish Durnovo and Trepov from the capital for having intrigued against him in such an inappropriate manner.[69]

By March 11 the crisis had been settled, Stolypin called Kokovtsov to say that the tsar had accepted his ultimatum. On the same day, the State Council rejected the Western Zemstvo Act in its entirety by a vote of 23 to 134.[70] The next day the tsar announced that the legislative chambers were prorogued for three days and on March 14 the Western Zemstvo Act was enacted under Article 87. When the legislative chambers reopened, Akimov received an order to inform Durnovo and Trepov of their suspension from the State Council until the following year.[71] There were also rumors that the tsar agreed to allow Stolypin to appoint thirty members of the State Council on the 1912 New Year's List.[72]

Although Stolypin had had his way, in the aftermath, all observers, press, and diplomats noted the alteration in his conduct. For one thing, both legislative chambers introduced interpellations against him. Also, according to the British ambassador, Stolypin no longer stood high in the tsar's favor and some trifling event could cause his resignation.[73] By May 1, the tsar was already wavering in his treatment of Durnovo, and Stolypin wrote to Nicholas pressuring him to remain steadfast, lest there be any doubts "of the final acceptance of the bill enacted by Article 87."[74]

Still, Stolypin's triumph had become a pyrrhic victory. The tsar was obviously losing confidence in his prime minister, who had misjudged the nature of his support in the Duma as well as in the State Council. For the remainder of the session, he avoided the legislative chambers, and observers noted his evident lack of self-assurance. His turn towards nationalism had not really changed the way reactionaries viewed his policies. For them, the legislative chambers, no matter how conservative, bolstered the odious constitutional system. Stolypin wanted to use the legislative chambers, but his miscalculation caused him to lose his ground in both the Duma and the State Council. The prime minister might have been able to reinstate himself the following session, but never had the opportunity: while accompanying the tsar on a state visit to Kiev, Stolypin was assassinated by a terrorist on September 1, 1911.

The State Council Becomes What Had Been Intended All Along

Stolypin's important accomplishments were not his alleged "constitutionalism," but rather the way he sought to complete his agenda. During his tenure, the Council of Ministers functioned as a "united government" in which ministers operated by consulting with one another, developing coordinated policies, and presenting – more often than not – a united front, characterized by a common agenda. With Stolypin's death, both the unity and the agenda disappeared from the Russian political scene.

Reactionaries tried to use Stolypin's style of "united government" as a weapon against him, insinuating that "he was eclipsing the emperor and becoming some kind of dictator." Empress Alexandra Feodorovna was even more sensitive to such accusations than her husband. When she first met Kokovtsov, she begged the new prime minister not to mention his predecessor "who had overshadowed his sovereign," and expressed the hope that Kokovtsov would "never go along with those terrible political parties, which dream only of seizing power or of subjecting the government to their will."[75]

Kokovtsov did not have any political parties on which to rely. The Octobrists were demoralized, found themselves in opposition and irrevocably split. The new prime minister had no nationalist credentials; nor were the Nationalists themselves sure of what direction to pursue. Nicholas II was pleased with the disarray in the Duma, and when Kokovtsov complained to the tsar about the absence of a disciplined, moderate, conservative majority, Nicholas replied, "Your relationship to the Duma – peaceful and non-party – is the only appropriate one."[76]

Yet although he kept his dealings with the Duma to the mostly trivial, Kokovtsov alienated many of its factions since he was not sympathetic either to the Right or the Nationalists. But while the Duma was impotent, the State Council was "hostile." And because Kokovtsov had also soon alienated the empress as a result of his antipathy to Rasputin, the fact of the matter was that he enjoyed neither Stolypin's support from the throne, nor the backing of either of the legislative chambers.[77]

The State Council began to fragment even prior to Stolypin's death. The committee elections on March 31, 1911 revealed the changes occurring in council groupings. Instead of three lists, as had been the case since 1907, there were five: the Left, the Center, the Neidgardt group, the Right and the non-party. The Center apparently consisted of the "basic group," the Polish *Koto*, and the Trade and Industry group. The Left and Neidgardt groups remained intact, and the Right managed to hold on despite the split over the interpellation against Stolypin. The "non-party" group included some former ministers who had drawn away from the Center and Right.[78]

When the seventh session of the State Council began, the fragmentation continued. The Right, overrun and plagued by internal dissension, barely managed to remain intact by creating a presidium composed of the two fraction's leaders, Durnovo and Stishinskii, pepetually at odds and breaking the Right into pieces "which remain unglued."[79] The Center was in no better shape, if only because it became smaller; according to the lists for fall 1912, there were about 62 members in the Center, and the following fall it numbered 56.[80] The Neidgardt faction was no longer part of the group, and the Center had suffered another important loss with the murder of P. N. Trubetskoi over the summer.

Yet, if the group had maintained its larger numbers, it would have hardly mattered since the State Council's role was finally the one its "reformers" had sought for it in 1905–6: it became a reliable obstruction to Duma legislation. Stolypin's successor had much less interest in using the legislative chambers as a vehicle to achieve institutional and political reform. Reform in the post-Stolypin era was carried out in localities – either in the zemstvo or the city dumas, but not through the government.

As we approach summer 1914, it became increasingly clear that the institutions created in 1905–6 were no longer at the center of Russian political life. The remnants of Stolypin's reform efforts had been buried, so that the version of local government reform rejected in the State Council in 1914 had very little to do with the bills introduced six years earlier. The government "virtually abandoned" any efforts to reform the zemstvo electoral system, and the Duma's effort to extend the zemstvo had become "the obsession of bureaucratic and noble opponents in the United Nobility and the State Council; indeed, it became the object of a striking alliance aimed at defeating the reform in the upper chamber."[81]

The State Council sent the Western Zemstvo bill to committee in February 1913 where representatives of the Right, A. A. Naryshkin, P. N. Durnovo, and A. S. Stishinskii, tried to convince other members to refuse to study the project by declaring it "not only harmful but directly fatal for Russia." During the course of over a year, the committee rewrote the bill, and even then only pressure from the president of the State Council forced a favorable vote (14 to 13) to bring it to the upper chamber. The State Council, after four days of "heated" debate rejected the bill, 96 to 72, without a first reading. According to reports in *Novoe vremia*, most of the Council's Right, Right-Center (the successor name for the Neidgardt group) and zemstvo group voted against the measure.[82] Interestingly, Stishinskii and Durnovo, assisted by their supporters, were once again working together to defeat what they regarded as a measure that would deprive government bureaucrats of their ability to maintain social and political order, representing yet another threat to autocracy, as well as endangering the status of the nobility.

By this time the State Council was indeed functioning as a "conservative buffer" to the Duma, whose members from the Octobrists to the Left became increasingly disillusioned with the tsarist government. In Hosking's words, "[t]he Emperor, various Ministers, the Duma parties, the nobles, the press and the public were all going their own way." The Octobrist leader, and president of the Duma, M. V. Rodzianko wrote to the emperor in December 1913: "Each minister has his own opinion. For the most part, the cabinet is divided into two parties. The State Council forms a third, the Duma a fourth, and of your own opinion the country remains ignorant. This cannot go on, your majesty, this is not government, it is anarchy."[83]

Hosking notes that the process of legislation through the Duma and State Council had been replaced by a system of cliques close to the tsar, much in the manner Rodzianko described. Each clique was determined to impede change and retain privileges advantageous to itself. There were no longer any real efforts to develop coordinated plans for direction in the Russian Empire. Needless to say, these tendencies inevitably debilitated Russia's military efforts after the beginning of the World War.

Ironically, the most perceptive warning to Nicholas II against entering into war against Germany came from P. N. Durnovo who asserted in his famous (and often cited) memorandum that were Russia and Germany to fight one another, their conflict would be profoundly injurious to the "conservative principles" of empire and would lead to social revolution in the defeated country, spreading from there into the land of the victor. He also prophesied that this revolution would not remain long in the hands of the Duma parties, but would slip into socialist control[84] – precisely as it did in 1917.

As to the State Council, it would of course be entirely inaccurate to regard the upper chamber as ever having been a firebrand reformist body; yet it was never monolithic in its composition or scope of opinion. The remarkable feature of its history is not that the State Council eventually became the conservative roadblock to reform that senior statesmen had visualized, but that it took so long for it to get that way.

Notes

1 The author would like to thank Xavier University for a Summer Research Grant and IREX for a 30-day Short-term Travel Grant that made it possible to include materials from the State Archive of the Russian Federation (GARF) in this article. Full responsibility for the article of course rests with the author.

2 Perhaps the best summary of these meetings is available in the second volume of Abraham Ascher's excellent two-volume work, *The Revolution of 1905: Order Restored* (Standford, CA: Stanford University Press, 1994), 60–5.

3 Ascher, *The Revolution of 1905*, 62–3.

4 State Council sessions paralleled those of the State Duma, with the first session corresponding to the First Duma, the second session to the Second Duma while its third, fourth, fifth, and sixth sessions correspond to the Third Duma period, just as the sessions numbered seven and up correspond to the Fourth Duma.

5 The new laws reforming the State Council provided that every January, the tsar would name the 98 appointed members of the State Council to serve in the restructured body. This meant that not all the life members of the State Council would be on the annual list to participate in the new legislature and that new life members could be named who would be able to participate immediately.

6 The Assemblies of Nobility met to elect 18 representatives; each provincial zemstvo sent one representative for a total of 34; and landowner assemblies from non-zemstvo provinces each elected one representative for a total of 22.

This last group included nobles from the Kingdom of Poland as well as Poles from the Western provinces where they were the largest landowners.

7 *Polnoe sobranie zakonov*, series 3, vol. 26, pt 1, no. 27425 (hereafter PSZ). Article 1, section 8 details the complicated procedure for electing delegates from the various trade and industry committees throughout the Russian Empire.

8 For example, one of the noble representatives, Prince V. I. Chavchavadze of Georgia was not only a Kadet, but he had also been arrested for revolutionary activities during 1905 (Alexandra S. Korros, "Activist Politics in a Conservative Institution: The Formation of Factions in the Russian Imperial State Council, 1906–1907" *Russian Review*, 52 (1) January, 1993: 1–19).

9 For exact statistics on the large numbers of marshals of nobility see, Alexandra S. Korros, "The Landed Nobility, the State Council, and P. A. Stolypin (1907–1911)," in Leopold Haimron, ed., *The Politics of Rural Russia, 1905–1914*, (Bloomington: Indiana University Press, 1979), 123–41.

10 V. M. Andreevskii, *Biograficheskie sosedeniia o zhizni i deiatel'nosti*, MS Bakhmeteff Archive, Columbia University, 60–3.

11 *Gosudarstvenny Sovet Stenografischeskie Otchety* (hereafter GSSO) mtg May 3, 5, 1906, 11–15.

12 *Gosudarstvenny Arkhiv Russkoi Federatsii* (hereafter GARF), f. 1178, op. 1, d. 1, l. 2.

13 GARF, f. 1178, op. 1, d. 34-, l. 1–2, 16–17. The membership roster for 1906 lists 103 members, and the one for January 1907 lists 97 members.

14 GARF, f. 1178, op. 1, d. 40, l. 14. The signature on this note is illegible.

15 GARF, f. 1178, op. 1, d. 40, l. 8.

16 Korros, "Activist Politics," 11.

17 Ibid., 11–12. The original correspondence can be found in Correspondence of the British Foreign Office, Record Class F.O. 371, vol. 127, Public Record Office, Kew, England: Nicolson to Grey, July 15 (3), 1906. Ascher notes that the bill's passage further discredited Goremykin in the eyes of the court and the tsar, 66–7.

18 Korros, "Activist Politics," 12. Minister of Agriculture, A. S. Stishinskii and Procurator of the Holy Synod, Prince A. A. Shirinskii-Shikhmatov were replaced by B. A. Vasilchikov and P. P. Izvolskii respectively. For more information on the new Stolypin regime, see Ascher, *The Revolution of 1905*, 216–63.

19 For more information on the agrarian reform see Ascher, *The Revolution of 1905*, ch. 7; one of the most authoritative works on the whole problem of agrarian reform is David A. J. Macey, *Government and Peasant in Russia, 1881–1906: The Prehistory of the Stolypin Reforms*. (De Kalb: Northern Illinois Press, 1987). See also Macey's "The Peasantry, the Agrarian Problem, and the Revolution of 1905–1907," in A. W. Cordier, ed., *Columbia Essays in International Affairs* (New York: Columbia University Press, 1972), 1–35.

20 GARF, f. 1178, op. 1, d. 8. l. 3. Center members from throughout the country gathered to discuss the mood of the population and formulate a series of positions to which the group could agree. The Center's conclusions affirmed the central place of the new constitutional system and stressed the importance

of returning the Russian Empire to a regime of law and order. The documents also placed great importance on the election of a State Duma capable of working with the State Council to create a legislative program to solve the ills of the Russian state. Leaders of the group were convinced that if the Center could boil down its views into a short political platform, they would appeal to other moderates in the provinces who wanted to support a conservative, constitutional monarchy. In some ways they imagined that they represented a substantial part of Russian opinion.

After a week of meetings, the Center prepared a document called "Conclusions Regarding the Problems under Review," in which it summarized its positions and articulated five principles based on the proposition that the constitutional monarchy would work only if the State Council and the State Duma could cooperate with one another. These included demands for agrarian and local government reform coupled with immediate lifting, by Article 87 if need be, of discriminatory laws limiting rights of nationality groups in the empire.

21   *Birzhevye vedomosti*, February 18, 1907.
22   Korros, "Activist Politics," 13. Stolypin's first speech proposed a program that would reestablish law and order, while at the same time stressing the need to approve the November 1906 land reforms, and enact local government legislation to introduce zemstvos, courts, and other necessary institutions at the *volost'* or village level. He described a program of reforms rationalizing Russian administration and eliminating the problems that had led to discontent in 1905.
23   See Korros, "Activist Politics", 13.
24   *Gosudarstvenny Sovet Stenograficheskie Otchety* (hereafter GSSO), session 2, 1907, mtg. 4, 27–47. See also, D. N. Shipov, *Vospominaniia i durny o perezhitom* (Moscow: Pechatnaia S. P. Iakovleva, 1918), 490–8.
25   GSSO, session 2, meeting 5, March 10, 1907, supplement 129–30, 72, 80, 93, 118–19, 121, 124.
26   Korros, "Activist Politics," 16.
27   For more details, see Korros, "Activist Politics," 17.
28   GARF, f. 1178, op. 1, d. 2, l. 20–1.
29   *Vsepodaneishii otchet predsedatelia Gosudarstvennago Soveta za tret'iiu sessiiu* (1907–1908), (St Petersburg, 1908), 43–4. Harvard Law School, Special Collections, Russia 600. In his *Vsepodaneishii otchet* to the tsar for the third session, State Council Chairman Akimov noted that at the conclusion of the second session, in order to avoid disputes over composition of these committees, the Personnel Committee had worked out a new procedure by using proportional elections. Each group submitted its lists of nominees to each committee and then the whole body voted. Members were assigned to the committees in proportion to the number of votes each list received. When the third session of the State Council convened on November 1, 1907, the elections to the standing committees were carried out in this manner.
30   GARF, f. 1178, op. 1, d. 39, l. 4. Dated May 15, 1908, entitled, "*Zhurnal gruppy*," it allocates places to the various subgroups on the lists for election to standing committees. Places 1, 2 and 5 were allocated to the "basic group,"

place 3 to the Neidgardt group, and place 4 to the Polish group – Committee on Legislative Proposals, and the Personnel Committee.

31 Under the new electoral law, the Third Duma was a smaller body (consisting of 412 instead of 524 deputies) with a vastly different composition from its predecessors. The landowners and big bourgeoisie received control of the lower chamber, worker representation was cut in half and the number of peasant representatives was reduced by over 50 percent. Half the total number of electors came from the landowning class (49.4 percent) while the peasants received only a one-quarter share. The parties of the Right gained substantial numbers of seats with 50 extreme rightists, 97 moderate rightists and nationalists, 154 Octobrists, 28 Progressists, 54 Kadets, 8 Muslims, 18 Poles and Lithuanians, 13 Trudoviks, and 19 Social Democrats elected in the fall 1907 elections. Although under the Electoral Law of December 11, 1905, suffrage had been neither direct nor equal, there had been a significant number of peasant deputies and urban representatives in the first and second Dumas. The June 3 system minimized their participation in favor of the propertied classes of the Russian Empire. In this new Duma, the Octobrist fraction was pivotal for the creation of a majority. Should the Octobrists vote "to the right," it would lead to a right Octobrist majority of 300; should they vote "to the left" with the Progressists and Kadets, they would form an Octobrist/Kadet majority of at least 260 votes. See: *Istoriia SSSR*, vol. VI (Moscow: Nauka, 1968), 209–11, 344–5 and A. Ia. Avrekh, *Stolypin i Tret'ia Duma* (Moscow: Nauka, 1968), 10.

32 The local government reforms developed by the Ministry of the Interior entailed an extensive reorganization particularly at the uezd (district) level. The proposed reforms would make the district Marshal of Nobility (*Predvoditel' dvorianstva*) into the representative of the noble estate, diminishing his responsibilities to guardianship of primary schools, chairmanship of the district zemstvo assembly, and of the district land committee. See RGIA, f. 1291, op. 50, d. 34, ll. 47–48–49. Memorandum of the Minister of the Interior, Report of December 1906, as cited in Hosking, *The Russian Constitutional Experiment: Government and Duma 1907–1914*. (Cambridge: Cambridge University Press, 1973), 156.

33 *Trudy IV s'yezda upolnomochennykh dvorianskikh obshchestv, 1908*. Thirty-two provinces. March 9–16, 1908. (St Petersburg, 1909), 19–25, passim. The minutes of the congress reveal that Stolypin's opponents were not only members of the State Council Right, but others affiliated with the Center group.

34 Having gained an advantage in influencing the appointments to the upper chamber, the Right pressed on the issue of naval rearmament. In the wake of the defeats of the Russo-Japanese War, a concerted effort began to reform the imperial Russian Navy. While all military appropriations and organization bills were important, the legislation pertaining to the Russian Navy was particularly sensitive. Stolypin's main supporters in the Duma, the Union of October 17, and especially its leader, Alexander Guchkov, were strong advocates of naval restructuring. They insisted on limiting expenditures on naval rearmament unless it was accompanied by reforms. Although Stolypin had

taken no public position on naval rearmament, the Octobrist fraction in the Duma was closely associated with a pro-government position. Since Stolypin needed their votes to pass his domestic agenda, local government reform, through the Duma, "conventional wisdom" associated with government circles presumed that the Chairman of the Council of Ministers would have to acquiesce to the Octobrist position on naval rearmament.

35 Ibid., 23–4.

36 GSSO, session III, meeting 36, June 13, 1908, 1701–9. Stolypin's speech was followed by a stormy debate pitting members of the same groups against one another over the issue of naval policy. There were rumors that even more Center members were wavering in their support for the government's position.

37 Immediately after the conclusion of the Russo-Japanese War, a temporary staff had been created under Article 87 of the Fundamental Laws. Thus, by spring 1908, the Duma had been requested to appropriate the necessary credits of 95,000 rubles to make the staff permanent. In performing this task, the Duma, at the request of Octobrist leader Alexander Guchkov's National Defense Committee, had confirmed the establishment lists, together with the salaries of the staff.

38 A. A. Polivanov, *Iz dnevnikov*, June 23, 1908, 47. P. A. Kharitonov, the state comptroller, disputed Schwanebach's view, claiming that it did not apply to the composition of the naval and war ministries. His views enraged Durnovo, Akimov, and other members of the Finance Committee, but when Prince A. A. Kasatkin-Rostovskii turned to the minister of war, General Roediger, seeking support for Schwanebach's position, Roediger replied that he fully concurred with the government. When A. A. Polivanov, the deputy minister of war, and a close associated of Guchkov, described the incident in his diary, he remarked that some committee members desired to attack Stolypin for supporting a bill that had permitted an unforgivable attack on the autocracy.

39 GSSO, session III, meeting 42, July 3, 1908, 2222–5.

40 *Golos Moskvy*, March 19, 1909.

41 GSSO, session IV, meeting 25, March 18, 1909, col. 1350, Durnovo's speech.

42 *Rech'*, March 20, 1909; *Birzhevye vedomosti*, no. 11017, March 20, 1909.

43 V. I. Gurko, Stolypin's deputy interior minister blamed the right wing of the Council: "In this as in other cases," Gurko wrote, "there was evidence of intrigue against Stolypin on the part of a group of State Council members." (V. I. Gurko, *Features and Figures of the Past: Government and Opinion in the Reign of Nicholas II*, ed. J. W. Wallace Sterling, Xenia Joukoff Eudin, and H. H. Fisher (Stanford: Stanford University Press, 1939), 514).

44 On March 21, *Russkie vedomosti*, a Kadet paper reported an "explosion" of displeasure over the bill's passage and that, led by "many influential members of the State Council," leaders of reactionary bureaucratic circles intended to circulate a report criticizing the government and suggesting cabinet changes. Three days later on March 24, the right-wing *Novoe vremia* noted that the unthinkable had occurred, "a Russian ministry responsible only to the Monarch, has allied itself with the liberal center (52 votes), but with the left Kadets (13 votes) and with the Poles (15 votes)."

45 *Russkiia vedomosti*, April 1, 1909; *Rech'*, April 1, 1909 and April 3, 1909.
46 F.O. 371, vol. 729, no. 17374, May 7 (April 24), 1909.
47 *Birzhevye vedomosti*, no. 11078, April 28, 1909.
48 Because the Western provinces had been acquired from Poland in the partitions of 1772, 1792, and 1795, Polish noblemen remained the largest property owners in these areas. Since the electoral law to the State Council was biased in favor of the largest landowners, the Russians, who were basically urban dwellers or smaller property owners, were excluded from representation. Ironically, in the Western provinces, the electoral bias that guaranteed limiting State Council representation to "trustworthy" individuals – the nobility of each province – privileged an even smaller minority in the west – Polish noble landowners!
49 *Birzhevye vedomosti*, no. 1025, March 24, 1909.
50 Ibid., col 1949.
51 *Birzhevye vedomosti*, no. 11096, May 9, 1909.
52 *Rech'* reported that the Center was so concerned about this apparent reversal of position on the part of the government, that it called a special meeting on May 4 to reevaluate its position on the Pikhno proposal because on the previous evening it had voted to reject the proposal. At the meeting on the fourth, A. S. Ermolov reported that the government intended to delay State Council elections from the Western provinces to introduce a bill guaranteeing the rights of Russians in the western region. After a long debate, the Center voted (32 to 18) to open a discussion of principle at the general Council meeting and then propose the Pikhno bill's rejection. In contrast, the 18 dissenters suggested sending the proposal to committee (not advocating actual support for the proposal itself) while only two of those present actually supported the bill.
53 See Robert Edelman, *Gentry Politics on the Eve of the Russian Revolution: The Nationalist Party, 1907–1917* (New Brunswick: Rutgers University Press, 1980) for the most authoritative discussion of the Russian Nationalist party. Robert Edelman argues that the Nationalists, more than any other political group, acted in the manner of a Western political party. At this particular moment their interests coincided with those of the State Council's extreme right although they were not attempting to use the Pikhno proposal as an embarrassment, but in order to attain their goal of increased Russian representation. Edelman writes that the Pikhno proposal was a "textbook example of a legislative proposal that germinated within a specific region, served the interests of its residents, and was advanced by its parliamentary representatives. The process by which it was elaborated and came to Stolypin's attention indicates the manner in which the future Nationalists came to serve their electoral base" (83).
54 For example, see Edward Chmielewski, "Stolypin's Last Crisis," *California Slavic Studies*, III, 1964; also his *The Polish Question in the Russian State Duma* (Knoxville, TN: Vanderbilt University Press, 1970); Hosking, *The Russian Constitutional Experiment*, 134–49; and Edelman *Gentry Politics on the Eve of the Russian Revolution*, 116–26. For Soviet discussions, Avrekh, *Stolypin i Tret'ia Duma* and V. S. Diakin, *Samoderzhavia, burzhuaziia i dvorianstvo v 1907–1911 gg.* (Leningrad, 1978), 213–17.

55 Chmielewski, *The Polish Question*, 86–7.
56 Ibid., 86–7. The six provinces were Volhyn, Mogilev, Kiev, Vitebsk, Podolia, and Minsk. The two north-western provinces of Vilno and Kovno were excluded because there were too few Russian landlords, while Grodno was dropped for the sake of administrative unity. Grodno's White Russian Catholics were said to be under strong Polish influence.

The percentage of a given nationality's population within a province was added to the percentage of zemstvo taxes paid by those holding land and immovable property who were of that nationality. The total was then divided by two, and the result determined the percentage of zemstvo voters for a given curia.

57 Ibid., 87–8.
58 Ibid., cols. 866–80.
59 Ibid., cols. 814, 853–66, 913–22, 835–9, 880–9.
60 Ibid., col. 979.
61 GSSO, session VI, meeting 25, March 4, 1911, cols 1199–203.
62 Ibid., cols 1240–1.
63 Ibid., col. 1256.
64 V. N. Kokovtsov, *Iz moego proshlago* 2 vols (Paris: Izdanie zhurnala Illiustrirovannaia Rossiia, 1933).
65 Witte explained the opposition of moderate nobles saying it was impossible for them "to make a distinction between nobles – Polish, and nobles – Russian . . ." See, S. Iu. Witte, *Vospominaniia tsarstvovanie Nikolaia II*, 2nd edn (Leningrad, 1924), vol. 3, 542. Yet, in their speeches, not one member of the "moderate nobility" voiced any consideration of the Poles. They were more concerned about the precedent that a lowered property qualification might have in changing the elections to the zemstvo in Russia proper.
66 Soviet historians such as A. Ia. Avrekh have stressed that the national curiae were simply an occasion to topple Stolypin, but that the Right actually supported such a measure. Avrekh is so bent on class analysis of the Stolypin era, that he does not give sufficient weight to the degree of support Stolypin might have gained had the national curiae been included in a bill that passed into law. He contends that if the arguments against the national curiae had been true, an arch-Right like Pikhno would have seen their value and not supported the curiae. In doing so, Avrekh fails to distinguish between the motivations of the Nationalists and the extreme reactionaries for whom nationalism was a convenient, but not necessary political attachment. See A. Ia. Avrekh, *Stolypin i tret'ia duma*, 319–22.
67 *Rech'*, March 9, 1911. The paper tells the same story with slightly different details. A. D. Golitsyn, *Vospominaniia*, Columbia University, Bakhmeteff Archive, 283. Golitsyn wrote that Stolypin had the impression that Akimov favored the bill. Kokovtsov, *Iz moego proshlago*, 452–3.
68 *Rech'*, March 9, 1911.
69 Kokovtsov, 454–5. The meeting of the Council of Ministers probably occurred on March 6, although Kokovtsov gives no dates. There is also a transcript of Stolypin's report in the archives, RGIA, f. 1262, op. 1, d. 325, ll. 1–2.
70 GSSO, session VI, meeting 28, March 11, 1911. See also *Rech'*, March 12, 1911.

71   Kokovtsov, *Iz moego proshlago*, 461.

72   A. A. Bobrinskii, "Dnevnik," *Krasnyi Arkhiv*, 26 (1928): 149.

73   F.O. 371, vol. 1217, no. 23857, June 14 (1), 1911.

74   "Iz perepiski P. A. Stolypina s Nikolaem Romanovym," *Krasnyi Arkhiv*, 30(7), (1928): 85–6.

75   Hosking, *The Russian Constitutional Experiment*, 197.

76   Ibid., 197. Hosking cites RGIA, f. 966 (V. N. Kokovtsov), op. 2, d. 11, l. 6 (letter of Nicholas II to Kokovtsov, November 18, 1911).

77   Hosking, *The Russian Constitutional Experiment*, 197.

78   *Rech'*, April 1, 1911.

79   *Birzhevye vedomosti*, no. 12583, October 15, 1911, no. 12589, October 19, 1911 and no. 12593, October 21, 1911.

80   GARF, f. 1178, op. 1, d. 34, ll. 35–6.

81   Francis W. Wcislo, *Reforming Rural Russia: State, Society, and Local Politics, 1855–1914* (Princeton, NJ: Princeton University Press, 1990), 291–3.

82   Ibid., 293.

83   Hosking, *The Russian Constitutional Experiment*, 213. He is quoting Rodzianko's memoirs, "Krushenie Imperii: Zapiski Predsedatelya Russkoi Gosudarstvennoi Dumy," in *Arkhiv Russkoi Revoliutsii*, vol. 17, Berlin, 1926, 52–4.

84   Robert Edelman, *Gentry Politics on the Eve of the Russian Revolution: The Nationalist Party, 1907–1917* (New Brunswick, NJ: Rutgers University Press, 1980), 221–2.

CHAPTER THIRTEEN

Church and Politics in Late Imperial Russia: Crisis and Radicalization of the Clergy

Gregory L. Freeze

While the vast literature on the Russian prerevolution has exhaustively explored virtually every facet of the profound social and political crisis overtaking the ancien regime, it has largely ignored the role of religion and church. In the absence of fundamental research, historians have inclined to draw upon stereotypes of the prerevolutionary intelligentsia (itself secular and anticlerical), the result differing little from the antireligious propaganda of the 1920s and 1930s.[1] That tradition was most pronounced in the case of Soviet historiography, which routinely equated the Church, clergy, and religion itself with reactionary monarchism.[2] Curiously, in this sphere Western historians – if they mention the Church at all – have accepted this picture, failed to tap the most rudimentary printed (let alone archival) sources, and blithely assumed that the Church was a "handmaiden of the state" staunchly committed to defending the tsarist order. Such analyses normally emphasize either a peculiar commitment to "other-worldliness" in Eastern Orthodoxy,[3] or the Petrine "bureaucratization" and "statification" of the Church, as the primary dynamics in transforming the Church into a "subservient handmaiden" of the secular state. That perspective informs, for example, the most recent general study of the Russian prerevolution by Richard Pipes, who (citing two hoary old studies) declares that "the monarchy governed Russia with the assistance of . . . the Orthodox Church," and avers that "the clergy stood by the monarchy in the 1905 Revolution."[4] Although some scholars (including

Pipes) mention the "liberal parish clergy," they marginalize clerical liberalism as a minor aberration and as inconsequential when compared to the "reactionary bishops."[5] And some indigenous scholarship, during both the perestroika and post-Soviet eras, also continues to recycle the conventional interpretation.[6]

That traditional interpretation, in the light of newer research, stands in need of radical revision. Above all, for the first time scholars have begun to use the basic corpus of printed and, more recently, archival materials, to explore the role of church and clergy in the politics of late imperial Russia. While this new work first appeared chiefly in the West,[7] in recent years a similar (if more cautious and contradictory) reassessment has come to inform scholarship within Russia itself.[8]

This essay, informed by this newer research but based primarily upon a systematic study of the printed and archival materials, will attempt to suggest a far more differentiated, nuanced picture of the role played by bishops and priests in the Russian prerevolution. Above all, it is important to distinguish not only between bishops and priests, but to delineate the sharp differences *within* these groups and, especially, how to establish their attitude toward the autocracy and old order evolved from the eve of revolution in 1905 to the fall of the monarchy in 1917. Were bishops uniformly "reactionary monarchists," not only during the 1905 Revolution, but in the critical interrevolutionary years? Were parish priests "mostly" reactionary in 1905 and enthusiastic members and supporters of the Union of Russian People? Were this the case, then why were the Church and clergy so wont to dissociate themselves from the tsarist regime in 1917?[9]

As this essay will suggest, by 1917 the Russian clergy – even the most benighted and "reactionary bishops" – had become thoroughly disenchanted with a regime that could neither reform nor repress, but only corrupt its elite and betray vital church interests. When the regime finally slid over the precipice into revolution in 1917, even the arch-conservative prelates in the Synod demurred to rise in its defense,[10] and a ranking lay bureaucrat in the Church estimated that 90 percent of its top officials welcomed the revolution.[11] Within a few weeks, diocesan assemblies gathered all across Russia to pass resolutions hailing the revolution, deposing unpopular "Rasputinist" prelates, and even endorsing the "just" social demands of the lower classes. The problem here is to explain why the liberal clergy (inclined to support the "liberation movement") proliferated, why the episcopate (even its arch-conservative wing) became disenchanted with the autocracy (and hybrid Duma Monarchy), and thus why the Church was neither able nor willing to continue serving as a "pillar of the old regime."

Episcopate: From Monarchists to *Frondeurs*

The Russian episcopate – some 175 prelates serving as metropolitan, archbishop, bishop, and suffragan bishop in the 71 dioceses – had itself changed significantly by the early twentieth century.[12] Although still vilified by old stereotypes and roundly disliked by many parish priests, the bishops had in fact changed radically since the mid-nineteenth century. To be sure, all were still in monastic orders, as mandated by Russian church tradition; however, far fewer belonged to the "learned monasticism" (*uchenoe monashestvo*), chiefly because the dearth of monastic graduates from the theological academies forced the Church to consecrate widowed priests, who thereupon took monastic vows and rose quickly in the hierarchy.

Still, as the twentieth century dawned, most prelates were indeed highly conservative in their outlook, with dignitaries like Metropolitan Antonii (Vadkovskii) of St Petersburg, who proved willing to tolerate and even sponsor Fathor Gapon of "Bloody Sunday" fame, being the exception. Not surprisingly, the bishops (and especially the Synod) were disposed to preach devotion to autocracy, as has been emphasized in the traditional literature. Apart from schoolbook catechisms,[13] and celebration of state holidays to glorify the royal family,[14] the Church took special measures to combat the revolutionary movement. Thus, in the wake of the tumultuous peasant disorders in Poltava and Kharkov in 1902, the Synod distributed a "model sermon" castigating the unrest as a "tragic and insane event, something hitherto unheard-of," where ill-intentioned "instigators" had deceived "the simple people" into committing an orgy of plunder and violence. The sermon enjoined the people to uphold law and order, whatever past wrongs might have been done to them.[15]

Nevertheless, on the eve of 1905, the church hierarchs became increasingly resentful and suspicious of the policies and power of the autocracy. These tensions had been mounting throughout the latter decades of the nineteenth century, especially after the appointment of K. P. Pobedonostsev as chief procurator; despite his reputation for omnipotence (more precisely, *because of* that reputation and his tactless meddling), ranking hierarchs had deeply resented his role ever since he acceded to his post in 1880.[16] At issue, however, much more than a question of personalities: church hierarchs had come increasingly to believe that the secular state was far more determined to pursue its own secular interests, even at the expense of the Church itself. Although the bishops had encountered such threats throughout the eighteenth and nineteenth centuries, in the early years of Nicholas's reign they encountered an unprecedented challenge to the special prerogatives and power of the Orthodox Church. Particularly alarming were the plans, actively encouraged by high-ranking officials, to "secularize" marriage – i.e., to transfer authority from the Church – and, more alarming still, to liberalize the Church's ban on separation and the fierce opposition to divorce.[17] A second, even more sensitive issue was religious tolerance; ever since the mid-nineteenth century, the government had inclined to jettison a policy of repression, especially in politically sensitive areas involving the influential Old Believers or the volatile borderlands, such as the Western provinces. Promises, as in the February Manifesto of 1903 to ameliorate the status of religious minorities, could only alarm hierarchs already alarmed by the explosive growth of Old Belief and sectarianism. Finally, prelates took offense at persisting attempts by government authorities to undermine the traditional religious *byt*, for example, by reducing the number of holidays or adopting the Western calendar.[18]

Significantly, it was not only the faceless bureaucracy, but the emperor himself who offended episcopal sensibilities. In response to the withering legitimacy of his regime, Nicholas II made a concerted attempt to "resacralize" autocracy – i.e., to reaffirm the special linkage between crown and cross. Certainly the clergy could only welcome some of his actions; the Manifesto of February 1903, for example, assigned a high priority to church reform and promised to increase financial support for the clergy.[19] At an important symbolic level, Nicholas personally interceded to address various problems facing the Church, ordering, for example, a formal inquiry into the manifold disorders in Russian monasticism.[20] Nicholas also expressed an interest in popular Orthodoxy, especially "Russian icon-painting"; citing the threat from cheap factory production, the emperor convened a special commission to consider ways to protect popular religious creativity from the heartless inroads of modern machinery.[21]

Most dramatic of all, Nicholas became personally embroiled in the issue of canonization itself. Church authorities had looked askance at popular requests for canonization (fearing, in most cases, machinations by local clergy to acquire a "saint," a relic sure to attract large throngs of generous and grateful believers); as a result, prior to Nicholas's accession, the Church had canonized just four saints in the course of the eighteenth and nineteenth centuries. And it had conducted such canonizations with extraordinary reluctance and caution, requiring not years but decades of investigation (to demonstrate that the candidate's relics had truly caused "miracles") before finally acceding to popular petitions. In 1902, probably at his wife's instigation, Nicholas determined to end the Church's procrastination on the canonization of Serafim of Sarov, an early nineteenth-century recluse who enjoyed particular popularity at court both because of certain predictions about a glorious reign for Nicholas and because of rumors that he could even solve the imperial family's desire to have a son and heir. Whatever the motive, Nicholas's intercession naturally had the desired effect, and within a year the Church conducted the formal rites of canonization, in which the tsar personally – amidst vast numbers of pious commoners – participated.

That episode, while much celebrated in elite memoirs and traditional historiography (as symbolizing a union of "tsar and people"), was a source of much anguish and conflict among the leading hierarchs. The very intrusion into so important a spiritual matter was highly opprobrious; however great the emperor's "worldly authority," it did not extend to canon law or to spiritual matters of such importance as canonization. Imperial pressure came in the face of disturbing evidence that, contrary to tradition and popular expectations, Serafim's remains had undergone corruption. As this unhappy revelation emerged (a formal church commission had reopened his tomb and attested to these facts), it triggered conflict among ranking clergy and devastating criticism from such diverse groups as left-wing intellectuals and contemptuous Old Believers. The canonization itself, held amidst an army of troops and police, bore more the imprint of the state than sanctity, much to the chagrin of believers.[22]

Once revolution swept the country in 1905, the church hierarchy did in fact seek to tame passions and avert violence. Bloody Sunday (January 9, 1905) brought the Church quickly to the defense of the regime: the Synod blamed the tragedy on evil leaders (even hinting at Japanese involvement),[23] while Gapon's erstwhile mentor, Metropolitan Antonii of St Petersburg, hastened to dissociate the Church from the errant priest.[24] Among the first to react was the archbishop of Novgorod, Gurii, who wrote the chief procurator to declare that he and his clergy remained loyal and fully opposed to the "internal and external enemies."[25] Bishop Germogen of Saratov induced a diocesan assembly, on February 10, 1905, to speak on behalf of preserving "the inviolable powerful autocratic authority."[26] While some bishops reacted favorably to news of the October Manifesto (for example, Bishop Filaret of Viatka),[27] others were plainly baffled by the tumultuous turn of events. When the prelate of Vladimir received word of the October Manifesto, the incredulous hierarch hastened to telegraph St Petersburg to verify whether such was really possible.[28] For the duration of the revolutionary turmoil, most bishops staunchly defended the existing order or, at the very least, urged their clergy and believers to eschew violence and disorder.[29]

Nevertheless, the government's response to the revolutionary turmoil of 1905 only served to deepen the episcopate's dissatisfaction with the regime. It took offense, in particular, at the overreaction of police to purported misdeeds of parish clergy; in a testy memorandum of December 20, 1905, the Synod protested the unwarranted arrest of parish clergy, particularly the failure to obtain church approval, adding that such actions only undermine the clergy's authority and influence "on the masses of the dark rural population."[30] More important still was the government's decision to promulgate the manifesto of April 17, 1905 granting religious tolerance – an edict that was to form a major watershed in the history of Church–state relations. Reflecting certain long-term tendencies in state policy, but obviously precipitated by a desperate attempt to reestablish order at any cost (including a sacrifice of church interests), the manifesto represented a major concession to minorities and essentially opened the door to an unimpeded exodus from Russian Orthodoxy (hitherto treated as "apostasy" and categorically banned). The manifesto of April 17, was the Church's Bloody Sunday, a flagrant and unequivocal violation of its "social contract" with autocracy. Already anxious about the threat of other confessions (especially Old Belief and sectarianism), the manifesto now opened the doors to massive reconversions – to Judaism, Islam, Protestantism, and especially Catholicism.[31]

Within two months of Bloody Sunday, the Holy Synod – apprised of plans for a concession to religious minorities – hastened to exploit the revolutionary upsurge and the regime's transparent weakness to press *its own* demands for reform.[32] Although such proposals had circulated for decades, the need for change now seemed more imperative than ever if the Church was to withstand the onslaught and challenge from other confessions.[33] And that, above all, meant a determination to undertake fundamental reform in the Church and to address the lengthy agenda of outstanding problems – parish organization, seminaries, material support of the clergy, diocesan administration, ecclesiastical courts, missions, religious practice (the liturgy, sermons), and even the Church's traditional relationship to the State. Above all, ranking churchmen hoped to convoke a national church council (*sobor*), which alone would have the authority to deal with issues touching upon canon law.[34] Although Nicholas declined to convoke a church council because of the "current circumstances,"[35] he authorized the Church to assemble episcopal opinion and to create a "preconciliar commission" to study individual problems and thus prepare for an eventual council. As the episcopal "replies" (subsequently published in three volumes) show, most prelates – even the most conservative – readily acknowledged the need for reform.[36]

Once the revolutionary turmoil had subsided and the Stolypin regime forcibly imposed law and order, the episcopate reaffirmed its support for the regime. Whether because of monarchist convictions, dismay and horror over revolutionary violence, or belief in a close link between revolution and irreligion, in 1907 the bishops were strongly disposed to support the new order and to collaborate in electing a conservative Duma.[37] Apart from electing clergy to the Duma, prelates like Metropolitan Vladimir of Moscow directed diocesan clergy to promote the election of people "faithful to the

Church, Tsar, and Motherland."[38] Vladimir, who also actively preached against radical social teachings,[39] seemed to typify the union of crown and cross that dominated revolutionary propaganda. Indeed, some bishops became closely identified with the Black Hundredists and actively urged parish priests to join and support right-wing parties. As before, the liturgical year continued to include a host of political ceremonies to celebrate the dynasty and its legitimacy.

Beneath this superficial identification with the autocracy, however, the interrevolutionary years witnessed a growing dissension between Church and state that would culminate in the episcopate's refusal to support the monarchy in 1917. While most prelates were still conservative, they became increasingly alienated from the new regime of a "Duma Monarchy."

One factor was the Duma itself – a secular institution, filled with many non-Orthodox deputies, which now dared to raise issues directly pertaining to the Church. Among the most sensitive were various proposals to expand religious tolerance,[40] to liberalize divorce,[41] to establish secular control over parish schools,[42] and to reconstruct the parish as an institution.[43] In the teeth of such incursions, the bishops grew increasingly critical of the Duma and its pernicious influence on Church affairs.[44] Indeed, from the very outset, the Church challenged the authority of the Duma to intercede in purely religious affairs; memoranda of 1907–8, for example, argued for the Church's sole authority in dealing with a series of important issues.[45] It was, in fact, the increasingly negative attitude toward the Duma that inspired ranking prelates to mobilize their clergy to campaign actively in the elections of 1912; only with a substantial clerical presence, they believed, would the Church be able to torpedo harmful proposals from the Duma.[46] Although the reasons for the failure of the Duma system are manifold (above all, neither the Duma nor the monarchy ultimately accepted the status quo), the Orthodox Church also played a certain role, using all its influence to stonewall and deflect reform proposals.

Even the purported alliance with conservative and right-wing parties, such as the Octobrists and Union of Russian People (URP), quickly disintegrated during the Duma Monarchy. The disenchantment with the Octobrists was most apparent, fueled in good measure by that party's flirtation with reform to aid the Old Believers, but gradually broadened into a full-scale break. More interesting still is the case of the URP, which had elicited the support and even membership of some prominent clergy in the wake of the 1905 Revolution. But this importunate right-wing party soon found itself at odds with diocesan prelates, even renowned conservatives like Archbishop Germogen of Saratov, who complained that the URP was not purely Orthodox (its charters failing to exclude Old Believers) and that it was attempting to appropriate the Church for political purposes, rather than lend its own support to Orthodoxy.[47] In response to repeated conflicts over demands by the URP that the clergy consecrate their banners, store their icons and banners in the parish church, and admit them (*qua* the URP) to march in icon processions, the Synod refused to endorse these demands and delegated all authority to local prelates to handle such issues.[48] That rule did little to deter the URP, which continued to file complaints – for the most part, without effect – against various bishops.[49]

The government itself, not just the Duma, increasingly loomed more like an adversary than protector. Many of the debates, over such issues as religious tolerance and censorship, elicited sharp differences between the ranking bishops and bureaucrats. When, for example, the government proposed to relax the rules against the elevation of sectarians into the officer corps, or to permit sectarian assemblies, the Church vociferously protested.[50] Similarly, despite repeated complaints about the press (which, in the wake of 1905, had been virtually freed of censorship), government authorities declined either to take punitive action or to prepare legislation to deal with the problem.[51] As a result, a prominent missionary, I. Aivazov, wrote privately that "Stolypin was constantly working against Orthodoxy."[52] As the extensive and testy correspondence between the Synod and Stolypin attests, relations between them rapidly deteriorated after 1907 and largely because of the government's attempt to construct a new regime, one better suited for a multinational and multiconfessional empire.

Significantly, it was not only the Duma and government, but the monarchy itself that became increasingly alien to the episcopate. Many, no doubt, were deeply appalled by the scandals involving Grigorii Rasputin, who exerted an influence on Church policy and appointments and did so much to bring disgrace on the monarchy. Rasputin himself took a highly deprecating attitude toward the church hierarchs, whom he dismissed as mere "officials"[53] a sentiment no doubt reinforced by attempts to charge him with being a sectarian "flagellant" (*khlyst*).[54] By all accounts, his dark influence led to the appointment of some unworthy figures to the episcopate, such as Varnava of Tobolsk – a man of limited education, whose sermons were the laughing stock of his new diocese, and someone who, with impunity, flouted the Synod's will by canonizing a local saint on his authority (and with the emperor's apparent blessing).[55] As one informed observer noted, "few of the prelates are favorably disposed toward [Rasputin]; the majority either regard him with indifference or as a pernicious sectarian, a flagellant."[56] Despite recent attempts to "rehabilitate" Rasputin,[57] he clearly exerted a pernicious influence on the Church, driving even the most conservative prelates – such as Antonii (Khrapovitskii) and Germogen – to denounce him.

Given the deteriorating relations between Duma, government, and court, and given the signs of massive "apostasy,"[58] growth of sectarianism,[59] and de-Christianization (even in the countryside),[60] the bishops were all the more determined to convoke a church council and rearm the Church for its struggle against all these ills and adversaries. Although the regime periodically mouthed a commitment to allowing such a council, it plainly had no intention of doing so. As the chief procurator declared, he himself yearned to see such a council, but hastened to add: "I do not find the present moment appropriate for realizing this most ancient dream, and God alone knows which chief procurator will be fated to see this happy hour."[61] No doubt the principal reason for the regime's reluctance to summon a council was political: many in the Church, including top bishops, now openly spoke about the need not only to reform the church internally, but to change its relationship to the state.[62] This desire to redefine the Church's status inspired ever more insistent demands for the reestablishment of the patriarchate, not from some vague sense of nostalgia, but because a patriarch could far more effectively represent the Church and, above all, repulse the demands of an importunate chief procurator.

As a result, in the final years of the ancien regime, not only radical priests but even conservative prelates became profoundly dissatisfied with the autocracy. In January 1907, the chief procurator sent P. A. Stolypin a memorandum outlining the Church's demands for a new, clear definition of its rights and status. It complained specifically about the recent concessions on religious tolerance, demanded that the regime recognize "the rights and privileges of the Orthodox Church," and urged the government to reaffirm for the Church "its complete freedom of internal rule" and to assist in convening a Church Council.[63] In the ensuing years, tensions only increased between the bishops and bureaucrats, with a special hostility toward Stolypin and his failure to protect church interests. Shortly after Stolypin's assassination in 1911, the bishop of Poltava publicly declared that the Lord had failed to intercede on Stolypin's behalf because the latter had dissuaded the emperor from attending a recent canonization.[64] An account of perlustration of letters in 1912 confirmed that indeed many prelates and their correspondents were deeply disturbed by the plight of the Church, especially the pernicious influence of Rasputin, the scandals involving Archbishop Germogen, and the harmful role of Chief Procurator V. A. Sabler. As the compiler of the report noted, "According to public opinion, the ecclesiastical domain experienced a kind of revolutionary movement in 1912." One letter quoted Archbishop Antonii (Khrapovitskii) as complaining that "the Russian bishops learn about appointments to the hierarchy simultaneously with the doormen and newspaper delivery boys." In one letter the same Archbishop Antonii, notorious for his extreme conservative views and later a key figure in the anti-Bolshevik Russian Church Abroad, wrote disparagingly about Germogen (even claiming that, "as a student at Novorossiiskii University, he castrated himself"), but acknowledged his respect for Germogen's willingness to denounce Rasputin: "I cannot fail to pay my profound respect to Archbishop Germogen for the fact that, having been himself a defender and protector of Rasputin and the Ioannites (flagellants), who had dulled his wits with the adulation he so much loves, Germogen – upon learning that Grigorii and the Ioannites were flagellants – openly, and with all his might, rose up against them (even though he owed his own summons to serve in the Synod to Rasputin's petitions)."[65] In private letters published only as an exposé in the Bolshevik era, Antonii inveighed long and hard against the degradation that had overwhelmed the Church on the eve of World War I.[66]

Many other prelates and conservative laymen shared this dismay. The bishop of Ufa, Andrei, for example, declared openly that "the life of the Church now presents an unprecedented picture of decline and decomposition. Worse still, even though the Church recognized its many failings in 1905, "almost everything remains just at it was."[67] The police intercepted a private letter from Archbishop Serafim, who wrote that "the tsar is a mediocrity, utterly without any talent," and no doubt many of his peers shared the same view.[68] And conservative lay believers, such as the correspondents with the bishops in 1912, expressed similar sentiments, merely giving greater force to their anger and bitterness. Perhaps the most influential was A. A. Papkov, a Slavophile-minded publicist prominent for his role in the church press. Yet his articles could just as easily have been written by a left-wing member of the intelligentsia, as he decried the catastrophic state into which the Church had fallen.[69] As the crisis deepened, amidst further scandals (such as the debacle involving Archbishop Varnava and the illegal canonization of 1915), the dismay and depression among ranking prelates only intensified as the regime drifted toward its final hours and sudden dissolution in 1917.[70]

Parish Clergy: Moderates, Liberals, and Radicals

Although the parish clergy had produced more than its share of radicals (like those who supported the rebellion under Pugachev), a broad-based "liberalism" gradually came to the fore only in the second half of the nineteenth century. In part, it derived from long-standing grievances held by the parish clergy against their superiors in the Church (whom, not without cause, they were wont to compare to haughty aristocrats and imperious officials).[71] It was also rooted primarily in the training and education at the seminary, which proved such a notorious hotbed of radicalism and dissent from the mid-century onwards.[72] Service too played its role: as the biographies and testimony of many priests confirm, they were also deeply affected by their everyday proximity to the common folk, whether factory worker or peasant, and hence had a keen appreciation for all their woes and weaknesses.[73] And a new Christology, which emphasized the need to bring the Church and clerical service (like Christ) into the world and to repudiate any one-sided "other-worldliness," gained ascendancy in the leading academies and gradually filtered down to the ranks of ordinary priests.[74] Fear and instinct for self-preservation no doubt played a role too: priests, especially those in isolated rural parishes, when surrounded by irate peasants, had particularly compelling reason to support their flocks.

While such liberal and radical sentiments had percolated, and occasionally erupted in the second half of the nineteenth century, they appeared in full public view only during the 1905 Revolution. To be sure, the revolution had its own powerful inertia, as many parish clergy were drawn – even against their will – into the revolutionary maelstrom of 1905. Given their material dependence on the parishioners (who provided the gratuities and land allotments that formed their main support), priests could ill afford to ignore the demands of their flock, particularly in the face of the utter breakdown of law and order all around them.[75] It took little to become "involved"; it sufficed only to perform memorial services for "those slain in the struggle" for political and social justice.[76] But it was more than fear that ignited clerical activism. Most important, no doubt, was the fact that the revolution encouraged parish clergy – like other social categories – to articulate and defend their own interests, often against their bishops, but invariably on the grounds that only radical reform could protect and renew the faith.[77] As a result, the clergy acted collectively to press their demands against bishops, to demand a radical improvement in their material support, and even to make attempts at forming a "union" of priests.[78] No less important, many priests had sons in the turbulent seminaries, where the violent demonstrations and strikes inevitably led to mass expulsions and school lock-outs that threatened their sons' very future.[79] And such disorders were as ubiquitous (whereby only four ecclesiastical schools – Minsk, Kholm, Arkhangelsk, and Volhynia – somehow failed to have a seminary disorder) as the reprisals were harsh and unforgiving.[80] Concerned that the seminaries not be closed and that their own sons not be among the expelled and blacklisted, even the most obeisant and subservient priests were driven to engage the "seminary question" and challenge the blind repression by panicky officials.[81]

Whatever the motive, parish clergy – primarily the priests, rarely the lower-ranking deacons and sacristans – became openly involved in the social movements of 1905–7. Just how many is difficult to estimate;

certainly the majority in most (but not all) dioceses demurred on active engagement. And a few even actively came to the defense of the existing order, sometimes obtaining official recognition for their attempts to pacify and to ameliorate social tensions.[82] As for the rank-and-file parish clergy, it proved highly difficult for them to organize and address social questions: they not only lacked independent organs of representation, but faced swift retribution by conservative bishops and arrest-happy police. As a result, many priests – probably the majority – preferred to prevaricate and dis- simulate, to bury their heads amidst the exploding social forces that were swirling all around them. As one cleric caustically observed: "Some [priests], like rabbits during a *battue*, hide in their burrows, do not come out, and wait to see whether misfortune will not pass them by."[83] When parish clergy finally did dare to challenge episcopal superiors, it was chiefly to press the demands of their own group. Thus a diocesan assembly of clergy in Nizhnii Novgorod (December 10–15, 1905) flouted the bishop's agenda and set its own; nonetheless, the group concentrated narrowly upon issues of concern only to their own estate.[84] An assembly of 40 priests in Saratov in 1906 met to discuss the social question, affirmed the need to fuse priest and parish into a "church community," but the major- ity declined to take a clear position, arguing that this responsibility rested with a Church council.[85]

Nevertheless, a distinct – and highly visible – minority became active in virtually every diocese and sometimes even succeeded in mobilizing the support of the entire rank-and-file clergy. This affected not only the dio- ceses of Moscow and St Petersburg (where urban radicalism and the influence of well-educated liberal clergy were predictable and paramount factors), but also several other central dioceses, such as Viatka, Smolensk, Kazan, and Vladimir. This activism of the parish clergy took three princi- pal forms: (1) public engagement in a radical clerical press; (2) collective discussions and resolutions at diocesan assemblies; and (3) individual par- ticipation of priests in social and political movements.

The church press, which had earlier been stultified and severely con- strained by ecclesiastical censorship, now acquired greater freedom and new organs as it directly engaged social questions[86] and openly summoned clergy to do the same through sermons, the press, and practical activity.[87] Particularly influential were the programmatic statements of the clerical "renovationists" (*obnovlentsy*), who sought to "renovate" – i.e., revitalize – the Church through this-worldly engagement.[88] They argued that such engagement was integral to the Church's spiritual mission: so long as the laity is oppressed by a despotic regime and social injustice, the Church "cannot instill in the people Christian feelings of fraternity and love, but, on the contrary, has as its consequence the enmity of some classes against others, of people set against one another."[89] The same kind of this-worldly theology informed the thinking of *Khristianin* (The Christian), a journal published by the Vifanskaia Seminary in Moscow, which espoused the need for a "Christian civic society" (*khristianskaia obshchestvennost'*) and proclaimed that "it is necessary to realize the universal truth here on earth, insofar as that is possible for man."[90] But perhaps the most celebrated clerical publicist was Father Grigorii S. Petrov, a St Petersburg priest whose numerous publications and lectures emphasized the fundamental duty of clergymen to become involved in social questions.[91] Above all, he propounded the need to remodel secular institutions and life after Christian precepts so that the entire world be regarded "as a sphere subject for transformation into Divine Kingdom by Christians."[92] In January 1906 Petrov opened a radical paper, *Pravda bozhiia* (God's Truth), its express goal being "to publicize the needs of the peasantry, factory workers, and all who perform heavy or dirty work."[93] He did not mince words on the import of his social gospel: "The upper classes rule over the lower ones. As a small handful they hold in bondage the entire remainder of the population, tens and hundreds of millions of the toiling; they have taken away everything from the lower classes – wealth, power, science, art, even religion."[94]

A second form of clerical engagement was collective statements, chiefly through local or diocesan assemblies. In addition to selective voluntary associations (such as the left-liberal group, "Union of Zealots of Church Renovation"),[95] official diocesan assemblies (*eparkhial'nye s'ezdy*) of parish clergy went beyond their usual agenda (finances and conditions in diocesan schools) to address the burning social issues of the day.[96] According to a police report of June 15, 1906, the diocesan assembly in Voronezh opened its doors to "women and correspondents," permitted rebellious seminarians to appear and denounce their teachers, discussed the question of giving land to the peasantry, and voted to dispatch the following telegram to the State Duma: "Instead of darkness and oppression, give us light and freedom . . . Long live the people's freedom, and may the Holy Church of Christ be strengthened and flourish!"[97] In September 1906, the diocesan assembly in another black-soil diocese, Tambov, warned of a dangerous gulf between the people and the Church and adopted the following resolution: "Recognizing the difficult condition of the peasantry and workers, we find the people's striving for a better future to be just and we sympathize with the liberation movement proceeding on the basis of the imperial manifesto of October 17, 1905, insofar as it goes by peaceful means and in accordance with Christian principles."[98]

Although most other diocesan assemblies were less radical (and indeed concentrated on their own plight or the crisis in the local seminary), they demonstrated clearly that liberal, even radical, sentiments were hardly confined to a few clerical "reds" in St Petersburg, but rather had substantial resonance among provincial clergy as well. Underlying such activism was a belief that the priest must not merely perform rites and rituals, but must confront community needs and such evils as drunkenness, ignorance, and injustice. As a diocesan meeting in Vladimir in late 1905 agreed, "the pastor of course must above all be a spiritual doctor, but he can exercise the appropriate spiritual authority only if parishioners are convinced that he is close and involved in their needs, which are determined by the demands of everyday, worldly life."[99] This meant, in particular, support for the liberation movement and even peasant interests: "The clergy should not remain apart, but should sympathize with the liberation movement in the spirit of the manifesto of October 17, without adhering to any political party, endorsing what is good and condemning what is bad, from a Christian point of view. From a practical point of view, the clergy should be sympathetic toward the moderate peasant party, endorsing its program, except for certain extreme points."[100] In Kherson, a meeting of clerical superintendents rejected membership in the Union of Russian People, declaring that its conservative land program was "contradictory to the cause of peace and love."[101]

The third form of clerical engagement was personal, individual involvement in the workers' and peasants' movements in the 1905 Revolution.[102] Press accounts, as well as official reports by bishops and the police, indicate that the level of involvement varied considerably, from hot spots like the two capitals and a few central dioceses (such as Smolensk, Viatka, and Kazan), to other areas where the priests apparently stood apart from the social unrest.[103] It is well nigh impossible to make an exact count on the number of clergy either accused or convicted of "revolutionary agitation": some accusations proved false or unproven,[104] while many other instances failed to come to the attention of central authorities (having been quietly handled by local church or state authorities). Indeed, the number of priests arrested for "agitation" may well reflect more the anxieties and capabilities of local authorities than it does the actual role of the parish clergy.

Nonetheless, the large corpus of archival materials – especially the voluminous police reports to Church authorities – do permit some generalization about clerical involvement in the "revolutionary" (not merely "liberation") movement of 1905–7. First, the number of card-carrying revolutionary priests was small indeed; although some did dare to join the left-liberal Kadet Party, few – predictably – joined or affiliated themselves with the Social-Democratic or Social Revolutionary parties.[105] Second, clerical engagement in the working-class movement was relatively weak, with Gapon being the great exception rather than the general rule.[106] The massive size of working-class parishes, the higher level of religious disaffection or indifference, the possibilities for tighter supervision by local authorities[107] – all this doubtless impeded clerical involvement. Third, the incidence of clerical involvement ran much higher in rural parishes, perhaps because of the weakness of state and diocesan authorities, as well as the closer ties and greater dependence on peasant parishioners. Although some priests were alleged to have instigated or supported disorders,[108] in most cases their offense had been to engage in some form of "agitation" – i.e. sermons and speeches that helped to radicalize and legitimize peasant expectations. For example, police in Penza reported that Father Aleksei Sokolov advised the peasants to stop renting gentry land (since they would soon receive it all gratis) and allegedly declared that "the land should be held in common. If the land is apportioned to peasants, this will be good; if not, there will be a general strike and a bloodbath."[109] Finally, clerical radicalism was most intense where it fused with nationalism, above all, in Georgia, where priestly radicals in 1905–7 (and indeed long thereafter) combined their social radicalism with a nationalistic demand for the reestablishment of an autocephalous Georgian Church.[110] Although radical priests were a minority in most dioceses, they had a significant impact because such behavior so contradicted expectations and seemed incontrovertible proof that even the last bastion of autocracy was defecting. The liberal church press and, especially, the radical speeches by clerical deputies to the first two State Dumas,[111] evoked a powerful resonance among the public and acute anxiety in police and episcopal quarters.

In the interrevolutionary years of 1907–17, such activism receded from public view. In large measure, no doubt, it was due to systematic repression – the purging and defrocking of radicals as well as the rampant intimidation of the rank-and-file clergy, not only from official quarters,[112] but from the Black Hundredist Union of Russian People.[113] In addition, many clergy probably shared the shock of the intelligentsia over the fearsome violence of 1905; the *Vekhi* syndrome had its equivalent in clerical quarters too. It was, further, compounded by growing anxiety about their flocks, not only those who became unbelievers, but those who claimed greater authority over the parish, especially its finances and its right to select clergy. In the wake of such concerns, and like their counterparts in educated society, the clergy turned from revolution to renewal, concentrating on "small-deeds" liberalism in the form of temperance, poor relief, and an assault upon other worldly problems. At the same time, few turned to the right; save the Western provinces (where clerical attitudes, fueled by ethnic and confessional competition, stood markedly on the right), most parish clergy remained cautious moderates, concerned more about their own needs and the Church's plight, hardly inclined to identify with a monarchy so tarnished by scandal and sectarianism. All this only buttressed the abiding distrust in official, conservative quarters about the true sentiments of rank-and-file parish clergy. Thus, in 1912, despite the trauma of 1905 and the repression that ensued, the Ministry of the Interior complained that the clergy in Voronezh diocese, "because of their extreme degradation and material dependence on the peasant population, are more inclined to vote for the left candidates than for the right."[114] Indeed, many shared the growing disenchantment of their bishops; by 1915 even the conservative clerical deputies in the Duma issued a public statement castigating the dismal status of Orthodox religious life and the failure to address, let alone resolve the central problems now confronting the clergy and Church.[115] As the monarchy fell in 1917, diocesan clergy – often in joint sessions with laity – hastened to welcome the revolution and the Provisional Government,[116] purge their dioceses of "Black Hundredist" bishops,[117] and express support for radical religious and social reform.

Conclusion

The foregoing analysis suggests several broader conclusions. First, it is highly misleading to assign the Church a purely conservative or reactionary role in late imperial Russia. On the contrary, much of the clergy, the hierarchs as well as parish clergy, became increasingly disenchanted and alienated, believing that the government was unable or even unwilling to protect its vested interests. In the wake of *Rasputinshchina*, concessions to other confessions, and other controversies, neither bishops nor priests came to the defense of the monarchy and "counterrevolution." Second, the profound differences within the clergy – between bishops and parish clergy, between the Russian heartland and minority borderlands – made it impossible to fashion a cohesive "clerical party," one capable of articulating and pressing ecclesiastical interests. Third, given this negative consensus (and lack of a common corporate program), the most effective strategy for the Church proved to be a "negative politics" – one devoted to obstructing reform, whether in the bureaucratic ministries or in the State Duma. Contrariwise, the state pursued much the same strategy, declining to convoke a church council and thus putting Church reform on indefinite hold. The deteriorating relations between regime and religion, the capacity of both to torpedo reform – all this reinforces the "pessimistic" view about the long-term prospects of the ancien regime, even before the catastrophe of war struck a final death blow to the old order.

Notes

1   Typical titles include A. K. Drezen, *Tsarizm v bor'be s revoliutsiei 1905–7 gg.* (Moscow: Gosudarstvennoe sotsial'no-ekonomicheskoe izdatel'stvo, 1936), and V. P. Kandidov, *Tserkov' v. 1905 g.* (Moscow: Moskovskii rabochii, 1930).

2   See, for example, Iu. A. Grintsevich, "Religiia na sluzhbe u reaktsii v pervoi russkoi revoliutsii," *Nauchnye zapiski Odesskogo kreditno-ekonomicheskogo instituta*, 3 (1956): 129–47, and E. F. Grekulov, *Tserkov', samoderzhavie i narod* (Moscow: Nauka, 1969); V. P. Andrievskii, "Iz istorii antinarodnoi deiatel'nosti tserkvi na Volyni" (Kand. diss., Lvov, 1968); P. N. Zyrianov, *Pravoslavnaia tserkov' v bor'be s revoliutsiei, 1905–1907 gg.* (Moscow: Nauka, 1984); N. V. Pavliuchenko, "Antinarodnaia rol' pravoslavnoi tserkvi v Belorussii v period pervoi russkoi revoliutsii, 1905–1907 gg." (Kand. diss., Grodno, 1979).

3   For a particularly clear, if unscholarly, statement (based on Max Weber, without any recourse to the primary sources), see A. Buss, *Die Wirtschaftsethik der russisch-orthodoxen Christentums* (Heidelberg: Carl Winter Univeristaetsverlag, 1989), which has been explicitly and uncritically incorporated in a defense of the traditional view of the Church by J. P. LeDonne, *Absolutism and the Ruling Class* (New York: Oxford University Press, 1991), *passim*.

4   Richard Pipes, *The Russian Revolution* (New York: Alfred A. Knopf, 1990), 61, 88. For similar comments, see also his *Russia under the Old Régime* (New York: Scribner, 1974), 221–45.

5   See O. Figes, *A People's Tragedy: The Russian Revolution, 1891–1924* (New York: Viking, 1996); A. Ascher, *The Revolution of 1905*, 2 vols (Stanford: Stanford University Press, 1988–92), 2: 329–36.

6   See, for example, Iu. F. Kozlov, *Soiuz korony i kresta* (Saransk: Mordovskoe knizhnoe izdatel'stvo, 1995), 222–8.

7   An early study, based exclusively on the abundant but neglected printed sources, was J. H. M. Geekie's dissertation, "The Church and Politics in Russia 1905–1917" (PhD diss., University of New Anglia, 1976). Since then, a number of archivally based studies have substantially revised the conventional picture of the Church and clergy in late imperial Russia. See, for example, G. L. Freeze, *The Parish Clergy in Nineteenth-Century Russia* (Princeton: Princeton University Press, 1983), pt 3; idem, "Handmaiden of the State? The Orthodox Church in Imperial Russia Reconsidered," *Journal of Ecclesiastical History*, 36 (1985): 82–102; J. Cunningham, *A Vanquished Hope: The Movement for Church Renewal in Russia, 1905–6* (Tuckahoe, New York: St Vladimir's Seminary Press, 1981); S. M. Dixon, "Church, State and Society in Late Imperial Russia. The Diocese of St. Petersburg, 1880–1914" (PhD diss., University of London, 1993); G. L. Freeze, "Subversive Piety: Religion and the Political Crisis in Late Imperial Russia," *Journal of Modern History*, 68 (1996): 308–50. Some of the most recent work has attempted to engage not only church, but religious history. See, for example, V. Shevzov, "Popular Orthodoxy in Late Imperial Russia" (PhD diss., Yale University, 1994); C. J. Chulos, "Peasant Religion in Post-Emancipation Russia" (PhD diss., University of Chicago, 1994); and N. Kizenko, "Making of a Modern Saint: Ioann of Kronstadt and the Russian People" (PhD diss., Columbia University, 1995); K. P. Herrlinger, "Class, Piety, and Politics: Workers, Christianity, and the Problem of Religious Identity in Russia, 1881–1914" (PhD diss., Berkeley, 1996).

8   To be sure, there were some useful early studies of prerevolutionary "clerical liberalism" – most notably, V. M. Andreev's "Liberal'no-obnovlencheskoe dvizhenie v russkom pravoslavii nachala XX v. i ego ideologii" (Kand. diss., Leningrad, 1971). In recent years, however, the reassessment has gradually pervaded a number of substantial studies: E. D. Zamakhova, "Deputaty ot pravoslavnogo dukhovenstva v Tretei Gosudarstvennoi Dume" (Kand. diss., Moscow, 1994); A. Iu. Polunov, "Vedomstvo pravoslavnogo ispovedaniia pod vlast'iu K. P. Pobedonostseva, 1881–1894 gg." (Kand. diss., Moscow, 1992); Iu. V. Simonov, "Analiz osobennostei sotsial'no-ideologicheskoi deiatel'-nosti Russkoi Pravoslavnoi Tserkvi v nachale XX v." (Kand. diss., Nizhnii Novgorod, 1993); N. K. Pashkina, "Rol' tserkovnno-prikhodskoi shkoly v utverzhdenii pravoslavnoi ideologii v Rossii (konets XIX–nachalo XX v.)" (Kand. diss., St Petersburg, 1991); E. V. Fominykh, "Proekty tserkovnykh preobrazovanii v nachale XX v." (Kand. diss., Leningrad, 1987); E. V. Denisova, "Differentsiatsii sotsial'noi pozitsii dukhovenstva v gody pervoi russkoi revoliutsii kak otrazhenie krizisa ideologii russkogo pravoslaviia" (Kand. diss., Leningrad, 1986); T. G. Leont'eva, "Tserkovnaia intelligentsiia Tverskoi gubernii v kontse XIX–nachalo XX v." (Petrozavodsk, 1902); O. V. Ostanina, "Obnovlenchestvo i reformatortstvo v russkoi pravoslavnoi tserkvi v nachale XX v." (Kand. diss., Leningrad, 1991).

9   For comparative perspectives, see H. Johnston and J. Figa, "The Church and Political Opposition: Comparative Perspectives on Mobilization against Authoritarian Regimes," *Journal for the Scientific Study of Religion*, 27 (1988): 32–47.

10 A. V. Kartashev, "Revoliutsiia i sobor 1917–1918 gg.," *Bogoslovskaia mysl'*, 4 (1942): 75–101.

11 N. D. Zhevakhov, *Vospominaniia tovarishcha ober-prokurora Sv. Sinoda*, 2 vols (Munich: Tipografiia R. Oldenburg, 1923), 1: 114.

12 Ia. Plamper, "Pravoslavnyi episkopat. Rossiia, 1721–1917: prosopografiia," forthcoming in *Litsa: biograficheskii al'manakh*; C. Patock, "Die russisch-orthodoxen Bischöfe der letzten 100 Jahre," in K.-C. Felmy et al., eds, *Tausend Jahre Christentum in Rußland* (Göttingen: Vandenhoeck & Ruprecht, 1988), 435–44.

13 See, for example, the text conveniently produced in Figes, 63.

14 See, for example, the description of liturgies held on Nicholas's birthday in 1903 in "Den' 6-go maia," *Novoe vremia*, no. 9758, May 7, 1903.

15 Rossiiskii gosudarstvennyi istoricheskii arkhiv (RGIA), f. 796, op. 183, g. 1902, d. 634, ll. 4–6 ob.

16 See Freeze, *Parish Clergy*, pt 3.

17 For a convenient account of the battle between the Synod and secular bureaucracy, see W. G. Wagner, *Marriage, Property, and Law in Late Imperial Russia* (Oxford: Clarendon Press, 1994), pt 1.

18 Ever since the 1860s, but especially after the turn of the century, state officials circulated proposals to reduce the number of religious holidays, chiefly in order to increase economic productivity. For the proposals, and adamant Church opposition, see the files in RGIA, op. 797, op. 72, g. 1902, otd. 2, st. 3, d. 232; op. 96, d. 230, ll. 2–9 ob.; f. 796, op. 185, g. 1904, d.

5997. For proposals to replace the Julian with the Gregorian calendar, see RGIA, f. 797, op. 69, otd. 1, st. 1, d. 41; op. 80, otd. 2, st. 3, d. 184.

19 "Vysochaishii manifest," *Tserkovnye vedomosti*, 9 (1903): 55–7.

20 In 1901, in response to complaints of crimes and misdemeanors in monasteries, Nicholas ordered a fullscale inquiry. See RGIA, f. 196, op. 182, g. 1901, d. 535, ll. 1–515.

21 RGIA, f. 797, op. 73, otd. 2, st. 3, d. 98.

22 For details, see Freeze, "Subversive Piety," 312–29.

23 RGIA, f. 796, op. 186, g. 1905, d. 576, l. 2 ob. See also *Vozzvanie Sv. Pr. Sinoda k russkomu narodu* (St Petersburg: Sinodal'naia tipografiia 1905).

24 For Antonii's reaction to Bloody Sunday, see his speech of January 23, 1905, reprinted as "Rech' k rabochim Putilovskogo zavoda," *Rechi, slova i poucheniia* (St Petersburg: Sinodal'naia tipografiia, 1912), 89–91. On the defrocking of Gapon himself, see ibid., d. 5618. The future patriarch, Tikhon (Beliavskii), was clearly aghast at the upheaval and, especially, Gapon's role: "God knows what is going on in Russia, especially according to foreign reports. It is becoming worse by the hour . . . There has even appeared some insane priest Gapon." RGIA, f. 796, op. 205, d. 752, l. 42.

25 RGIA, f. 797, op. 5, otd. 3, st. 5, d. 31, l. 3.

26 RGIA, f. 797, op. 75, otd. 3, st. 5, d. 31, ll. 22–3.

27 RGIA, f. 797, op. 75, otd. 3, st. 5, d. 31, ll. 474–5.

28 RGIA, f. 796, op. 186, g. 1905, d. 894, l. 4.

29 Liberal bishops were rare indeed. For the case of a suffragan bishop, Isidor in Nizhnii Novgorod, who had denounced *Moskovskie vedomosti* and collaborated with the more liberal *Russkie vedomosti*, see the complaint by police authorities and the reprimand by the Synod in RGIA, f. 796, op. 186, g. 1905, d. 686, ll. 3–4. The Ministry of the Interior also complained that the bishop of Perm', Nikanor, was showing undue leniency toward radical clergy; see Gosudarstvennyi arkhiv Rossiiskoi Federatsii (GA RF), f. 102, g. 1905, op. 5, d. 2270, l. 34.

30 GARF, f. 102, op. 5, g. 1905, d. 2270, ll. 37–8.

31 RGIA, f. 796, op. 186, g. 1905, d. 3085; V. Rozhkov, *Tserkovnye voprosy v Gosudarstvennoi Dume* (Rome: Opere Religiose Russe, 1975), 8–128.

32 RGIA, f. 796, op. 186, g. 1905, d. 657, l. 25; op. 205, d. 248, l. 23; op. 186, d. 657; f. 797, op. 75, otd. 2, st. 3, d. 75; A. R., *Istoricheskaia perepiska o sud'bakh Pravoslavnoi Tserkvi* (Moscow: Tipografiia I. D. Sytina, 1912).

33 Circular letter from Metropolitan Antonii to diocesan bishops, April 4, 1905 (RGIA, f. 796, op. 187, g. 1906, d. 6972, ll. 22–3 ob.)

34 Valliere, "The Idea of a Council Russian Orthodoxy in 1905," in: R. Nichols and T. Stavrou, eds, *Russian Orthodoxy under the Old Régime* (Minneapolis: University of Minnesota Press, 1978), 183–201. For contemporary expectations, among the parish clergy as well, see: *Trudy moskovskoi komissii po tserkovnym voprosam* (Moscow: 1906), and N. Ognev, *Na poroge reform russkoi tserkvi i dukhovenstva* (St Petersburg, 1907).

35 RGIA, f. 796, op. 186, g. 1905, d. 657, l. 25.

36 *Otzyvy eparkhial'nykh arkhiereev po voprosu o tserkovnoi reforme* (3 vols; St Petersburg, 1906). For a summary of these valuable materials, see J.

Meyendorff, "Russian Bishops and Church Reform in 1905," in *Russian Orthodoxy under the Old Régime*, 170–82, and P. E. Immekus, *Die Russisch-Orthodoxe Landpfarrei zu Beginn des XX. Jahrhunderts* (Würzburg: Augustinus Verlag, 1978).

37   Clerical deputies to the Third and Fourth State Dumas were distinctly conservative, with only a rare cleric voting on the center or liberal-left. For the political profile, see Rozhkov, 363–4, 391–2. See also F. Jockwig, "Kirche und Staatsduma," *Wegzeichen* (Würzburg: Augustinus Verlag, 1971), 437–50.

38   RGIA, f. 797, op. 82, otd. 1, st. 1, d. 241, l. 310. The Synod had made a similar recommendation for elections to the Duma in 1906; see ibid., op. 71, otd. 1, st. 1, d. 115, ll. 116–17. See also Gavriil, *Golos arkhipastyria k vyboram v IV. Gos. Dumu* (St Petersburg, 1912).

39   Vladimir, *Nasha pastyrskaia zadacha v bor'be s sotsial-demokraticheskoi propagandoiu* (Moscow, 1909); see also Aleksei (Dobronitsyn), *Khristianstvo i kommunizm* (Kazan, 1909).

40   See the discussion and references in P. Waldron, "Religious Reform after 1905: Old Believers and the Orthodox Church," *Oxford Slavonic Papers*, 20 (1987): 110–39, and idem, "Religious Tolerance in Late Imperial Russia," in: E. Edmondson and O. Crisp, eds, *Civil Rights in Imperial Russia* (Oxford: Clarendon Press, 1989), 103–20.

41   RGIA, f. 1412, op. 241, dd. 15, 22.

42   Rozhkov, 128–215.

43   At issue was the juridical status of the parish and, especially, the power of the laity to control church finances and the appointment of clergy; hostile to Duma meddling (as an encroachment on ecclesiastical prerogative and violation of canon law), church authorities bitterly fought Duma plans for parish reform. See A. Papkov, "Iavochnyi poriadok dlia osushchestvleniia prikhodskoi reformy," *Novoe vremia*, February 11, 1914 (no. 13621); RGIA, f. 797, op. 75, g. 1905, otd. 2, st. 3, d. 518; op. 84, otd. 2, st. 3, d. 396; f. 796, op. 189, d. 2229/b.

44   See the critical comments by a well-connected layman, A. A. Kireev, in G. Dobrynin, *Tserkovnyi listok*, 13 (June 20, 1912): 1.

45   RGIA, f. 797, op. 83, otd. 1, st. 1, d. 49, ll. 70–2; op. 78, otd. 2, st. 3, d. 122/b, ll. 50–76.

46   See the Synodal resolution of July 14, 1912 (RGIA, f. 796, op. 194, g. 1912, d. 1207, l. 10–10 ob.) and a typical episcopal directive (from the bishop of Kostroma in f. 797, op. 82, otd. 1, st. 1, d. 241, ll. 34–6).

47   For Germogen's conflict, see RGIA, f. 796, op. 187, g. 1906, d. 775, l. 35.

48   See the Synod resolution of March 19, 1908 in RGIA, f. 796, op. 191, ch. 2, otd. 6, st. 3, d. 112.

49   For typical cases of URP rejection, see the file on Ekaterinoslav in 1911 (RGIA, f. 796, op. 193, g. 1911, d. 1770), Vladimir in 1909 (op. 190, otd. 6, st. 3, d. 88), Kiev in 1914 (op. 195, d. 1633). In 1909, when a URP supporter such as Archbishop Antonii (Khrapovitskii) sought to have the Synod reverse this policy, it stood firm (ibid., f. 190, otd. 6, st. 3, d. 258, ll. 2–3).

50   On the issue of military officers, see RGIA, f. 796, op. 190, d. 146/b; op. 195, otd. 6, st. 3, d. 1552; on the question of religious meetings, see f. 796, op. 191, otd. 6, st. 3, d. 2.

51 RGIA, f. 797, op. 83, otd. 2, st. 3, d. 224. For complaints about the press
    and stage performances, see f. 797, op. 78, otd. 2, st. 3, d. 358; op. 81, otd.
    2, st. 3, d. 107; op. 84, otd. 2, st. 3, d. 373. Contrariwise, the *government*
    complained about excesses in the ecclesiastical press, especially the anti-
    Semitic themes (f. 797, op. 83, otd. 2, st. 3, d. 361, 266; op. 79. op. 2, st. 3,
    d. 408).

52 RGIA, f. 1101, op. 1, d. 1111, l. 1.

53 For Rasputin's denunciation of bishops as "bureaucrats," see "U Grigoriia
    Rasputina," Nikolaevsky Collection, Hoover Archive, folder no. 129.2.

54 GARF, f. 612, op. 1. d. 13; RGIA, f. 797, op. 82, otd. 2, st. 3, d. 77.

55 Freeze, "Subversive Piety," 342–8.

56 "Rasputin i ierarkhi tserkvi," *Peterburgskii kur'er*, July 6, 1914. See also
    "Pravda o Grigorii Novom (Rasputin)," Nikolaevsky Collection, Hoover
    Archieve, folder no. 129.2.

57 O. A. Platonov, *Zhizn' za tsaria (pravda o Grigorii Rasputine)* (St Petersburg:
    Voskresenie, 1996). See also J. T. Fuhrmann, *Rasputin* (New York: Praeger,
    1990).

58 For data on the defections during 1905–9, see RGIA, f. 797, op. 79, otd. 2,
    st. 3, d. 494, ll. 36–8.

59 See the assessment in 1909 in RGIA, f. 796, op. 186, g. 1905, d. 657, t. 2,
    l. 221.

60 Although the question of de-Christianization is far too complex to treat here,
    suffice it to say that most bishops, while discerning an "improvement" in
    piety after 1907, nevertheless conceded the presence of significant prob-
    lems, especially in the case of the youth, migrant workers, intelligentsia, and
    townspeople. For a typical assessment, see the report from Vladimir diocese
    in 1912 in RGIA, f. 796, op. 442, d. 2507, ll. 46 ob.-49 ob. These reports,
    in a one-sided fashion, were widely used in Soviet historiography; see, for
    example, L. I. Emeliakh, *Istoricheskie predposylki preodoleniia religii v sovetskoi
    derevne sekularizatsii* (Leningrad: Gosudarstvennyi muzei istorii religii i
    ateizma, 1975).

61 "K uvol'neniiu ep. Germogena," *Rech'*, January 15, 1912.

62 "O patriarshestve," *Strannik*, 3 (1919): 467–9.

63 RGIA, f. 797, op. 77, otd. 2, st. 3, d. 33, ll. 4–6 ob.

64 RGIA, f. 796, op. 195, d. 8477, l. 1–1 ob. (MVD to chief procurator,
    December 13, 1911).

65 RGIA, f. 1101, op. 1, d. 1111, ll. 1–10.

66 "V tserkovnykh krugakh pred revoliutsiei," *Krasnyi arkhiv*, 31 (1928):
    204–13.

67 A. Papkov, "Arkhipasytrskii prizyv," *Novoe vremia*, no. 13652 (March 15,
    1914).

68 GARF, f. 102, DP OO, g. 1915, d. 355, l. 27, 92–92 ob. (MVD report to the
    emperor, January 20, 1916).

69 In March 1914, for example, he wrote a review of the most recent annual
    report of the chief procurator on the state of the church, and the subtitle of
    the book – "horrifying book" – aptly describes the tone of his essay. See A.
    Papkov, "Trevozhnoe sostoianie nashei tserkvei (strashanaia kniga),"
    Tserkovno-obshchestvennyi vestnik, no. 10 (March 16, 1914): 5–7.

70 On March 7, 1917, the Synod greeted the new order with this declaration: "The Lord's will has been done. Russia has entered upon the path of a new state life. May the Lord bless our great Motherland with happiness and glory on its new path." RGIA, f. 796, op. 204, otd. 1, st. 5, d. 54, l. 48–48 ob.

71 Such sentiments run deep in Church history; for references, see Freeze, *Parish Clergy*. They quickly emerged in 1917; as a diocesan assembly in Novgorod declared, "in most cases [the parish clergy] did not love their prelates, but only feared them." RGIA, f. 796, op. 189, d. 2229/b, ll. 344–5 ob.

72 For an introductory account, see B. V. Titlinov, *Molodezh' i revoliutsiia* (Leningrad: Gosudarstvennoe izdatel'stvo, 1924). For a typical case, where seminarians denounced their schools for training them to "instill darkness and superstition in the people," see RGIA, f. 796, op. 185, g. 1904, d. 582, l. 53. For incidents that same year, see dd. 247–8 (Kutaisi), 185, 249 (Blagoveshchensk), 557 (Saratov), 543 (Tobolsk), 553 (Kaluga), and 225 (Vladimir).

73 As a priest in Moscow, Ioann Moroshkin, wrote in a 1906 appeal for reinstatement (after being suspended for joining the Kadet Party), "I must confess that I sympathize with much of the Kadets' program, insofar as it has as its goal the welfare of the poor, the amelioration of the fate of the toiling and oppressed." RGIA, f. 796, op. 187, d. 6405, l. 2. Another priest, a prominent radical in the Duma, explained that "from childhood I lived among the poor peasant population and received an education at their expense. The marvelous soul of the simple Russian peasant was an open book for me; in this book I read the entire, endless sadness of the people, all their grief, needs, and lack of rights." RGIA, f. 796, op. 187, d. 6881.

74 G. L. Freeze, "A Social Mission for Russian Orthodoxy," in: M. Shatz and E. Mendelsohn, eds, *Imperial Russia, 1700–1917* (DeKalb, Ill.: Northern Illinois University Press, 1988), 115–35.

75 In 1907, the Ministry of the Interior communicated reports that, in parts of Orel diocese, "all the Churches have been plundered, the clergy subjected to attacks, church wardens murdered, and the clergy [left] starving" (RGIA, f. 797, op. 77, otd. 3, st. 5, d. 116, l. 1–1 ob.) While the report proved a gross exaggeration, it did reflect the fact that parish clergy, especially in rural areas, *were* under strong pressure to support their peasant parishioners' cause.

76 For typical cases involving "revolutionary" memorial services, see the files Moscow, Perm, Tver, and Vologda in RGIA, f. 796, op. 187, g. 1906, d. 6608, l. 19–19 ob.; d. 6573, l. 2–2 ob., and d. 6849, ll. 11–11 ob.; f. 797, op. 76, otd. 3, st. 5, d. 10, ll. 130–1); reports of such services also appeared in the church and secular press (for example, accounts on Vologda and Saratov *Tserkovno-obshchestvennaia zhizn'*, no. 11 (1906): 414, and *Saratovskii dnevnik*, January 10, 1906.

77 Apart from individual statements castigating the episcopate, even some diocesan assemblies dared challenge the bishop's authority. Thus the diocesan assembly of Viatka clergy in 1906 asserted its right to "discuss the bishop's resolutions" on their decisions and even asserted that, if a diocesan

decision did not contradict the law, if it had been endorsed twice over an episcopal veto, it was nevertheless to be implemented immediately (V. Beliaev, A. Viktorov, and M. Mansurov, *Eparkhial'nye s'ezdy. Sbornik deistvuiushchikh zakonopolozhenii ob eparkhial'nykh s'ezdakh* (St Petersburg, 1908), 26.

78   In Kherson diocese, 14 priests assembled to issue an appeal to create a clerical union and to address their difficult material conditions. See RGIA, f. 796, op. 187, d. 6577, ll. 1–46. For an analogous attempt to establish a clerical union in Stavropol, see ibid., d. 6576, ll. 1–3.

79   Although the seminarians focused primarily on their own problems (scholastic curriculum, denial of access to secular literature, oppressive controls and, most important, barriers to transfer to secular schools and universities), they sometimes showed a concern for social issues. Some seminarians, like those in Arkhangel'sk in May 1905, sometimes even became embroiled in public demonstrations (see the case of 27 students expelled for joining a May Day demonstration in RGIA, f. 796, op. 186, d. 405, ll. 1–16). For a recent overview, see J. Morison, "The Church Schools and Seminarians in the Russian Revolution of 1905–6," in G. A. Hosking, ed., *Church, Nation and State in Russia and Ukraine* (Basingstoke: Macmillan, 1991), 193–209.

80   RGIA, f. 802, op. 16, d. 196, l. 5. The relative importance of seminarian disorders is not to be underestimated: according to police records, 69 of 125 disorders in secondary schools occurred in seminaries. A. V. Ushakov, *Revoliutsionnoe dvizhenie demokraticheskoi intelligentsii v Rossii 1895–1904 gg.* (Moscow: Mysl', 1976), 203.

81   For the case of Vladimir diocese, where the clergy actively lobbied on behalf of their seminarian sons, especially their right to transfer to the university, see the resolution in "Sobranie v dome Ego Preosviasshchenstva," *Vladimirskie eparkhial'nye vedomosti*, 20 (1905): 591; Gosudarstvennyi arkhiv Vladimirskoi oblasti (GAVO), f. 556, op. 1, d. 4423, ll. 22–3, 25.

82   Thus a priest in Riga, Petr Grinval'd received a medal of commendation for actively opposing the revolutionary movement (RGIA, f. 796, op. 187, g. 1906, d. 102, ll. 1–2). Similar awards were given to military chaplains (RGIA, f. 796, op. 1897 g. 1906, d. 63–4), priests in Poltava, Khar'kov, Kursk, Vologda and Vitebsk (ibid., d. 75; f. 797, op. 5, otd. 3, st. 4, dd. 152 and 191; f. 796, op. 189, d. 30).

83   Memorandum from Ekaterinburg priest E. Landyshev to Metropolitan Antonii, January 21, 1906, RGIA, f. 796, op. 205, d. 794, ll. 1–4.

84   Specifically, it called for a church council with parish clergy and lay representation (not merely bishops), the election of deans, abolition of church censorship, the establishment of small-scale "episcopates" and parish communes, and replacement of the diocesan consistory by a council of priests ("presviterate") elected from rural and city clergy, with lay participation. It also demanded that monasteries be required "to assist orphans and the general needs of the clergy in the diocese." The ecclesiastical radicalism of the group, which nonetheless ignored secular issues, is revealed by its decision to retain traditional clerical dress, implying that at least a vocal minority opposed the existing requirement on cassocks and beards. See RGIA,

f. 796, op. 187, d. 873, ll. 1–10. Similarly, the discussion at an assembly of clergy in Iakutsk in February 1906, which focused exclusively on ecclesiastical issues – the convocation of a national church council, the voluntary defrocking of ordained clergy, and the election of deans and diocesan officials. RGIA, f. 796, op. 188, g. 1907, d. 697, ll. 2–3 (*zhurnal* February 20, 1906).

85 See "Korrespondentsiia iz Saratova," *Tserkovnyi vestnik*, 41 (October 13, 1905): 1297–9.

86 See, for example, the typical complaint by deputies at the diocesan assembly in Kazan in September 1905 – namely, that their diocesan organ (*Izvestiia po Kazanskoi eparkhii*) was dull, narrow, useless, and irrelevant to contemporary needs. See "Zhurnal zasedanii Kazanskoi eparkhial'nogo s'ezda," *Izvestiia po Kazanskoi eparkhii*, 43 (November 15, 1905): 1274–5.

87 For example, see the demand that the clergy use their sermons to confront social conditions in Myshtsyn, "Iz periodicheskoi pechati," *Bogoslovskii vestnik*, 2 (1905): 641–2.

88 See N. S. Gordienko and P. K. Kurochkin, "Liberal'no-obnovlencheskoe dvizhenie v russkom pravoslavii nachala XX v.," *Voprosy nauchnogo ateizma*, 7 (1969): 313–40; V. M. Andreev, "Liberal'no-obnovlencheskoe dvizhenie v russkom pravoslavii nachala XX v. i ego ideologiia" (Kand. diss., Leningrad, 1971).

89 See "Ob otnoshenii tserkvi i sviashchenstva k sovremennoi obshchestvenno-politicheskoi zhizni," *Tserkovnyi vestnik*, 11 (March 16, 1906): 329.

90 "Nashi zadachi," *Khristianin*, 1 (1907): 14. Similarly, a clerical paper in Kiev, *Narod*, urged the clergy to develop "Christian public opinion," to bring Christianity into all spheres of life, and "to expose the injustice of capitalist exploitation and contemporary land relations." See "Mneniia i otzyvy," *Tserkovnyi vestnik*, 16 (April 20, 1906): 502–3.

91 See, for example, a typical work such as *Tserkov' i obshchestvo* (St Petersburg, 1906).

92 The quotation comes from the charter of the "Fraternity of Zealots for Church Renovation," which was compiled under Petrov's leadership and signed by 47 other priests. The charter received a provisional three-year approval, as an "experiment," by the Holy Synod May 24, 1906. See RGIA, f. 804, op. 4, d. 565, l. 1–2 ob.

93 *Pravda bozhiia*, 1 (1906): 2.

94 *Pis'mo sviashchennika Gr. Petrova Mitropolitu Antoniiu* (St Petersburg, 1908), 3, 5. From all accounts, Petrov enjoyed considerable popularity among the provincial clergy. See N. P., "Sredi dukhovenstva," *Vladimirskie eparkhial'nye vedomstva*, 1 (1905): 17; A. Bobrov, "Po povodu korrespondentsii, 'Sredi dukhovenstva,'" ibid., 4 (1905): 106–12. As might be expected, he came under severe attack from conservative quarters (including the Union of Russian People) and was eventually defrocked and expelled from the clergy. For the role of the Union of Russian People and the metropolitan of Moscow in Petrov's case (especially because of his periodical and because of alleged agitation among the middle social strata and clergy), see RGIA, f. 796, op. 187, g. 1906, d. 6668, ll. 1–55; f. 797, op. 77, otd. 3, st. 5, d. 59;

Tsentral'nyi gosudarstvennyi istoricheskii arkhiv v S. -Peterburge (TsGIA g. Spb.) f. 19, op. 98, g. 1906, d. 21, ll. 1–13. Even after his defrocking, Petrov remained a focus of conservative attention. See, for example, the complaint by Bishop Germogen of Saratov about lectures that G. Petrov had given locally, in RGIA, f. 797, op. 81, otd. 2, st. 3, d. 500, ll. 1–7.

95 Committed to social justice, the Union observed that "our Russian Church and its official actors had to adhere to the principle of non-intervention in worldly affairs, i.e. state and social," which had served to alienate leaders of the liberation movement and had left the Church silent on basic issues of social justice for workers and peasants. See Soiuz revnitelei tserkovnogo obnovleniia, *Ob otnoshenii tserkvi i sviashchestva k sovremennoi obshch-estvenno-politicheskoi zhizni* (St Petersburg, 1906). More radical still was the group of 45 delegates who convened in Moscow in July 1906 to form a "Russian Christian-Socialist Party," with the express aim of seeking to promote "the organization of the toiling masses in a wide cultural struggle for the realization of Christian socialism on earth . . . [and] to support every peaceful opposition movement which aims to transform the existing economic and political struggle" *Tserkovno-obshchestvennaia zhizn'*, 31 (July 21, 1906): 1054. For the radical "Christian Fraternity," see V. Svenitskii, *Khristianskoe bratstvo i ego programma* (St Petersburg, 1905) and TsGIA Spb. f. 19, op. 97, g. 1905, d. 53, ll. 1–2.

96 Established by the seminary reform of 1867 for the purpose of finding the means to finance and improve the local ecclesiastical schools, the assemblies were under the strict control of the bishops, who set the agenda and modified resolutions at will. Nonetheless, a number of diocesan assemblies expanded their competence to address not only broader issues of church reform but also the burning issues in the secular domain. For the vigorous challenge by clergy in Viatka, with threats of a priestly strike, see RGIA, f. 796, op. 187, d. 6677, ll. 1–28. Similarly, the clerical assembly in Nizhnii Novgorod, which convened from December 10 to 15, 1905, boldly discarded the bishop's agenda and addressed issues of greatest concern to the parish clergy – radical church reform. See RGIA, f. 796, op. 187, d. 873, ll. 1–10.

97 Gendarme report of June 21, 1906 in GARF, f. 102, DP OO, op. 236 (2), d. 750, ll. 1–2.

98 The bishop rejected the assembly's resolution and denounced its advocates as supporters of "the Constitutional-Democratic party, which is directed against the government." RGIA, f. 797, op. 76, otd. 3, st. 5, d. 10, l. 734–34 ob. (report to the chief procurator, February 17, 1907), ll. 734–43 ob. (consistory resolution, December 21, 1906). See also "Po eparkhiiam," *Tserkovno-obshchestvennaia zhizn'*, 43 (December 13, 1906): 1441. For other collective statements, see the declarations by the clergy in Yalta (f. 796, op. 187, d. 6571), Smolensk (op. 186, d. 6576), and Ekaterinoslav (op. 186, d. 657, ll. 303–14).

99 "Sobranie v dome Ego Sviashchenstva," *Vladimirskie eparkhial'nye vedomosti*, 20 (1905): 622.

100 GAVO, f. 556, op. 1, d. 4423, l. 7. (November 29, 1905).

101   RGIA, f. 797, op. 77, otd. 3, st. 5, d. 3, ll. 53–4.
102   The substantial number of archival files, which have hitherto been ignored
      by historians, are disucussed in fuller detail in G. L. Freeze, "The Parish
      Clergy in the Revolution of 1905" (paper presented to a conference on
      Imperial Russia and the German Empire, University of Tübingen, December
      1993).
103   For example, one report in June 1906 listed some 400 radical clerics, who
      were particularly concentrated in a few dioceses (Nizhnii Novgorod, Kazan,
      and Smolensk), whereas dioceses like Chernigov apparently had none. See
      Tserkovno-obshchestvennaia zhizn', 26 (June 16, 1906): 875 and 29 (July 7,
      1906): 987. The files from some dioceses, however, indicate few incidents of
      clerical radicalism sufficiently flamboyant to attract the attention of author-
      ities. Typical is the report from the secretary of the diocesan consistory in
      Samara (February 13, 1906), identifying seven priests, one deacon, and
      three sacristans (RGIA, f. 796, op. 187, d. 6670, l. 2–2 ob.).
104   False denunciations and arrests were by no means uncommon, the product
      of personal enmity, popular misreading of clerical sermons, and the hyste-
      ria of local police. See the cases from Smolensk diocese, where the govern-
      ment had unjustly arrested clergy, provoked sharp censure from the Synod
      (March 10, 1906) on the pernicious effect of such actions (RGIA, f. 797, op.
      76, otd. 1, st. 2, d. 51, l. 4–4 ob.) Jittery landlords were sometimes respon-
      sible for the false denunciations. In one case involving a priest in Poltava
      diocese, the bishop defended the cleric against a complaint by a local squire;
      as it turned out, the priest had tried to pacify, not incite, his parishioners
      (RGIA, f. 796, op. 187, d. 6711, ll. 1–8). A similar case was reported by the
      bishop of Kostroma: contrary to claims that the priest, Ia. Vigilianskii, urged
      peasants to pay no taxes, send no recruits, and engage in plunder, he had in
      fact preached just the opposite – viz., that the faithful should remain non-
      violent (op. 187, d. 6532, ll. 3–5). For other cases, see the files on two priests
      in Volhynia (op. 187, g. 1906, d. 6725, ll. 1–14); a priest in Pskov (op. 188,
      g. 1907, d. 7021); a priest in Nizhnii Novgorod (op. 187, d. 6837); a priest
      in Perm (ibid., d. 6571); a sacristan and priest in Kazan (op. 187, d. 6292);
      a sacristan in Minsk (ibid, d. 6581); a priest in Podolia (op. 188, d. 7145);
      a priest in Novgorod (op. 187, d. 6885); and priests in Nizhnii Novgorod (op.
      187, dd. 6883 and 6837).
105   Such cases were indeed rare and of marginal significance – for example, the
      accusations that a radical sacristan in Tver, D. Nikol'skii, had disseminated
      revolutionary literature (RGIA, f. 796, op. 188, d. 7152, ll. 1–3). A radical
      deacon, Vasilii Vostorgov, evidently acting under the influence of his two
      sons, belonged to the revolutionary underground and concealed a secret
      typography that printed materials for both the Social Democrats and the
      Social Revolutionaries (RGIA, f. 796, op. 188, g. 1907, d. 7096). A priest in
      Iaroslvl, Aleksandr Kremlevskii, was alleged to have agitated against the
      Union of Russian People and on behalf of the liberal and left parties, includ-
      ing the Social Democrats, who seemed more inclined to help the poor (RGIA,
      f. 797, op. 76, otd. 2, st. 3, d. 109, ll. 21–8).
106   Nevertheless, radical priests acting on behalf of the workers do sometimes
      figure in the official records. One was Father Evgenii Leskov, who served in

a factory parish in Okhanskii uezd and whom the police described as "a person of secular and liberal tendency" and disposed to defend the workers and their need to strike. GARF, f. 102 (DP OO), op. 5, g. 1905, d. 2270, ll. 304 (local bailiff to the governor, March 5, 1905). It was alleged that, "at every convenient opportunity," Leskov criticized the government, supported the workers' demand for an eight-hour working day, and castigated factory-owners (who "live at the expense of the workers and drink their blood, while the workers starve"). RGIA, f. 797, op. 75, g. 1905, otd. 3, st. 5, d. 28, l. 61 (report by the bishop, dated 9.4.1907). Even larger groups, such as a clerical assembly in St Petersburg, concurred that "factory-owners are required by law to do too little for their workers." RGIA, f. 796, op. 442, d. 2105, l. 58 (annual report for St Petersburg in 1905). A commission of St Petersburg clergy admitted inattention to the worker cause, emphasized the need to preach not only in the parish church but also in the factory, but summoned clergy not only to appear with "the Word alone," but also to provide real material assistance (by using church funds for charitable purposes). See the report from suffragan Bishop Kirill to Metropolitan Antonii (October 1905) in TsGIA Spb, f. 19, op. 97, g. 1905, d. 7, ll. 47–8, 51 ob.–52.

107   See, for instance, the annual report for St Petersburg diocese in 1905 by Metropolitan Antonii, who instructed subordinate clergy to exercise greater caution in dealing with workers. See RGIA, f. 796, op. 442, d. 2105, ll. 54–57 ob.

108   For example, the bishop of Tauride, Aleksei, dispatched a telegram (December 19, 1905) to the Synod reporting that some clergy in his diocese had been participating in "agrarian disorders" and revolutionary movement (RGIA, f. 796, op. 187, d. 6608, l. 2). According to a gendarme report of December 28, 1905, a priest in Tula diocese, Nikolai N. Borisoglebskii, actively propagandized radical ideas among peasants, criticized the government for the Russo-Japanese War, and incited peasants to "seize gentry land, to cut wood from their forests, to confiscate the grain, hay and livestock, and entire property of the squires, and to expel the latter from their estates." He also urged them to paralyze the state by refusing to pay taxes or to send military recruits; see GARF, f. 102, (DP OO), op. 5, g. 1905, d. 2270, l. 18–18 ob.). A priest in Vladimir diocese, Aleksei Rozhdestvenskii, was also arrested for participating in disorders (RGIA, f. 796, op. 187, g. 1906, d. 6592). Another priest in the same diocese, Aleksandr Arkhangel'skii, elicited complaints from local authorities, who accused him of seeking to dissuade military units from taking action against disorderly peasants. See the complaints, filed on August 11, 1906 from a police officer, in GAVO, f. 556, op. 1, d. 4595, ll. 1–3 ob. A deacon in Poltava diocese, Konstantin Shust, was alleged to have encouraged peasants to attack the estates of gentry land and was eventually sentenced to exile in Tobol'sk province for 3 years (RGIA, f. 796, op. 187, d. 6622, ll. 2, 4). Similarly, a priest in Orel diocese, Vasilii Vvedenskii, was purportedly inciting his parishioners against the gentry, although some of the laity (even a few landowners) denied the allegations. See the report from Bishop Serafim to the chief procurator, March 27, 1906, in RGIA, f. 797, op. 75, otd. 3, st. 5, d. 28, l. 119.

109 In August 1907 the police arrested Sokolov as the ringleader of "a criminal band" that was seeking to turn the population against government and that was responsible for thirteen arson cases. RGIA, f. 796, op. 187, d. 6689, ll. 2, 9 ob., 46.

110 For a theoretical defense of the Georgian Church's claim to autocephalous status, see K. Tsintsadze, *Istoricheskaia spravka po voprosu ob avtokefal'nosti gruzinskoi tserkvi* (Tiflis, 1906). For a typical collective statement of the Kutais clergy (demanding autocephalous status), see the telegram in RGIA, f. 796, op. 187, d. 6413, l. 1. Another assembly in Ossetiia demanded a constituent assembly, among other reforms (RGIA, f. 796, op. 186, d. 866). The Synod also received reports about the activities of individual radical priests (op. 187, dd. 6541, 6568, 6579, 6580) as well as more general complaints from the Ministry of the Interior (op. 187, d. 6575). For the ongoing attempt by the Synod to mediate and pacify, see RGIA, f. 796, op. 186, d. 965; f. 797, op. 79, otd. 3, st. 4, d. 101; op. 80, otd. 3, st. 5, d. 80. Predictably, the seminary in Georgia – Stalin's training ground – was long a hotbed of radical, especially nationalist, passion; see the materials on 1905 in RGIA, f. 796, op. 186, dd. 296, 351.

111 Thus a priest from Voronezh diocese, A. V. Poiakov, supported the peasant demands for a transfer of land, adding that "what the people want, I also desire." Gosudarstvennaia duma, *Stenograficheskii otchet*, I sessiia, 1: 130–1. Another fellow deputy-priest similarly demanded that the state "allot the peasant land, and [give] the poorest of them funds to purchase everything necessary and essential for working and tilling the land as the nobles do." Ibid., 2: 876–7.

112 For a general file on repression cases in 1910–17, see RGIA, f. 797, op. 80, otd. 3, st. 5, d. 12, ll. 1–288. On the defrocking of radicals in the 1905 Revolution, see the case of F. V. Tikhvinskii and others in RGIA, f. 796, op. 187, d. 6881, as well as V. V. Brusianin, *Sud'ba pervykh deputatov* (St Petersburg: Sovremennik 1906). For the famous case of G. S. Petrov, who was finally defrocked for publishing a public letter defending his behavior and reproving his bishop, see RGIA, f. 797, op. 77, otd. 3, st. 5, d. 59, l. 12–12 ob.

113 For typical cases, see the files on priests in Taganrog, Moscow, and Ekaterinoslav in RGIA, f. 797, op. 78, otd. 3, st. 5, d. 583; op. 83, otd. 3, st. 5, d. 5, l. 50–1; op. 84, otd. 2, st. 3, d. 583.

114 RGIA, f. 797, op. 82, otd. 1, st. 1, d. 240, l. 8–8 ob.

115 "Pechat' i dukhovenstvo," *Missionerskoe obozrenie*, 11 (1915): 286–8.

116 Typical was a telegram from a clerical assembly in Polotsk, which resolved "to welcome joyously the new condition of life of our fatherland as a surety for the powerful development of the Russian national spirit" (RGIA, f. 796, op. 204, otd. 1, st. 5, d. 54, ll. 73–5). Clergy in another diocese declared that "the collapsed order had long since outlived its time," and the "first free diocesan assembly" in Tula declared that the Church "will be reborn to a new, bright life on the basis of freedom and conciliarism" (ibid., ll. 107–107 ob., 117). See also the resolutions by clergy in Vladimir ("Telegramma," *Vladimirskie eparkhial'nye vedomosti*, 9/10 (1917): 41), Novgorod (RGIA,

f. 796, op. 189, d. 2229/b, ll. 344–5 ob.), and Kaluga ("Protokol kaluzh-skogo eparkhial'nogo s'ezda," *Kaluzhskii tserkovno-obshchestvennyi vestnik,* 1917, no. 24/25: 18).

117 For the files purging the bishops of Orel, Minsk, Eniseisk, Riazan, Nizhnii Novgorod, and Vladimir, see RGIA, f. 796, op. 204, otd. 1, st. 5, d. 113, 294, 95, 78, 124; op. 445, d. 7).

Index